BRET HARTE
From the portrait by J. Pettie, R.A., 1890

THE LETTERS OF
BRET HARTE

ASSEMBLED AND EDITED BY
GEOFFREY BRET HARTE

With Illustrations

BOSTON AND NEW YORK
HOUGHTON MIFFLIN COMPANY
𝕿𝖍𝖊 𝕽𝖎𝖛𝖊𝖗𝖘𝖎𝖉𝖊 𝕻𝖗𝖊𝖘𝖘 𝕮𝖆𝖒𝖇𝖗𝖎𝖉𝖌𝖊
1926

The Riverside Press
CAMBRIDGE · MASSACHUSETTS
PRINTED IN THE U.S.A.

TO THE
DUCHESS OF ST. ALBANS
ONE OF BRET HARTE'S OLDEST FRIENDS
THIS COLLECTION OF LETTERS
IS INSCRIBED

PREFACE

AMONG the many publications devoted to Bret Harte the excellent biographies by Edgar Pemberton and Henry C. Merwin stand apart. Whereas the former has naturally suffered from the inhibitions due to a work written in the lifetime of the subject, the latter has been collected mostly from printed sources, so that, although remarkable literary studies in themselves, neither, perhaps, can be said to throw an exact light on the personality of Bret Harte. Moreover, his extreme distaste for publicity of a personal nature would not, even after his death, have simplified their task.

There is no more vital or faithful picture of a man than the one revealed by the intimacy of his correspondence, and if the compiler of the present work has ventured to disregard the natural inclination of the author, in offering these letters to the world, it is by reason of their importance in disclosing the true character and life of Bret Harte, which he firmly believes never before to have been done.

The greater part of this collection relates to the author's life abroad, from the period of his consular duties in Crefeld and in Glasgow up to the time of his death, and covering the twenty years of his residence in England of which so little has been written. They will, therefore, it is to be hoped, offer the advantage of supplementing what may have been found lacking in the various works dealing with his life, and in particular with this period, which was by no means a less important part of his brilliant career as a writer and personality. They will be found to contain many passages worthy of his literary work, together with admirable descriptions of nature and people, showing the sentiments of the man who painted with such consummate art the masterpieces that have placed him among the greatest writers of his country.

It has been thought advisable to precede the present letters with a short biographical sketch for the benefit of those who are not already acquainted with the general outline of his life.

It is a special pleasure for the compiler of this work to render thanks to the Duchess of St. Albans for her courteous contribution of a few of the most interesting letters of Bret Harte in her possession; also to the Marquess of Northampton for the portrait of the late Lord Northampton, his father, and pictures of Compton Wynyates, of which he has been kind enough to authorize the reproduction, as well as for his repeated search for letters in the archives of his family; to His Excellency the Marquess of Crewe, British Ambassador to France, who has taken much trouble in connection with letters in possession of his sister, the late Mrs. Henniker; to Mr. and Mrs. A. S. Boyd for their invaluable contributions, to Mrs. T. Edgar Pemberton, to Miss Chappell, to Mr. A. A. Froude, son of the eminent historian, and to Mr. A. P. Watt, all personal friends of the late Bret Harte. Thanks are also due to the family of the late C. M. Kozlay, and to all those who both in America and in England have so generously given him the assistance without which the assemblage of the present work would have been impossible.

La Retraite
Coppet, Switzerland

CONTENTS

CONTENTS

ILLUSTRATIONS

ILLUSTRATIONS

BIOGRAPHICAL SKETCH

BRET HARTE was born at Albany, State of New York, in 1836, of descent three quarters English, and a quarter Dutch. The son of Henry Harte and Elizabeth Ostrander, his family was among the first settlers in America. Bret was the name of his paternal grandmother, who in turn was the granddaughter of Roger Brett, descendant of Sir Balliol Brett, the first Lord Esher. Roger Brett came to New York in 1700 with Lord Cornbury, who was at that time Governor of the Province. He and his wife owned immense estates on the Hudson including the Fishkills and vast forest lands. Bret Harte was particularly proud of his descent on his mother's side from a Truesdale, Son of the Revolution, for he was an ardent patriot, and the long years of residence in Europe only strengthened his profound belief in the ideals of his country.

He was a precocious child, reading Shakespeare at the age of six, continuing with Fielding, Goldsmith, and others through the great masters of the English language. His father was a well-known scholar of Greek, so that the boy was well versed in Greek and Latin. His mother was a clever literary critic, and in his home life reigned an atmosphere of culture, to which must be attributed much of the perfection of style that later characterized his work. In this respect he was not a self-made man, but inherited from his ancestors, as well as from his immediate surroundings, a keen insight into human nature and an appreciation of the finer shades of life. He had been admirably and unconsciously schooled for the great place he was to occupy in the history of American Letters.

Henry Harte died when his son was still a boy. His

widow remarried and went to live in California. It was to
join her in 1852 that Bret Harte crossed the continent at
the age of eighteen, little knowing that his name was to
be forever associated in the annals of literature with the
great foundation of the History of the West.

After a short stay in the home of his stepfather, Colonel
Williams, he started out for Sonora, Calaveras, the centre
of the gold country. Like all young men, with the enthusiasm of his age he wished to try his luck so near at
hand. Bret Harte's own description of his arrival is too
graphic to be omitted. 'Here I was thrown among the
strangest social conditions that the latter-day world has
perhaps seen. The setting was itself heroic. The great
mountains of the Sierra Nevada lifted majestically their
snow-capped peaks against a sky of purest blue. Magnificent pine forests, of trees which were themselves enormous, gave to the landscape a sense of largeness and greatness. It was a land of rugged cañons, sharp declivities,
and magnificent distances. Amidst rushing waters and
wildwood freedom, an army of strong men in red shirts
and top boots were feverishly in search of the buried
gold of the earth.' It yielded him a wealth far greater
than gold, a unique opportunity for observation which
his eager mind was quick to perceive, although at the
time, as he admitted, he did not realize the value.

Seeing that there was no chance for him among them,
he accepted the post of messenger on the Wells Fargo
Express. It was a daring one that required both skill and
nerve, and was not without attraction for those whose
enjoyment of it was the recompense of their audacity. It
consisted in protecting from attack the safe containing
the gold carried from the mining camps to San Francisco.
Bret Harte's predecessor was shot through the arm by
highwaymen; his successor they killed. Armed guards

were sometimes carried within the coach, but usually he was alone to protect its treasure from the 'hold-ups' that were by no means infrequent.

These two brief periods of his life, lasting in all less than a year, were the chief inspiration of Bret Harte's life's work. Shortly after, he returned to San Francisco, entering the offices of the 'Golden Era,' where he rapidly rose to the editorial room. To this paper he contributed his earliest stories, the most important of which was 'M'liss.' Later, in 1864, he was contributor to 'The Californian,' the famous periodical for which Mark Twain, Stoddard, and other brilliant contemporaries were writing, and in 1866 the 'Overland Monthly' was founded, of which Bret Harte was the first editor. He chose the name, designed the vignette, and published in its columns his first great story. He was thirty-two when 'The Luck of Roaring Camp' brought him immediate fame, not only from the East, but throughout the English-speaking world, and praise from no less a pen than that of Dickens, who wrote, urging him to come to London, as contributor to 'All the Year Round,' of which he was editor. The letter arrived only after the sudden death of the great writer, and Bret Harte, who had an intense admiration for him, wrote his beautiful poem 'Dickens in Camp' without knowing that a letter from the master was on its way. An interesting contrast to note was the violent antagonism opposed to the appearance of 'The Luck' in California, where the prudery of a few misguided individuals almost prevented its publication.

If 'The Luck of Roaring Camp' was a great literary triumph, 'The Heathen Chinee,' written two years later, gave him widespread popularity, bringing his name to the masses in England as well as in America.

Apart from his fame as an author, he was occupying a brilliant position in San Francisco, being Secretary of the United States Mint, Professor of Literature at the University of California, and successful editor of the 'Overland.' In 1862, he married Miss Anna Griswold, of New York, to whom the greater part of the following letters are addressed. In 1870, for reasons that find their explanation in the course of this work, Bret Harte left California to go to the East, where he was under contract with Fields, Osgood and Company, proprietors of the 'Atlantic Monthly,' for ten thousand dollars for his literary work for the year. The journey across the continent, which, as an insignificant youth, he had taken seventeen years previously, was now in the nature of a triumph. He had arrived unknown and unnoticed; 'now he was,' as Mr. Merwin says, 'the most distinguished person in California, and his departure marked the close of an epoch for that State.' Indeed, his fame was so great that his journey was recorded in detail throughout the country, and in England a well-known paper humorously maintained a 'Bret Harte Circular,' with a daily account of his progress from coast to coast.

Not long after his arrival, he undertook a series of lecturing tours, in the East, Middle West, and South, a full account of which is given in his letters of the period. Bret Harte made his home in New York and Newport for the next seven years, until 1878, when he was offered the post of First Secretary of the American Legation at the Court of Russia, which he, however, declined, fearing to have insufficient private means for the maintenance of such a position. Instead, he accepted the minor but more profitable one of Consul at Crefeld on the Rhine, a rich silk industrial town, where he remained for three years. Later the Department of State transferred him to the more important post of Glasgow, which he held until 1885. Together with the period when he was Secretary of the Mint in San Francisco, Bret Harte held for fifteen years in all a Government position, afterward taking up his residence in London, which remained his headquarters until his death. It was during these remaining seventeen years, of toil as well as of universal fame, that he created the greater part of his literary work.

Although Bret Harte never allowed himself to be lionized, his reserved and sensitive nature abhorring publicity or notoriety, yet he maintained in the most aristocratic circles of English society many faithful friends, who showed him that courtesy and hospitality which he found nowhere else to the same extent. His interest in mediæval history created an attraction for him in several of the famous homes where he was a frequent guest.

As has been said before, Bret Harte was intensely patriotic, and revered with profound conviction the ideals of his country. It was a source of bitter disappointment to him, in the later years of his life, to feel a certain lack of appreciation and comprehension on the part of his countrymen, which made it impossible to earn his livelihood among them. No letter can better illustrate how deeply he was attached to his country than the one written to his little son Frank, from Crefeld in Germany, when Bret Harte was Consul there:

We drove out the other day through a lovely road, bordered by fine poplar trees, and more like a garden walk than a country road, to the Rhine, which is but two miles and a half from this place. The road had been built by Napoleon the First, when he was victorious everywhere, and went straight on through everybody's property, and even over their dead bones. Suddenly, to the right, we saw the ruins of an old castle, vineclad and crumbling, exactly like a scene on the stage. It was all very wonderful, but Papa thought, after all, he was glad his boys

live in a country that is as yet quite *pure* and *sweet* and *good;* not in one where every field seems to cry out with the remembrance of bloodshed and wrong, and where so many people have lived and suffered that to-night, under this clear moon, their very ghosts seem to throng the road and dispute our right of way. Be thankful, my dear boy, that you are an American. Papa was never so fond of his country before as in this land that has been so great, so powerful, and so very, very hard and wicked.

Bret Harte was in many respects different from what he has been so often portrayed, as his correspondence clearly shows. He lived as he worked, seriously, conscientiously, and laboriously. Profoundly religious of sentiment, he evaded no duties or trials, and was always ready with a helping hand for those who perpetually appealed to him. Infinitely painstaking in an art of which he was a self-exacting and perfect master, he worked throughout his life, never knowing that haven of rest and peace which has been the recompense of less courageous lives. An invalid, he heroically supported the terrible illness that carried him away, never making it the excuse for the alleviation of a single day's task. When at last the end came, it found him still at his desk, with before him the opening sentences, many times corrected, of a story that was never to be finished. Bret Harte died at Camberley, on the second of May, 1902.

LETTERS OF BRET HARTE

PART I
AMERICA: 1866–1878

LETTERS OF BRET HARTE

∴

PART I

AMERICA: 1866–1878

THE early letters are few and far between. The first we come to is addressed to Mr. Anton Roman, publisher, who later founded the 'Overland Monthly,' of which Bret Harte was to become first editor, and deals with a book of Californian verse compiled by him, but which contained none of his own poems. The little book of sketches to which he refers was published a year later, in 1867, under the title of 'Bohemian Papers,' and consisted mostly of reprints from 'The Californian' and 'The Bulletin,' the two great periodicals of the time. It was Bret Harte's first book of prose.

SAN FRANCISCO
January 8, 1866

A. Roman, Esq.
New York

MY DEAR SIR,

I have to thank you for yours of the 9th ulto., and the Eastern notices of 'Outcroppings.'

You will learn from Mr. Allan that the book has created considerable excitement here, and that the compiler has been abused beyond his most sanguine expectations. All of which ought to make the volume sell.

I understand that Miss Tingley disavows your right to use her selections. I trust you have written to her before this, and relieved me of responsibility in the matter.

From your remarks concerning the cost of the volume,

etc., am I to infer that you propose to recompense me from the profits of the edition? I do not think we made any agreement whatever as to the amount or manner of remuneration, but I certainly cannot consent to any that is to be *contingent* upon the success of the volume, if that is your intention. I may misunderstand you; pray write to me more particularly upon this point. It is better we should understand each other at once. If you will recall our interviews, you must remember that I was not sanguine of the success of this venture, and certainly did not base my ideas of payment on such contingency.

I have some idea of publishing a little book of my California sketches and burlesques including the 'Condensed Novels,' which have been widely copied and seem to be popular in the East. Let me know what you think of it. Of course, I should depend entirely upon its sale in the East. Yours very sincerely

Fr. Bret Harte

Three years later 'The Luck of Roaring Camp' had made his name famous throughout the English-speaking world, in spite of the violent antagonism it created in the West. Bret Harte was thirty-two years of age, successful editor of the new 'Overland,' and Secretary of the Mint in San Francisco. That he was also a kind but exacting critic is seen in the gentle advice given to his friend Charles Warren Stoddard, at that time contributor to the 'Overland,' in the following letter written in 1869.

SAN FRANCISCO
March 22, 1869

Charles Warren Stoddard, Esq.

MY DEAR CHARLEY,

In the few minutes left me to write this — and I am

very sleepy, and the mail goes early to-morrow — I can think of nothing to interest you. Nobody to my knowledge has been born into, married, or died out of this régime, in whom you had any concern. The 'Overland' marches steadily along to its fate, which will be in July — but what I know not. Decency requires that you should be present in prose or poetry, at these solemn moments, so send along your *mess*.

I have used the best you have sent me, Charley; you would not have thanked me for publishing some which was not so good. I have looked after the pecuniary matters as you desired. Command me further as you want — don't wait for me to write as I do now.

You do not want my advice; I should give you more than I should take myself. But you have my love already, my boy, and whether you stay with the bananas or return to beans, I am always

Yours
F. B. H.

In the midst of the universal praise which formed such a striking contrast with the incomprehension shown by California for their greatest writer, came a letter from Fields, Osgood and Company, proprietors of the 'Atlantic Monthly,' the great Eastern periodical, requesting upon 'most flattering terms' contributions from the author of 'The Luck.' This was followed by another containing a proposal for republication in book form of the stories which had already appeared in the 'Overland.' From Bret Harte's reply we have an insight of the strain of his work as editor, which, in addition to his duties as Secretary of the Mint, left little time for the literary work of so painstaking an author.

ROOMS OF THE OVERLAND MONTHLY
SAN FRANCISCO, *April 23,* 1869

Messrs. Fields, Osgood and Co.

      Boston

GENTLEMEN,

In regard to your proposal to examine a collection of my California sketches, with a view to republication, I fear that you have overestimated the number of my contributions to the 'Overland,' which are (of stories) but two: 'The Luck of Roaring Camp' and the 'Outcasts of Poker Flat,' the latter one in the January number.

I am writing a little sketch similar in style for the June number, and have in view three or four more, when the pressure of my editorial duties shall be lifted, either by the suspension of the magazine or a division of its editorial work, which, since the inception of the 'O. M.,' has fallen entirely on me. One or the other will happen about the 1st of June. I have one or two California sketches published before (but not in the 'Overland') and not included in the 'Condensed Novels,' but even these would not, together with 'The Luck' and the 'Outcasts,' make a volume of the size suggested.

As my contract with Carleton of New York expired with his first and only edition of the 'Condensed Novels' (fifteen hundred copies), would it not be possible to translate one or two sketches from that?

Will you be good enough to tell me also what the 'Atlantic' would pay for stories like these proposed?

                Yours very truly

                    FR. BRET HARTE

A new man succeeded Mr. Roman as publisher of the 'Overland Monthly,' and between Bret Harte and him there had been a good deal of disagreement. The 'editor' was greatly overworked, and under very uncomfortable conditions. The fateful month of June, mentioned in the previous letter, had arrived, and the discussion culminated in the following ultimatum, which, together with the brief note that comes after it, settled matters definitely, and was accepted without modification.

SAN FRANCISCO
June 7, 1869

John H. Carmany, Esq.

SIR,

I will continue in the editorial charge of the 'Overland Monthly,' upon the following terms:

1. That I have the exclusive control, as formerly, of its literary and critical conduct.

2. That I shall be privileged to select and occupy, for that purpose, a private office as formerly — where rent shall not exceed thirty dollars per month chargeable to the 'Overland.'

3. That I shall receive as compensation two hundred dollars per month, payable weekly, and receive the same amount paid other contributors per page, for all contributions to the body of the magazine exclusive of Etc. and Book Reviews.

4. That when the business or magazine shall justify the expenditure, I shall have exceptional editorial assistance.

5. That this contract shall continue in force for one year.

F. BRET HARTE
Editor Overland

June 9, 1869

J. H. Carmany, Esq.

SIR,

I repeat my answer of yesterday, that the only terms upon which I will continue in the editorial charge of the 'Overland,' are those which I offered two days ago, which I have never changed and do not intend to change.

Yours very truly

F. BRET HARTE

In the interesting letter to Cincinnatus Hiner Miller, who later won fame as a poet under the name of Joaquin Miller, Bret Harte makes use again of his critical powers to the best. Impartial and thoroughly sound, yet full of kindness and encouragement for the art of which he was such a self-exacting master, he writes:

ROOMS OF THE OVERLAND MONTHLY
SAN FRANCISCO, *August* 19, 1869

C. H. Miller, Esq.

MY DEAR SIR,

Although I shall not be able to use either of your poems, I think that I fairly appreciate the merit of their performance and promise. I cannot say that I greatly admire your choice of subjects, which seems to me to foster and develop a certain theatrical tendency and feverish exaltation, which would be better under restraint, just now. I see nothing in you worse than faults of excess, which you can easily check by selecting less emotional themes for your muse. You are on your way to become a poet, and will, by and by, learn how much strength as well as beauty lies in repose. The best thing in 'Peccavi' is the quietest — the very felicitous and natural *lie* at its close. The rest is ecstasy, relieved by good phrasing, or a theme worn threadbare already, by the best poets of your kind.

Yet I would not have you false to your dramatic tastes, but only suggest to you to develop your other faculties equally.

I have to thank you for your volume. Let this informal and well-meaning attempt at criticism take the place of a notice in the 'O. M.'

I should be glad to receive something else from you. Try and condense something as long as 'Sackcloth and Ashes' into thirty or forty lines.

Yours very sincerely
FR. BRET HARTE

Seven years previously, in 1862, Bret Harte was married to Miss Anna Griswold, the daughter of Mr. and Mrs. Daniel Griswold, of New York. They had two children and lived at San Rafael. When the following letter was written, he had been recently appointed Professor of Literature at the University of California, retaining at the same time his post as Secretary of the Mint, and his editorial charges.

In spite of his seeming prosperity, he was not happy in California. There was an accumulation of resentment toward all those who, during his brilliant career among them, had done all in their power to make his struggle for success a difficult and bitter one, by reason of their constant opposition to every honour that was finally shown him. It was not, however, for another two years that Bret Harte and California were to take leave of each other forever.

This is the first of the many letters to his wife which find their place in this volume, and in it he speaks of a possibility of a journey to the East.

Rooms of the Overland Monthly
San Francisco, *Wednesday* p.m. [1869?]

My dear Anna,

Felton asked me to dine with him at Piochi's to-night to meet Professor Pierce and some of the Regents. I declined at first, saying that I wished to go to San José to-night, but he pressed it on the ground of practical utility, and I assented. I suppose this is the way these things are done in California. Yet I would rather have a 'dinner of herbs' in San José than the 'stalled ox' up at Piochi's, but that there is a prospect of the East and Europe in the distance.

I suppose you will be doubly disappointed that Mrs. Leach does not come down to-night, but she says she will not be able to leave here until Saturday night, when she and Leach will go down — the latter to return Monday, the former to stay later, if we stay.

I met Mr. Beard, of San José Mission, in the cars yesterday. He repeated his old invitation, and in very shame I at last accepted, promising to bring you and the boys on Saturday morning, by the railroad to Washington Station, where he will meet us with a carriage to take us to the Mission, a mile or two distant, where we are to spend the day, returning by the evening train to San José. So don't make any other plans for Saturday.

I've seen Barrett. He will not make any other than his first offer, and of course I declined to accept it. But of this I will say more when I see you to-morrow (Thursday night).   Your affectionate

Frank

The affection which dictated the next letter to Charles Warren Stoddard was very gracefully returned in the latter's tribute to Bret Harte, when he wrote that 'to

his criticism and encouragement I owe all that is best
in my literary efforts.'

SAN RAFAEL, *April 24*, 1870
Charles Warren Stoddard, Esq.

MY DEAR CHARLEY,

'The Albatross' is better, but not best, which is what I
wanted. And then you know Coleridge has prior claims
on the bird. But I'll use him unless you send me something else. You can, as you like, take this as a threat.

In 'Jason's Quest' you have made a mistake of subject.
It is by no means suited to your best thought, and you're
as much at sea in your mythology as Jason was.

You can do, have done, and must do better. Don't
waste your strength in experiments. Give me another
South Sea Bubble, in prose, tropical picture — with the
cannibal — *who is dead* — left out. It's time, too, that
you began to work with a long aim.

In haste, yours
H.

A year later, Bret Harte, with his wife and children,
started out for the East. The extraordinarily widespread
interest which accompanied their journey across the continent is described by Messrs. Pemberton and Merwin,
in their respective biographies. Upon his arrival in New
York, he stayed first at his sister's house, at 16 Fifth
Avenue, and shortly after paid a visit to Boston, to see
his publishers, where he was for two weeks the guest of
W. D. Howells, editor of the 'Atlantic Monthly.' In his
'Literary Friends and Acquaintances' the latter gives us
a delightful description of this visit, during which Bret
Harte encountered everywhere that courtesy and refine-
ment characteristic of New England. During his stay

there, he made the acquaintance of most of the great literary men of the day, among whom were Emerson, Lowell, and Longfellow, for whom Bret Harte had a great admiration, and on whom he subsequently wrote an essay, recording his impressions of their meeting. Upon his return to New York, he entered into contract with Fields, Osgood and Company for his literary work during the ensuing year, in consideration of the amount of ten thousand dollars. It has been frequently suggested that Bret Harte wrote only one story during that time, thereby taking an unjust advantage of the contract. That this was, however, so little the case can be readily seen from the next two letters, which include both his acceptance of the agreement and his fulfilment of the same. There were, furthermore, a stipulated number of contributions, twelve in all, and not 'whatsoever he may write, be it much or little,' as had been erroneously stated. That he gave his full measure cannot be doubted, from his second letter at the close of the agreement, which, as Mr. Merwin justly remarks, represented a year of very hard work.

NEW YORK, *March* 6, 1871

I accept your offer of ten thousand dollars for the exclusive publication of my poems and sketches (not to be less than twelve in number) in your periodicals for the space of one year commencing March 1, 1871. I have had some talk with Eytinge this morning, and think I gave him several ideas about the 'Heathen Chinee' and his Pagan brother — the California miner. I have also promised to mark the passages in 'The Luck,' etc., which I thought best fitted for illustration, with marginal notes and directions, etc.

The following letter shows plainly that he *did* give

full value for money received and according to his contract.

MORRISTOWN, NEW JERSEY
December 12, 1873

MY DEAR OSGOOD,

I confess I was considerably surprised by your note, as you had given me no intimation, when I asked for my account in Boston a few days ago, of the position you intended to assume. Neither did I know anything of your plans to dispose of the 'Atlantic' — and so render it out of my power to furnish you with the single article we agreed upon as due you in the spirit of our contract — until after you had consummated the sale of the 'Atlantic.'

When I offered you 'Mrs. Skaggs's Husbands' for the 'Atlantic,' according to our contract, you agreed to waive your right to it in the magazine in consideration of its freshness for the new volume — accepting it, however, as the substitute for two articles for the 'Atlantic.' This left the matter furnished to you on my contract as follows:

Prose

1 The Poet of Sierra Flat
2 The Romance of Madroño Hollow
3 Princess Bob
4 How Santa Claus came to Simpson's Bar
5⎫
6⎭ Mrs. Skaggs's Husbands
7 Lothaw (in 'Every Saturday')

Poetry

8 A Greyport Legend
9 A Newport Romance
10 Grandmother Tenterden
11 Concepcion de Arguëllo
12 Idyl of Battle Hollow
13 Half an Hour before Supper
14 Chicago ('Every Saturday')

In addition I offered you 'Handsome is as Handsome Does,' written for 'Every Saturday,' but on account of your relations with Charles Reade you declined it.

There seemed, however, to be some misunderstanding between us regarding the 'Every Saturday' material being applied to the contract, and I offered to furnish you at some future time a sketch or poem in addition without charge. The last time I met you in the city I spoke of this — saying that I was writing a Spanish legend for your magazine and for a new volume of verse about which I wanted to consult you. I had the poem nearly completed when I received the news of the 'Atlantic's' sale — of which you had not then or at any time given me any previous intimation.

Remembering these circumstances, I think you can understand my surprise at your note. I should like also to know what is your proposition, and, in any event, I think I am, at least, entitled to a statement of my account with you.

Very sincerely yours

BRET HARTE

To Jas. R. Osgood, Esq.

In the next two letters to his wife, written during the summer and short visits to Boston and Manchester, he speaks of his meeting with Mr. and Mrs. James T. Fields, and his appreciation for the New England country.

BOSTON, *Monday* P.M.

My dear Nan,

We did not arrive until after two o'clock, and even had I intended to telegraph for you to come down, it would not have reached you in time. I felt much better, however, and, although I shall not get off to New York before to-morrow (if at all), I shall stay with Clark to-night and you need be in no fears of my lacking ministration if worse. I enclose a letter from Mrs. Sherwood, which I suppose you will hardly believe that I opened without observing that it was for *Mrs.* Bret Harte.

Mother telegraphs to me (via Newport) that she wants to know if I intend to come down or whether she shall come to Newport. If she has received my letter, this is about as cool a piece of pertinacity as I know of. Should I not get off to-morrow, I shall telegraph you to come down and expect you to be here in time to return to New York Tuesday night. Don't worrit.

Affectionately

FRANK

BOSTON, *September 6*, 1871

MY DEAR ANNA,

I received your telegram some twelve hours before your letter. I am glad that you happen to like Mount Vernon in spite of its good report from other people.

I finished the poem — which is poor stuff — the night you left. The next morning I met Mr. Fields, who of course pressed me again to go with him that afternoon to Manchester, and I did, returning this morning.

Mrs. Fields met us at Beverly with the pony carriage, and drove us to Manchester over a pleasant road past quaint old-fashioned farmhouses. There was an autumnal suggestion in the air that was very fresh and sweet.

The New England coast here is much finer than at Newport — the rocks are more picturesque and the trees — which are large and generous — almost overhang the ocean. We stopped on the way to call on a Mrs. Cabot (I think), a friend of the Fields, whose house for really beautiful surroundings surpassed anything on our foggy little peninsula. There was very little wind — no fog. The sea even was sad and silent. There was a thoughtfulness over everything, as if the whole landscape had been surprised into reflection over some subtle premonition of the coming winter that we could not detect. I never believed that autumn could be so tenderly beautiful.

I have had a telegram from Watrous saying that he would send me some copies of the 'News Letter,' but as yet nothing has come from him or San Francisco, and I must wait here until it does. I shall try to go up to Mount Vernon to-morrow afternoon; if not, will come with Mr. Clark on Friday. I am not very well and sleep and eat but little.

Yours affectionately
FRANK

It was at the beginning of 1871, a year after his arrival in the East, that Bret Harte undertook, upon the advice of his friends, to give a series of lectures on the early days of California. Only the lure of freedom from financial anxiety induced him to overcome his extreme distaste for notoriety and his horror of the 'platform,' which, it will be remembered, was shared also by Mark Twain, and others. The lecture was entitled 'The Argonauts of '49, California's Golden Age,' and on the first tour was delivered at Albany, Boston, Washington, and Pittsburgh, from which city the following letter to his wife is written. Letters of this period are all very interesting. There is an underlying note of melancholy which makes them very human, and which, together with admirable descriptions of nature and people, rank them among his best.

MONONGAHELA HOUSE, PITTSBURGH, PA.
January 9, 1872. 2.50 P.M.

MY DEAR NAN,

I telegraphed you twice from Washington and once to-day from Pittsburgh. And I now send you many happy and happier returns of your birthday, dear little woman!

I've gone along thus far very fairly and without delay. My Washington lecture was crowded; the audience almost as quick and responsive as the Boston folks, and the committeemen, to my great delight, told me that they made money by me.

You will be sorry to hear that I felt dreadfully lonely on my Washington trip, and you will be sorrier to hear, you infamous woman, that my loneliness was mitigated by meeting Miss Binney Banks and her mother in the train. You may remember that I met Miss Binney Banks at Burlingame's little dinner — but I don't know that I told you that she was *lonely*. She and 'her ma' went with me to the lecture.

I called on Charlton at the British Minister's and had some talk with Sir Edward Thornton which I have no doubt will materially affect the foreign policy of England. If I have said anything to promote a better feeling between the countries, I am willing *he* should get the credit of it.

I took a carriage and went alone to the Capitol of my country. I had expected to be disappointed — but not agreeably. It is really a noble building worthy of the Republic — vast, magnificent, sometimes a little weak in detail, but in intent always high-toned, grand, and large-principled. I felt very proud until I looked in upon Congress in session — then it was very trying to compare the house with its tenants.

How you would have enjoyed the trip with me!

Finding that I would be two or three hours in Baltimore on my way to Pittsburgh, I telegraphed to Chris Mayer to meet and sup with me. He met me at the depot. We went to 'Guy's' — a famous restaurant — and had a nice supper, and then we spent the last half-hour of my limit at Brantz Mayer's home with your cousins. 'Miss Kate' and 'Jinny' were on their way to a party, and there were one or two other sisters, whom I had not seen before. They all regretted you were not with me, and made me promise to bring you in early spring to spend a few days.

All that I saw of the road between Baltimore and Pittsburgh was beautiful. Its scenery is noted, I believe, but in the early grey morning it came upon me, with its great white distances of Alleghanies and coursing rivers, as a special revelation. We passed the 'blue Juniata,' where you remember the 'bright Alfaretta' roamed and wept. The spot where she wept is plainly to be seen, and is still damp.

I am looking from the windows of my hotel on the Monongahela River, with all sorts of queer flatboats and barges passing and repassing.

How you would have enjoyed it!

The mail leaves in a few moments. I conclude you are better or you would telegraph me. Kiss the chickens for me, Nan, and look for the safe return speedily of your own

FRANK

A second lecturing tour was undertaken in February, 1873, and took him through Canada. The lectures were delivered at Toronto, Montreal, and Ottawa, where he was the guest of the Governor-General and his wife, the Earl and Countess of Dufferin, at Rideau Hall, but, like the previous one, it was not a financial success, and at the end of March he returned to New York.

EAST SAGINAW,
February 26, 1873

MY DEAR NAN,

I telegraphed you from Toronto, Detroit, and — an hour ago — from this place. I sent you a telegraphic order for one hundred and fifty dollars from Toronto and another for two hundred dollars from East Saginaw.

I turn my face East again, very gladly, to-morrow. To-night will make my third lecture and the other three are on my way home. This has been, by far, my most anxious and difficult experience. At Toronto, the audience waited for me an hour and a half as I flew towards them in a special train (an engine and a single car) which I telegraphed ahead for, and in which I dressed myself, at the rate of seventy miles an hour — the most rapid and unsatisfactory toilette I ever made. Again, on my way to Detroit the engine broke down, and although I had given myself three hours' leeway, it was taken up by this delay, and we arrived in Detroit at five minutes to eight — I dressing myself again in a compartment of the Pullman car, into which I had my trunk brought from the baggage car.

Nevertheless, thus far the trip has been successful, in more ways than one. They were so well pleased with me at Toronto — an English audience, and, I fancied, quite a pleasant forecast of the reception I should meet abroad — that I made an arrangement to return in the latter part of March and deliver ten or twelve lectures throughout Canada. Again I had a long talk with a prominent Canadian publisher at Toronto and have entered into a contract to prepare a complete edition of my works in one volume — which will probably set-off Mr. Hotten's pirated edition and give me copyright in England. Don't laugh at the word 'contract' — it simply means the getting up of such a book as I sent Tauchnitz — a few hours' work.

Who can you imagine is sitting with me in my room at the usual dismal hotel? Mrs. Rose's husband — Mrs. Rose herself being at Clifton. I was delighted, as you can imagine, to find somebody to talk with, although I had never met him before; he is very much like her — bright, original, and intelligent, and bridges over the dreary intervals before and after the lecture.

I'll write again from Cleveland. Kiss the chickens.

Your affectionate
FRANK

MONTREAL, March 25, 1873

MY DEAR NAN,

I telegraphed my arrival in Ottawa on the 21st and to-day my arrival here. But I did not write because I really did not know and do not now know whether I shall not have to give up the Canada engagement entirely.

In Ottawa I lectured twice, but the whole thing was a pecuniary failure. There was scarcely enough money to pay expenses, and of course nothing to pay me with. Kirby has no money of his own, and, although he is blamable for not thoroughly examining the ground before bringing me to Ottawa, he was evidently so completely disappointed and miserable that I could not find it in my heart to upbraid him. So I simply told him that unless the Montreal receipts were sufficient to pay me for my lecture there and a reasonable part of the money due me from Ottawa, I would throw the whole thing up. To-night will in all probability settle the question.

Of course, there are those who tell me privately that he is no manager and a man of unfortunate reputation, but I really do not see but that he has done all that he could and that his only fault is in his sanguine and hopeful nature.

I did not want to write this disappointment to you as long as there was some prospect of better things. You can imagine, however, how I feel at this cruel loss of time and money — to say nothing of my health, which is still so poor. I had almost recovered from my cold, but in lecturing in Ottawa at the Skating Rink, a hideous, dismal, damp barn — the only available place in town — I caught a fresh cold and have been coughing badly ever since. And you can well imagine that my business annoyances do not add greatly to my sleep or appetite.

Apart from this, the people of Ottawa have received me very kindly. They have vied with each other in social attention, and if I had been like John Gilpin, 'on pleasure bent,' they would have made my visit a success. The Governor-General of Canada and his wife — the Earl and Countess of Dufferin — invited me to stay with them at their seat, Rideau Hall, and I spent Sunday and Monday with them. Sir John and Lady Macdonald were also most polite and courteous.

I shall telegraph you to-morrow if I intend to return at once. Don't let this worry you, but kiss the chickens for me and hope for the best. I would send you some money, but 'there *isn't any* to send' and maybe I shall only bring back myself.

Your affectionate
FRANK

P. S. 26th.

DEAR NAN,

I did not send this yesterday, waiting to find the result of last night's lecture. It was a *fair* house, and Kirby this morning paid me one hundred and fifty dollars, of which I send you the greater part. I lecture again to-night, with fair prospects, and he is to pay something on account of the Ottawa engagement besides the fee for that night. I will write again from Ogdensburgh.

Always your

FRANK

Bret Harte always had a preference for the first 'M'liss,' which was incidentally also his first story, and by some considered to be his finest. He had started to make a longer version of it, which, however, had never satisfied him, and which, as he says, he gave up in disgust. How the incident, mentioned in his letter to Osgood, by which he discovered that this beautiful story had been still further lengthened and completed by another hand, must have angered him can well be imagined. After his departure from America, the story was further desecrated through its conversion into a variety entertainment, where it attained great success, much to the author's despair and in spite of all his efforts to prevent it.

45 FIFTH AVENUE, *April 2*, 1873

MY DEAR OSGOOD,

Yours of the 27th March was forwarded from Toronto and only received by me to-day. If you think a 'complete' edition would pay you here, by all means get it up.

I have your answer to my dispatch of yesterday, saying that Hotten had not responded in any way. In the face of enclosed note, which I received three weeks ago, his conduct seems to me inexplicable. Is he not responsible to you directly?

I am *not* going to England next month, as you might have known from the papers saying that I *was*. I have too much unfinished work to complete here. I think I will 'keep' to another year with my English friends.

I am very much irritated by the discovery of another California swindle upon me. In 1860, I wrote the 'Story of M'liss,' as it appears in 'The Luck,' etc., for the 'Golden Era,' a weekly San Francisco paper, with which I was connected. Three years after (1863), at the request of the proprietor, Colonel Lawrence, I attempted to create a longer story or novel out of it, but after writing nine or ten chapters I wound it up in disgust. As I always preferred my first conception, I adopted *that* when I put it in 'The Luck.' I find now that the 'Golden Era' is reprinting the second story in three columns with an advertisement saying that it will be completed in 'sixty-two' chapters. Of course this means a swindle on the public, or a *forgery*. I regret to say that they are quite capable of doing either in California, and, as I have received no explanation or notice from them, I expect the worst. I have written a 'card' to be published in the 'Bulletin' of San Francisco and have sent a private note to the editor. Can you not frighten them by copyright? The whole transaction is infamous!

I have copyrighted my lecture in Canada, on England, having heard that an English order had been sent to New York for a stenographic reprint. As I copyrighted a 'proof' or printed slip of it, this will prevent Hotten or any other pirate from printing it.

Yours   HARTE

Bret Harte's attachment to the South and the Southerner is well known, and all who love the immortal Colonel Starbottle will be interested in this letter, written from Virginia, in which he gives such a charming description of his favourite type.

BERKELEY SPRINGS, VIRGINIA
Saturday [July 10, 1873 ?]

MY DEAR NAN,

Pettis said he kept my note until he reached Washington instead of posting it at Baltimore, so that it must have reached you two days late. I telegraphed yesterday, thinking you might be worried.

I hardly believe I shall ever be able to leave Virginia. At least, if I do, I shall come back here instead of going to Europe. *Such people* as I have seen! Imagine my sitting down to dinner with a gentleman in the dress of the early century, ruffles, even *bag-wig*, complete — a gentleman who has visited these Springs for the last forty years! Who remembers 'Madison, Sir,' and 'Monroe, Sir,' and asked me what I thought of the poems of Matthew Prior! I have seen people that I believe never existed off the stage — gouty old uncles in white flannel; stiff old dowagers who personify the centennial. And all this undiscovered country within four hundred miles of New York! I never had such a chance in my life — I look back upon poor Colonel Starbottle as an utter failure. If I could dress Robson, and get him to speak as I heard the real Virginian Colonel Starbottle speak yesterday, I could make him famous.

I shall return Monday or Tuesday next, I think — until then I hope you will not be worried. I am better physically and, I think, in every way. Don't mind my incoherency. I am writing just now to keep up with the 'Post Boy' — a real 'Post Boy' who is to pass here on his pony in a few minutes.

Your affectionate

FRANK

The third lecturing tour was started in October, 1873,

and continued into the spring of the following year. It took him throughout the Middle West. It was again not a financial success, partly owing to bad planning on the part of the agents, and, when expenses had been paid, the profits were so small that the lectures often proved not to have been worth the trouble, to say nothing of the tremendous effort which they cost him. People seemed also disappointed in not finding him the person whom they had pictured. The late Charles Meeker Kozlay, who compiled and published 'The Lectures of Bret Harte,' says in his preface, 'As a lecturer, Bret Harte was no more successful than some of our other noted American writers who, like him, attempted this line of work. Tall and slender, a gentleman of distinguished bearing, his first appearance was a disappointment to many who had expected to see a typical Californian in dress and manner.' However, as he goes on to say, and as Bret Harte himself confesses, he was not an orator, not having the fire and action, nor indeed the necessary strength of voice for the purpose. Yet everywhere he met with success and appreciation.

The following group consists of several letters written during this period.

St. Louis, *October* 19, 1873

My dear Anna,

As my engagement is not until the 21st at Topeka, Kansas, I lie over here until to-morrow morning in preference to spending the extra day in Kansas. I've accepted the invitation of Mr. Hodges, one of the managers of the lecture course, to stay at his home. He is a good fellow, with the usual American small family and experimental housekeeping, and the quiet, and change from the hotel is very refreshing to me. They let me stay in my own room — which, by the way, is hung with the chintz of our 49th Street house — and don't bother me with company. So I was very good to-day and went to church. There was fine singing. The contralto sang your best sentences from the *Te Deum*, 'We believe that Thou shalt come, etc., etc.,' to the same minor chant that I used to admire.

The style of criticism which my lecture — or rather myself as a lecturer — has received, of which I send you a specimen, culminated this morning in an editorial in the 'Republican' which I shall send you, but have not with me at present. I certainly never expected to be mainly criticised for being what *I am not*, a handsome fop, but this assertion is at the bottom of all the criticism. They may be right — I dare say they are — in asserting that I am no orator, have no special faculty for speaking — no fire, dramatic earnestness, or expression, but when they intimate that I am running on my good looks — save the mark! — I confess I get hopelessly furious. You will be amused to hear that my gold 'studs' have again become 'diamonds,' my worn-out shirts 'faultless linen,' my haggard face that of a 'Spanish-looking exquisite,' my habitual quiet and 'used-up' way, 'gentle and elegant languor.' But you will be a little astonished to know that the hall I spoke in was worse than Springfield and *notoriously* so — that the people seemed generally pleased, that the lecture inaugurated the 'Star' course very handsomely, and that it was the first of the first series of lectures ever delivered in St. Louis.

My dates in Kansas are changed thus, Topeka, 21st; Atchison, 22d; Lawrence, 23d; Kansas City, 24th; but they are not distant from each other and I shall probably get any letters without trouble.

I hope to hear that you have got a house and are settled, in your next letter. I shall write again this week, probably from Kansas City.

Your affectionate

FRANK

LAWRENCE, KANSAS
October 23, 1873

MY DEAR ANNA,

I left Topeka, which sounds like a name Franky might have invented, early yesterday morning, but did not reach Atchison, only sixty miles distant, until seven o'clock at night — an hour before the lecture. The engine as usual had broken down, and left me, at four o'clock, fifteen miles from Atchison on the edge of a bleak prairie with only one house in sight. But I got a saddle-horse — there was no vehicle to be had — and, strapping my lecture and blanket to my back, I gave my valise to a little yellow boy — who looked like a dirty terra-cotta figure — with orders to follow me on another horse and so tore off toward Atchison. I got there in time; the boy reached there two hours after.

I make no comment: you can imagine the savage, halfsick, utterly disgusted man who glared at that audience over his desk that night, and d——d them inwardly in his heart. And yet it was a good audience — thoroughly refined and appreciative, and very glad to see me.

I was very anxious about this lecture, for it was a venture of my own, and I had been told that Atchison was a rough place — energetic, but coarse. I think I wrote you from St. Louis that I found there were only three actual engagements in Kansas, and that my list, which gave Kansas City twice, was a mistake. So I accepted an offer to take Atchison on shares. I made one hundred dollars by the lecture and it is yours, for yourself, Nan, to buy 'minxes' with, if you want, for it is over and above the amount Eliza and I footed up on my lecture list. I shall send it to you as soon as the bulk of the pressing claims are settled.

Everything thus far has gone well. Besides my lecture of to-night, I have one more to close Kansas — and then I go on to St. Joseph.

I've been greatly touched with the very honest and sincere liking which these Western people seem to have for me. They appear to have read everything I have written — and seem to appreciate the best. Think of a rough fellow in a bearskin robe and blue shirt repeating to me 'Concepcion de Arguëllo.' Their strange good taste and refinement under that rough exterior — even their tact — is very wonderful to me. They are 'Kentucks' and 'Dick Bullens' with twice the refinement and tenderness of their Californian brethren.

And, of course, as in all such places, the women contrast poorly with the men — even in feminine qualities. Somehow a man here may wear fustian and glaring colours and paper collars and yet keep and mature his gentleness and delicacy, but a woman in glaring 'Dolly Vardens' and artificial flowers changes natures with him at once.

I've seen but one that interested me — an old negro wench. She was talking and laughing outside my door the other evening, but her laugh was so sweet and unctuous and musical — so full of breadth and goodness — that I went outside and talked to her while she was scrubbing the stairs. She laughed as a canary bird sings — because she couldn't help it. It did me a world of good, for it was before the lecture, at twilight, when I am very blue and low-toned. She had been a slave.

I expected to have heard from you here. I've nothing

from you or Eliza since last Friday when I got yours of the 12th. I shall not write again until I hear further. I shall direct this to Eliza's care, as I do not even know where you are.

Your affectionate

FRANK

DAVENPORT, IOWA
October 29, 1873

MY DEAR ANNA,

I have heard nothing from you since yours of the 17th, which reached me at St. Joseph. If anything could add to the dreariness of this usually dreary hour with me, and the landscape, without my window, whitening fast under a driving snowstorm, it would be the thought that you might still be at the Grand View House in Morristown, from which your last letter was dated. I fervently hope that you are settled somewhere comfortably by this time and that the letters informing me of the fact are on their way to me now. But you said in your letter of the 17th that you would telegraph as soon as you found a house, and here it is almost the first of November and no word.

I was getting so low-spirited and nervous a few hours ago that when the committeemen offered to take me out to dine, although it was snowing hard, I accepted. We drove to Rock Island, the Government Reserve and Arsenal, a beautifully wooded island in the Mississippi. As we drove on through the storm, under the great Gothic-arched trees, with our wheels slowly muffling with snow, I was struck with the quantity of rabbits, squirrels, and even deer, and, although it was late in the season, the birds, quail, and partridges sitting securely in the coverts, and then my companion told me that, since the Government had taken charge of this beautiful spot, it had protected sacredly all game, and made it an offence to fire a gun within the limits of the island. The result was that all the birds for miles around came to this haven of refuge. And yet here, remember, lay all around the terrible implements of war, guns lying unlimited on the ground. I saw a squirrel running in and out of a twenty-four-pounder. The idea struck me at once as being so quaintly beautiful in its contrast, that a poem sung itself to me at once. My friend said that the birds had increased so that Professor Henry came here from Washington to study the new varieties. And all this in an Arsenal — think of it! While in Omaha I bought of an Indian trader a bearskin for a rug for my desk. It was the skin of a young Montana grizzly, very full, and I think very fine. I also bought a beautiful bearskin, very large for the kind and very soft — for Totty. I don't know what, under Heaven, she can do with it, but it was very pretty. And I couldn't resist getting two mink skins — real 'minxes' — for you, Nan. But you can make something out of them — they are remarkably beautiful skins. I sent them by express to 45 Fifth Avenue.

I am very grateful that I have got on so well. My cough, I think, is more from nervous weakness than anything else, and, although it sometimes keeps me awake, it seldom troubles me on the platform. The strain and travel necessary for me to keep my appointments — for losing a single train here would make me lose half a dozen engagements — keeps me rather limp as to strength, and completely upset my pretty plans about writing *en route*. I usually lie down until the time to dress — after my arrival. But I am — they say — a great success out here, and have larger and more appreciative audiences than ever known. I have had half a dozen applications for other cities in my route, but, of course, with every night engaged, could not well take them. And that reminds me, I must stop this and get ready to dress. Good-night, Nan.

Your affectionate

FRANK

SOUTH BEND, INDIANA
31st October, 1873

MY DEAR NAN,

No letter from you yet or telegram telling me you have found a home. A few lines from Eliza says you are still seeking in the country for the home, and winter, that here, at least, has already come with snow and wind, is already upon us.

I stopped at Chicago an hour and a half on my way here this morning and found there two notes enclosed; an hour ago the telegram arrived. My dates after the 6th and until the 12th are uncertain and I may be sent back again from Canton to the vicinity of Chicago. I cannot tell until I hear from the Bureau. It would be pleasant to have them come back with me.

I have missed no engagement yet. But I am drawing hard on my vitality to keep up. I was full of things to tell you, but I am so worn out, Nan, that I must lie down a few hours before the lecture to-night. I have only just arrived here, and to reach this place left Bloomington at half-past two last night.

Good-night; Heaven keep you and the babies.

Your affectionate

FRANK

SARATOGA SPRINGS, *Saturday Morning*

MY DEAR NAN,

I telegraphed fifty dollars to you yesterday and enclose to-day a draft for one hundred and fifty dollars.

Of course the telegram assured you that I reached Gloversville in time to lecture, although it was a very close shave. It kept me in a high state of nervousness all day, and when I did arrive, at half past eight — the audience waiting — I went on the platform, without changing my dress, or taking any refreshment, solid or *spirituous*.

I lectured here last night, to a very large, but rather cold audience. Heaven knows what, or who, they expected to see! I was disappointed in not finding the Carrolls at home here, although the old gentleman met me at the cars. The family are in Troy, and he was stopping at the hotel here, having only arrived the day before, on business. So I had to go to the hotel, too. I shall leave here this P.M. *en route* to Buffalo, although I may stop at Troy; if invited it will save me a day's expense, which is considerable when the money is so hardly earned.

I am pretty well — although dreadfully lonesome and wearied with travel. I think you had better give Arnold Bliss one hundred dollars of the within.

I shall write you and telegraph again from Buffalo. Love to all. Kiss the chicks; always, dear Nan,

Your affectionate
FRANK

HORNELLSVILLE, January 19, 1874

MY DEAR NAN,

That long ride and wonderful night over the Erie Road is past, and I am beating a tattoo on the pane of my dreary little window in the gloomy hotel, and looking out upon as blue a prospect as I ever saw. It is a January thaw with a feeble drool of rain — 'bad weather,' the committeeman says, 'for a lecture.' The people seem to be preternaturally serious and depressed, as if they had come from my lecture instead of going to it. Just now a man came into the barber's shop where I was getting shaved and asked, in his lugubrious tones, 'who this Bret Harte was, who was going to show this evening.' The barber instantly began to telegraph violently over my head — (I saw the whole performance in the mirror) — and the man said 'Eh? Eh?' and finally brought out the remark, 'O, it's him!' and then subsided.

Don't get worried or lonely. When you are particularly blue, think of me and let your cerulean tint pale before my deeper indigo.

Take care of the children, teach them to avoid becoming lecturers, caution Totty against marrying a poet, and, believe me, Nan, dismally your

FRANK

BINGHAMTON, March 7, 1874

MY DEAR NAN,

I sent you a telegraphic transfer for fifty dollars to Morristown to-day. I should have sent more, but the cheque for one hundred and twenty-five dollars for the Binghamton lecture to-night was sent to New York. I've telegraphed Carter to send it to you. Whether he will or not I can't say, but I shall send one hundred dollars more from Batavia on Monday or Tuesday, when I will write again.

I do not know when I have been so agreeably disappointed as in my Ithaca audience. They were by far the most appreciative I have had, not excepting Boston and New York. From the time I made my first appearance on the platform, they had made up their minds to be pleased, and followed me through, rising at all the delicate points like a trout at a fly. I never saw a finer collection of bright young faces than those that looked up to me from the crowded benches.

Well, the secret of it was, Ithaca is the seat of Cornell University — a fact I had quite forgotten when I came. There they were, grave professors, students, girls and boys! My dear friend President White may well be proud of his cubs. Harvard cannot show such young *gentlemen* as met me in the committee room. There was all the culture — without the conceit!

Of course, my anonymous friend of the 'Cornell Era' was among the first to welcome me, and he proved to be Professor Corson, Professor of Early English Literature and the famous commentator on Chaucer. He was a capital good fellow — as sweet and gentle as the old poets he lives among — and he gave me his picture. I had to sit for mine, for the students, before I left there this morning.

I'll write again from Batavia, which I shall reach to-morrow morning.

Good-night — with kisses for the chickens.

Always your affectionate husband

FRANK

In October of the same year Bret Harte lectured again, this time in the South and West, visiting Georgia, Omaha, Nashville, down to Augusta, Milledgeville, Macon, Chattanooga, and back to Morristown. The letters from Macon are of particular interest in connection with his impressions of the Southerners and of their way of living, in contrast with the Northern temperament, and convey vividly their charm, and that of the country, which he describes so delightfully.

OMAHA, NEBRASKA
Sunday, October 26, 1874

MY DEAR ANNA,

Here I am at the extreme western limit of my journey, my trip half completed, and just two weeks to-night since I left New York. I am very grateful that thus far all has gone with me so well. I lecture here to-morrow night, and the next day (Tuesday) turn my face again toward the East. It will be a long and in some respects even more anxious and wearisome journey, for some of my appointments are out of the main highways of travel, but you will remember, each night, Nan, that I am drawing so much nearer home.

I found your letter of the 17th waiting me at St. Joseph; one a week old, yesterday. I did not have time to write you from there, for the mail closed up an hour after I arrived, and I had to leave St. Joseph at midnight, after the lecture, to come here. I only enclosed a draft to Eliza with a few lines to indicate my arrival and departure.

Your letter, Nan, was thoroughly good and welcome, but I felt dreadfully when I found you were still at the 'moated grange' in Morristown. I have, during these long weary nights and days, time to think of you as occupying your mind and hours at some new home that I hoped to hear about in your letter, but when I heard from you, as being alone in that deserted house, I felt like giving up my trip and going home at once.

Nevertheless, now that you are willing to live in the country, provided that you can get a comfortable house, I think it is for the best. I should have felt no anxiety in leaving you the mistress of such a house as that near Nast's, in a cheerful neighbourhood, and I should and would now come home to it with intense satisfaction. Oh, Nan, I weary of boarding or living in a house with others. If we can find some quiet home of our own, this winter, in some country place, near New York, even if Morristown be out of the question, I think we will not regret it. So I wish to hear you telegraph me of your success. Even if you have to pay one hundred and twenty-five dollars per month, I think it would be better. We must have a good *comfortable* home — for the boys' sake if not for our own.

When I left St. Joseph last night it was raining. As I rode into Omaha this morning the streets were dumb with snow, and winter, savage and pale, looked into the windows of the cars. My route lies a little northward of this, and I trust I shall not be blocked up with snow before I get away from this bleak northern plateau.

Imagine a hotel as large and finely appointed as the Occidental in San Francisco, and think of there being such a one at Omaha. Yet here I am — in a very pretty furnished parlor of the 'Grand Central' on the very outpost of the West, the cars of the Union Pacific starting on their long overland trip but a few blocks away. Do you remember anything of Omaha? We saw nothing of it from the cars when we came East. Yet it is a large, bustling town. Verily the West is wonderful. I spoke last night in an opera-house at St. Joseph — as large and beautifully decorated as Booth's Theater. I have no words to describe the lordly and magnificent conceit of rebuilt Chicago! Rather I have only slang — as I told one of their citizens 'they have "seen" their former glory and gone one hundred better.' Being a Western man, he understood the gambling simile perfectly.

I am doing very well. Although without knowing that I had a cold, I have somehow got a cough and a hoarseness that at times, at night especially, is troublesome. I suppose it is from speaking so much. I spoke five nights successively, last week.

I keep my cheerfulness pretty well, although there are one or two hours at twilight and midnight when I am very blue. I always enter a new place with distrust and leave it with hope.

Kiss Totty and tell the boys to be good. Always your affectionate   FRANK

MILLEDGEVILLE, GEORGIA
November 4, 1874

Mrs. Bret Harte
      The Willows
            Morristown, New Jersey

MY DEAR NAN,

I despatched a few hurried lines to you this morning before I left Augusta, merely that you should hear from me, and to enclose two drafts for three hundred dollars. I had concluded to come here to Milledgeville, the old capital of Georgia, partly because it was on my way to Macon and I had a day to spare, and partly because I was invited to lecture here with the assurances that my expenses would be paid — even if I got nothing more. Chattanooga was already stricken from my list, as the agent there refused to run any risk; and I began to fear that my trip would be, financially, considerably below my expectations, particularly as the Bureau had just written me that Savannah had withdrawn from the date and wanted to engage me later in the season. I am hesitating whether to go there on the same terms as I came here (which have been offered me by telegraph) after lecturing at Macon. I have a day to spare and should not lose anything but my travelling expenses. I will telegraph you if I go.

Do not blame me if I do not write you more frequently, and longer letters. I am usually tired out when I arrive in any town, and am so depressed in spirits that my letters would be very despondent. I will tell you all about my trip — which has been, in some respects, a striking experience to me — when I return. I have been in better health than I had reason to expect, and have been very pleasantly received by the people, but nothing remarkable. I have had occasion to change my views of the South very materially, and from what I have seen am quite satisfied that the North is profoundly ignorant of the real sentiments and condition of the people. They affect me very deeply and sadly.

I am very anxious to hear from you again, particularly to know about your health, of which you said nothing in your telegrams and letters. I hope everything has gone well. I have sent in all five hundred dollars, and would have sent one hundred more, but I deemed it advisable, in this uncertain and very expensive trip, to keep more money with me than I have usually done.

Pay Rosen and Cooper and Tivell, equally, instalments as far as you can without leaving yourself without money. I am anxious to know why Bliss has not sent the draft — it seems strange.

I hope you got the dates from the Bureau; they are right, except Chattanooga.

Good-night, dear Nan; kiss the chickens for me, and don't worry about me; the 16th will soon come and with it

Your own

FRANK

MACON, GEORGIA, *November 7, 1874*

MY DEAR NAN,

I found yours of the 30th awaiting me here, and telegraphed this morning acknowledging it. I trust you have Bliss's draft by this time; I think it would have been paid simply on your telegram signed by my name. At all events, you must have received the other one hundred dollars long before I received yours.

I have no engagement until the 9th at Montgomery, Alabama, and will probably rest here quietly to-day and to-morrow. I abandoned the idea of Savannah, as I was fearful of making a pecuniary failure there on account of the brief time necessarily given to the announcement of my lecture — only two days. It was provoking: I wanted to see Savannah and wanted the one hundred and fifty dollars it ought to have yielded me, but I did not dare to take the risk on my own account at so short notice. But I am full of the idea of making it the excuse for a little trip down here later in the season, with *you*. I want you to see something that I have seen here — I want *you* to share the strange experience I have had. I think you would be affected very much as I have been.

I have had several applications to lecture here at different places, but none of them could be made to suit the dates of my present trip. Perhaps I could arrange for two or three later — still, I would be content to come down for about ten days to Savannah, for only that one lecture, if we could manage to come here together. Think of it well. I believe it would do you 'a heap of good,' and there is no roughness in the journey that your condition would make dangerous.

I seem to have been away from home a year. Never before in any trip has my experience been crowded so full of strange observations and impressions. Since I left Louisville, I appear to be travelling in a foreign land, and among a foreign people. I am too full of it to talk about it; I have done nothing — I can do nothing — but absorb. I have tried to write, but my novel seems a far-off thing; even my lectures never before appeared so vapid. How could I expect to interest a people who were infinitely

quainter and more original, more pathetic, more ludicrous than the life I had to talk about? Perhaps I am
only lazy — affected by the climate, which seems to me
the most perfect realization of an indolent, luxurious lotus-
eating dream. It is Indian summer here — an Indian
summer purged of all grossness and asperity, dependent
upon no beauty of colouring or fascination of any particular sense, but affecting you in the subtlest and most in-
toxicating way through all the senses, and lapping your
nerves into a most delicious and profound tranquillity.
No wonder the people are what they are! No wonder they
stare with great hollow eyes at the profound statesmen
of the North who project themes for their well-doing
based upon the temperature of New England and the
habits of labour. They don't know how to work here.
Their attempts at what they conceive to be it are inde-
scribably amusing. I have watched them and heard them
talk about it, until I was divided between a laugh and a
cry — as, indeed, I have been continually divided ever
since I came here. I cannot keep the smile from my lips
when I am with them — or the moisture from my eyes
when I think of them, alone. They are so shiftless, so
helpless — so like spoiled and petted children, who have
been suddenly punished and brought face to face with
duty — that I can't think of them seriously as men and
women. And more mysterious than all, their unrestrained
and continual familiarity with the negro has wrought between them a strange, weird sympathy and even affection
which neither slavery *nor freedom* has changed, and which
makes their fate almost identical. What that fate is to be,
God knows! I dare not think. The outlook is hopeless.

You wonder, dear Nan, to hear me talk so strongly of a
political question — knowing how little interest I have in
it usually. But I never before had such a fateful problem

brought before my eyes — I never before stood by the bedside of a ruined and slowly dying people. If I were a statesman, I should devote my life to save them. I can think of no loftier ambition for any man — any Northern man, I mean; for they are helpless: any Northern man who was large enough to see that it is not only the ex-slave to be saved, but the ex-master.

And the 'nigger' — the innocent, miserable, wretched, degraded, foreordained by race and instinct and climate to be forever helpless and a useless part of the nation. This 'curse' lolls in the sunlight, slouches in the shadow, evades his responsibilities, is truant to his duty, to his future, to the North, to the South — and is miserably free and wretchedly happy. He works only when want drives him to it, and even then will drop his work to go on a picnic, or on the excursions or political meetings that occur every day. And when he goes to the political meeting, he is as likely to vote against what are called the 'radicals' as he is in favour of what are believed to be his own principles. He has but one virtue — he still loves his old master — it is his only fidelity. And it is a fact — this was told me by a Northern man — that the ex-master is apt to be more kind, humane, and considerate, and less impatient, than the Northern man in his treatment of this quaint, utterly original, and utterly useless people.

All through the South, over the old battle-grounds, and among the very people who have fought upon them, I have been pained with the spectacle of the utter devastation and ruin brought by the war — and struck *always* with the noble resignation of those that have suffered. I have heard no complaint nor bitterness. 'You will hear no unforgiveness or hatred from the men who have fought,' said a Confederate general to me, and our own general in command at Nashville, at whose table I heard the statement, endorsed the fact. The ill-feeling, the Ku-Klux outrages, are kept up by the men who stayed at home during the war. I have never heard a word of insult or prejudice from these poor fellows — only an anxiety to show me that they had been maligned. I have listened in the cars, during this election excitement, to the conversation of the old 'rebels,' who did not know a Northern man was listening to them, and have heard only a desire for peace and the restoration of the dying South.

Personally I have been fortunate in only knowing intimately the *best* — and then only on rare occasions has there been any allusion to the past. They have been uniformly kind and courteous to me — without much effusion — and I think they like me. They are old-fashioned in everything — in literature, in art, in dress; but their manners are frank and easy. I have heard no better English spoken anywhere — nor as good — as among the wives and daughters of this State of Georgia. And in manner, natural grace, and gentle womanliness, they are far superior to the New Englander. They are not generally as pretty, but always are finer ladies. They dress outrageously — their slim purses and a certain kind of local pride keep them 'ever in the rearward of the fashion,' but they always act like ladies.

My audiences generally have not been large — but I get the best — and the people are few. To many a lecture is a novelty of which I am the sole introducer in the Far South. I think the better class are always pleased — there is, of course, a class in the audience who stare and — are disappointed. I am sorry to say that some of these are Northern men who have come in since the war.

But my dominant impression — above everything — is one of sadness. The wasted, ill-kept fields, the scattered negro cabins, the decaying and fallen plantations, the badly dressed people, the helpless and hopeless negro, and the dumb, ill-regulated, but earnest striving of the best people for a better state of things, and their childlike trust in the power of the great North to help them — all are pathetic, and form a picture over which this tender sky and this delicious atmosphere hang with an irony that is hopeless and cruel.

But that'll do, Nan. I am so full of this that I couldn't help talking about it. Don't think I am not longing for you and the dear children even while I am being absorbed by the life around me. Give my love to Mother, and say to her I would write if I could find time. Remember me kindly to the Colonel. You do not say that Aunt Caddy is with you. Don't get low-spirited or worry. In less than ten days I will be back again, better in health than when I left. I weigh more than I ever weighed before — one hundred and fifty-two pounds. I am a little languid from the climate and tired from my journey, but I'm ever so much better than when I left. I enclose a draft for you, one hundred dollars, and will send another from Montgomery.

Always, dear Nan,

Your affectionate

FRANK

MACON, GEORGIA
Sunday, November 8, 1874

MY DEAR NAN,

I wrote you a long letter yesterday morning, and am afraid that I bored you with a lot of political talk of which I was full. But I enclosed a draft for one hundred dollars as an evidence that I remembered I was still in debt, and had a heap of practical work to do yet before I rode ahead redressing political grievances.

I go to Montgomery to-night at seven o'clock. But I

don't get a 'sleeper' before midnight — which is the way they do things in the South. The trains travel about fifteen miles an hour over the worst rails you ever saw (to go faster would be dangerous) and stop at every station. No train ever comes in on time. An hour or two hours late is nothing here. Nobody ever keeps an appointment promptly. Punctuality is not a Southern virtue. There is a delightful irregularity and uncertainty about all these things which in the North are confounded with regularity and certainty; the mails occasionally omit altogether; the morning papers come out in the afternoon. But nobody complains — and really, after you have been here a week, you look upon it as a matter of course.

I rode out yesterday with one of my committeemen. Macon is the principal city of the old cotton-planting aristocracy, and on the heights around are still standing some of the lordly houses of the great slave-owners. They are often very beautifully equipped and have a certain broad ease and munificence (everything is broad here — the streets are like public squares, the houses are low and large! the bedroom I am writing in, at the hotel, is as large as our parlour) — but even about the best there is somewhere the old primeval note. There is somewhat always the suggestion of barbarism. And they all — even those inhabited and kept up — have a *triste* look — a deserted, kind of heart-broken air. The ivy, the real English ivy, and another dark funereal-looking vine, whose name I can't remember, have a way of hanging from porch and pillar like black crape. The gardens are most always neglected. One of the finest houses belonged to a young man who owned thirteen hundred slaves and was the largest cotton autocrat in the district. He died before the war — was killed by an overseer with whom he was remonstrating for the *overseer's ill-treatment of a slave!* This was so much unlike the usual stories current in the North that I took pains to verify it by a Northern man here. It was true. Both men were passionate — but the cause was as I have stated. While my friend was telling me this, he made another remark exceedingly characteristic of the habits of the people. Speaking of this dead planter, he said, 'By the way, Mr. Harte, you remind me very much of him. He was about the same build and had the same *quick, energetic, decisive way with him that you have;* he was quite unlike the rest of us, though he was born here.' You can imagine what an idea they have of energy and quickness when *I* am looked upon as an example. But they all dawdle and loll and talk, and wonder what you are in such a hurry for, and have an unbounded faith in yesterday, and no particular regard for to-morrow.

We drove to the cemetery, which was, I think, my perfect idea of a burial-place — if cremation doesn't become popular. It stood on the banks of a beautiful river, over which trees with mourning bands and streamers of ivy bent and wrung their hands and sorrowed and lamented. There were winding ways strewn with dead leaves, leading up, up, terrace by terrace toward the patient sky. There were tombs, ivy-shrouded, and black with age, but always showing some sign of recollection in a bouquet of yesterday or an attempt to restore the half-concealed inscription. With that passionate fondness for the Past, they love to linger here — they will not take the lesson that Nature is never weary of teaching them, but, as fast as she tries to cover up their sorrows, they bare the spot anew. For all that, I think she has generally triumphed — the cemetery is now rank with overgrowth. Of course here were the Confederate dead — of Macon; a thousand on the hillside, each name recorded on the little headboard. Yet even here I was struck with a circumstance which indicated the absence of a refined taste, or a sense of the ludicrous, among these sincere mourners. Over the entrance to the Confederate burial-place was a large arch and painted upon it was this singular inscription, 'We mourn our Dead — Badham & Jarvis.' Of course Badham & Jarvis didn't particularly mourn the dead, but they were the painters who had painted the sign and their names were nearly in as large letters. My guide assured me he had not noticed this infelicity before. It appeared that Badham & Jarvis were a pair of local Yankees who came down South and did these things by contract. I did not point out the irony of the coincidence, for my friend was full of the Past, and I don't think he would have seen it.

We drove home through the soft melancholy twilight. My friend pointed out the various tokens of progress — a new cotton mill, a new church, a new driving-park and State Fair Grounds, and a new cottage fresh with damp brick and mortar — with that kind of nervous eagerness with which even the proudest of these sad, strange people try to impress you with an idea of their regeneration; but the cemetery seemed to me to cover the whole town — the planters' sombre houses were mausoleums, the few listless people we met who looked up were only ghosts of their dead selves wandering around aimlessly, and waiting to be covered up again.

When I got back to the hotel, I was glad to pick up a New York 'Herald.' But it was a week old — and somebody in the next street was reading the other part of it.

At Milledgeville I stayed with Dr. White, an old planter, slave-owner, ex-United States Navy Surgeon, and ex-Confederate soldier. But I'll keep my social reminiscences for you when I return. I have been treated very kindly — not with any excess or extravagance of hospitality like that of California, or what I have been told was the Southern custom — but always in good taste and consideration. I have seen a dozen 'Bell Whites' in Tennessee — but she is not a type of the best Southern girl, who is remarkable only for the general elegance of her speech and the absence of any dialect. They have occasionally odd expressions: they speak of a 'full suit of hair' meaning a fine growth of hair; the 'evening' begins after one o'clock P.M.

I am getting better of my cold, although this weather, delicious as it is, saps my energy and does not allow me to throw it off. On the 10th I turn my face again North, stopping only at Knoxville, on my way home. I shall strike across through Virginia and come home by way of Washington, and possibly may reach New York Sunday night — a week from to-day.

What a blessed peaceful Sabbath it is! There is not a sound in this large hotel — not a figure to be seen upon the broad street below — nothing but the belt of pines beyond the sleeping town and the grey haze that seems to linger over it like a benediction. I have seen more beautiful landscapes, but never have I seen or felt such an atmosphere; it is an intoxication but an intoxication without exaltation, without levity, without hopefulness. It is the resignation, the silence, the sweetness, the tenderness, of death.

Nevertheless, I must get ready to go to dinner, and finish this. Remember you are to keep up your spirits. Tell Mother I hope to find her better. Tell the boys that Papa has put some pieces of sugar cane into his trunk for them — to the great danger of his best clothes. Kiss Tot, and say that Papa has been kissing all the little girls down here for his 'baby.' Don't worrit, Nan, but wait patiently for   Your affectionate

                                              FRANK

I enclose an ivy leaf from the cemetery and the tomb of that young planter.

These ended his important lecturing tours. Afterward he occasionally made short ones, such as the one mentioned in the following letter, which seem to have been more successful than the previous tours, although it was each time a greater strain upon his health and nerves.

ROCK ISLAND, *January 26*, 1875

MY DEAR NAN,

I am just back from Jacksonville — an all-day ride — desperately tired and going to bed. I leave to-morrow morning at five o'clock for Iowa City. Then I turn homewards, taking Fort Wayne and Toledo *en route* Oregon, Illinois, is off, I suppose; at least I have not heard from them or the Bureau, and they were to telegraph to me.

I have had very fine audiences — large and appreciative, both here and at Jacksonville. Even the lyceums have been astonished at the size and quality of the audiences I have drawn. I am very well satisfied — but dreadfully tired and worn out. This kind of work grows more and more laborious to me each time I have tried to write in the cars, but have done very little beyond reading and correcting the proofs I found at Jacksonville.

I sent you a telegraphic transfer on Monday for fifty dollars. I enclose now a draft to your order for one hundred dollars. You have only to sign it on the back and any of the Morristown tradesmen will pay it.

I am very anxious about you, dear Nan, and shall not feel at ease until you telegraph me or until I return. I trust you are better, and are free from that nervousness —I don't apprehend anything worse than that, until later.

I am writing by a miserable gas-light and can hardly see the ink. Kiss the children. God bless you, dear Nan.

Your affectionate

FRANK

SAINT JAMES HOTEL
IOWA CITY, IOWA
28th January, 1875. 4 A.M.

DEAR NAN,

I leave in half an hour for Rock Island *en route* to Fort Wayne and Toledo and home. I enclose one hundred dollars for Arnold, unless something else is more pressing.

I am very tired and have been quite sick. Kiss the children for me. I hope you are better, Nan.

Always your affectionate

FRANK

The next letter to Bliss in connection with his only long novel, 'Gabriel Conroy,' shows his careful attention to all the details that go to make a perfect unity.

MORRISTOWN, NEW JERSEY
Sunday night [*April 27*, 1875]

MY DEAR BLISS,

I enclose another chapter complete — thirteen pages — over four thousand words.

I find the book winds up slowly. It requires as much care — even more — in *ending* than in beginning. I have already blocked out five more chapters to conclude — that is about fifty pages of manuscript. Of course there may be more — certainly not less; and I expect to have everything in by the first of May.

I have sent back the designs with my criticisms. Much depends upon the excellence of the illustrations. Better *good* cuts for this novel or *none* at all. Try and make the artist think that his reputation is equally at stake with mine. He is a good artist and a thoroughly practical and picturesque one — if he only would read my text a little more carefully.

About the table of contents I am at sea! I don't know any better or other table than the chapter headings, and I certainly would prefer those *in the book*. I don't care what you send to your agents, and am willing to trust to your judgment of what will sell. But I think with your *page lines* the suggestion of the novel is sufficiently plain and exciting — *in the book!*

As to the title I am afraid that we may differ. I am — after mature deliberation and consultation — in favour of a single title: the name of the hero and central original figure — 'Gabriel Conroy.' Believe me, the shorter the title, the better the chance for its quotation and longevity. Two names live longer than half a dozen.

But I think that we ought to meet and talk with each other by or before the first prox., on these and other matters. Say when! I am at your service.

Always yours
B. H.

P.S. Osgood is anxious to bring out his book of my latest sketches (reprints), now in his hands this four months, waiting this novel. I and he both agree that the one book will help the other. I have held back, thinking that you ought to be consulted. I would advise you to let it precede yours. It will be a gratuitous advertisement. Please let me know by telegraph. Hastily

B. H.

Bret Harte gives vent to his keen sense of humour in the amusing letter to Osgood, composed chiefly of afterthoughts, in the form of postscriptums, and includes a burlesque set of verses about his literary agent.

713 BROADWAY, NEW YORK
May 26, 1875

MY DEAR OSGOOD,

I've been moving out of Jersey into town or I should have written you before. Thanks for your news about the Hingham Cottage. I won't be able to come to Boston this week, but if you are coming down next week I will arrange to go back with you. Hingham is near Cohasset, I believe — a place already suggested to me by Barrett, and another actor — whose fortune I am about to make - Stuart Robson.

I have got tired of enriching only publishers.

The 'more thousands' is good! I don't know how true it is. Six thousand was the exact sum to be paid to Bliss, he afterwards accounting — to me — and the entire receipts of the English sale of the serial for myself solely. This is *entre nous;* indeed, I supposed that the fact of the sale was not to be made public at all, until I saw that paragraph.

Smith, the great! Smith, the well-born and hyphenly-connected, is my agent. I reject with scorn the small shifts and brutal sallies aimed in your note at that truly great man. One thousand pounds is the sum he is to get from the English publisher for me. I have, I fear weakly, consented to take five thousand pounds for the right in Europe, Asia, and Africa — reserving Australia and certain penal settlements in the Pacific, where my works are popular. I can imagine how your breast will dilate with envy when you read of Roswell Smith's presentation at Court with a copy of 'Gabriel Conroy' in one hand and 'Bonnicastle' in the other.

P.S. Am I never to see you again? Shall 'ginger be hot i' the mouth' again, or have you reformed? Did you read the burlesque of 'Nicholas Peppermint' and good Dr. Holland in the 'Sun'? Did you see my report of the Patent Office fire?

B. H.

P.S. Here I can acknowledge $150,000 by telegraph. And are those notes all paid, and won't you please send me that statement of account — due, I think you said, in December?

B. H.

> People in Cremorne Garden
>   When twilight was falling,
> Smith! Smith! Smith! Smith!
>   They were crying and calling.
>
> Smith without a 'y' or 'e'
>   Nothing can enliven,
> But as bad as bad can be
>   Is Smith with a hyphen.
>
> See, old Welford's at the door,
>   Sampson & Low are snarling,
> Go back, O Smith, across the moor —
>   You are not our darling.

I know how fond you are of 'Maud,' so I expect you to set this delicious little song to music and sing at that dinner which I greatly fear you will kill.

Yours
B. H.

How comes on the Jarndyce v. Jarndyce decision. Are they going to settle my ability to live in the State of Massachusetts and do business before vacation?

B. H.

The lovely autumn will do for the book, I suppose. The cheque I am willing to receive before. There is nothing mean about me.

B. H.

Bret Harte's charming and clever reply to Charles Godfrey Leland has already been published in the latter's biography by Elizabeth Robins Pennell, and alludes to the curious mistake which occurred in connection with the publication of 'The Dancing God.'

February 18, 1876

MY DEAR MR. LELAND,

I confess I was a little astonished yesterday in reading in the 'Tribune' a statement, made with all that precision of detail which distinguishes the average newspaper error, that I had written a story for the 'Temple Bar' entitled 'The Dancing God.' But the next day I received my regular copy of the magazine, and find your name properly affixed to the story. The error was copied from the English journals evidently before the correction had been made.

Nevertheless, let me thank you, my dear sir, for your thoughtful courtesy in writing to me about it. You are a poet yourself, and know his 'irritability,' to use the word the critics apply to that calm conceit which makes us all shy from the apparitions of a praise we know belongs to another. But I am glad of this excuse to shake hands with an admirable and admired fellow-countryman across the water, and I beg you to believe, dear Mr. Leland, that I would not pluck one leaf from that laurel which our appreciative cousins have so worthily placed on your brow.

Always your admiring compatriot and friend,

BRET HARTE

Bret Harte was not a master of modern English only, but could also cleverly imitate that of 'My Lord Shaftesbury,' as in his witty and delightful letter, written from Washington, to his old friend Colonel Brantz Mayer.

WASHINGTON, D.C.,
July 8, 1877

HONOURED SIR:

Forasmuch as some vain, trifling Fellow hath, in sheer Wantonness and after an Antick fashion, writ me an Epistle having the Import of yr. Hand and Carry'd by Post from Baltimore, it seemeth to me but Just and Honourable that I should lodge Information against this Miscreant Scoundrel and Losel Knave by apprizing you of his Trait'-rous Act. For, as my Lord Shaftesbury hath Justly Observed: 'the Style or Fashion of an Authour being his Own, it "May not be Imitated by Another."' Whereas, not only hath this Knave imitated yr. Style but hath Vilely misused the King's Majestie's English by Glaring Anachronisms of Expression, thereby casting Discredit and Reproach upon an Honourable Gentleman.

But that I am lying Ill of a Sore Distemper that cometh from the Fogs and vile airs that the fens and Marshes of the Capitol Exhale at Night this matter should not have Delayed.

But of These more at Another Season — when I shall Chance to Lie at yr. House on my journey by easy Carriage to New York. Trusting, Honourable Sir, that Faring thither I may see yr. Face

I am yr. Honour's Obt. Svt.

BRET HARTE

These to Brantz Mayer, Gent.,
   late Col. in the Forces of the
      United States of America,
         at Baltimore.

In 1877, a scheme was started by John J. Piatt, to found a magazine in Washington, under the name of 'The Capitol.' Bret Harte was to collaborate as editor and contributor, upon terms of five thousand dollars a year, or, if he preferred, a smaller amount, with a half-interest in the paper. Coming after the financial disappointment of his lecturing tours, during which he had been able to accomplish only very little literary work, this appeared as a godsend, in which he placed great hopes for the stabilization of his position for the future. The letters written to his wife from Washington, where he went to supervise the undertaking, give a clear idea of the project.

RIGGS HOUSE, WASHINGTON, D.C.
27th July

DEAR NAN,

I enclose draft for fifty dollars and have sent Eliza the same amount. I am hurrying on with my story, which begins in Sunday's paper, but the last few days' heat has taken considerable sap out of me. I wonder how I stand it; but I am careful in my diet and expose myself but little to the direct sun.

Piatt's latest offer is three thousand dollars a year and one half the paper; he is to furnish me with a statement of the affairs of the company, and if I am satisfied I think I'll close, although I shall make the suggestion that I will take the five thousand dollar salary with the privilege of coming in within a year on the other sharing plan.

Do you know that _I_ should have to live here? — and that it is very unhealthy in summer for children, although there are some country places not far away where some of the citizens go. The question is a little too large to be dismissed or settled at once. It is in every way a new departure for me, and once embarked I must see it through.

God bless the babies; tell the boys I'll see them soon. If I can find time I'll write again to-night.

LIMICK

WASHINGTON, D.C., Sunday, P.M.

DEAR NAN,

I had no opportunity to write you yesterday, and nothing to write. I have nearly finished my story, besides writing another article for 'The Capitol.' Dana has sent me a telegram saying the story read so well he wouldn't bother me with proofs, and would not publish until next Sunday. He may give me something extra for the story, as it is longer than my usual one hundred dollar sketches; whatever he may send I'll send to you.

Piatt, the editor and proprietor of 'The Capitol,' to-day made me an offer of five thousand dollars per year (put in bank to my credit and payable monthly) if I will share with him the editorial labors — or he will give me a smaller salary (secured) and a half-interest in the paper. Both offers are good; perhaps the five thousand dollars in hand is worth the half interest in the bush — but I'm going to look into it to-morrow. It is a weekly paper — it will only require about two columns of writing per week or about as much as a single article for the 'Sun,' and will leave me, as Piatt says, ample time for my literary work elsewhere.

Washington is the place for a literary man to make money.

Think of it. Remember the money will be secured me by deposit in bank as the one thousand dollars is for my story. Let me know your advice. You must also remember that the payment of five thousand dollars is not dependent upon my finishing so much copy — it is a *salary;* if I should be sick or unable to do anything, I could still draw it. And if I can write as well and as rapidly as I am writing now, I can easily double it in the 'Sun,' by the articles Dana still wants.

Now I am utterly bewildered as to what *you* are to do — *just now.* I sent you fifty dollars and will send you more to-morrow, at least enough to enable you to go anywhere you like, with a month's board in advance in your pocket. But just now don't go to the Catskills — it's too far for me; and if you can possibly *wait* a few days longer for my return — do it. I want to get in another instalment of my story, and get Piatt's offer into a definite shape and contract to submit to you.

Every moment here is pecuniarily valuable to me. I will try and come early next week, and, if the roads are blocked by strikers, shall come by sea.

God bless you all. I think the tide is turning. At least I begin to feel my way ahead, slowly.

Your own
LIMICK!

P.S. I am writing with an old quill and can hardly read this, and my eyes are giving out. When you write or when you receive letters, remember that Morristown is as far by mail from Washington as Boston is, and that by telegraph it is farther and twice as expensive as Chicago.

THE CAPITOL, WASHINGTON
Wednesday P.M., 1877

MY DEAR NAN,

I am waiting to get a statement of the affairs of 'The Capitol' so that I shall know what my *half*-interest will be.

I've only a few instalments more to write for the paper, and then I can leave.

If I determine upon taking Piatt's offer of three thousand dollars and one half interest, before I leave here, you must trust to my judgment, and the papers will all go through a lawyer's hands.

But I don't want to say positively 'yes' or 'no' until I talk with you — unless I am obliged to.

In haste.

Your own
FRANK

P.S. I'll write to-morrow; I send fifty dollars to you and fifty dollars to Eliza. Make it go as far as you can for the present.

Matters, however, were not going so smoothly as he had anticipated, and the first serious disappointments appear in the following letters, in which he shows his anxiety. In addition to this, his health, which was never very strong, had completely broken down under the strain of uncertainty.

WASHINGTON, D.C., *July*

MY DEAR NAN,

I have written to you twice and telegraphed you twice within the past ten days, but have received no answer from you or Eliza. The last letter I sent to Eliza's care. To-day I mailed fifty dollars.

I have made the contract with 'The Capitol,' who have deposited one thousand dollars in bank for me to check against as I furnish instalments — one hundred and twenty-five dollars for each instalment if it be only a chapter. This *secures* the money to me, and, as Washington papers are not very rich or secure, I am satisfied so far. But I have been grievously disappointed regarding the advance; Piatt promised me two hundred and fifty dollars, but on Monday he told me that the other member of the Capitol Publishing Company thought it was enough if they paid for an unfinished story in instalments, particularly as they should not begin to publish it until it was all complete. Nevertheless, Piatt himself handed me seventy-five dollars (fifty dollars of which I send you) and promises to send me the other within a day or two. Meanwhile, when I finish the first chapter, I will get according to contract one hundred and twenty-five dollars, which will make my complete remuneration eleven hundred and twenty-five dollars for the little story — as Piatt's advance is an individual act and based upon what we are both to get from Thompson, which he says will amount to over two thousand dollars more. I do not build much on this — but from what I know of T. he will certainly do something more.

I shall try to finish the work in a month, for I have nothing to invent — only romantically and dramatically cast a really wonderful *true* story. I shall have to stay here a few days longer to collect my materials — *probably*. I can't tell until to-night. That done, I shall return, although when I reach the climax of the story I shall have to go back to Washington for a few days. Meanwhile, remember I don't, at this writing, know where *you* are or where *I am returning to*. I have just telegraphed Eliza to know your whereabouts.

I am better — but very slowly recovering. I have a good old Virginian doctor who promises to make me strong again, not temporarily but permanently. For the first time in my life I have attended to my diet. I've lived the last few days on beef-tea and broth — eschewing all vegetables, liquors, or stimulants. I had to be half killed before I could show my self-control.

God bless you, Nan. I've no time to ask any questions — I know you answer them all instinctively. I trust you altogether and I know only the want of money cramps you. Always

LIMICK

WASHINGTON, D.C.
September 21, 1877

My dear good, patient Nan, if you did not already know how foolish I am about not writing bad news, you would guess, as I see by your kind letter you have, that I have had great trouble and perplexity here. The non-appearance of my story, the annoyance — even to the meanness of its having been alleged by the 'World' that I was bought off or frightened by a decision of the Attorney-General's, in the New Idea Case — when, as you and I know, only the necessity of writing other things to pay my daily expenses caused the omission. It was, still, a dreadful mistake. It lost me, I fear, many friends. It put me again in the shameful attitude of breaking my engagements. All of which there was no answer to, dear Nan. It was my own fault, and I cannot blame people for not knowing everything.

When I handed Piatt the contract, he said he was very sorry, but that some old debts against the paper had lately come up unexpectedly and that he could not fulfill his promise regarding the account I have. Of course, I believed this only an excuse and that he had thought better of his bargain. But since then he assures me that he is most anxious to complete it; that he hopes to arrange matters so that we can go as he intended — and honestly (and this is one reason I have not told you this before), *I do not even now know whether he is sincere or not*, or whether he will, if sincere, be able to do what he offered. I have been kept for a week in the most wretched, lamentable state of anxiety.

But I shall to-night finish the story. It is longer than 'Thankful Blossom' — longer than I first intended, but I could not bear nor dare to put in poor work or hurry it. Please God, I may yet get a couple of hundred dollars out of it from Osgood, and, mayhap, something from England. It isn't a bad story — some of it has been written in the sorest trouble I have ever had.

Dear Nan, I have had no money since I have been here. I shall have none until the story is finished. I do not blame them. But it is hard. But it is not so terrible to me as the reflection that you are left alone, penniless, at that strange hotel, with no money. If I could do anything by being *there*, more than I am doing here, I would come. *But I must come with money.*

God bless you, Nan; be patient a day or two longer.

FRANK

WASHINGTON, 19*th October*, 1877

MY DEAR NAN,

I wrote you yesterday, and to-day enclose in great haste, to catch the midday mail, this cheque for fifty dollars. You can endorse it and give it to Devine. I am promised one hundred dollars more to-morrow, and, if I get it, will send it at once. I shall stay a day or two longer in the hope of getting something from 'The Capitol.' Meanwhile, I cannot advise you. Do what you think is for the best, then — or the least worst, poor Nan, for I know how hard your life must be — harder just now than my disappointments, but you have all that I can wring of comfort or sustenance out of it.

God bless you.

FRANK

P.S. I shall telegraph you to-day. I have paid *all the expenses of telegrams from Glen Cove*, so don't let them swindle you out of any extra charge.

The crash came at last with the failure of 'The Capitol,' and its seizure by creditors in 1878. Following upon one disappointment after another, one can easily imagine what a blow it was to Bret Harte, in his serious difficulties.

Thursday Night [1878?]

Thank you, dear Nan, for your kind, hopeful letter. I *have* been very sick, very much disappointed, but I'm better now, and am only waiting for some money to return. I ought to have, for the work that I have done, more than would help us out of our difficulties. But it doesn't come, and even the money I've expected from 'The Capitol' for my story is seized by its creditors. That *hope* and the expectations that I had from the paper and Piatt in the future amount to nothing. I have found that it is bankrupt.

Can you wonder, Nan, that I have kept this from you? You have so hard a time of it there that I cannot bear to have you worried if there is the least hope of a change in my affairs as they look, day by day. Piatt had been gone nearly a month, was expected to return every day, and only yesterday did I know positively of his inability to fulfill his promises. Neely Thompson came here, three days ago, and in a very few moments I learned from him that I need expect nothing for the particular service I had done him. I've been vilified and abused in the papers for having received compensation for my services, when really and truly I have only received *less* than I should have got from any magazine or newspaper for my story.

I sent you the fifty dollars by Mr. Dana, because I knew you would be in *immediate* need and there is no telegraphic transfer office on Long Island. It was the only fifty I have made since I've been here.

I am waiting to hear from Osgood regarding an advance on that wretched story: he writes me he does not quite like it. I shall probably hear from him to-night. When the money comes, I shall come with it.

God bless you and keep you and the children safe, for the sake of

LIMICK

Bret Harte had, however, staunch friends in political circles who were anxious to use their influence in obtaining for him a Government position which would free him from financial worry and enable him to continue his literary career, besides the fulfillment of his duties. It is not generally known that he was offered the post of First Secretary of the American Legation to Russia, which he declined, fearing not to be able to maintain it with his insufficient private means. After a few weeks of parleying, it was finally decided to appoint him Consul at Crefeld in Germany. A curious and interesting insight into the manner of this appointment is given in the following letters to his wife, written at the time.

MY DEAR ANNA, RIGGS'S, *Friday Night*

I am considerably worried at not hearing from you. I have finished my poem; it makes over four hundred lines, and I have written Lee to send you a cheque for one hundred dollars. I suppose he will. I see no reason why he should not be prompt, but people always take their own time, and only to-day have I got an answer from the 'Independent,' to whom I sent a poem last Thursday, with a request for them to send cheque at once. And the answer is — 'that the editor had *written* to me.' Doesn't it beat anything?

I have seen Stanley Matthews and he has promised me all his assistance, and has, I hear from others, expressed great indignation at my having had to ask for a consulate. He told a friend that he would *make* the Administration *offer* it to me. I cannot help smiling at all this — but it may mean something.

I wrote to Watrous five days ago to see Dix for me. No answer.

Here at last is something tangible. The proprietor of the New Brazilian line of steamers will personally invite me to go on the first trip of the new steamer to Rio Janeiro. If all else fails, here is a trip and a rest for two months, sure.

God bless you. I wish I could send you something more definite.

LIMICK

P.S. Don't forget to write — even if you have nothing new.

Sunday evening, WASHINGTON

NAN! NAN! NAN!

I have not written you because there was really nothing to say, and because I was so faint-hearted that I really could not feel that I could say anything. When I telegraphed to you that 'I had succeeded,' I meant that the

President, the Secretary of State, and Carl Schurz, the Secretary of the Interior, had all recognized my claims and had assured me *personally* of their intention of sending me to the Netherlands, Switzerland, or perhaps *a little higher up in the diplomatic scale.* I have been so faint-hearted and ridiculously modest that until the day I telegraphed you I did not dare to believe in my success. But, when after an interview with the President, the other day, in the Cabinet (where never before another civilian had been admitted), the President said that 'he would unite with the Secretary of State' in giving me an appointment and told me that he did not mind saying that Mr. Evarts (from whom I could not extract a word of positive encouragement before) 'had sent in a list of proposed names and among them my own' — why, I could not help sending you that joyful telegram and feeling, as dear Colonel Laking said to me, that I was 'all right.' No one could have been kinder to me than this noble Teuton; no one has ever, I think, received such uniform courtesy and intelligent appreciation as I have. Whatever I receive from the Department of State I have won by *my own individual efforts;* I have not had to wet the sole of my shoe in the political mire; even the Masons with their 'cousin-ry' have not done anything for me, and in the beginning I saw at once that I must stand alone.

I am so full of my experiences that I cannot write. Wait until I can see you. Then I will talk for half a day. In my whole life I have never had such an experience, and one so fateful for good or ill.

You imagine, I think, Nan, why I have delayed here. But when you remember that I came here with twenty dollars in my pocket, and that until I sent to New York to-day I had nothing more, you will know why I have lingered. And yet you will be glad to know that every moment's delay has helped me — as I will explain to you.

God bless you; know that I will come when I can, and that I am perhaps making the turning-point of my life.

LIMICK

RIGGS HOUSE, *Friday night*

MY DEAR NAN,

I had an interview with Mr. Seward yesterday, which resulted in his confirming all and more than Stanley Matthews had said, and satisfied me, as far as evidence could go, that it was *the plan* of Mr. Evarts to do something for me. Mr. Seward said 'kindly' (like Frankie's schoolmistress), 'Mr. Harte, wouldn't you like to take the map and look at some of the places talked of for you. You know, however, that you are not supposed to know anything about it — until you are offered some place. But here is 'Crefeld,' near Düsseldorf, in Germany, on the Rhine, not much to do and it's worth about two thousand dollars now and may be raised to three or four thousand. What do you think of it? — Mr. Matthews was looking at it for you and we've stopped the application of others for it at present. It is vacant now, and has the advantage that you could take it at once.'

Of course, I was wise enough not to commit myself — although you can imagine that, with all my disappointments, this seemed like a glimpse of Paradise. That it was well to wait, my interview with Matthews again this morning satisfied me, for he told me I could have the position of *First Secretary of Legation to St. Petersburg*, salary twenty-six hundred dollars, if I wanted it!

Of course, this is away *up* as honours go, but St. Petersburg is costly and very 'swell,' and I could barely keep up appearances on the salary. It would be pleasant, of course, to be with Stoughton, who is the Envoy, but I frankly told him why I thought I had better not take it, and he understood me. In looking over the 'blue book,' I noticed his hand and eye always rested on 'The Hague,' and always came the remark, 'That's what you ought to have — the *Mission* there! But it's filled, and *I don't know yet how we can get that man out!*' I only tell you this to show you that the estimation of my needs is increasing — the plans spoken of are successively better — not that I expect or have a right to expect anything better. But being in the saddle I shall try to go as far as I can before I dismount.

And I have something else to tell you, which, happily, is a *fact accomplished*, and which, whatever is done hereafter, cannot be undone. A paper or petition to the Administration in my behalf has been circulated in Congress, and has received I dare not say how many great names and expressions of good-will recommending me to a diplomatic or consular appointment. It was an almost spontaneous movement in which they all have joined, irrespective of politics or party, Democrats and Republicans, Northern and Southern men. One of the Senators told me that in the history of the American Congress, no such honour or compliment was ever before given to an illustrious citizen. He said I should be proud of it — if it brought me nothing; but he added, with a laugh, that no Administration was strong enough to dare to put themselves on the record as ignoring it.

There! — that'll do for to-day, Nan. I am to see Evarts to-morrow, and I'll write.

No, I must tell you something else — in one respect *best of all!* I heard that — as, indeed, I had all along feared — enemies were trying to poison Mr. Evarts's ear with reports of my debts, extravagancies, etc. My friends took hold of the matter on the ground that Mr. Evarts would be influenced by it, as this statement, if true, might show my unfitness for any financial trust. In this extremity I remembered that I had held a pretty responsible position in the Mint, honourably, for seven years. They were overjoyed at this news. I remembered also that John Jay Knox (now the Comptroller of the Currency), a very high official, came out to California to investigate the Mint while I was there. I went to see him: he wrote a letter to Matthews (which Matthews sent to Evarts), saying that I had held a most responsible position, and that in Innis's absence I was, virtually, Superintendent of the Mint, and had been in the confidence of one of the best business men in California. So that, in one blow, all the stories of my extravagance, debts, etc., so far as they affected my having a responsible position under Government, were demolished! More than that, Knox's praise of me absolutely clothed me with virtues of integrity, fitness, etc., I didn't know I possessed.

So it's all right, Nan — there!

I'll stop now and give you a rest. But I wanted you to get this before Sunday, and have it to read over and think over then.

All that worries me now is money. I'm at work writing again, although night and day I keep at the other business. Matthews tells me to stay as long as I can. So be patient.

And God bless you and the chicks!

LIMICKY

RIGGS'S, *Tuesday*, P.M.

MY DEAR NAN,

The Chief Clerk at the State Department this morning told me that my matters were arranged, and that my commission had *been ordered to be made out,* and that it would be ready for me with my instructions, etc., etc., in the next two days. It is *Crefeld* — and I am beginning to think that perhaps it is, as Mr. Seward says, the best thing for a beginning.

So I telegraphed you at once saying 'All Right' and that I would write, but since then your anxious letter has come and I am fearful you might not have comprehended the full meaning of 'All right' — *that the long suspense was over and that I had a place at last.* I thought you knew that I would write. I thought you knew that I was sure of something, and I am worried now to think you were worried.

I can do nothing about money matters until I return. I will write again to-morrow. There will probably be a small balance of copyright account with Osgood which I can get when I return. I've been quite sick and my cold and cough has returned; but I'm ever so much relieved and hopeful now. I'm scribbling this to catch the mail.

Kiss the children.

LIMICK

From Washington, Bret Harte returned to New York, to join his family, before sailing, from where the letters to Osgood and Howells were written. W. D. Howells, it will be remembered, was the first to receive Bret Harte upon his arrival in Boston from California.

713 BROADWAY, NEW YORK
November 9, 1877

MY DEAR OSGOOD,

I was delayed on my return from Washington and only got your proofs yesterday. I return them herewith.

I also send you an English collection of the sketches I submitted to you last summer. I wish you would read them over again — particularly 'My Friend the Tramp' — which, by the way, is a 'taking' title for the book. I have written two or three other sketches, one of which I enclose with the book, another which is one of the 'Condensed Novel' series, being a burlesque on the awful 'Young America' novels — called 'The Pirate Prodigy, by Jack Whackaway,' and to be published in the New Year's number of 'Godey's Lady's Book' ('Godey' is coming to the fore — let the 'Atlantic' tremble!), another Christmas story for the 'Spirit of the Times,' etc., etc., enough to make a book respectable in size and not so d——d bad as to quality.

To come back to 'The Story of a Mine,' which might be called 'That Mine of Mine' if we cared to go into this vulgar possessive case business by way of burlesquing it. I'll try and look up another title. Meantime there is no great hurry to get the book out, and some prospects of profitable sale if we can let it follow on the heels of some sensational developments regarding land-claim frauds which Congress will probably ventilate about 1st December. But I'll read proof and return it promptly. I don't expect to go to Washington again for a couple of weeks at least — unless Evarts sends to consult me regarding the Patagonian mission — in which case I should inform you by telegram.

Truly yours
BRET HARTE

217 EAST FORTY-NINTH STREET
June 22

MY DEAR HOWELLS,

I enclose a poem for the 'Atlantic' — one of half a dozen I hope to write, when the soul that is in me shall germinate. I want to make some dramatic dialogues and monologues like my 'Jim' and 'Cecily' — minus the dialect and the California flavour, for I find men and women pretty much the same on Fifth Avenue as in Dutch Flat, and there is abundant material here. I don't think anybody is likely to follow me in this, and I know no one has preceded me. I purpose another to be called 'Ten Minutes before Dinner'; another, 'Over the Piano' — all dramatic and I think not inconsistent.

My story still hangs fire, but I think you shall have it in a day or two. In the last two months the baby has occupied my attention as an author to the exclusion of all else. Let me know if the poem will do, and what you think of my plan.

Ever yours
BRET HARTE

W. D. HOWELLS, ESQ.

PART II
CREFELD: 1878–1880

PART II

CREFELD: 1878-1880

In June, 1878, Bret Harte sailed for England, on his way to his post, 'little thinking,' as Merwin says, 'that he was never to return.' He sailed alone, his wife and children remaining temporarily in America. How very hard this separation was for him is seen from the letters that follow. Bret Harte was a man essentially in need of a home and sympathetic surroundings, and no one was to feel the lack of it more keenly than he did in the first years of his residence in Europe. One good result, at least, has been the outcome of it, inasmuch as the letters written to his wife during this time throw such an interesting and important light upon his life and character, and enable one to understand and better appreciate his exceedingly sensitive and remarkable personality. It is curious to note the sense of solitude and awe with which he was impressed by the city where he was, very shortly after, to make his home for the rest of his life.

TAVISTOCK HOTEL
LONDON, *July* 9, 1878

MY DEAR NAN,

As soon as I landed at Plymouth, yesterday morning, I telegraphed you, but, on arriving last evening, I found myself so fagged out that I did not write as I promised.

I know you are most anxious to hear about my health. I wish I could write more encouragingly, but I fear the voyage did me not even a temporary good. I was not seasick; I was simply heavy, dyspeptic, and sleepless. I do not think I have had one good night's rest since I left New York, except last night. In short, the voyage was a great disappointment to me — although from my recollection of my previous experiences at sea, I ought not to have built up much hope on that. Nevertheless, the trip was interesting — the weather, with the exception of one or two foggy days, delightful, and the sea, but for one or two days of rolling and roughness, quite calm and beautiful. I was not taken off my sea-legs, but spent most of my time day and night on deck; was thought to be a very good sailor, and secretly envied the passengers who were down in their berths, dreadfully seasick, and soon over it. Osgood was very jolly; Mr. Waring very kind; the Colonel bright and self-complacent; and the few other passengers whose acquaintance I made were very pleasant. A——, of the United States Coast Survey, was on board and gave me a chart on which I marked each day our reckoning, and which I sent to Wodie by mail. It was a pleasant occupation and somewhat broke the monotony of the voyage. I made one or two notes of certain little experiences, of the exquisite colours of the ocean, which were new to me, and which I shall use hereafter.

The run up, by rail, from Plymouth through southern and woodland England was so beautiful that it half atoned for the voyage. I never saw anything like it. There is nothing like it elsewhere. It is all I expected — and more! The island is one strong reality of vivid colour and verdure, but by no means a vision. Everything is comfortable and wholesome, even in its beauty. Nowhere is the earth so beautiful, but nowhere so thoroughly 'of the earth — earthy.' There was to me something so new, and, as it seemed at the time, so comprehensive, in the resolution of England and the English character — a revelation I do not think has been made to any other writer,

BRET HARTE
1878

that I think I shall be able to make something of it. If
I can get my health again — which I sometimes doubt —
I think I can say some new things of England.

I am stopping at a quiet little hotel (Osgood's choice
and selection) and have been already to see Routledge
and Company, and sent my card to Charles Reade with
Boucicault's letter last night. I have not heard from him
yet. Nobody has been to see me yet — it takes a long
time, I suppose, for people to find you are in London,
there being no publication, as with us, of hotel arrivals.
It seems probable that I may be obliged to leave to-
morrow, without seeing anybody — and that Joaquin
Miller's ridiculous advice may be right, after all. But I
would rather go away unnoticed than follow it. And the
programme Osgood and I propose may obviate it, which
is this: I shall, unless I hear from Reade to-day, leave
to-morrow for Paris, stay there a day, and go to Crefeld,
take my place, present my credentials. Then a week
later, when I have everything in order, a Vice-Consul
appointed to act for me, I shall return to Paris, to meet
Osgood there, stay a day or two with him, and then return with him to England, when anybody, if they come
to see me, can find me. It seems to be the best thing to do
at present. I may find some other place. At all events, I
will write you from Paris or Crefeld, as again from here
should I stay over to-morrow. Mr. Trübner, of Trübner
and Company, Osgood's friend, wants me to go down
with him to see George Eliot and stay a day, but I dare
not accept yet.

I have ridden four or five hours through London, and
(from a hansom cab) have seen Saint Paul's, Westminster, and a few other noted points. But I reserve even a
thought about them for the present.

I have only one very strong dominant feeling in this

great, solid, earthly, powerful, and practical London. I am *awfully* lonely!

FRANK

P.S. It was foolish of me not to ask you to write to London, for I shall not hear from you until I reach Crefeld.

Alone, friendless and homesick in a strange land, one can easily picture the feelings of Bret Harte upon his arrival at Crefeld, which account for the melancholy, almost despair, of the first letter he wrote from it.

CREFELD, July 17, 1878

MY DEAR NAN,

At last! I arrived here at eight o'clock this morning, after a long, sleepless ride of twelve hours from Paris, and found your letter of June 28th waiting me. It was only a day's later news, but it was the first one I had from home since I left three weeks ago.

I left London Friday morning and reached Paris the same night, intending to come here the next day, but I found myself so worn out that I lingered at Paris until last night — three days. I saw Dora and Gertie — they were both glad to see me, were very kind, and found a nice little hotel for me, and helped me in many ways in my lingual helplessness, although I was dreadfully disappointed that they could not come to Crefeld with me, where so much depended upon my having some friend with me who understood the language. But I have audaciously travelled alone nearly four hundred miles through an utterly foreign country, on one or two little French and German phrases and a very small stock of assurance, and have delivered my letters to my predecessor and shall

take possession of the Consulate to-morrow. Mr. W——
the present incumbent, appears to me — I do not know
how far I shall modify my impression hereafter — as a
very narrow, mean, ill-bred, and not over-bright, puri-
tanical German. It was my intention to appoint him
my Vice-Consul — an act of courtesy suggested both by
my own sense of right and Mr. Seward's advice, but he
does not seem to deserve it, and has even received my
suggestion of it with the suspicions of a mean nature.
But at present I fear I may have to do it, for I know no
one else here — I am to all appearance utterly friendless;
I have not received the first act of kindness or courtesy
from any one, and I suppose this fellow sees it. I shall go
to Barmen to-morrow to see the Consul there, who held
this place as one of his dependencies and under whose
direction W—— was — and try to make matters
straight.

It's been uphill work ever since I left New York, but
I shall try to see it through, please God! I don't allow
myself to think over it at all, or I should go crazy. I shut
my eyes to it and in doing so perhaps I shut out what is
often so pleasant to a traveller's first impressions, but
thus far London has only seemed to me a sluggish night-
mare through which I have waded, and Paris a confused
sort of hysterical experience. I had hoped for a little
kindness and rest here. Perhaps it may come. But you
must know that the only courtesy extended to me in
London was through one of Osgood's friends, Mr. Trübner, of Trübner and Company, who invited me to his
house, while Reade, whom I saw finally by going to him,
was barely civil, made a lame excuse of intending to write
to me, and said Boucicault had *not* written to him and
that he (Reade) never had anything to do with the new
paper. But to-day I found here (forwarded from London)

a kind letter in response to my card, from Froude, who invites me to come to his country place — an old seaport village in Devonshire. If everything has gone well here — if I can *make* it go well here — I shall go back to London and Paris for a vacation of a few weeks — and see Froude, at least.

At least, Nan, be sure I've written now the *worst;* I think things must be better soon. I shall, please God, make some friends, I think, in good time — and will try and be patient. But I shall not think of sending for you until I see clearly that I can stay *myself*. If the worst comes to the worst, I shall try to stand it for a year, and save enough to come home and begin anew *there*. But I could not stand it to see you break your heart here through disappointment as I mayhap may do.

Gertie told me that the French and English papers copied all the ugly things that were said about me. That may account for some of the incivilities.

I shall write again in a day or two when I have taken my place.

Your affectionate
FRANK

P.S. My health is pretty fair. It would be unfair to judge of it now until I get over my worries.

Although highly emotional, Bret Harte was always perfectly sincere. Fearing that, in the despondency of his first impressions, he may have gone too far, he followed the previous letter by a second one, written the same night, in which he attempts to rectify what he thought might have been exaggerations. He was, however, never fond of Germany, nor was he ever happy there, in spite of his appreciation for its history and art.

CREFELD, *July* 17, 1878, *Midnight*

MY DEAR NAN,

I wrote and mailed you a letter this afternoon that I fear may sound rather disconsolate, so I sit down to-night to send another which I hope will take a little of the blues out of the first. Since I wrote I have had some further conversation with my predecessor, Mr. W——, and I think I can manage matters with him. He has hauled in his horns, considerably, since I told him that the position I offered him — as far as the honour of it went — was better than the one he held. For the one thing pleasant about my office is that the dignity of it has been raised on my account. It was only a dependency — a Consular Agency — before it was offered to me.

I feel a little more hopeful, too, for I have been taken out to a 'Fest' — or a festival — of one of the Vereins, and one or two of the people were a little kind. I forced myself to go; these German festivals are distasteful to me, and I did not care to show my ignorance of their language quite so prominently, but I thought it was the proper thing for me to do. It was a very queer sight. About five hundred people were in an artificial garden, beside an artificial lake, looking at artificial flowers, and yet as thoroughly enjoying it as if they were children. Of course there was beer and wine. Here as in Paris, everybody drinks, and all the time, and nobody gets drunk. Beer, beer, beer — and guzzle, guzzle, guzzle, food and drink, and drink and food again. Everywhere the body is worshiped. Beside them, we are but unsubstantial spirits.

I write this in my hotel, having had to pass through a mysterious gate and so into a side courtyard and up a pair of labyrinthine stairs to my dim, spark-like 'zimmer' or chamber. The whole scene as I returned to-night looked as it does on the stage — the lantern over the iron gate, the hotel, half inn, half warehouse, strutting out into the street with a sidewalk not a foot wide. I know now from my observations, both here and in Paris and London, where the scene painters at the theatres get their subjects. Those impossible houses — those unreal silent streets all exist in Europe.

Good-night.

LIMICK

I send Frankie a little book of songs which were sung by the people at the 'Fest.' Tell him to look at page 13, and try to get it translated, and imagine how his papa felt when he heard these grave men sing it. I think you will recognize it at once.

CREFELD, GERMANY, *July 22*, 1878

MY DEAR NAN,

I've received yours of the 4th and the boys' two letters of the 5th July.

And I've finally settled the matter of my Vice-Consul, which was worrying me dreadfully — for everything depended upon my having a good man. He backed out again the next day after I had written to you, but, with the help of Mr. Stanton, the Consul at Barmen, who has been a very good friend to me, although my appointment lost him one of his dependencies, I've finally found one — who speaks English, French, and German — who will act as my deputy, provide me with a suitable office, etc., etc., and take all the work of the Consulate off my hands for all the fees above twenty-five hundred dollars per year — unless they should run above thirty-five hundred per year, when he returns the balance to me. This, of course, limits my income to twenty-five hundred per year, but it really was the only way in which I could assure myself of that. The entire fees will but average over three thousand per year, so that the arrangement simply means that I pay out five hundred dollars for office rent, clerk hire, and some one to act as my deputy. Stanton, of Barmen, says it is most advisable, and I have made it only for six months — the first six months when I shall be so helpless.

So that I am *sure* — reasonably sure — of twenty-five hundred dollars a year income from my office. This is at least one step gained in my outlook for the year. It is only subject to this one limit — which I and you must always keep before us — that I am likely, at any moment, with or without cause, or why or wherefore, to be *removed*. Mr. Stanton is one of the oldest and most efficient consuls in the service and has been treated like a child. This place was taken from his district to give to me — without word or apology.

Now with this patent fact before me I've been trying to figure ahead.

First: I've found out all about the cost of living in Germany, and my conclusion is this: You cannot live — *in any respectable or decent fashion — on less than you can live decently in America,* BUT — you can live on a modest sum — say nine thousand marks or three thousand dollars — infinitely better than you can live in America for the same sum. It is the little *luxuries* and ornaments of life that are cheap here — not the *necessities*. House rent is, of course, cheaper, but furnished houses are unknown, and you must risk buying furniture at about New York prices. Servants' wages are trifling, but you require more servants. You cannot economize and live here, without dropping below the class to which you belong, and that is fatal to an American official. There is no intermediate stage here as in France. You must spend three thousand dollars and live comfortably as a gentleman, or spend about one thousand dollars and live like the petty shop-keepers, over your shop, and be regarded as them. There is nothing between one thousand or three thousand. Stanton and I went over the various items carefully and came to that conclusion. He lives in a handsome house, spends forty-five hundred dollars, but lives in a style that would cost ten thousand in New York, and he — like most of the other American officials of my grade — has a little private income. In all the nonsense told me about the cheapness of living in Germany I find but one grain of truth — it is incomparably the best place for a man of moderate means and assured income to live.

Now, there is five hundred dollars for me to make up for our living — to make up out of other work. Of course, if I keep my health I can — indeed I *expect* to make at least twenty-five hundred dollars per year more, in literary work. But suppose I should fall sick — or be removed?

Of course, I expect to somewhat modify these figures (all but the *income*), and it would be foolish for me to speak finally now, but before you can *think* of bringing the family here I must have some further experience. It is difficult to say yet whether this climate and country is best for me, or will enable me to do the most work. At present I cannot write *at all* — of course, I know I ought not to in this excitement — but I've had an article in hand, for which I expect one hundred and fifty dollars from England, unfinished for ten weeks. I'm far from well, and suffer from headaches incessantly, and am so *lonely* that, as I told you before, I dare not dwell on it. I've been twice over to Barmen — sixty miles — to Stanton's to dinner, and here had a childish comfort in hearing my own language spoken and having some kindness shown me. Stanton has a very sweet German wife who speaks English well — but what I have done meanwhile, when I was not at the consulate, I don't really know. Without a knowledge of the language, it is impossible to do anything — to say nothing of conversations and mere social intercourse.

You must remember, Nan, that I've scarcely been two weeks in this country — indeed, I can hardly believe that it is not yet a *month* since I left New York — and you must not expect me to be able to do more than record my experience for some weeks yet to come. And before anything more is thought of your coming (all of you), there must be at least eight hundred dollars ahead — clear of all other expense. And I'm almost afraid, if I can have that, I'll take it and *return.*

I have been hoping to return to Paris in a day or two — it is only a day's ride — and see Osgood, who has written me to go to Switzerland with him. Perhaps if I went the trip and mountain air might do me good. The hotel here is miserable in its lodging, and I have not yet found rooms. The German cooking is damnable. This is the Rhine district, where beer is unknown, but everybody drinks wine, and in enormous quantities. Every man drinks a couple of bottles at dinner, but nobody gets drunk. I've heard this before of Germany — but, looking carefully at the men, I find that, while they are stout and ruddy, they are inclined to be pimply about the nose and streaky in colour in the face, and that, after all, the Gentle Bacchus has somehow put his seal on them. Miserable dyspeptic that I am, God help me from ever becoming one of these fat-witted rosy satyrs. Since I have been in Europe I've grown sick of meat and drink, I fancy.

Tell the boys I'll write to them in a day or two. Tell the girls that out of England, among the upper classes, Papa never saw any so sweet as his own little Ethel and Tottie.

Should I not go to Switzerland from Paris, I'll go to see Dora and Gertie — who is to sing for the Competition Prize on the 25th. Should I go to Switzerland, I shall return to Crefeld before I go to England, postponing my visit there. In any event, I'll write you soon again.

Don't mind this scrawl. I write hastily — as I eat — or I shouldn't *eat* or *write* at all. Remember that half the time I'm expecting to modify what I have said, and that half the time I fear I'll worry you with my worries, or distress you by my silence.

You remember that I told you how odd my hotel looked one night when I entered it through the gateway. Crefeld is a modern town — and about the most uninteresting place you ever saw; but I was surprised to learn today that the hotel was over four hundred years old and that the soldiers during the Thirty Years' War held it. Candour compels me to state that, in spite of that historic glamour, the room I'm writing in is the most uncomfortable hole I ever was in. The city is a cramped Philadelphia without its neatness, with all its whitened glare. Look any way, walk any way, north, east, south, and west, the same little blocks of stucco-fronted, shutterless houses, with windows from which no face ever shows through the muslin-shrouded panes. A man, two blocks away, looms up like a tree. At morning and evening, the people hurry by on the newer sidewalks and through the middle of the street between these blank walls as if they had taken a short cut through an alley and were anxious to get home.

God bless you and the children.

FRANK

P.S. Address your letters always to me as Bret Harte, etc., United States Consul, Crefeld, Germany.

In August of the same year, having already put the affairs of the Consulate upon a sound footing, Bret Harte returned to London for a short vacation and rest. He had not a strong constitution, and at this time was far from well, being subject to violent and increasing attacks of neuralgia which left him sleepless and weakened him considerably. He speaks again in the following letter of the demoralizing effect of his perpetual ill-health, and of his increasing difficulty in fighting against it.

LANGHAM HOTEL
LONDON, *August* 11, 1878

Mrs. Bret Harte
    Sea Cliff Hotel
        Sea Cliff, Long Island.

MY DEAR NAN,

Two weeks ago I left Crefeld for Paris. I did not write to you from that wicked place, for I was so thoroughly steeped in iniquity and dissipation while there that I did not wish to write to you. I'm comparatively clean now, although my hair still stands on end.

And yet I was not happy, nor, what is more important, in better health. I am hoping that a visit to Froude down in Devonshire on the seacoast may do me good, although the English climate affects my throat and brings back my cough. I dislike to write so much about myself and my ailings, but my miserable health spoils everything — the landscape, the scenery, the people — everything is merged in me. I have no appetite and sleep badly. I wish I had gone to Switzerland, and, if I do not pick up at Froude's, I'll go there yet. It is not far from Crefeld and the mountain air may do me good. The doctor in Crefeld recommended it.

Did I tell you that there are few homœopaths in Ger-

many now? My German doctor pooh-poohed them, and
wanted to physic and blister me! He tried to get me to
take chloral to make me sleep, and finally presented
valerian, but, when I opened the vial — which was exactly like the medicine bottles you see in pictures, with a
flaming label, *tied on the neck* — I smelt the sickening
odour of *chloroform* and threw it out of the window. Then
I got better.

I have got all your letters. Don't think, Nan, because
I have not spoken of them, that they are not anything to
me, and that all you tell me of the children and their say-
ings, and your own thoughts, is not as grateful as the blue
sky to me, but I try to stop thinking of you and them and
the distance between, and how much yet has to be done,
and how I must keep up my strength to do it; for, when I
do, I become utterly despondent. I know everything will
come right when I get stronger, and I believe all that you
tell me, Nan, even to your talk about the stimulants —
but I cannot use them. They simply make me sick. But
I did, for a while, I think, improve on the Rhine wines
at Crefeld.

I've half filled my little drawing-book with rough pencil sketches — and, when I'm a little stronger, I'll write
you about them. I've done some work, too, and pretty
good work, I think. And I'm full of new ideas and suggestions for stories — and sketches. But I feel that I
ought not to write a line for at least six months. Nevertheless, I did write a story, for which I expect to receive some
money this week, so that I can send you a draft. And you
will have also what 'Scribner' or the 'Atlantic' give for
it. I've some little things for you and some medals for
the boys, which I shall send you by Osgood, who returns
to America on the 27th. He'll tell you how I am, although
my prolonged stay at Crefeld knocked our little excursion

on the head, and I have not seen him since I left him in London a month ago.

Give my love to Eliza and remember me kindly to Denis. Tell the boys I'll write to them soon again. Kiss the little girls from their own papa.

FRANK

P.S. I shall write you from Froude's.

One of the principal reasons for Bret Harte's choice of England, for his short leave of absence, was to enable him to visit James Anthony Froude, the famous historian, for whom he had a great admiration. Froude was to become one of Bret Harte's most intimate friends, their friendship lasting until the former's death. In the letter to his wife he gives a charming description of an old English home, together with clever and humorous observations on the differences of English and American life.

'THE MOULT,' SALCOMBE
KINGSBRIDGE, DEVONSHIRE
August 19, 1878

MY DEAR NAN,

I have just received yours of August 2d, forwarded to me from Crefeld. I can understand your alarm at not receiving a letter from me for two weeks, because, after writing you on the 8th July, I did not write again until I had arrived at Crefeld, nearly two weeks. I think I have received all your letters, I think you have all mine.

I wrote you from London a day or two ago. Since then I came down here to visit Froude (the historian), who is the only Englishman who has yet treated me with any particular kindness. After I left London, a month ago, I got a line from Houghton at Crefeld inviting me to dinner the next day, but since then I have not heard from him.

I sent my card to Froude when I first arrived. He quickly responded with an invitation, but I could not then leave Crefeld; then he sent a second letter, which I enclose, and so I came down here. This damp English climate is depressing to me, and, of course, this place on the southwesterly coast of England is almost like being again at sea, but I don't regret coming here.

It is, without exception, one of the most *perfect* country houses I ever beheld. Imagine, if you can, something between 'Locksley Hall' and the 'high wall garden' where Maud used to walk, and you have some idea of this graceful English home. I look from my window down upon exquisite lawns and terraces all sloping toward the seawall and then down upon the blue sea below. I walk out in the long high garden, past walls hanging with netted peaches and fruits, past terraces, looking over the ruins of an old feudal castle, and I can scarcely believe I am not reading an English novel, or that I am not myself a wandering ghost. To heighten the absurdity, when I return to my room I am confronted by the inscription on the door 'Lord Devon' (for this is the property of the Earl of Devon, and I occupy his favourite room), and I seem to have died, and to be resting under a gilded mausoleum that lies even more than the average tombstone does. Froude is a connection of the Earl's, and has hired the house for the summer.

He is a widower, with two daughters and a son. The eldest girl is not unlike a highly educated Boston girl — and the conversation sometimes reminds me painfully of Boston. There is the usual sly grimace, with the usual much 'put-upon' look, and an awful dowager, widow of a Bishop — or perhaps, Heaven knows! a Bishop herself — in awful silks, with a voice like Mrs. Siddons. When she asks me questions about America, and you and my chil-

JAMES ANTHONY FROUDE

dren, it seems like a voice from the Past. The youngest daughter, only ten years old, told her sister in reference to some conversation Froude and I had that 'she feared' (this child!) 'that Mr. Bret Harte was inclined to be *skeptical.*' Doesn't this exceed any English story of the precocity of American children? The boy — scarcely fourteen — acts like a boy of eight (an American boy of eight) and talks like a man of thirty — as far as pure English and facility of expression goes. His manners are perfect — yet he is perfectly simple and boylike. The culture and breeding of these English children is something tremendous. But sometimes — and here comes one of my 'buts' — there's always a suggestion of some repression — some discipline that I don't like. Everybody here is carefully trained to their station — and seldom bursts out beyond it. The *respect* the whole family show toward me is something fine — and *depressing.* I can easily feel how this deference to superiors is ingrained in all.

But Froude — dear old noble fellow — is *splendid.* I love him more than I ever did in America. He is great, honest, manly — democratic in the best sense of the word — scorning all sycophancy and manners, yet accepting all that is round him, yet more proud of his literary profession than of his kinship with these people, whom he quietly controls. There are only a few literary men like him here, but they are kings. I could not have had a better introduction to them than through Froude, who knows them all, who is Tennyson's best friend, and who is anxious to make my *entrée* among them a success. I had forgotten that Canon Kingsley, whom you liked so much, was Froude's brother-in-law until Froude reminded me of it. So it is like being among friends here.

So far I've avoided seeing any company here, but

Froude and I walk and walk and talk and talk. They let me do as I want — and I have not been well enough yet to do aught but lounge. The doctor is coming to-day, and, if I am no better, I shall return in a day or two to London and then to Crefeld.

I'll write you from London and send some money. God bless you all.

LIMICK

During his stay in England, Bret Harte visited Newstead Abbey, the famous historic home of Byron, where he was the guest of Mr. and Mrs. Webb, who later became his intimate friends. He had always been deeply fascinated by Byron's genius and personality, and the unusual engraving of him in his scholar's robes was presented to Bret Harte by Mrs. Webb with the charming dedication: ' . . . in memory of his first visit to his English home, Newstead Abbey, to his English first cousins.' In the following very interesting letter to his wife, he gives a beautiful description of the old place and of the charm which the memory of its past held for him. It was a tribute to their very real hospitality when he wrote that 'leaving Newstead was like leaving home.'

NEWSTEAD ABBEY
NOTTINGHAM, September 6, 1878

MY DEAR NAN,

I came up from Froude's to London quite ill, and yet I had to wait here a few days for Osgood, who was going back to America, and who I trust has sent you my note and a few trifles I gave him for the boys. While waiting here, however, I got an invitation from Mrs. Webb, the hostess of Newstead Abbey, to visit her there. I think I am indebted somewhat to Mr. Miller for this first introduction to some of the best people in England — for he was visiting the Abbey at the time — but after I arrived here, and since I have been here, all the kindness and excessive cordiality shown to me I think I won for myself. For I have heard much of English hospitality, but never was so pleasantly convinced of it. I have been told that this beautiful house must be considered my 'English home' — to come here whenever I want, do as I like — and always feel that my English 'first cousins' would be glad to see me. And even the few days I have spent here quite draw me to believe in this pleasant illusion.

You have, of course, read all about this old home of Lord Byron's. Washington Irving was here when it belonged to Byron's old schoolfellow Colonel Wildman, and has written about it. There are many pictures of this old Norman abbey (and some I shall send you) and perhaps you already know *how* it looks; but neither photograph nor written description can give you an idea of its beauty, of its wonderful mixture of the romantic, the historical, the legendary, and the modern opulence of a *perfect* English country seat. I thought Froude's place was beautiful, but here is so much beauty, with history, with a certain grandeur, and, above all, with all the melancholy of Byron's genius instinct in every line of the ruined chapel. It is grand and lovely as Byron, and as — sad. For the man has become a very real person to me since I have been here, and what I have always looked upon as his fancies and his affectations I can see were doubtless very genuine and sincere. To be *here*, where *he* played as a boy, and know how dreadful it must have been for him to part with it; to see the great house of 'Annesley' and even the 'antique oratory' where he stood with Mary Chatworth and feel in some queer way *why* he was unappreciated here — a feeling which the ludicrous self-conceit of these people has perpetuated by a hideous picture of an agonized Byron in a dark corsair's cloak looking in a window on her perfect happiness — to come back to the abbey, and at night hear the wind sighing through the ruined central window of the chapel, and the wall left standing like a great screen, or to come up from the billiard-room at night, through the old cloisters, when the light of your bedroom candle is but a foot from you, and from every arch the figure of the 'black friar' seems to steal forth — then you begin to understand something about this proud, handsome, sensitive, lame boy. I never thought I should ever feel like crying over Byron. But I walk here alone in a dream, with only this beautiful, wicked, foolish, but awfully pathetic figure appealing to me out of the past, until I forget everything but that.

It was during his stay at Newstead Abbey that Bret Harte made the acquaintance of the Duchess of St. Albans, who, with her husband, became a devoted friend. He frequently stayed with them in later years. Yet in spite of the courtesy and kindness of which he was the object, and which he deeply appreciated, he was always homesick for his own country.

10th September, LONDON

I take this up after leaving Newstead on my way back to Crefeld. I'm afraid you can't read it, but I leave it for you to puzzle over. Leaving Newstead was like leaving home; in the week that I was there I felt more at ease than I have felt anywhere since I left America. These people have very truly made it my 'English home.'

Among the little photographs I have put away to send you is one of *my room* — 'the Duke of Sussex Room,' as was called. It was next to the great ruined screen-like wall of the Abbey, and overlooked the lake. I tried to write you here and began a letter to the boys, but I was so full of everything I saw that I could not write a line. I slept one night in the Byron room — the haunted chamber — of course, without anything coming of it; but that night I wrote a funny ballad called the 'Good Lord Byron' — being a sort of relief to the dreadfully gloomy stories of the dreadfully wicked Byrons, and gave it to Geraldine Webb — whose picture I send you — for her album. It was a great success, and the whole countryside were anxious to have it to copy. I'll get a copy from the lady and send it to you. I remember only that it was very ridiculous and audacious, and that all the Byron ghosts, headed by George Gordon himself, would have been justified in haunting me the next night.

I met many pleasant people. Among them was the Duchess of St. Albans — a sweet, bright, sympathetic, graceful lady to whom I took a great fancy. I lunched at her house and she came over the next day with all her party from 'Bestwood Lodge' to luncheon at the Abbey. She had, she confessed to me, set her heart upon taking me away from the Webbs and installing me at 'Bestwood,' and she at last got the Webbs to consent. But I knew they felt a little sore about it and they had been very kind to me, and so I declined as graciously as I could, and got out of it by promising to make the Duchess a visit in October if I could come to England. She sent me her photograph, which I will send you, and a book which she wanted me to read. I met her once or twice in my wanderings with the Webbs out toward 'Annesley' and Hucknall, and have a very picturesque recollection of her coming through the graveyard at Hucknall Church, where Byron is buried, with a train of some of the prettiest women in England behind her — but herself the nicest of them all. It was pretty to see the suggestion of graceful deference paid her by those other women — who were mostly her old schoolfellows and friends and who called her by her Christian name — and the sweet little graceful way she accepted it — the whole thing more a sentiment than a formality. It was the only indication I ever saw of her rank — of her being the wife of the second oldest Duke in the Kingdom. I always felt more at ease in her presence than I ever felt among American women. She was perfectly *natural;* and so indeed were they all. We had, a day or two afterward, a picnic in Sherwood Forest, and a visit to Lord Manners's great house, and Mrs. Scott-Murray and her sister, and a Mrs. Percy-Gore and her daughter (two beautiful women of apparently the same age) helped me to poke fun at the paintings, and pretend to appraise the value of the furniture as if they had been two mischievous American girls — say the God-wins. This reminds me that I met Annie Godwin in Paris at the Hôtel Splendide. Her father and mother were in London; she was in company with a very 'fast' American woman and her daughter, and of course there was no end of wickedness that she informed me she had been up to. I could not help laughing, but I could not help remembering what those Frenchmen think about our American girls. And I must say that the extravagance of some of our 'fast' girls justifies them somewhat. Gertie told me that she had to fight against the prejudice of the best people to the American girls when she first entered the Conservatory, and that she did not dare to be even civil to a gentleman.

The Webbs told me to tell you that you are to come to them as soon as you come to England, and the boys are to have the lake to row on and to fish in. They have been very kind — but for all that, I cannot say that I like

England or should like to live there — or that I am very anxious to go there again. I am always heartsick for my own country. I do not feel as if I could stop long in any place — and the thought of two years longer here sometimes makes me feel utterly hopeless.

My eyes are troubling me, so that I must stop writing. They have been very weak lately. Hence this scrawl.

I hope Osgood sent you a cheque for some copy I gave him; for I cannot send you anything until I get back to Crefeld. God bless you. I'll write from there.

FRANK

The next letter, to his son Francis, although written upon his return to Crefeld, is still a remnant of his stay in England. Bret Harte was essentially a patriot, and nowhere more than in the letters to his children can be seen that strong and dominant adherence to the principles of a free race which never forsook him throughout his long residence abroad.

BRET HARTE
UNITED STATES CONSUL

CREFELD, *September* 11, 1878

MY DEAR FRANKIE,

I began a letter to you at Newstead Abbey, but I cannot find it now among my papers, and imagine I must have torn it up. You will say 'that's like Papa' — but it contained nothing more valuable than an account of some things at the Abbey which I thought might interest you. I'll try to remember some of them, and the photographs I have sent to Mamma by mail will explain the rest.

You know, or ought to know, that the Abbey was founded by the King Henry who murdered 'à Becket,' and that this Abbey was built in expiation or apology for the offence. Kings always wiped out a murder or a crime of any kind by making a bishop or a pilgrimage or a church. Then another king — you'll find out who he was in history (of course, Papa knows!) — took the church away from the friars or monks who lived there and gave it to a Lord Byron who had killed people in battle. Killing was always a good business in England, and two thirds of the noblemen and their estates owe their titles to slaughtering or were perfected by homicides. But what made Newstead most interesting to Papa was that here Lord Byron (when he was a lame, melancholy boy) lived with his mother, and he loved the old place, and was filled with its beauty and its gloom and its traditions, and that he buried his 'only friend,' as he called his dog 'Boatswain,' here, and that he planted an oak tree that still stands here, and that he cut his name and that of his sister Augusta on another tree that still bears it. But they have cut it down lest the growth of the tree should obliterate the lettering, and they keep it sacredly in a glass case in the Abbey. For there are many varieties of the British oak at Newstead, but there was only one Byron, and he made that one tree famous 'with his little penknife.'

Then Papa liked the people who are there *now* — much better than the people who *were* there — always excepting Lord George Gordon. The place is owned by Colonel William Frederick Webb, a retired officer of the English Army, and a famous African traveller and sportsman. The great halls and galleries of the Abbey — even the cloisters where the monks used to walk — are filled with tigers' heads and buffalo horns, elk horns, rhinoceros heads, and as you enter the eastern porch you are confronted by a big (stuffed) lion with a bullet-hole in his forehead still showing where the gallant Colonel's bullet passed through. The Colonel was a mighty hunter —

and a great friend of Dr. Livingstone, the explorer. It seems to me that he ought to have had a title and estates given to *him* — but it's the English custom to reward only *man*-killing, and so he's a simple gentleman, but rich enough to buy the estate himself, and not be 'beholden' to a king for it. He is tall — over six feet — and as brave and good as he is tall and strong.

I've told you he was rich. Very rich. He owns a coal mine that runs under half a county, he has a railway station *of his own*, a stable filled with seldom-used horses, an army of servants, etc., etc. He is very good to his tenants and work-people, and both he and the Duke of St. Albans have built some picturesque cottages for their working-men and colliers, that are finer than anything I ever saw in America. The other day we were riding out together, and I saw among the trees the clustering roofs and gables of a beautiful building. 'Whose place is that,' I asked? 'Oh,' says the Colonel — 'that! — that's nothing. It's only the schoolhouse and library I put up for my farmers and labourers. *It was too far for them to send their children to Mansfield!*' He seemed to be quite pleased that I liked it, and said he had thought perhaps he had been foolish to spend twenty thousand pounds (or one hundred thousand dollars) in that way.

And yet — you would hardly believe it — this really noble, generous fellow, sitting as Chief Magistrate in the next town, sent two or three men to jail for picking turnips in a field — 'Trespassing upon property.' For this is England — here property is everything. Men are an afterthought. All property is sacred — even the blackberries on the hedges belong to somebody. A weary tramp walking the highroad may not rest himself in the hedge for fear of frightening the partridges out of it into somebody else's domain. Property again.

I want you to respect and like England — as I do — but I want you to be thankful — very thankful — that you are born and live in a country where Nature owns something — and where everything has not been taken away from God, until you really fancy that the sunshine has been 'preserved,' you so rarely see it.

The daughters of the house were all called 'children' — except the eldest; did not come to the table, but lived with their books and the governess in the schoolroom. They are very nice, and very large, and very natural. Mabel Webb — aged fourteen — being bantered by her sister as to her strength, took me up in her arms and carried me half the length of the terrace, fifty feet. She was a little larger than Miss Fanny Faulkner. I felt very much as if I had been carried away by a lioness. There is only one boy — Algernon — the son and heir to all this property. He was about ten, as tall as you. He wore an immense 'good boy' collar, which was always getting under his ears and hiding him, and he was always having his hair pulled by his athletic sisters.

I must stop now, for my eyes — which are very poorly — are quite giving out. The song I sent you, 'Wandering is the Miller's Joy,' was one of your old kindergarten songs taught you by the 'kindly' Miss Jordan in Oakland. I'm afraid you don't remember yourself as well as 'Papa' remembers you. Tell Wodie I'll write to him to-morrow.

Your affectionate Papa
Frank

All was now going well with the Consulate, and Bret Harte, relieved from anxiety, although far from well and still very much a stranger, was slowly getting accustomed to his surroundings. He was arranging to lecture in Wiesbaden, which proved to be very successful, and he was also planning through his friend Froude a series of lectures in England for the winter. His niece, Miss Gertrude Griswold, to whom he frequently refers in letters of this period, had a remarkably fine voice, and later became prima donna at the Grand Opera in Paris. He was always very fond of her, and assisted her throughout her short and sad career.

CREFELD, *September* 14, 1878

MY DEAR NAN,

I enclose draft for one hundred dollars and will send you duplicate by some other steamer. I hope Osgood has disposed of my story, and has already sent you the proceeds. I expect in a few days to hear from the German publishers, and will send you some more. I've had to lay out considerable money for the Consulate (which will all come back to me at the end of the year), and my travelling expenses have been considerable.

But the business of the Consulate will, I think, fully realize all my expectations. My literary work, as soon as I am able to get fairly at it, will pay me well, and I have just concluded an arrangement to lecture at Wiesbaden this winter for one hundred dollars. It's a great compliment and a great sum for Germany — considering that the lecture is in English for the benefit of the American and English residents at this great Continental wateringplace. I'm keeping back from making any English engagements for the winter to lecture, for when I do I want to strike high. I want to get the ear of the best people, and I think from my late experience in England I can. I told Froude what his brother-in-law Kingsley said, and he will help me at the right time. But I shan't hurry matters.

I spent my birthday rather dismally in London (I'm answering your last letter, wherein you speak of it — or I should not), working away feverishly and hurriedly to finish a story for the 'Belgravia,' a proof of which I have just sent to the New York 'Sun.' When I was most nervous and homesick, it suddenly occurred to me that it was the 25th. Two days afterward I had a letter from my Vice-Consul saying that they had drunk my health in Crefeld on that day, and I dare say that had I been there I should have had a *fête* as you suggested. But I was very much touched at receiving a letter from United States Consul Winser, of Coburg, whose daughter — a little girl of fourteen — had been fellow-passenger with me from New York, thanking me for my kindness to her and her aunt, and enclosing me a letter from her with a birthday present of a paper-knife. How she remembered or knew of my birthday I couldn't find out.

I should have told you before that the afghan was found all right, and that it has accompanied me on all my voyages. I should have told you, too, that Gertie Griswold sang for the prize, didn't get it, but got a very handsome notice in the papers and from the critics. Her mother says they told her that if it had not been Gertie's *first year* at the *Conservatoire*, she would have had the prize — but it was not the custom to give prizes to such *new* pupils. I did not hear her, for I was not in Paris at the time. They are now at *La Bornboule*, a watering-place in the South of France, for Gertie's health, which, by the way, is miserable. She looks like an intelligent and self-absorbed ghost. She has written me a long and very bright letter describing the place and the scenery, with a wonderful appreciation of Nature which I, and I don't believe you, would have suspected.

I hope the photographs and leaves will come safely to you. Did I tell you that I cut from the base of the ruined screen of Newstead Abbey two small slips of ivy, that I kept them carefully in water and have given one to a German friend and admirer of Byron's, and the other I shall plant in a little flower-pot and, if it grows and takes root, I shall send it (by some good-natured passenger) to you?

I haven't sent you any *silk* — for I expect to have it presented to me when I visit Mr. Schoebel's factory. *That*, I am told, is the custom — but Schoebel is away in Switzerland now.

At Newstead I wrote two long letters to the boys, but with my usual carelessness I tore them up, I suppose, with other papers. I reproduced a letter to Frankie as nearly as I could remember, and I shall give an hour or two to Wodie to-day. I am glad the boys got the boat. I don't know what to say about the theatrical performances. I want them both to study the languages — and write good English, and learn good manners. I'd rather always they would be honest *boys* — than imperfect, cheap, *men*.

You *must* send me pictures of Ethel and Totty. Everybody asks me about them. I got a long letter from Eliza, and as soon as I get a little time I'll answer her. God bless you all.

Limick

Crefeld, *October 5*, 1878

My dear Nan,

I was conscience-stricken and horrified when your letter came, to look back and find it was nearly three weeks since I had last written. But they were *very busy* weeks to me, all the business that had collected in my office during my absence to England, and all my first quarterly reports to the Department, had to be got rid of. It is so late now that I must only send you a few lines with a draft for one hundred dollars — and a promise, which I shall *surely* keep, to write again within the next week and send you another draft. I wish I had more money to send *now*. For I want you to be able to make your arrangements to leave Sea Cliff, before the 1st November. You must not on any account stay there during the winter. I've so much to say to you for and against coming here this winter that I must not open the subject now. All I can say now is that, from *my own experience* (and it has been pretty general), I know of no happiness, comfort, pleasure, mental or bodily, that can be had by a residence in Germany, that cannot be had in America with less trouble and expense. You probably think I exaggerate — wait until I write again and I'll give you a few details — and personal experiences. I am not speaking of a visit or the novelty of travel and sight-seeing. I speak particularly of a home.

I think my health is better, although I came back from England with a cold very much like my cold of last winter. I think I have broken it up, however, by a very simple German remedy — so simple that I want you to try it. I take a goblet full of equal parts of hot *milk* and cold Selters water, every morning before rising. You know how I dislike milk; but the Selters water takes away the buttery taste, and makes a palatable drink — very much as I imagine cream soda-water tastes. There is enough salt in the Selters to give it a flavour. Try it: one half glass of *hot* milk, one half glass of Selters, mixed before rising. It is a sovereign cure for a cold in the beginning.

You ordered me to try the German wines. I did, but they did not agree with me, and the doctor ordered me to drink red wine (Bordeaux). It's too bad, for the wines here are good and cheap. But almost every form of wine or alcohol disagrees with me. My dyspepsia has taken a new form of terrible distress and distension after each meal. I go often without my meals, fearing to eat. But I'm bet-

ter, I think, in other ways. I'm stronger. I can walk —
without dizziness or trouble; and I walk nearly four times
as much as I did in America. When I can afford it, I shall
get me a horse. They are to be had cheap here — I mean
on hiring.

I was at first frightened as to my *work*. But I think I've
got back my old strength and pleasure in my pen again.
It's a great relief not to have to write against *time*, and to
work for my own pleasure at my own leisure. And I shall
have no difficulty in disposing of my work here, at good
prices. I think I can make from my pen nearly twice as
much as before. I hope to get something from the German publishers, and am in treaty with them now. The
London journals write to me for copy. I've already
accepted an invitation to lecture in Hull, England, for
two hundred and fifty dollars this winter, and Froude
thinks I will have no difficulty in making ten or a dozen
lectures in England.

My English friends have been very anxious to have me
return to them for a visit. I enclose to you a letter from
the Duchess of St. Albans with an invitation I had to
decline on account of my work here. . . . She's a very nice
woman. When I write again, I'll send you her photograph, though it breaks my heart to part with it, of
course!

Kiss the little girls and say that Papa has their pictures
on his desk. Tell the boys I'll write to them presently,
but *not* until after I write you again. Remember me kindly
to Mr. Devine. Ask Mr. Dana if he got my sketch in
time to publish it. I might have sent it elsewhere and
got you a hundred dollars for it, but I thought it better to send it to Dana to begin to pay up the money he
so kindly advanced. It will be all the better in the end
if you can hold your own for a month yet. You will not

then be troubled at all for want of money. My first settlement of accounts here makes me nervous about drawing money, and I have kept one rule rigidly here. *I will not make a single debt.*

God bless you.

FRANK

P.S. I can't find St. Albans letter, but I send a note of hers as a specimen of her handwriting.

CREFELD, *October* 17, 1878

MY DEAR NAN,

Since I wrote you yesterday about the silk I wished to send you, I have seen Mr. Otto Andreae, the exporter, and find that I *can myself* select the silk here, and send the *very* piece I select to their house in New York through them. So you will be sure to get the piece I buy, and yet not have the trouble of the Custom House. Mr. Andreae will give me a letter to his New York house, which I will enclose to you, and all you will have to do will be to present or send the letter as an order for the goods. Perhaps, if you can, you had better go yourself. He has promised to send me the letter to-day — if it comes in time I will enclose it; if not I'll send it by next mail. The case in which it is sent will not arrive in New York until a week or ten days after you get this letter. I merely apprize you of its arriving so that you may make your calculations accordingly. It's a rare piece of silk as far as I can judge — twenty-two metres long or about twenty-five yards, of a quality sold only in Vienna or Berlin. It is not a 'charged' silk, as they call it here (i.e., dyed to make it heavy), but of a lasting colour and material. My Vice-Consul, who knows, says it's splendid. I hope you'll like it, Nan. I won't tell you the price — but it cost me less than it could be bought in Berlin or Vienna, and less than half what it would cost in New York.

In haste to catch the mail.

FRANK

We see from the following letter that Bret Harte had returned to England again, this time on a visit to the Duke and Duchess of St. Albans. There is a strange pathetic power in his description of Bestwood and its inmates, which shows also his insight and comprehension of character.

BESTWOOD LODGE, ARNOLD, NOTTS
November 3, 1878

MY DEAR NAN,

I was so much relieved to get Frankie's letter a few days ago, and to-day — forwarded to me from Crefeld — your own acknowledging the safe arrival of the Newstead pictures. Strangely enough, it comes to me here — only a few miles from Newstead — for I at last have managed to make my long-promised visit to the Duchess.

Delightful as the place and people are, I should not have come to England simply for this visit. But it was necessary for me to come to London to make my arrangements for my lectures this winter. And with this nation of snobs it does not hurt me to be the friend of a Duke and an inmate of his house. As, for example, the Lord Mayor of Nottingham dined here yesterday, and the Duke took him aside and told him I *might* be induced to lecture this winter. Whereat the Mayor took *me* aside, and begged that they might have the honour of entertaining me in Nottingham if I would come there to lecture, and that they would pay sixty pounds (or two hundred and fifty dollars) for a single lecture.

I suppose I ought to — and can — make two thousand dollars this winter in two weeks lecturing in the principal towns, and if I am only strong enough I *will*. But the climate I find still depresses me; I am chilly all the time, and cough a good deal. The weather is frightful for the nerves — being gloominess personified, and there is no dry, bracing air to stimulate. All the kindness of these people scarcely keeps me from the blues. There is a wonderfully strong German expression '*graue Elend*' — literally, 'grey wretchedness' — which is a perfect picture of myself at times. I don't wonder that the Englishman always was supposed to commit suicide in November. Think of the gloomiest day you ever knew at Sea Cliff, add to it the snow chill of those Morristown spring days, and fling over all the foggy pall of a San Francisco afternoon, and you have the regular English November.

The Duke of St. Albans is one of the oldest Dukes in England. The first Duke was the offspring of Nell Gwynne and Charles II, and the present Duke bears a singular likeness to the Stuart family; not the *Second* Charles, but the *First*. That melancholy face and half-morbid, unhappy eye — which look down upon one from every picture gallery in this vicinity, and which hangs above me as I write (it is a Van Dyck and they say a perfect likeness) — is carried about by the present Duke. Everybody sees the likeness. He is a shy, reserved, sensitive man, with a passion for gambling and the turf — in a grave, cold way. We are very good friends — and he is a great study to me — and I don't know why, but I feel sometimes awfully sorry for him. I would rather be my own dyspeptic, miserable self than he, and the lord of this princely house and its solemn woods. The other afternoon we were sitting together in the hall and the likeness to his melancholy, unfortunate ancestor came out so strongly in the twilight that I felt as if the picture had stepped out of its frame. It was very uncanny. It's odd that, as Byron made Newstead quite 'spooky' to me, so Charles I renders Bestwood Lodge very uncomfortable. I ought to tell you that all the broad woodlands called 'Bestwood' were given to Nelly Gwynne by her royal lover on a queer condition. He told her she might have all the land she could ride around before breakfast. It's needless to say that Mistress Nelly rose early and put spurs to her horse. But she had the good sense to choose the loveliest bits of woodland to circumscribe — for, like all the royal families of England, she was brighter and better than the man.

I've told you how I liked the Duchess. I'm glad to hear from all who know her that my first impressions are correct, and that she is one of the brightest and most noble-souled women in the peerage. I did not send you her photograph because I did not think it did her justice, but she has promised me a second one, and I'll send you that.

I shall write again from London. God bless you and the chickens.

FRANK

LONDON, *November 6*, 1878

MY DEAR NAN,

I enclose a picture for Ethel and have written a note to her, which, of course, you will read and translate. The picture is a photograph of Her Grace St. Albans' *second* son — the Marquis of something or other — I've forgotten the title. But the Duchess gave it to me for Ethel and wrote his name on the back.

It's a pretty picture of a little fellow 'born to the purple,' but too young yet to be spoiled by the knowledge of it.

I left Bestwood yesterday, and am on my way to Crefeld. I shall write you as soon as I arrive and send you what money I have.

I have just remembered something, which, of course, you have already seen — and so I wrote to the Duchess to-day that I must have *another* picture for Jessamy.

God bless you all.

LIMICK

CREFELD, December 7, 1878

MY DEAR NAN,

I was becoming very nervous over your long silence when I received yours of the 22d. It pains me, Nan, to think that you had any worry over money, but it was not entirely my fault. I trusted to your receiving money from Scribner and Company for a story I had sent them; when I did not hear from them, I became alarmed, and telegraphed you, instead of sending by post one hundred and fifty dollars — on the 22d November. It was a blessing that I did so.

When I left New York, Mr. Smith absolutely begged me to send my stories *directly to him*, saying that if he did not take them for his magazine he would dispose of them elsewhere for me. His action in regard to the 'Great Deadwood Mystery,' which I sent him by Osgood, was so prompt that I felt assured there would be no delay, and when I sent him a proof of 'The Heiress of Red Dog,' over six weeks ago, I looked upon it as being the same as sending a draft to you for one hundred and fifty or two hundred dollars. He has that story now on hand, I suppose, for I have not heard from him yet, and also another by this time, and you should be in receipt of the money for both, but not daring to trust to this uncertainty I have telegraphed you again to-day, one hundred dollars.

This makes seven hundred and fifty dollars in all, but I calculated that, in the half-year, you should have received one thousand dollars, which if Mr. Smith had disposed of the stories would have been correct.

It may be that he has not been able to dispose of them, and has sent them to Dana, of the 'Sun' — which I told him to do as a last resort. Then, of course, they go to pay up my indebtedness to Dana, and are not lost. Indeed, if I could afford it just now I'd rather send everything to him directly.

I shall not hereafter trust to the selling of manuscripts, but send you what I can regularly, twice a month on the 15th and 1st, either by draft or telegraph. I have not got so far ahead yet that I have even one hundred dollars in advance — I do not take from my fees except after they have accumulated over our office expenses, so I may have to telegraph it. But cheer up, Nan, it will all be right.

I do not know how much you were owing when the last one hundred and fifty dollars reached you, sixteen days ago. At all events, I hope and pray that the one hundred dollars sent to-day will keep you along until Scribner sends you some money — or until the 15th, when I will send you another draft, by mail. That should reach you by the 1st January. God keep you from beginning the year in debt or even anxious about money. In the next two or three days, if the money due in from England arrives, I shall send fifty dollars for Christmas presents *for yourself and the children exclusively.* I beg you not to use it for anything else.

I enclose a circular from my agent in London regarding the lectures. He has been highly recommended to me, and I hope he will do well for me. If I can only get a couple of thousand dollars in this way, *ahead*, I'll go through the agony and misery of the lecture work. I shall not have to travel such distances as I did in America. I shall not begin to lecture before the latter part of January, if the arrangements are made. So I have a month ahead yet to get strong. I think I am a little better. I feel more cheerful, for I went to Wiesbaden to lecture on the 2d December — an all-day journey from here — and was not as much fatigued as I expected and feared. It was a lovely journey — along the Rhine all the way — to one of the famous old watering-places with its 'Kursaal' and promenades, and its strange polyglot English, American, French, and Italian residents who winter there. Another time I'll tell you all about it.

I also enclose you the Duchess's picture. You'll see she doesn't look a *bit like Mrs. Salter*, and indeed is not. She is really a very true, noble gentlewoman. She has gone over with St. Albans to Ireland, and sent me a note the other day, saying she would send me another picture of her boy for Jessamy, and regretting I could not go with them. Write to me regularly.

I have just received a letter from Gertie saying that Ned is engaged. As soon as I get a lazier day, I'll write to the boys. Give them my love and kiss the girls for me.

FRANK

In the letter to his friend Trübner, partner of Messrs. Kegan Paul, Trench, Trübner and Company, the well-known firm of English publishers, Bret Harte asks for some books that interested him, on Italian painting. It had always been his desire to go to Italy, which, however, unfortunately was never fulfilled. He refers again to his lecture in Wiesbaden, and to the 'Sierras,' to which his heart had always remained faithful.

CREFELD, *December* 8, 1878

MY DEAR TRÜBNER,

'Sandy Bar' and Mrs. Jameson's 'Lives' are duly arrived. I made a stupid mistake regarding the latter. I have not seen the book since I was a boy, and had forgotten that the biographies were confined to the Italians. I wish to recall some facts about Rubens and Rembrandt. But no matter: the book will keep.

Send me Taine's 'Art in the Netherlands' — in English. You might also let me know the price of his other books on Italy or Venice. An American publisher published them separately in small 16mo volumes, I think.

I don't think I can afford 'Flaxman' at all, but if 'Marshall' is well commended and is illustrated plainly, I'll get it, later. You might let me know what artists think of it. Ask your friend Fritt. I was greatly shocked to hear of poor Lewes's death. I had no idea he was in extremity when we spoke of him last. How does his wife bear it? I fear there is no philosophy in the literary life which lifts its votaries above the level of weak humanity. I have known a poet actually to feel bad over the death of another man's wife. But he was an exception in other ways.

I suppose Petrie, Philps and Company's consignment will come in time. I think I have nothing else just now to bother you with.

I lectured at Wiesbaden on the 2d inst., to about four hundred English people in the Kursaal. I rather enjoyed the journey there and my first glimpse of the spectacular Rhine. May I be pardoned for saying, in confidence, that it seemed to me slightly theatrical and somehow looked like very nice landscape gardening and grotto work.

I said nothing of this in the lecture, of course, but gossiped away quite cheerfully for an hour, with my thoughts in the Sierras, where there were valleys in which the Drachenfels and Loreleiberg might lie hidden overlooked and forgotten. Keep this heresy to yourself and don't expose me. I dare say I am all wrong, and, like the prince in the Arabian Nights, I want my cream tarts made with pepper.

Of course, I know Fairchild, and a devilish good fellow he is to know, too. Give him my love.

With regards to Mrs. T. and your family,

Always yours
BRET HARTE

A. TRÜBNER, ESQ.

There is, throughout these letters to his wife, a strong, dominant note of sadness, to which he abandons himself only in the intimacy of his letters to her. From the contrast between them and those written to his friends, it is easy to realize that the whimsical 'insouciance' which he exposed to the world was only a shield behind which was hidden the deep melancholy of his over-sensitive nature. Alas, the rest he has so pathetically underlined, he was never to know, and with old age came only more and greater difficulties. Little did he know that these were, in spite of all, still the 'hay days' of his labours.

CREFELD, December 17, 1878

MY DEAR NAN,

I've nothing from you since yours dated the 21st November, when you had just received the one hundred and fifty dollars I sent by telegraph that day. I have since written you twice and on the 8th December sent you by telegraph again one hundred dollars. The cost of telegraphing is of little account to the absolute safety of sending you money by this method, as I pay it into the hands of a Crefeld exporter, who telegraphs his house in New York to pay to you.

I've been trying *so* hard to get well and strong enough for my lectures six weeks from this, but I've lately been attacked by rheumatism — not of an alarming kind, but just positive enough to give me a hint to take very good care of myself. I've a very good German doctor, who has promised to build me up for these awful lectures, and I've great confidence in him, which is better than medicine. Meantime, I 'flannel' myself throughout.

The winter is here already — grim, black, bitter, and awfully lonesome. They say it is *exceptionally severe* — you know what a faculty I have always for getting into such climates — and the accounts from England and Berlin go to prove it. I saw more thunder and lightning in England last summer than I ever did in America in one season: — that they said was also 'exceptional.' We have had two *earthquakes* at Crefeld, *since I've been here* — unknown before to their records.

I have sent for a copy of the Wiesbaden paper with an account of my lecture, which I shall send you, having already sent my only copy to England to my agent. It was a very handsome notice. Another account spoke of me as being of a slim, elegant figure in spite of my probable *fifty* years! It was in German, and '*fünfzig*' looks even older than our 'fifty.' It's of no use, you see, for me to try to appear young, Nan — but, really, I've got *very old* lately. I feel it in many ways — perhaps it is better that I should, as it makes me less nervous and anxious. I've only one idea now — to get enough money to *rest*.

I think of you and the children continually. I should feel very, very lonely, I suppose, and discontented, but I have ever before me that *awful, terrible last winter!* I don't know — looking back — what ever kept me from going down, in *every way*, during that awful December and January. So I contrast it with to-day, and I know I feel more hopeful and am thankful, and I know you are no longer anxious or worried as you were then — about me, nor, I trust, Nan, about yourself. I do not think you will again have any worry about money, at least.

It is queer that I do not hear from Scribner about my manuscripts. However, I do not calculate upon that, but shall send a draft to you in a day or two by telegraph.

I've begun a letter to the boys — but I had to put it aside on account of my eyes. They are very weak. God bless you all.

FRANK

CREFELD, *December* 30, 1878

MY DEAR ANNA,

I have the boys' two letters and your postscript of the 13th inst., to say that Smith had written you that he had sold my sketch for one hundred and fifty dollars, and would send you the money. I hope he did so, and that you felt relieved even before you received my last telegraphic order for one hundred dollars on the 23d. I hope you took it as my Christmas present to you and the boys and that you applied it as such.

I wrote to Mr. Dana that I valued the two sketches he had received and published at three hundred and fifty dollars. This would clear off that two hundred and fifty dollars I owe him and leave him in my debt one hundred dollars, which he ought to send you; but he had written to me that he thought the two stories ought to just 'make it square.' However, take anything he may send you, but don't *expect* anything. I shall be satisfied to know

that in six months I have untied myself out of *one* debt!
— at least.

Tell the boys I will write to them as soon as I find a
little more time. For a month longer I shall be very busy
sending off my reports.

I am glad to hear that you are all better of your sore
throats. I was greatly worried about you. It was a dreadful story, that of the Grand Duchess of Hesse Darm-
stadt losing one child, and then dying from the kiss she
received of the other that recovered. St. Albans wrote
me about it, his letter being in mourning.

Diphtheria is frightfully prevalent here in Germany.
My friend Lutyen's children had it, and my Vice-Consul's
baby also. Give my love to 'Lize and say that I wanted
to send her a draft for Christmas, but I could not.

God bless you all.

FRANK

CREFELD, *January* 1, 1879

MY DEAR ANNA,

Happy New Year!

There is a pretty German custom belonging to this
day which has filled the shop windows with all kinds of
pretty valentines, and I could not resist buying a few for
the children. In fact, Saint Sylvester, who takes care of
New Year's Eve, is a kind of Saint Valentine, and everybody here uses the post-office to send to his friends some
little token of good-will or '*Glückwünsch.*' So don't be
surprised or disappointed at the pretty little 'nothings'
I am sending. I only want the children to see Germany
as I am seeing it to-day. '*Mit besten Glückwünsche.*'

FRANK

Bret Harte had already been translated into German
before his arrival in Europe, and he always was greatly

appreciated there. Besides the lecture which he delivered at Wiesbaden, the great German daily the 'Berliner Tageblatt' made a request for a series of articles containing his impressions of Germany, which were, however, never as outspoken as those of the present letters.

CREFELD, *January* 13, 1879

MY DEAR NAN,

I have just received yours of the 26th December — that to me already seems years ago. I had quite put out of my mind Christmas and all that it meant, and your letter made me quite sad. I'm glad the boys had their presents and I hope you bought yourself something from me.

My first lecture in England is the 28th inst. I dread it, for I am far from well. But it will be in London, and the next dates are near London, so I shall have little travelling to do. Thank Heaven for the little island — there are no such tremendous distances as in America.

I have often felt like sitting down to write you a long letter about Germany and my impressions — beyond what I have already told you — but I am *tired* always, and I feel I ought to try and write it for some periodical — when it would pay you the money we both need more than long letters. The 'Berliner Tageblatt,' for whom I wrote the article on Bayard Taylor, has made me an offer to write for them a series of articles giving my frank, honest impression of Germany. I have accepted, and you will consider the letters are sent to you, as the money shall be.

It is bitterly cold weather and everything is frozen up. It is awfully dreary here, Nan. Kiss the children, tell the boys to write to me and I will write soon, and God bless you all. FRANK

P.S. Tell the boys that instead of buying all the presents they suggested for me, I took what these presents would cost in money, and added enough to it myself to buy a *watch* for myself. It is a gold watch — very good make — and cost only thirty dollars. Poor Frankie's — or is it poor Wodie's — silver watch was no longer presentable or decent. Never mind; I'll send you and the boys all watches soon — if the lectures pay.

You have forgotten to give me the number of your house in Washington Square. I wish I had some regular address, besides Eliza's, to always find you at.

Roswell Smith was Bret Harte's literary agent in America. Amusing reference to him will be remembered in Bret Harte's letter to Osgood, in '75. 'The Legend of Cologne,' and 'The Legend of Sammstadt,' the former a poem, the latter a short story, were both the fruit of his pen in Germany.

CREFELD, *January* 16, 1879

MY DEAR MR. SMITH,

I enclose to you 'A Legend of Cologne.' 'Belgravia' will publish it in the March number, issued on the 20th February, 1879. You ought to be able to produce it simultaneously in America, in 'Scribner's.' I don't know what to say about its price. It ought to be worth about one hundred and twenty-five dollars to you, if anything. I could get more for it, if I were in America, I dare say, but I am willing you should have it at that price. It's a good honest length, and I've an inner consciousness that it will take.

Don't bother with it much if *you* don't want it, and cannot readily find a purchaser, but send it to Mr. Dana, of the 'Sun,' without price, merely saying that I desired you to so enclose it. I'll write to him.

I have received your letter regarding 'The Legend of Sammstadt,' but by the next mail a letter from Mrs. Harte informing me that the 'Sun' had sent her a cheque for one hundred and fifty dollars, by which I presume that there was some hitch in the 'Herald's' purchase. Touching the suggestion you kindly made me about writing for the 'Herald,' at present I hardly think it practicable.

The 'Berliner Tageblatt,' the great German daily, has made me an offer for a series of frank, outspoken 'impressions' of Germany. I have accepted. They will be published semi-weekly in small instalments, but I estimate they will make a half dozen good-sized monthly articles for a magazine, and can be published almost simultaneously in America. As they will appear first in German, and I get a copyright here, it matters little if there are a few weeks' difference in time. Do you care to make me an offer?

Very truly yours
BRET HARTE

ROSWELL SMITH, ESQ.

Bret Harte, in his contemplation of a lecturing tour in England, was anxious to guard against the financial failures and bad management of his American experiences. He was, however, not at first successful, as we see later on.

BRET HARTE
UNITED STATES CONSUL

CREFELD, January 17, 1879

MY DEAR ANNA,

I sent you by telegraph yesterday one hundred dollars, and expect to send you one hundred more by the 1st February. I wrote you a few lines on receiving yours of the 26th: and sent you yesterday 'Vanity Fair,' with a caricature of myself as its weekly cartoon. I think it's poor and does not contain any one of my characteristics, but still it might be *worse*, and is not as bad as one they had of the Prince of Wales, or a terrible one of poor St. Albans. It's considered a very *swell thing* here to be caricatured in 'V. F.,' and I suppose it will help my lectures. At least so they all say.

I'm worried about this lecture tour. My agent is an honourable man, but I fear he is *too sanguine* and he is *too* anxious for me to speculate with him; time tells, etc., all of which I refuse to do. I shall not add *that* anxiety to my other nervous dreads. So I've had a contract drawn up by my own lawyer in London, guarding me against any evil contingencies, and, as it is just *possible* that he may not sign it, perhaps the lectures may fall through.

I shall know in a few days and will write you. I am *pretty* well; only so so. God bless you all.

FRANK

The next letters to his two sons are delightful examples of Bret Harte's letters to his children.

CREFELD, *January* 18, 1879

MY DEAR FRANKIE,

I had not time to answer your letter before, but you must never wait for that, but write to me as often as you can. It is the business of 'The Private Secretary' to write letters *to* as well as *for* the United States Consul.

It has been thus far a very cold, severe winter here. All the streams and ponds and *canals* — for the country here is flat, like Holland, and very low — have been frozen over, and even the banks of the Rhine, where it has overflowed, are glittering sheets of ice. As a consequence everybody is skating — except in this very business town of Crefeld — men, women, and children. On Sunday last I noticed that the whole population of Düsseldorf seemed to be doing nothing else. Sunday in Catholic Germany, anyway, is always a holiday, and in Neuss and Linn the people bring their skates to church. Our large pond in the Hofgarten was reserved entirely for *sliding*. That is to say, about five hundred people were all sliding in rows — as New York boys do in the gutters.

You would be surprised at the sleds here, or, as they call them, 'Schlitten.' (By the way, a skate is a 'Schlittschuh,' literally a 'sled shoe,' and skating is 'Schlittschuhlaufen,' literally, 'to run on sled shoes.' The sled is made exactly like an armchair on runners, and in it they sit and are pulled or shoved on from behind. Generally the boys or girls — one on each side — propel the sled forward — sometimes running, sometimes sliding, sometimes skating. The sleds are often very beautiful with curved gilt runners, like swans' necks, but I have never seen a sled like our American ones, on which I used to go 'pony gutters' when I was a boy.

Germany is the great storehouse of toys, so you can imagine how interesting the shops were on Christmas. Papa could remember when the 'Private Secretary' and even his big brother 'Wodie' were both little boys and loved toys, and Papa, for their sakes, and partly because he was lonely, went into the shops. They were all very cheap, of course — so Papa bought a few for his Vice-Consul's children and they cost him one mark and fifty pfennig — or about thirty-seven cents; and they made the children very happy. I sent you some of the New Year cards, which are half-toys, and are sent here to one's friends, like valentines.

Do you remember reading about the *stork* in the German story-books? I was greatly disappointed at not finding any here — but they are not in this part of Germany, and I did not see one until the other day, being just over the Dutch frontier, in a little village, I saw one perched on a chimney. While I was looking at it, three little children, scarcely older than Ethel, ran out and, taking hold of each other's little hands, began to sing to it. I was so much impressed with the simple, childish words that I made them sing it again, for the promise of some pfennig to buy cakes — for German children are always ready for cakes. This is the song and I want you to teach it to Ethel. Remember that the words are pronounced exactly as they are spelt, and the letters, with the exception of the 'w's,' which are always pronounced like 'v's' are the same as ours.

> 'Storch, Storch, Steiner!
> Mit den langen Beinen
> Und den kurtz'n Knieen,
> Jungfrau Marie hat ein Kind gefunden
> War in geld gebunden,
> Flieg über Beckerhaus, hol' drei Kecks heraus.
> Mir einen, dir einen, und dem Andern auch einen!'

Perhaps I have not got it exactly right, I only trusted my ear. The English of it is:

> 'Stork, Stork, Steiner!'

'Steiner' is a children's word 'made up,' and means nothing.

> 'With the legs so long-like
> And the knees so short-like,
> Virgin Mary has a child found
> That was all in gold bound,
> Fly over Bakers' house
> Bring three cakes to us,
> One for me,
> One for you,
> And one for the other too!'

If you could have seen those little things swing their hands up, and scream at the top of their voices, and in perfect trustfulness,

'Mir einen, dir einen, und dem Andern *auch* einen!'

you'd have understood, as I did, all about German children, in an instant.

They believe storks bring good luck and always carry a baby in their bills as a present. Hence the allusion to the Virgin Mary.

Now begin with this as your German lesson. Don't turn up your nose at it because it's childlike. Papa has begun to study German like a child, and has been in the third and fourth reader, and has broken his heart and worn his eyes out, over translation of 'Rothkäppchen' — ('Little Red Riding Hood'), etc., etc.

But I must write no more to-day. God bless you, Frankie. Take good care of Mamma, and love your

PAPA

CREFELD, *January* 21, 1879

MY DEAR WODIE,

I hope you've got over your sore knees by this time, and although the 'housemaid's lameness' is not a very elevated disease, still, I am very thankful that you did not have an aristocratic broken leg or a high-toned ulceration. Still, Papa wants his big boy to grow up as *strong* as he is *tall*, and, if Papa is to be obliged to 'look up' to his eldest son, he wants to have something nice to look at.

Now, my dear boy, I want you to 'pitch in' and study as hard as you can. I have not heard that you are *not* studying, but I tell you this because I know that, if you were here in Germany with me, you would be a little ashamed to see how hard these German boys study, and

how much they know. They all study English and
French as a rule, and some speak both languages fluently.
Yet they are not naturally *bright* boys. It's all *hard work*
with them, but they keep at it conscientiously. They
begin their studies as early as seven o'clock in winter and
do not leave school till four o'clock, and study in the
evening. Everybody here has the greatest belief and
admiration for American clever children, and I should
not like, and you and Frankie would not like, them to
find you both backward, or not up to them in mere study.
I only say this Wodie, dear, by way of caution to you and
Frankie, and now Papa has done his preaching.

I was wondering to myself the other day what would
most amuse you here. I am afraid, after the first day or
two at Crefeld, you would find it very dull and stupid —
and see nothing to interest you in these long dull streets.
There is no peculiarity of costume or architecture to
make this city look any different from Morristown or
Newark. But if you walked about two miles from here
toward the Rhine, you would suddenly come to a little
village with an arched gateway, and as suddenly you
would come upon as perfect a picture of a ruined castle
as any you ever saw in the books. It is hidden by high
trees, *within* as well as *without*, for it is roofless, and the
trees have grown up in what was once the dining-hall,
since the old days when one of Köln's archbishops lived
here. It is quite hidden from the road; only the highest
tower with battlements is seen above the trees. It belongs
to a rich old lady, who lives in quite a modern house adjoining it, and who generally looks after it, and keeps it
from being torn down or overrun by visitors. I spent an
afternoon there alone — as thoroughly alone as if there
was nothing more modern within a thousand miles, nor
any one living since the people who inhabited it. As I was

climbing through the broken window of the gateway, I was startled by seeing two figures standing by a ruined window of the chapel gazing at me. They appeared to be monks, with cowls on their heads, and were regarding me with a fixed, stony stare. Everywhere else the sun was shining brightly — and I rubbed my eyes, thinking it a delusion. At last, when I couldn't stand it any longer, I jumped down into the courtyard and went up to them, and found they were two *wooden figures*, perfectly painted, but put there purposely, doubtless, by the queer old lady to frighten off intruders. It was a startling likeness. Before I went away, however, I took an old newspaper and folded it into the shape of a soldier's chapeau, such as children make, and put it on the head of one figure, and put a cigar in the mouth of the other. I don't think they startled anybody — but the old lady — after that.

You would have your fill of soldiers in Germany. Every other man you meet at Düsseldorf, Coblenz, and Mayence is a soldier. By the law every citizen is obliged to serve three years in the army; — hence this drilling, marching, and counter-marching. You get tired at last of this incessant blare of trumpets and glitter of uniforms. Yet some of the uniforms are wonderfully fine. Take our best-dressed soldiers — the Seventh Regiment, for example — and they would look like civilians beside these gorgeous 'hussars,' 'lancers,' and helmeted infantry, who all seem more like the soldiers you see in pictures than anything you have seen in reality.

The general who commands at Düsseldorf — General von Rauch — is a friend of mine. We were at dinner together at a friend's house one evening, and then went to a public concert given in honour of the Emperor. The general, to do honour to the occasion, was in full uniform and blazing with orders, stars, ribands, and crosses. We occupied a front box together with two officers similarly gorgeous. As I had only very ordinary black evening dress, compared to these gentlemen, whose breasts were hung with a clothes-line full of ribands and decorations, I felt like a crow who had suddenly got into a cage with some tropical parrots. Von Rauch was good enough to tell a friend of mine that I did not look like an American or Englishman, but he would have taken me for a Prussian officer — which, of course, he considered the highest compliment could be paid to any one; so I told the friend, in return, that I thought Von Rauch looked like an American general — Burnside — as he did.

The officers generally are very fine fellows — and have good manners. They have very strict rules among themselves. They are not allowed to marry unless they have a certain income more than their pay, to support their families in case they are killed. They are not allowed to enter certain expensive regiments unless they can fully afford it. They are expected always to be in uniform, and never to do anything that would be inconsistent with it. They must not carry a cane nor an umbrella nor a parcel. If they are walking with a lady, they must not offer to take her bundles or bags. I have seen the wife of one, loaded down with shawls, travelling bags, etc., etc., and her husband strutting solemnly at her side, with nothing heavier than his long sword trailing at his heels.

But it's time to stop. I'll tell you some other time something about the Rhine. Good-night now; take care of your little sisters and be the big boy of

Your affectionate
PAPA

Mrs. Bret Harte was very musical and had a very fine

voice. He was himself fond of music, and had a great appreciation for opera, to the exclusion, however, of Wagner, as he clearly shows in this amusing letter to his wife, which has been published in part in Merwin's biography.

CREFELD, *January 22,* 1879

MY DEAR NAN,

Mrs. Bayard Taylor has sent me a book of her late husband's and a very kind note, and it occurs to me to enclose to you to-day the letter I received from her in answer to one I wrote her after hearing of her husband's death. You remember that I did not feel very kindly toward him, nor had he troubled himself much about me when I came here alone and friendless, but his death choked back my resentment, and what I wrote to her, and afterwards in the 'Tageblatt,' I felt very honestly.

I have been several times to the opera at Düsseldorf, and I have been hesitating whether I should slowly prepare you for a great shock and tell you at once that *musical Germany* is a humbug. It had struck me during the last two months that I had really heard nothing very good in the way of music or even *as good* as I have heard in America, and it was only a week ago that, hearing a piano played in an adjoining house, and played badly at that, I was suddenly struck with the fact that it was really the *first* piano I had heard in Germany. I have heard orchestras at concerts and military bands, but no better than in America. My first operatic experience was 'Tannhäuser.' I can see your superior smile, Anna, at this, and I know how you will take my criticism of Wagner, so I don't mind saying, frankly, that it was the most diabolically ludicrous and stupidly monotonous performance I ever heard. I shall say nothing about the orchestral

harmonies, for there wasn't anything going on of that
kind unless you call something that seemed like a boiler
factory at work in the next street, and the wind whistling
through the rigging of a Channel steamer, but I *must say
one thing!* In the third act, I think, Tannhäuser and two
other minstrels sang before the King and Court to the
accompaniment of their harps — and the boiler factory.
Each minstrel sang or rather declaimed something like the
multiplication table for about twenty minutes. Tannhäuser, when *his* turn came, declaimed longer, and more
lugubriously and ponderously and monotonously than
the others, and went into 'nine times nine are eighty-one'
and 'ten times ten are twenty,' when suddenly, when he
had finished, they all drew their swords and rushed at
him. I turned to General von Rauch and said to him that
I didn't wonder at it. 'Ah,' said he, 'you know the story
then?' 'No, not exactly,' I replied. 'Ja wohl,' said Von
Rauch — 'the story is that three minstrels are all singing
in praise of Love, but they are furious at Tannhäuser
who loves Hulda, the German Venus, for singing in the
praise of love so *wildly*, so *warmly*, so *passionately!*' Then
I concluded that I really did not understand Wagner!

But what I wanted to say was that even *my poor* un-
educated ear detected bad instrumentalism, and worse
singing in the choruses. I confided this much to a friend
and he said very frankly that I was *probably right* — that
the best musicians and choruses went to America!

Then I was awfully disappointed in 'Faust' — or, as
it is known here on the play-bill, 'Margarethe.' You
know how I love that delicious idyl of Gounod's, and I
was in my seat that night long before the curtain was up.
Before the first act was over, I felt like leaving — and yet
I was glad I stayed. For although the chorus of villagers
was frightful, and Faust and Mephistopheles spouted and

declaimed blank verse at each other — whole pages of Goethe — yet the acting was good. The music was a little better in the next act and the acting was *superb*. I have never seen such a Marguerite. From the time she first meets Faust with that pert rebuke, until the garden scene, she was perfect. The prayer in the church — the church interior represented with kneeling figures and service going on, such as they dare not represent in England — was most wonderful. I can see her yet — peering from one to another of the kneeling groups as the women draw away from her, and, as she knelt in a blind groping way with her fingers mechanically turning the leaves of the prayer-book, and the voice of Mephistopheles mingling with the music, until, with one wild shriek, she throws the book away. Then it was that I jumped up in my seat and applauded. But think of my coming to Germany to have opera badly sung, and magnificently acted. I saw 'Der Freischuetz' after this, but it was not so well acted — and awfully sung. Yet the scenery was wonderfully good, and the costumes, historically perfect. The audiences from Cologne to Düsseldorf are all the same. Stiff, formal, *plainly dressed* — all except the officers — and undemonstrative. The opera audience at Cologne looks like an American prayer-meeting.

I have written Frankie and Wodie. Unless my lecture tour is postponed, I shall not write you again until I get to London. And then I shall be so busy I can only give you the news of success.

God bless you all,

LIMICK

The first days of February, Bret Harte returned to England to carry out his plan of lectures. As he had feared, they were well received but did not bring in what he had hoped for. He returned to Crefeld very much disappointed, but with the expectation of returning again under more favourable auspices.

LONDON, *February* 7, 1879

MY DEAR NAN,

I came here a week ago to begin my lecturing tour, but my agent has blundered so in the beginning that my friends think it better for me to postpone the tour until later in the season — at least a month. Instead of taking me directly to London, Mr. Carte opened with me at the Crystal Palace at Sydenham, which would have been about equal to an *entrée* in New York at ——. I was so fearful of a repetition of the Redpath business, and my solicitor telegraphed me so positively that I *must* come, that, although knowing it would be a business failure, I came. You can imagine, Nan, how all this added to my usual nervousness — I am glad the tour is postponed for that reason alone. But there are, like the Crystal Palace, three or four other places where I *must* lecture, and I may get a few hundred dollars out of it. The pay for lectures here is very poor; my half-share of the Crystal Palace receipts amounted to about seventy-five dollars. Think of that!

In other ways the lecture was well received, as you will see by the papers I send you. 'Punch' in particular said a few kind, brotherly words. I am asked out everywhere — and have all kinds of attentions shown me — but I have lost my taste for that sort of thing long ago.

I am afraid, Nan, that I have given you uneasiness about money. I sent you one hundred dollars on the 17th January and one hundred dollars yesterday. I tried to get it all *within the month*, but I could not. I only take the money as it comes in at the Consulate. I've sent a poem to Smith; I do not know if he has sent you any money for it yet.

I am so nervous and sick that I may return to Crefeld right away. I'll let you know if I do. The three lectures would keep me here a week longer.

God bless you and the children.

FRANK

P.S. I enclose the Duke's picture; you have all the family now.

CREFELD, *February* 21, 1879

MY DEAR NAN,

I have received two letters from you in the past two days, and one from Wodie and Frankie. Tell Wodie I shall send his interesting account of the 'fifty dollar Schooner' to Mrs. Webb, of Newstead, who has taken a great interest in him and his vessel. Tell Frankie I shall write a line or two to Boucicault for tickets for himself and Wodie — if it be not too late.

You see I am back again at my post. The tour was a miserable failure financially — just as I feared. It has been now postponed for a month or six weeks — *provided* Mr. Carte, my agent, can send me a list of engagements (*secured sums*) sufficient to make it pay. I was in England three weeks and lectured *five times*, and cleared only about two hundred dollars above my expenses. I was bound in honour to perform them or I should have returned when I found how I was *swindled*. Only a fear of repeating the 'Redpath' experience kept me from doing it.

Of course I was, as far as the public and press were concerned, very handsomely received. I had to decline many invitations, and it is proposed now, if I return, that I shall be offered a public dinner. But my return to England rests entirely on my being able to make the lecture tour profitable.

I sent you one hundred dollars yesterday by telegraph through Schroeder and Company.

God bless you all.

LIMICK

In the following letter to his wife, he speaks of a possible change of consulate. His post in Crefeld had been very unsatisfactory, in all ways, his health had greatly suffered, and Germany was not congenial to him. In October of the same year, Bret Harte wrote to the State Department, requesting a transfer, together with a leave of absence, which latter was immediately granted. Bret Harte's modesty does him an injustice. 'I shall have made,' he writes, 'a good record here, by luck, I fear, more than by good management.' Crefeld was the chief town, not only of Germany, but, with Lyons, of the whole of Europe, for the manufacture of silks and velvets, of which the exportation to America was very considerable. It was due to Bret Harte's organization that this exportation was increased by over two hundred thousand dollars quarterly, or eight hundred thousand dollars a year under his administration, and this by reason of the great simplification introduced by him into the previously existing methods regarding invoices, etc.

CREFELD, *March* 15,. 1879

MY DEAR NAN,

I've just received yours of the 27th February. I was inexpressibly shocked to hear of poor Brantz Mayer's death. Since I have been here I have lived so much in the atmosphere of old recollections that I suppose it was not strange that for the last two or three weeks I have

been thinking of him and of my visit to Baltimore just a
year ago. His death, which I saw in the telegraphic news,
came home to me at once.

I am very much worried about Frankie's illness; and
in fact I am dreading the horrible spring weather of New
York and its effects upon you and the children. The only
consolation I can give you is that it is as inclement and
sickly here. This district is full of diphtheria and scarlet
fever, and my Vice-Consul's children have been very sick
with both. I, who have been suffering from a succession
of colds — almost a repetition of my last year's experience
at Sea Cliff — became quite alarmed last week at the
state of my throat, and feared I had 'caught something,'
for my office is in the V.-C.'s house. But the doctor said
it was only a kind of 'epidemic sympathy,' etc., etc.

Worse than that, I've been tempted by an offer of
eighty-five guineas (nearly four hundred and fifty dollars) to lecture at Manchester in about ten days, and
perhaps elsewhere; and here I am, down sick before the
time comes. I hope to pull through it some way, however — and get the money.

I am seriously thinking of asking the Department to
change my location. Germany is no place for me — I
feel it more and more every day. So that if I do not hold
out any hopes to you, it is because I do not know if I
will stay here. There are so many places better for my
health, for my literary plans, for my comfort, and — for
my purse — than this. I shall write quietly to one or two
of my Washington friends to see if it can be arranged.
I shall have made a good record here; — by good luck,
I fear, more than by my management, the consular
business will exceed this year any previous year, and I
can hand over to the Government quite a handsome sum.

I sat down to write you a long letter, but my cold

leaves me so weak to-day I can hardly write, and I must keep up my strength to sign and record invoices.

God bless you all.

LIMICK

In his letter to Miss Philip, who had set to music one of Bret Harte's poems, we see that he is again in England for the fulfilment of an engagement to lecture at Manchester, the details of which he gives in the second letter to his wife.

LANGHAM HOTEL, PORTLAND PLACE
LONDON, W., *April* 6, 1879

MY DEAR MISS PHILIP,

Pray accept my very hearty thanks for your little sheaf of music. There is no more delicate flattery to an author than the intimation that his work is good enough to suggest something to a sister Art, and I dare say you have given 'Fate' a new lease of life in your composition. Very many thanks, also, for your musical transcript of Charles Kingsley's melodious verses.

I doubt not that Mrs. Bret Harte has already acknowledged your courtesy to her, by letter.

I was unaware of your great loss. If my sympathy and condolements be not too tardy and frail, pray accept them as the sincere expression of

Yours very truly
BRET HARTE

CREFELD, *April* 17, 1879

MY DEAR NAN,

I've just returned from England, where I've been lecturing. Deducting my expenses, which were enormous, and commissions, which were equally exorbitant, my profits amounted to very little. Lecturing here is so different from the American system, and these English people, with all their kindness and compliment to me, do not understand that Americans lecture for *money* alone, and seem to think they have done their duty when they attend, applaud, and praise afterward — at one shilling each. I was very handsomely received at Birmingham and Manchester — they cheered and applauded me — *even when I stopped to drink a glass of water* — during the lecture — they made speeches about me when I got through. At Brighton a deputation waited upon me, and presented me with an *illuminated scroll!* — a very elegantly and eloquently prepared piece of parchment, like a patent of nobility.

I found *two* letters from you, one of the 15th and the other of the 26th March, when I returned. I am sorry you were disappointed in my postponing the dinner. But I had not yet received my leave of absence and could not leave Germany. Again, there was some feeling expressed by some other gentleman that the proposed dinner was not properly gotten up nor by the *right* people, and these English never forgive a man for making a mistake in his introduction. Nevertheless, I would have accepted it could I have gone at the time, although perhaps it's for the best. The compliment, at least, has been advertised. I am invited to the dinner of the Royal Academy — which is the great swell dinner of the season — on the 3d of May and am expected to make a speech. *That* terrifies me: — but I shall prepare myself for it, if I go. I shall send the first 'Tageblatt' letter to Dana by this mail. I suppose he will print it soon and send you the money. By the way, I was not able to send you but one hundred dollars last month, nor anything this month until last week, when I telegraphed you two hundred dollars.

Unfortunately, the only letter which contained your

address in West Washington Place I have lost or mislaid, and in the very letter in which you beg me to be particular to send there hereafter, you give no address whatever at the top of the page. I do not wonder that you all dream about my *not* knowing what must have been patent to you that I could not know from your letter. I am dreadfully afraid that it will be too late now — even if you answer this at once — for me to get your address before Eliza leaves 45 Fifth Avenue, unless you should, providentially, write it in your next letter, due in a few days. It is most important in my sending you *money!*

You have done right — very right — about sending the boys to the Commercial College, although I don't believe in *commercial* colleges. But it keeps them up — until I can do something better for them. I have plans for this autumn — Heaven only knows if I can fulfil them.

I'll write next week again. My love and kisses to the kids. God bless you all.

FRANK

The result of this second venture in the lecturing field, which was his last, is seen in the following letters. The Royal Academy Dinner was the great event of the London season, and Bret Harte was asked, as a special compliment, to answer the 'Toast to Literature.' Merwin gives, in his 'Life of Bret Harte,' an interesting and correct explanation of the complications of which his acceptance and subsequent refusal were the cause. 'He received the compliment of being asked to respond for Literature at the Royal Academy Banquet, in 1879, and, with his constitutional unwillingness to give a point-blank refusal, he had promised or half promised to be present. Meanwhile, he had returned to Crefeld, and the prospect of speaking at the dinner loomed more and more horrific in his imagination.' Finally, he telegraphed his inability to attend. Bret Harte, however, did do so the following year, and his speech, which was a great success, has been included in Mr. Kozlay's collection of his lectures.

My dear Nan,   Crefeld, *April 25*, 1879

I've been trying for a long time to so arrange matters that you would hereafter be *secure* in regularly receiving money from me. The principal trouble thus far has been that I did not know from month to month how *much I could send you*, and how much I could depend upon your receiving from *the sale of my writings in New York.* I have at last arranged with Schroeder and Company to pay you regularly one hundred and fifty dollars per month — in such sum or sums as you may like on the 1st or 15th of each month. This is to be a surety — and you can depend upon it. Of course, Nan, you understand that I will send more *if I can* — and that in all probability the sale of my writings will amount to fifty dollars or perhaps one hundred dollars more, and that you are pretty sure of calculating upon two hundred dollars each month; but I want you to feel that you can depend regularly upon *something*, until my year in this consular service is over, which will be on the 18th July, and I will know how and where I stand.

I am not very hopeful of the future *here*.

I am hesitating about returning to England to go to the 'Royal Academy Dinner' and the 'Literary Fund Dinner' and the 'Dinner of St. John's College' at Cambridge — to all of which I am invited, and where I should be expected to make a speech. I am trying to leave out my personal feelings and look at it purely as *business*. It will be a good *advertisement*, and make some people I

know of in New York and Boston ashamed — but it will
cost me *some money* — at least seventy-five dollars —
and in all my other trips I have made my lecturing pay
my expenses. There is no lecture to come in as an excuse
— and a recompense pecuniarily. And I am afraid that
in America something may be said about my absence
from my Consulate and my being continually in England. I have a leave of absence of seven weeks from the
Department, and have not used it all — I have still a
week at my disposal; but that they don't know, and they
might make a fuss in the paper, which, of course, the
Department would not condescend to *answer*, but might
wish had never occurred. Again, I find that this absence,
if only for a week, retards my learning German greatly,
and interrupts my study and, besides that, I am getting
backward in my story-writing. If I wrote one or two
things — particularly good — it would do quite as much
to keep up my reputation as a dinner — if not more. I
wish you could advise me *what* to do!

I shall not continue my German sketches at present.
Writing them for a German paper and living in a German
community, and above all holding a half-diplomatic
position here, cramps my pen. Did I not tell you that
the people of Crefeld were very much annoyed by the
'Legend of Sammstadt' — taking the extravagant
speeches I put in C.'s mouth as my own utterance?
Well, when I found them so thin-skinned, with the fear
of truth before my eyes, when I sent my manuscript to
the 'Tageblatt' I asked them to be frank and point out
any passages that might be open to misunderstanding.
They did — very frankly and kindly — condemning the
ridiculous sensitiveness of their countrymen, offering to
print as I scribed — but pointing out three or four of my
best passages as being 'likely to be misunderstood.' I

have consequently written but the one article — and shall bide my time for the others.

While I am writing this, and just after I had satisfied myself that I *ought not* to go to London, comes a letter from Sir Frederick Leighton, President of the Royal Academy, asking me if I will respond to the *toast of 'Literature,'* as they wish to deviate from their regular custom of asking a British author, *in honour to myself!* What shall I do?

Kiss the babies for Frank — while I make up my mind.

P.S. Can you read this scrawl?

CREFELD, *May* 6, 1879

MY DEAR NAN,

I concluded finally to decline the invitation to the Royal Academy Dinner, and the illness of my Vice-Consul afforded me a good excuse. You will probably see by the papers that, instead of losing by the omission, I really gained something by it, as Froude (dear good friend) spoke for me, complimented me handsomely, and got the fact that I *was* thus honoured before the world, which was all I wanted. So it's all right now, Nan. I'll send you the invitations, cards, etc., etc., I've received, and you can let people see — if you care to — what is thought of me out of my own country.

Besides, I can rub along at the German, and write a little, and use the leave of absence this summer to go to Switzerland for my health's sake, which is most important, as I do not seem to get any better. Some of the most unpleasant symptoms that I used to have in America are not quite so persistent here or are gone entirely, but I suffer terribly from *neuralgia* — the most frightful *toothache* (a thing I have always been spared) I can imagine is all it can be compared to. Then I am very sleepless. I sleep — no matter what time I go to bed — exactly four hours — no more, no less.

I was invited to a large dinner given by the Provincial Diet of the Rhenish Provinces at Düsseldorf last night. It was a long, tedious affair — everybody in uniform and glittering with orders — much wine-drinking, sentimental speech-making, etc. The Prince of Hohenzollern asked to be introduced to me, and said very nice things to me, and so did his cousins and uncles and his aunts. I've been very little in society here and care nothing for it, for I rather think the people of Crefeld, who are of the middle classes, think a Commercial Agent is something like a commercial traveller or drummer, and because I do not wear a uniform like the other Consuls, am rather indifferent in these courtesies. It is rather amusing that in any other part of Germany and all over England there is but the expression of astonishment. 'Why did your Government send you to Crefeld?' I blush, but I don't say that I had to take this place or nothing. The English Consul-General was inclined to look down upon me, too, until he heard that St. Albans was a friend of mine, and he became civil. But if I had been valued at the estimate my Government put upon me — Heaven help me!

You must take care of yourself, Nan: it perplexes and worries me to hear you hint so vaguely of your health. Is it a cold — or is it debility? You must not worry about me or the future — things will come right in the end. I know that since I have been here I have been able to send you more money than I expected, and yet have kept myself free from debt. I hope even by the end of the first year of my Consulate — and my *exile from home* — to have a little over. I shall have been here a year on the 18th July — that is a year in the Service. I cannot make any preparation for the next year or know what I

shall do until then. My salary is not what it should be.
When I was at Bradford, a small town in England, the
American Consul told me he made eight thousand dollars
a year from his office. Think how a place like that would
have answered all our wants and saved me breaking my
heart over this horrid German language and ruining my
already weak digestion with their filthy fat and vinegar!
I am very glad to know the boys are prospering so well
in their studies. Tell them Papa wants them to keep up
their good work. Kiss Tottie and Ethel and say that
Papa's heart is lifted whenever he hears about them.
God bless you.

FRANK

Bret Harte was always fond of animals, dogs especially, and they have been the heroes of more than one of
his sketches. At Birmingham, during one of his lectures
there, he greatly admired a beautiful Saint Bernard belonging to the friends with whom he was staying, and
gratefully, but perhaps somewhat rashly, accepted one of
her two pups. 'Shem' grew up without ever seeing his
master, who, as time went by, and the dog became bigger
and bigger, was more and more at a loss to know what to
do with him. The following letter to his friend is one of a
series connected with 'Shem,' a few of which are published
here. Edgar T. Pemberton was an intimate friend and
collaborated with Bret Harte in several plays. He later
wrote the first biography of him.

UNITED STATES CONSULATE
CREFELD, *May 25*, 1879

MY DEAR PEMBERTON,

I think I prefer, all things considered, 'Shem.' 'Ham'
might be preferable if he had the colour attributed by the
best authorities to his Noachian namesake. A black

Saint Bernard would be as beautiful and as terrible as a thunderstorm. But I am very grateful, my dear fellow, for 'Shem.' 'Shem' let it be, then. Vivat Shem!

You have forgotten to tell me how old he is. So I cannot tell if he will be able to bear the fatigue and excitement of Continental travel. I don't want to expose him prematurely to foreign temptation and habits, without some previous experience, or to take him out from you and his mother rashly. Therefore, please let me know at once. Meanwhile consider him *mine;* act for me vicariously; let him have the best at my expense.

Procure for him a collar with a silver plate — not *too* expensive, but suitable to *my degree*, and his — which shall bear the legend 'Shem.' Let him do as he likes, short of active aggression upon the persons of your family, and send the bill to me.

Give my best regards to your wife, and beg her to bear with him yet a while longer, for my sake, and believe me, anxiously awaiting your reply,

Yours ever
BRET HARTE

T. EDGAR PEMBERTON, ESQ.

Meanwhile Bret Harte, who was far from well, seemed to be getting worse, so much so that the doctors ordered complete rest and a change of climate. The following letters to his wife speak of this, and of his projected request for a transfer of consulate.

UNITED STATES CONSULATE
CREFELD, May 29, 1879

MY DEAR NAN,

On the 18th of July I shall have served the Government one year at this post, and I am thinking very seriously of applying to the Department for a transfer or *exchange* (I dare not hope for any *promotion*) to some other locality. My strongest reason is my *health*, and I can get any number of certificates from the best German physicians here that this part of the country is injurious to my temperament and condition. You will perhaps smile and remember how you used to accuse me of making the like charges against every place where I have lived. I only know that certain symptoms disappear when I leave Germany, if only for a week or two, and inevitably return when I am here. Although I was by no means well in Paris and London, I am much worse here, and lately *neuralgia*, in all its most disagreeable forms, has fixed upon me. I used to have little pity for people with the toothache, but since I've suffered with my jaws bound up in a towel, night after night, I can imagine nothing worse. I've had dentists examine my teeth, doctors stick things into my ears, and indulge in all sorts of speculations, until they finally concluded that it was really *neuralgia*.

I should have asked for an exchange before, but when I write to the Department I must have *outside friends* to urge and speak for me. I shall write a private letter to Mr. Seward, but *that* is not sufficient, and at present I cannot think of any one with influence enough in Washington to assist me. If I could hold on until a change in the Administration, I might be reasonably sure of success, but I cannot ask for an extended leave of absence, by reason of taking already so much in my lecture trips to England, and the doctor says I must go to Switzerland, or the seashore, this summer positively.

You may have wondered why I did not ask before. I was quite ashamed so soon, but the belief that I cannot live here and be a strong and healthy man with the power to work has been slowly forcing itself upon me, and has been at the bottom of all my indecision in the plans of the future. I am only too glad that I have made none, and that the change — if I have to make one — will involve the movements of nobody but myself. It would have been no light matter to have moved a family.

I'll write to you again, and more decidedly as to my intentions — *when I know them.* I hope you are in the country by this time, although it is but a shade or two warmer than an American March at this season here, and I sincerely hope you are all better. Don't worry about me either! The doctors here, who have examined me and probed me all over, say it is nothing but the climate acting upon a nervous, sensitive American constitution.

God bless you all.

FRANK

CREFELD, *July 5,* 1879

MY DEAR NAN,

I suppose you have been worried at my silence, but I have been really quite ill for the last three weeks, and have been waiting to get better before I wrote. My trouble was neuralgia and rheumatism brought on by this always bad climate and this exceptionally cold and wet weather. At last the doctors pretended that they found another predisposing cause in one of my teeth, and I have had two dentists punching at them and latterly have had the nerve 'killed,' as they call it — which seems, as far as I can make out, giving it the lively activity of forty toothaches. It has been 'dead' four days, and I have serious thoughts, if it keeps on, I won't survive it. The fact is they — the dentists and doctors — here are the most profound humbugs in the world. Why young Americans are ever sent to Germany to study science or

art is beyond my comprehension. They do not know the
latest inventions and the latest medicines. When my
eyes were very weak after my last lecturing tour and the
study of German, I went to the greatest oculist in Germany, *Dr. Moorau* — a name known all over the world —
who lives in Düsseldorf, and whose patients come even
from China and San Francisco. He told me the nerves
of my eyes were '*tired*' — which Dr. Gunning had told me
— and gave me — as a 'rare prescription' — the very oint-
ment which poor dear old Dr. Mackintosh gave me in
San Francisco fourteen years ago! D——n Germany!

Another thing kept me from writing. I am trying to
finish a story or romance for a German paper so that
I might get some money to go to Switzerland with —
for, Nan, I have not overmuch cash to spare for travelling, and *there* it is very expensive. But I persevered and
finally wrote a long story, in spite of the doctors, the
dentists, and the weather, and I shall go to Switzerland
in a few days.

Since I wrote last I have received two letters from you,
one from Eliza, and one from Wodie. You must tell Eliza
that I will surely answer it as soon as I can, and tell Wodie
that his papa was very proud of his 'big boy's' improved
handwriting. I'll answer the letter in a day or two. I
know the two authors of the 'Pinafore,' and when they
come to America, I'll have the boys see them. You, too!
You would, I think, like Arthur Sullivan. He invited me
to dine with him and the Prince of Wales, but I had to
lecture that night in Birmingham.

I am quite anxious to know if my lecture on 'American
Humour' — the one I wrote for the Mercantile Library
— is among the papers you discovered. I cannot find it
among my things *here*, and it is of great importance to
me. Please send it if you can find it. If all the papers —

including Miss Coolbrith's packet — do not make *too* large a bundle, you might send them to the State Department ('care of') addressed to me here. They will send it to me in a despatch bag.

I will write again in a few days, as soon as I know what day I shall leave for Switzerland. I am glad you are again at Morristown and expect to go to Sea Cliff — only, I suppose, because I can 'place' you there. I have never 'seen' you in New York at all. I couldn't imagine any of the places you were at.

Kiss the chickens for me.

Yours
Limick

P.S. My hand is so rheumatic I fear you cannot make out this scrawl. I must go to Switzerland.

Finally, in August, he took his brief holiday in Switzerland, from where the lovely letter to his little son Frank was written, in which he describes the famous clock of Strassburg in his charming half-serious, half-humorous manner. The two other letters, to his wife, give an account of his short vacation, and contain some fine descriptions of nature, and a very interesting reference to his struggle over the publication of the story that made him famous.

United States Consulate
Zurich, 31*st July*, 1879

My dear Frankie,

I began a letter to you a day or two ago before I left Crefeld to go to Switzerland, but I've forgotten whether I finished it or not. But no matter now. You ought to prefer this, as it's written on the hills overlooking the

Lake of Zurich, with a few of the snow-capped Alps in sight. I am sitting at an old table one hundred years old, say; in a room panelled with oak and about three hundred years old, and in a queer house one half of which is as old as the Swiss people. The house is called 'Bochai,' is a *pension* and was an old *Jägerhof* or hunting-house of a Zurich Burgomaster of the old days. I wish I could say that the hills were finer than the Californian Coast Range at Oakland, that the waters of the lake were bluer than Lake George, or that the sky was fairer than any American sky — but it is not. Rather, I won't say anything about it, but leave you and Wodie to say what you think about it when you come here with Papa — in the days to come. But it is *Switzerland*, and I'm here after a few days' leisurely journeying up the Rhine.

I went first by rail to Rolandseck, on the Rhine, opposite the famous 'Drachenfels' and the ruined castle of the old robber knight, which looks exactly as it does in the pictures. I stayed there one night, and the next morning took the train to Coblenz, an old fortified town with a high stone wall surrounding it — looking again exactly like the pictures; then I took a steamer, one of the largest of the Rhine 'Schnelldampschiffs,' but not as *large* nor half as *comfortable* or quarter as *fast* as the old 'Sewanhaha.' Every mile of the nine thence to Mayence was historical and crested with old ruined castles, looking like scenes in the theatres, and all very strange and new, but around me on the steamer were Americans and English, and everything on board the boat was less foreign than my home at Crefeld. From 'Mayence' or 'Mainz,' as they call it — for they have German names for all the towns that are historical to us — I went to Strassburg to see the Cathedral and the famous clock. Long before I reached the town, I saw the tall spire of this very ugly cathedral rising over the plain, but one of the most beautiful plains I had ever journeyed over, perfectly brilliant and resplendent with poppies, corn-flowers, and tawny yellow grasses. If you have not read about the famous clock at Strassburg, Mamma will tell you about it, and you won't be satisfied with knowing that I went to *see* it strike the hour. It was five o'clock when I stood before it. The clock struck 'five' like any ordinary clock. But suddenly the figure of a skeleton in one of the galleries of the clock case struck a bell with a hammer, denoting an hour passed; an angel, holding an hour-glass, reversed the glass; a little child started out of another semi-circular gallery to denote the beginning of another hour, just as an old man passed away from another gallery to denote that the last hour had fled. The clock is wound up every eight days, and is arranged to run nine hundred and ninety-nine years. I don't know why the maker didn't add another year to make it one thousand — but perhaps he got tired. It shows the day of the week, month, year, leap-year, the state of the moon, eclipses, etc., etc., and is really very wonderful. During the siege of Strassburg by the Germans during the last war, the Cathedral was almost destroyed by shells, but the clock was miraculously preserved.

I have just returned here from Zurich and am very tired. I'll write you and Mamma again in a few days.

Your loving papa
FRANK

UNITED STATES CONSULATE
ZURICH, *August* 11, 1879

MY DEAR NAN,

I wrote a few lines to Frankie last week, but I have had no time to write you the long letter I expected to write from Switzerland. I have been running around from place to place, hoping to find some beautiful spot to spend my vacation in — but in vain. Unfortunately, I cannot afford to go to the most frequented places, for the prices and the altitude are equally *high*, and if I stay in Switzerland I must find some spot that is cheap. Therefore, my health has been no better; I did not expect to be delighted with the scenery, so I am not disappointed there, but I did hope to be strong enough to take long walks and to climb a little. The weather here has been intensely hot, and although it has cooled off a little within the last few days, I am still weak. I shall go to the Rigi — about four thousand feet up — in a day or two; if I do not feel some exaltation or improvement from it, I shall leave Switzerland and go to the seaside in Holland.

I have tried, when my head or my stomach was not aching, to appreciate Swiss scenery. I am living in the hills overlooking Lake Zurich — (whence the poem 'By the margin of fair Zurich's waters') and I regret to say that the Zurich waters are *not* 'fair,' and that the Californian mountains and Coast ranges are vastly superior to these famous Alps — in every respect. As the Rhine is inferior to the Hudson, so is Switzerland to California, and even to the Catskills in New York. The snow peaks visible from my window are fine, but I have seen finer views from a wayside hotel in California country.

Last night some infamous wretches extemporized a 'yodel' call or cry which you probably remember to have read of or heard sung in the opera. It was like the caterwauling of fifty cats, with an obbligato from a donkey.

I will write you after I have returned from the Rigi. I have not received anything from you since the 25th of July — but I have not had my letters sent here from Crefeld and your letters may be awaiting me there.

God bless you all.   LIMICK

MY DEAR NAN,

I wrote you a few hurried lines yesterday as soon as I got back from Switzerland. I thought to write you a long letter, describing some of the things I had seen, but I find the little enthusiasm I had has gone out — and I recall only a few things in which I was not disappointed.

Do you remember a certain ride we once took over the Santa Cruz Range with Mr. R. and family. There was nothing in Switzerland more wonderful than that except that the roads are finer and better kept. There is nothing in Switzerland *grander* than the Sierras — there is much, however, more singularly *beautiful*. I was not struck with the isolated grandeur of the Rigi until I saw the clouds slowly forming on some peaks opposite, and really seemed to be *in the manufactory where they were made.* Not the usual misty sheets and veils and ribbons one sees on small mountains, but these just piled up ice-cream masses that lie high up in the sky before a thunderstorm. I felt no exhilaration at this height, five thousand feet, because perhaps I had often been ten thousand feet up in the Sierras. The isolation of this great sugar loaf rising out of Lake Zug was its point of interest to me, and at night, when the wind rose, I felt the joy as if I were again at sea. More remarkable to me were one or two days at Wesen on the Wallen See, where I had the peak of Glärnisch before me and the Speer behind me, all rising from a perfectly level billiard-table-like valley triangular in shape, having for its apex the Glärnisch. To watch the play of light and shade and colour, the coming and going of clouds, the dreamlike unreality of these great lovable giants, as they seemed occasionally to thrust a foot or an arm, or even to lift their heads up out of this wonderful, shifting, gauzy drapery, was wonderful and even to my eyes — accustomed to the hard, stern outlines of the atmosphereless Sierras — I actually grew weak and faint with exhausted nervous sensation: 'dazzled and drunk with beauty,' I suppose, but such beauty as makes all other beauty seem as naught — all other sensation as grossness. The alpine glow was also *not* a disappointment. I don't mean the rosy light on the snowfields known by that name; but the cold, ghastly, bluish-white that succeeds it — which is Death made visible, and awfully beautiful. The Jungfrau one night looked to me as I suppose the Angel of Death looked in the days of Solomon when it was visible.

Between my awed and hushed reverence for the great, reposeful gentleman-and-lady-like mountains, I had to struggle with a violent and active resentment against the natives — the 'hardy,' 'liberty-loving' Swiss — who are the biggest frauds I ever met. A race of 'Yankees' — more intolerant and bigoted than the poorest downtrodden peasants I ever met — are these 'hardy mountaineers,' with their sham sentiments, their sham liberty, their sham chamois (an ugly cross between a goat and a jackass), their sham *jödel* — that awful falsetto as musical as a cat's serenade; and nothing real about them but their hideous *goitres*. How the mountains must despise 'em so that all the mountains every now and then take a shy at 'em with an avalanche. I saw the descendants of the survivors of three buried villages below the Rigi — I looked at them and looked up at the mountain, and thought it was merciful!

I spoke of Roman! Read the enclosed slip and imagine how furious I was to read it in Switzerland, where I couldn't get at anybody to set them right, or tell them that they *lied!* Do you remember the day you lay sick at San José and I read you the story of 'The Luck,' and took heart and comfort from your tears over it, and courage to go on and *demand* that it should be put into the magazine. And think — think of fat Mrs. Roman claiming to be its sponsor!!!

Good-night.

LIMICK

How deeply Bret Harte felt the separation from his wife and children is apparent from the letters that follow the short note written upon his return from England. 'The Twins' are those of 'Table Mountain,' which had been written during his stay in Germany, and which had just been published in America. Things were rapidly maturing in connection with his change of post, and he was planning for a complete rest during the two months' leave that had been granted him, but which he had not yet made use of.

LANGHAM HOTEL
LONDON, *September 9*, 1879

MY DEAR NAN,

I've just returned from a week's visit to Colonel Webb at Newstead Abbey, and am now on my way to Crefeld. I've met some very charming people, have been in better health, and have two long letters to you and the boys with photographs and relics, etc., etc., packed in my trunk.

I only sit down a moment to catch the steamer mail, lest you should be worried by my silence. I'll write you as soon as I get to Crefeld.

God bless you all! In great haste,

FRANK

CREFELD, *September* 13, 1879

MY DEAR NAN,

I have yours of the 27th August and a characteristic letter from Master Frankie, consulting me on 'the subject of his education.' I'll answer him in a day or two with the mature deliberation his questions require, but at present let him go in and study like a Trojan, and if he misses fire at 'Columbia,' remember that there is still a very good School of Mines at Freiburg.

I am expecting daily to hear from the 'Sun' about my story of the 'Twins' which they published on the 17th August, but which I suppose you had not seen when you wrote ten days later. If they sent you the money, it might have justified you in going to Sea Cliff, even at a greater expense — for I want you, Nan, always *to do what you think best for yourself and the boys*, and know that it will always please Limick. You say you are lonely even with those dear children around you. I don't like to tell you how lonely I feel at times, nor do I care much to think of it myself. If I could travel around much, I could shake it off, but to sit here, sometimes with the grim *routine* of my work before me, and so little — apparently so *very* little to look ahead to, even when I work hard, is dreadful. I sometimes wonder what kind of work I am doing. I never see anybody whose opinion I value; I never hear any criticism. I grind out the old tunes on the old organ and gather up the coppers, but I never know whether my audience behind the window blinds are wishing me to 'move on' or not. Tell me — very frankly — what you think of 'The Twins.' I wrote it when I was half dead with neuralgia.

I hope they will exchange me. I shudder to look forward to the dreary autumn and drearier winter that is coming. There seems to have been no summer at all —

in this dull level of monotony. But I am not going to growl any more, leastways beforehand. Kiss the boys for me and hug the girls, and tell them to be patient and wait for Papa.

LIMICK

CREFELD, 11th October, 1879

MY DEAR NAN,

The English and Continental newspapers have been circulating paragraphs about the effect of the Crefeld climate on my health, and that I am thinking of resigning. Many of the reports are very much exaggerated, and I fear may be copied in American newspapers and worry you.

The facts are that I am far from well (although the neuralgia is better), but the famous German doctor here — Dr. Von Kohlwetter — says I cannot get better in this climate, and I have written to the State Department, *first*, for a leave of absence of two months; *second*, for an *exchange* of locality if I do not get better in that time. I wrote a private note to Mr. Seward regarding it and have asked for an answer by telegraph. I suppose the newspapers got hold of it from some passage in a private letter to friends in England, and the newspapers here are as active in personal paragraphing as the American press — with the saving grace that they are more respectful and kind.

I have yours of the 17th and 26th. It cannot be helped if you have drawn from Schroeder. Your drafts there will always be honoured as long as I remain here and don't get very sick. You understand that I expected you would get about three hundred and fifty dollars from the 'Sun' and one hundred and fifty dollars from Osgood — that was why I wrote.

Osgood is acting in that queer un-Osgood-like way into which he sometimes falls; I am asking no favour from him! He has taken the volume to publish, and he has always advanced the price of fifteen hundred copies — one hundred and fifty dollars — on the receipt of the manuscript. It is queer. I am only afraid that some creditor may come down upon him. I have written him again.

I sent Dana another story — for which he ought to send you one hundred dollars.

I will write again soon. I may probably go to Paris in a day or two. But you shall hear from me as soon as I hear from the Department.

God bless you all.

FRANK

UNITED STATES CONSULATE
CREFELD, *November* 1, 1879

MY DEAR NAN,

I have just received yours of October 17th. I feared that the newspaper paragraphs concerning my health would take some garbled shape, and that was why I wrote you so particularly concerning it.

The Department have telegraphed me two words, 'Granted, Seward,' which is dear good Seward's consent to my application for a leave of absence. Of course, I shall not know until two weeks later, by official correspondence, what they intend to do about 'exchanging' me. I am furious with myself for not asking a leave of absence *to include a visit to America*, as these 'leaves' have to be granted *separately* — and I might have come home, and perhaps have arranged with the Department to better advantage. It is possible that they may make some such suggestion in their correspondence. I should avail myself of the leave to come, anyway, only I fear that my presence there, uninvited, might prejudice my case.

They scruple about removing a man when he *is at his post*, but when he is at home, they seem to think it quite easy to do so.

If I do not come to America, I shall try to find some cheap place in Italy to spend a month or six weeks. I *must* have a change; the climate here is so depressing, so dead-and-alive, so sunless, dark, and gloomy that it is like being in a mine, and I fear that if I got *very sick*, I should never recover from it. You can imagine what it is when I assure you that it is really less depressing in the house than out of it. When you are faint — to go into the open air only makes you worse. And this is only the *beginning* of the winter. The sun has shone two hours in twenty-seven days. If it *stormed*, it would be a relief. But it is the gloom and quiet of a sepulchre.

I am shocked to hear of the accident to Eliza and but thankful that they escaped with so little injury. I have been, I dare say, instinctively conscious of all this — for it has been a month of deep nervous apprehension to me, and there have been days when only the most desperate effort of my will — kept up for hours — prevented me from leaving everything at once and going back to America.

I am writing another long story as long as 'The Twins,' but it progresses *so* slowly — sometimes I cannot write more than a page in a day. I do not write late at night as formerly. I haven't the strength.

God bless you all. I sent a line to Frankie the other day with a note enclosed to Mr. Boucicault.

As soon as I have any news or come to any determination I'll write again. Kiss the kids for

FRANK

The depressing note of the preceding letters is alleviated by the following interesting one to the Duchess of

St. Albans, in which Bret Harte gives a very sincere expression of his patriotic feelings. It contains also a clever literary criticism of Henry James.

CREFELD, *November 6,* 1879

MY DEAR DUCHESS,

I was very honestly interested in your sister's book, and cannot understand why it should not be popular, unless a majority of mankind are Freemasons, and this very wholesome exposition of a mystery, which seems to be no mystery at all, should be distasteful to them. I am not a Freemason, and I was delighted to hear that this historical brotherhood was, really, a very *recent* affair. Your sister must be awfully learned. *I* should be quite afraid of her.

You ask me to tell you about Mr. James. I think I met him in Boston some years ago, when I first came from California, but I dare say I would not be able to recognize him now. Of his work, I have only read 'Daisy Miller.' It struck me as being quite fresh and entertaining. My impression of the man, however, is that he is an American who has lived long enough abroad to be critical of his countrymen and countrywomen, and to be nervous, in a nice ladylike way, at the spectacle of their unconventionality. I think he hardly sees below the surface, nor understands what that unconventionality means. Seeing and feeling superficially, he never has any plot or design or moral in his work. Poor little Daisy Miller's fate is almost absurdly illogical. She might have gone in a conventionally proper way to the Coliseum, and yet caught the malarial fever, and died. You cannot believe her dying for love, any more than you can believe the cold-blooded hero, who notices all her defects, as a lover, or a creature such as a girl could love. I have known two or three Daisy Millers, but they did not culminate in that fashion. 'The International Episode' in the same volume is very good, as far as regards the American sketching. Nothing could be more truthful than that picture of Newport life, but here again Mr. James sees only something odd in the spectacle of that New York husband, working to keep up the Newport court of his queenly wife, and loyally accepting his own separate existence. Mr. James does not see the pathos of this figure, nor how perfectly characteristic it is of our woman-worshipping race, no more than the Englishman did.

It vexes me to see this misunderstood. I love my country (as you pretty well know) and I revere its women-reverencing men. I find no such people anywhere else. Forgive me if I flap my wings, not so much over a country of free men as of free women.

The English side of 'The International Episode' you can better criticise. I never met gentlewoman, titled or untitled, who behaved as Lord Somebody's mother and sister. Perhaps they exist.

I'm afraid I have talked too much. You must hold my criticism to yourself. A literary man can hardly estimate a contemporary fairly, and I may be quite wrong in my ideas of Henry James.

I would like you to read Howells's 'Lady of the Aroostook,' and, when you have done so, give me your opinion. I have my own.

The Department has granted me, by telegraph, a leave of absence. I am hesitating whether to go to Italy or whether to make a brief visit to America. In either event, I shall come to England for a week or two before I go. I am very far from being strong — what little activity I have resides in my nerves.

Pray send me that wonderful receipt for neuralgia.

I have written to Paris to know why that envelope was torn. I handed the letter to the *portier* of the hotel to post. It must have fallen into strange hands — possibly Freemasons'. Write me soon.

Yours very truly
BRET HARTE

It was at the approach of Christmas that he most felt the separation from his family, as he always attached a deep sentiment to being united at that time, and always, even to his friends, thought of some little presents to give them pleasure and to be remembered by.

CREFELD, *December 7, 1879*

MY DEAR NAN,

I have written Schroeder and Company to send you at once fifty dollars, over and above and independent of any money you may have been obliged to draw from them. And I want you to apply it solely to the purchase of Christmas things for yourself and the children. I wish it was more, but I am trying to keep out of debt entirely this year and have a trifle — if only a trifle — over on the 1st of January.

I send also to-day, consigned to Schroeder and Company, a small box containing some trifles for yourself and the little girls. That you should not expect too much and that you may be sure to get even the little I send, I enclose a list of the contents of the box. I give a duplicate list to Schroeder and Company, that they may get it through the Custom House. I am almost ashamed to send such trifles, but they are all local and have been collected by me from time to time. I hoped to be able to send you a watch — but I could not.

Osgood wrote me that he has sent you one hundred and fifty dollars; Dana also writes that he has sent you one hundred dollars for 'Peter Schroeder.' Meantime I hope you have not wanted for money, but have drawn from Schroeder. I shall send by the next mail a story to Dana — longer than 'The Twins' — and ask him to send you a cheque at once. I do not know how much it will be.

I sent you the other day two pieces of music, one the Malkeston March, a very favourite German march here played by the military bands and very characteristic, and the other a Norwegian composition which I have heard played by some Norwegian young ladies in a family here. One of them dressed the German doll, an Alsatian peasant, and requested me to send it to my little girls with her compliments.

I also send you the little Christmas song that the children sing here on 'Weihnachts' around the Christmas tree. As certain airs or songs represent certain places to me more or less characteristically, this one is identified in my memory with a German Christmas.

Where *I* may be Christmas, I cannot say. I shall not return to America until my letter asking an exchange is answered. I think I shall go to England. But wherever I go, I cannot hope to be less lonely than I am. I think my health has improved a little under a sharp snap of frosty weather, quite unusual here, but it has made me feel homesick, and even a heavy snowstorm that I delighted in only brought back old memories. Just now I am suffering from the hands of a German dentist who has filled one of my teeth and left me for the past two days in exasperating pain.

I want you to be all very happy on Christmas and very hopeful. I want the children sometimes to think of Papa

alone here, but not too much or let it stand in the way of
their happiness. God bless you all, Nan, prays

LIMICK

CONTENTS OF BOX

1 Album of Swiss Photographs	Mamma
1 German doll	Ethel
1 French doll	Tottie
1 Pair wooden shoes	Tottie
1 Work bag	Mamma
containing	
1 Celluloid ornament for the hair	Mamma
1 Locket and chain (silver)	Mamma
1 Thimble and case	Mamma
1 Portemonnaie	Tottie
1 Portemonnaie	Ethel

Bret Harte knew most of the great literary men of his
day, some of whom became intimate friends, as in the case
of William Black, Sir Wemyss Reid, Jerome K. Jerome,
and others. He relates in an interesting manner, in the
following letter to his wife, his meeting with the famous
English writer George Eliot, as well as with Thomas
Hardy, and the well-known artist Du Maurier.

LONDON, January 7, 1880

MY DEAR ANNA,

I sent you yesterday a few New Year's and Christmas
cards for Tottie and Ethel — some of them sent by my
kind hostess, Mrs. Trübner, and her little daughter. It
is the European idea of a New Year's call, and is a very
pretty custom, I think. In Germany it is sentimentality
mixed up with Saint Valentine, but I sent the children
the German cards and wrote all about it, I think, last
year. Do you remember?

I spent a delightful hour with George Eliot (Mrs. Lewes) on Sunday last at her house. I was very pleasantly disappointed in her appearance, having heard so much of the plainness of her features. And I found them only strong, intellectual, and *noble* — indeed, I have seldom seen a grander face! I have read somewhere that she looked like a horse — a great mistake, as, although her face is long and narrow, it is only as Dante's was. It expresses elevation of thought, kindness, power, and *humour*. It is at times not unlike Starr King's — excepting King's beautiful eyes. Mrs. Lewes's eyes are grey and sympathetic, but neither large nor beautiful. Her face lights up when she smiles and shows her large white teeth, and all thought of heaviness vanishes. She reminds you continually of a man — a bright, gentle, lovable, philosophical man — without being a bit *masculine*. Do you understand me?

Of course, her talk was charming. It was wise and sweet and humorous. It was like her books — or her written speech when she moralizes — but I thought it kinder and less hard than some of her satire. She said many fine things to me about my work, and asked me to come again to see her, which was a better compliment, as she has since Lewes's death received no one.

I saw Hardy — the novelist — at the club the other night. A singularly unpretending-looking man, and indeed resembling anything but an author in manner or speech. I had a pleasant chat with the artist Du Maurier, who draws the lovely children in 'Punch,' and met Henry James, Jr., the American novelist, who is creating quite a reputation here. He looks, acts, and thinks like an Englishman, and writes like an Englishman, I am sorry to say, excellent as his style is. I wish he had more of an American flavour — but this is the effect of extreme Boston culture and European travel. The club is a new one — just being formed — the Rabelais Club it is called — and I had been proud to become a member. At the dinner last night Sir Frederick Pollock presided as President, and to my astonishment at the end of the dinner nominated *me* to preside as president next time, to everybody's apparent applause and satisfaction but my own.

The weather is gloomy and horribly foggy — worse than Crefeld was. I fear I will be obliged to cut short my stay, for my neuralgia is troubling me again. I will write you when I leave. Love to the kids.

LIMICK

Then follows one of the fondly humorous and interesting letters to his son Frank, which is typical of the letters to his children.

CREFELD, *February* 9, 1880

MY DEAR FRANKIE,

I am very glad to hear from your letter — which, by the way, is very well written — that you are 'studying very hard' and that 'Peck's Manual' and 'Davies's Legendre' are your '*constant* companions.' Nevertheless, I would not, if I were you, breakfast with 'Peck's Manual' *every* morning, nor dine with 'Davies's Legendre' *every* day. Be moderate with Peck and Davies — that's Papa's good little boy!

You must write to me all about your friends, and who they are (always excepting those inseparable companions of your youth — Peck and Davies!) and tell me *what* you do these pleasant evenings. I wish you could spend some of them with Papa — although he is getting rather too old to be company for you now.

I think, though, that you would have enjoyed yourself

at Cologne during the Carnival. There was a great '*Zug*' or procession yesterday — all of which I saw from the balcony of a friend's house on the *Neumarkt* — one of the great squares of Cologne.

I think I wrote you last year something about Cologne, and of the famous 'Dom' or Cathedral, part of which was begun as early as A.D. 1200, and the rest — the spires — being still in course of erection. It will be completed this summer, when the building will be higher than Saint Peter's at Rome. At present it is a mere mass of scaffolding from the body of the church up.

Diagonally across the square from my balcony is a high house, from one of the upper windows of which two white stone horses' heads protrude. They appear to be looking into the square. They are placed there to perpetuate an old legend which runs somewhat after this fashion:

Many years ago, during a plague in Cologne, the wife of a certain Count died, and was hastily buried in the churchyard of the church on the next corner. She was, however, only in a *trance*, and was awakened from it by two grave-robbers, who entered her tomb to steal her valuable rings, which they proceeded to do, after the clumsy fashion of the period, by '*cutting them off with a knife.*' The loss of blood revived the poor lady, frightened the robbers, who fled, leaving her to find her way, only a few steps, to her husband's house. She knocked. He opened the window, and demanded, 'Who was there?' 'Your wife,' she replied. 'That is too thin!' he answered (I mean, he probably used the Cologne slang of the period). She repeated her story, which he said 'wouldn't wash,' and then told her she might as well tell him 'that his horses, securely locked in the stables, were looking out of the window with him.' Instantly a trampling noise was heard on the staircase, and his two horses entered the chamber, and, solemnly approaching the window, looked out of it. Of course, the Count came down then, and, of course, had his ears soundly boxed for his skepticism. (I dare say, however, he took privately *his* revenge on the horses the next time they drove out.)

Frankie, *I* don't believe that story! Because *one* horse would have done as well as *two*. The extra horse is fatal to the story. But there are the two horses' heads still looking from the window on the *Neumarkt*, and I stared at them all day, yesterday, when I wasn't looking at the procession.

The spectacle was very fine. There were groups of jesters, clad in stripes and motley; men in armour, heralds, pages, soldiers in the uniform of the last century, chariots with allegorical figures in them, carriages with burlesques of local officials and political satires (nobody — not even the Government — dares take offence at anything during the Carnival), monkeys, bears, elephants (all personated by men), giants who shut themselves up like telescopes when they didn't care to overlook the crowd, a brass band dressed like cats (imagine your Mamma's horror!), one great sledge filled with polar bears (a satire upon the very severe winter). Some of the costumes were most extraordinary. One man I remember was dressed entirely in *matchboxes!* (the ordinary lucifer matchbox), stitched together in some queer way. Another was dressed in china tiles! The procession formed on the square, then marched round it, being nearly an hour passing our balcony. Add to this, remember! the fact that nearly *all* the spectators in the streets and balconies were also in costume! The effect of this great multitude of bright-coloured figures in a square as large as Washington Square was very wonderful and extraordinary.

In the afternoon we rode through the streets in a carriage, making a party composed of my friend and his wife, the American Consul and his wife, and myself. We had provided ourselves bountifully with *bonbons* and candies to throw to the little children, who were also in costumes, thronging the streets. Sometimes we could barely force our way through the crowds. Naturally the poor little children whom we threw our candies to *didn't get them* — for the bigger children made a rush after them, and finally became so bold as to invade our carriage. Two girls — of fourteen or fifteen — laid hold of me and tried to wrench my packet of sweetmeats from my side. Finally, some fellows also climbed into the carriage and tried to kiss the ladies, and *then* we had to lay about us right and left, the coachman whipped up his horses, and we got through without any more trouble. The ladies were dreadfully scared, and, I must confess, for a little time, I did not see exactly where the fun came in. The other Americans felt as I did. But you are not allowed to get angry at anything during Carnival time. Nevertheless, I felt like echoing Dr. Warner's question, 'How many of these fellows would be shot in an American crowd like this?'

It — the Carnival — is now a *Volksfest* or holiday of the people. Formerly the better classes took part in it. I cannot better describe the Carnival spirit than by saying it is a kind of frenzy or madness like that produced by liquor, and is not funny any more than drunkenness is. I believe that many — men and women — were actually drunk! We *walked* afterward in the streets, without the ladies, of course. A dozen men and a dozen women in the space of two squares stopped us and either embraced us or pinched us. Being a foreigner evidently, and my grey hair looking as if it were *powdered* for the Carnival, I came in, I think, for more than my share of hugging and pinching. I was breathless and sore in twenty minutes. At twelve at night — last night — the madness ceased. The Carnival was over.

I've written you a long letter, and have not yet said what I wanted to say. I must wait until next time. You must share this letter with Wodie!

Your affectionate papa
B. H.

In the meantime, 'Shem' has been growing up, and his new master is planning to take him from his friend's house, on his next visit to England. Bret Harte is daily expecting notification of his transfer, and quite cheerful at the prospect of going anywhere in preference to remaining at Crefeld.

UNITED STATES CONSULATE
CREFELD, February 27, 1880

MY DEAR PEMBERTON,

Pray do not for one instant give way to the belief that I have forgotten 'Shem' or his kind entertainers. Only the fact that I have asked my Government for an 'exchange' from Crefeld, and am now waiting to know where I am to go, has kept me from sending for him. As matters stand, I must ask you to bear with him and his discomforting greatness a little longer. I should not like a good dog to share the uncertainties of an American official.

But I am delighted to hear of his progress, his physical welfare, and his moral advancement. Yet, my dear Pemberton, you say nothing of his *spiritual* tendencies. Does he know the interior of a church? Can I take him into a cathedral with me? (if it were large enough). Has he ever been known to bark at a Bishop or a beneficed clergyman? These are not light questions, but momentous ones! A terrier of my acquaintance has been known to follow a priest two squares, violently objecting to him, and has gone out of his way, in a cathedral, to insult the hypocritically crossed legs of the effigy of a Crusader!

I am coming to Oxford and Cambridge to lecture after Easter. Somewhere about that time I shall visit you and 'Shem.' But of this more particularly later.

Pat 'Shem's' head for me gently, but not patronizingly, and read him this letter. Make my best regards to your wife, and say I have not forgotten the pleasant time I spent in her household at Birmingham.

In haste.

Yours always
BRET HARTE

T. EDGAR PEMBERTON

Bret Harte's outlook was much brighter, knowing that in any event it would not be long before he was transferred. In spite of his previous refusal, and although James Russell Lowell had just been appointed Ambassador in London, Bret Harte was again requested to return the 'Toast to Literature' at the coming Royal Academy Dinner, which was a special mark of English esteem and appreciation. The ridiculous letter which he quotes is almost worthy of a Mark Twain story, in its unbelievable absurdity.

CREFELD, March 18, 1880

MY DEAR NAN,

Since I wrote to you that Hay had written me a long letter full of kindness and promised to do his best to help me to an exchange, but with very little *hopefulness* in his own ability, I have a letter from Clarence King, much in the same vein, very charming and pleasant, in which he says Hay is working and will work his best to help me.

King writes because Barlow — who appears to have been *a very good friend of mine* — has evidently been stirring them all up. Says King: 'I at once pitched into Evarts and others. Evarts has been particularly busy, but is well inclined. I think the matter can be soon arranged. If it is made to your satisfaction, you will owe it chiefly to Hay, who has never lost an opportunity to work for you.'

And so — I wait. I am, though, chiefly pleased at the way dear, old, *fat* Sam Barlow has *not* forgotten me, but has, gratuitously, and without a word from me, set this all in motion. I had not expected it of him; we saw very little of each other, you remember, except socially, or on that dreadful boat when I used to go hopelessly and helplessly back and forth to the city, and he might have naturally forgotten me. I know that his very sweet Christmas letter, which came to me at Christmas time on one of the loneliest of my lonely days, brought the tears to my eyes. I have got so into the habit of believing myself in a kind of banishment here that a word of kindness or encouragement, outside of my own family, from across this wide ocean affects me greatly. It used to be a relief to me at first when I came here not to see the daily papers, or hear the ugly things said about my poverty, my debts, and my 'failing honours,' as they called it. Do you ever see Barlow? Or Dana? Or any of my old friends? How is Mrs. Sherwood?

I am surprised at that paragraph about the Academy Dinner. When I was in London, Frith, the painter, and R.A., asked me if I would come this year. I said 'yes,' and then he said it was all right. Immediately on receiving your note, I wrote to Froude asking him to find out from Sir Frederick Leighton if I was expected to speak. Froude has not yet seen Sir Frederick, but it would be quite natural if Lowell were asked to speak, he being the new Ambassador and the older man. Of course, I shall accept if I am asked, but if not I shall be equally satisfied. The invitations are not yet sent.

I am suffering from a bad cold. I had been so hopeful — having been free for the whole winter, but now I have 'Schnupfen,' which is the expressive German for 'cold in the head,' and a throat that 'strains at a gnat and swallows a camel's-hair pencil of lunar caustic.'

I have received many queer letters in my life and have some very odd European ones which I have kept to show you some day. But I send you a literal translation of one I received yesterday which I think transcends everything! Here it is:

VIENNA, 12 *March*, 1880

HIGH AND WELL-BORN SIR:

As a great admirer of your grand literary productions I am very sorry to learn that your health is poor, which made me think how happy I would be to undertake the duty of a faithful and attentive nurse.

I would willingly change my home for yours, and consider your wishes my commands.

Should you be able and willing to grant my request, which comes from the depths of my heart, a soon reply would greatly oblige me, and you would find me perfectly willing to answer any questions with the greatest sincerity.

With the greatest esteem
(Signed) M. STARK

1. LG. SCHOTTEN GASSE 3
   VIENNA

How is this for high-German sentiment? Suppose I put that letter in a German sketch, how the critics would go for me and my extravagance! I shall have to answer it, or the gentle Stark may come down upon me any day at the Consulate with her bandboxes. Of course, she's old, fifty at least, with pale, inexpressive eyes and glasses.

I send a very sloppy kiss to the children. I am regularly beaten with this cold.

Your sneezing
FRANK

Here at last was the good news, and better than he had expected. Bret Harte was given the Consulate at Glasgow, which was not only a transfer, but also a promotion. Here his salary would be almost double, and, although the climate, as far as his health was concerned, was not much of an improvement, he would be in far more congenial surroundings. His dislike for Crefeld was so intense that he was all the more grateful for the exchange. The three letters that follow give all the details of this new event in the story of his life.

CREFELD, 1st April, 1880

MY DEAR NAN,

I've been quite sick with a sore throat (which clings obstinately to me) since I wrote you last, and was ten days shut up in the house. During this time I saw a despatch in the London 'Times' saying I had been nominated Consul to Glasgow. Since then I have received all sorts of congratulations from England — the 'Daily Telegraph' devoted an editorial of fervent welcome to me — but *I have yet not a word from the Department at Washington*. Perhaps it may not be true. Perhaps it is the Department's brusque way of doing a favour, but I cannot help thinking it strange that they did not write me a line or send me a telegram. Possibly I may not be confirmed by the Senate.

If it is *true*, although the change is not all that I would seek in the way of a climate, it is better and more healthful than Crefeld. There are fogs — but they are sea fogs and the winters are sincere and cold. In every other respect it is a grateful change and an improvement. First, it is *promotion*. Glasgow is a full Consulate and is the second largest city of Great Britain. The salary is three thousand dollars per year, and one of my colleagues writes me that there are other emoluments which make it at least four thousand dollars. Then it is near Edinburgh — and not very far from London, and, as my English friends write me, 'you belong now to us.'

But I'm writing all this quite in the dark as to the future and quite ready to hear that there is some mistake. I must go to England on the 19th to lecture; before that time I ought to hear from the Department, and while in England I will run up to Glasgow and examine the ground. It is scarcely possible, I am told, for all the formalities of the transfer to be concluded before two months.

I will write soon again. Tell Frankie I have his earnest, honest letter and will answer it as quickly as I can.

Love to all. God bless you all.

LIMICK

Please pardon my scrawling hand to-day, but I've been writing much and my eyes are giving out.

UNITED STATES CONSULATE
CREFELD, *April 2*, 1880

MY DEAR ANNA,

A line to say that a private note from John Hay, received this morning, confirms the news of my appointment. By the same mail I am worried to hear from Frankie's letter that you are ill with an inflamed ear —

and cannot write. I *know* it must be painful, but I do not think it can be dangerous, and I do hope before this reaches you you will have forgotten which ear it was. In great haste, and with love to all,

LIMICK

P.S. My sore throat is obstinate, and I've lost some strength by it, but I think it is better.

UNITED STATES CONSULATE
CREFELD, *April* 15, 1880

MY DEAR NAN,

I have just received yours of the 3d inst., and am greatly alarmed to hear you have had a return of the earache. I had hoped it was only a temporary trouble and that you would have forgotten it by this time. I wish you would at once leave town — unless the weather is very backward — and take the children with you to recuperate in some little watering-place. Above all, and over all things, don't let yourself get 'run down' now.

I am fearful that it may be two months yet before I can be formally exchanged — particularly as I have yet received no *official* notice of my promotion. I know it is all right — but it is very tantalizing, this delay.

As I wrote you before, I am all in the dark about my future movements in Scotland until I have seen my new post. I shall, however, see it within the next two weeks when I go to England to lecture, and I will write you fully all about it. I hear it is a rather *expensive* place. But Germany was always quoted as 'cheap' — and is quite the reverse in my experience.

I have a dreadful amount of work and business anxiety crowded into the next two weeks. I must lecture three times — at Oxford, Cambridge, and Norwich —

while here, at the last moment, I have a note from Sir Frederick Leighton that he expects me to answer to the 'Toast to Literature' at the R. A. Dinner. I had hoped the rumour was not true. It will require me to prepare a speech — which I don't like — and speak it — which I *dread*. And, besides, there is all the work incident to the transfer of Consulate, while I am far from well. I ran down — five hours distant — to Holland on Sunday last and stayed three days. It broke up my cold, I think. I'll write you all about it another time — as I will write you about England; but you must be content with a few lines only until I have seen Glasgow, and know what we can do.

Love to all. God bless you.

LIMICK

The fifty dollars was all right. The 'Chronicle' offered me that sum for 'Jeff Briggs,' and I told them to send it to you. I am too poor to lose fifty dollars, which I can honestly earn, even of an enemy. They might have *stolen* 'Jeff Briggs,' too, and I couldn't have helped myself.

No man was more abstemious in his daily life than Bret Harte. As Merwin, his biographer, wrote, 'he smoked a good deal, drank very little, and took exercise every day, etc.' One can gather, in consequence, how furious the reports of his so-called drunkenness that were circulated among the German papers must have made him, and his disgust to discover that they had originated in no other than his own country. It was one of the many little hurts that were not forgotten.

CREFELD, *April* 17, 1880

MY DEAR NAN,

No news yet from the Department. I go in a day or two to England to lecture. I may not have time to write you again until I return.

A line in Frankie's letter worried me a week ago; it alludes 'to some trouble I had had in Germany.' As I *have had* some trouble here — but only recently, and before you could have an opportunity of hearing it, it surprised me.

I should not allude to it now and worry you with it if it were not all over — and settled. While I was confined to my room with sore throat, I received a paragraph cut from a German newspaper by an English friend in Düsseldorf. The paragraph said that 'I was sick of Germany and was going to resign.' It then added that it was 'well known' that the 'genial poet' was beset with an ungovernable passion for 'fire-water' (*feuerwasser* — brandy) brought on by his early habits in California: that his Government had sent him to Germany hoping to cure him of it (imagine a man addicted to drinking sent to this land of swilling sots for a cure!), but that, alas, it was all in vain, and now the 'genial poet' was about to return to San Francisco 'where he could indulge himself freely.'

I need not tell you how furious I felt. I at once wrote to a lawyer in Berlin and began to demand a retraction or prosecution against the paper. Meantime the very few friends I have here, but who knew me thoroughly, were indignant too. My little doctor — Von Kohlwetter — who is one of the most famous of physicians in this district, was furious. He wrote an indignant letter to the 'Kölnische Zeitung,' saying that he had attended me *daily*, that it was all an infamous lie, etc., etc., and hinted pretty plainly that if all Germans were as abstemious as

I was, it would be better for them. Mr. Leutzer, my old Crefeld friend, and a member of Parliament, declared that I had been an inmate of his family, and he knew me perfectly, and that it was a gratuitous and infamous slander. You see, anybody who really knew me — or saw me in company or at dinners — knows that I drink sparingly (I think I told you that I could not take any stimulants here), so that to them the story was absurd. Dr. Von K. went further, and said he knew from my nature and habits, and above all my symptoms, that I not only was *not*, but never *could have been*, a drunkard, etc., etc. Meantime the Berlin paper, frightened, apologized and took it all back. Another paper came out and said it was all an infamous lie. The other papers copied the retraction — and so the matter ended. I triumphed. But, Nan, I knew — what I didn't dare tell my friends — that paragraph — *that slander came from America!* God bless you all. Tell Frankie I will write to him as soon as I have seen Glasgow.

LIMICK

Bret Harte answered the 'Toast to Literature,' on May 1, 1880, before a distinguished assemblage, including the Prince of Wales, the Duke of Cambridge, and other members of the Royal family, the ministers, foreign ambassadors, and members of the two houses of Parliament. He was introduced by the president in a short speech, welcoming 'in its midst the great American Humourist.' Bret Harte's reply was brief and greatly applauded, and has been included in the collection of his lectures by the late Charles Meeker Kozlay.

LONDON, *May* 11, 1880

MY DEAR NAN,

I leave for Crefeld to-morrow, having got through my lectures, the Royal Academy Dinner, and the visit to Glasgow.

The lectures were *not* profitable; my expenses in travelling here equalled my very small fee. It enabled me to go to the R. A. Dinner (which I did to please *you*), but I don't think even *that* paid. I made a neat little speech — not bad and not very good — the Prince of Wales asked to be introduced to me (he's more like an American than an Englishman), a lot of swells were 'glad to make my acquaintance,' etc., etc., and that was about all. It was a good deal of trouble for very little result.

As to Glasgow. It's a big city — about as big as New York — very smoky, very damp, they say. But it's a relief to Crefeld.

I'll write you from Crefeld, where I am returning only to pack up and turn my office over to the new Consul. I wrote you that it would be perhaps two months before I could take my place — but I find I can probably go there sooner. Kiss the children — I suppose Wodie and Frankie will not come under that category any more. God bless you.

LIMICK

PART III
GLASGOW: 1880–1885

PART III

GLASGOW: 1880–1885

BRET HARTE left Crefeld in June, after the arrival of his successor. He had, however, not yet received his commission of appointment to Glasgow, and was temporarily without a post. The prospect of a Scotch climate, as he was discovering it, did not fill him with joy, but he was greatly to modify his opinion of the people, among whom he formed many devoted friends.

LONDON, *July 9*, 1880

MY DEAR NAN,

I am still waiting for my commission. I cannot take charge in Glasgow until that comes, and so I wait in London, where — as I am staying with the Timmins — it is less expensive. I expect, of course, that the Government will allow me to reckon my salary from the time I left Crefeld, but I cannot draw anything until I actually take charge.

Since I wrote you from Scotland, I have received yours of the 15th June. I am rejoiced to hear that you are out of town; even if Morristown is the same old bigoted, self-righteous, hypocritical place, it is better than being in a New York boarding-house in summer. But will you not find some pleasanter place? As soon as I 'take charge,' I will see that you have the two hundred dollars regularly every month, and will probably send it through some bank, but until then you may draw upon Schroeder as before.

The question of your coming over this summer with the children, Nan, is one that must be at once seriously considered. In the first place, we must both bear in mind that my position in the Government service is sure only up to the 4th of next March and the duration of this Administration. I believe that Garfield will be elected; Captain Mason, who knows him intimately, says, if he is elected, I may expect not only to be retained but promoted. Even if the Democrats succeed, it is possible that they will not interfere with me — a literary man and not a political appointee. *But none of these things are sure.* I do not — I *must not* take them into my calculations. So that the real question is, Can we afford to undergo the cost of bringing the whole family over when the additional expense of returning may be added in six months? If I were to leave the Government service, I could not make enough money by mere literary work in England to support my family. I should be obliged to return to America at once.

I can easily reckon what the expenses of the trip here and back would be, and when I get to Glasgow ascertain what the expenses of living there for six months would be, and add these sums together for the total.

The question, therefore, is whether it is better to take this risk *now*, or wait until after the 4th of March, when the risk is past. If it is better to wait, I shall try to get a leave of absence this winter to visit America, get promoted if I can, and then bring you back with me — I hope *not* to Glasgow. For I do not think I could stand it long, and I go there only with the hope that I may be 'changed' with the change of Administration.

I hope I may be disappointed in the Scotch people. All I hear of them is dreadful; all I have yet seen of them is not hopeful. The climate is certainly a very slight improvement on Crefeld. It rains every day, but I suffer most here from the utter absence of all the warmth and

A FAMILY GROUP TAKEN ABOUT 1900
Standing: Bret Harte and Mrs. Francis King Bret Harte (daughter-in-law)
Seated: Ethel Bret Harte (youngest daughter) and Anna Bret Harte (wife)

graciousness of summer. It is not to be found in northern
Europe. There are occasional *tepid* damp days, but never
any dry sunny summer weather when the shade is really
grateful. I always find an overcoat comfortable in England, but what is more perplexing I find that I seldom
have an opportunity of perspiring. You remember how
easily I always perspired; since I have been in Europe I
do not know what it is. I think much of my neuralgia and
throat trouble is owing to this inactivity of my skin and
its pores. Other Americans tell me the same thing.

Returning from Oban by rail, I passed through the
Highlands of Scotland. I never saw scenery that, to me,
seemed to typify the character of the people so strongly;
rather, I ought to say, has impressed itself so strongly on
the character of the people. I do no longer wonder that
a Scotchman cannot take a joke. Nature never smiles
upon him. I can understand why they are bigoted;
their highest mountains never rise above the clouds and
fog and mist of their own creating. There is not a mountain summit in Scotland above the clouds. Accustomed
to see Nature stern and forbidding and scant in her kindliness to him — he makes his own religion and practises it.
I wish you could see what they call a 'fine day' in Scotland — you would understand their idea of the Sabbath.

Apropos, I must tell you a good story of them — new to
me. A gentleman going to church one Sunday found himself too early for the service and would pass the time
away by walking in an adjacent park. But the park-
keeper opposed him and informed him he must not de-
secrate the 'Sawbath' by walking in the park. In vain the
gentleman pleaded that he was only *waiting to go to church*.
The park-keeper was unflinching. Then the gentleman,
a little indignantly, informed the park-keeper that Our
Lord not only walked in the fields with his disciples on

the Sabbath day, but plucked some ears of corn and ate them. 'Aye,' said the park-keeper. '*And I'm na thinkin' the better o' him for that!!*' This is the most perfect exposition of Scotch theology I ever heard.

I have been very kindly treated and made much of during my stay in London. But I am more pleased at meeting my old friends of ten years ago, and finding them still loyal and true, than in making any new acquaintances. I have found the Webbs of Newstead, the Duchess, the Franks, and the Timmins, just as I left them. The poor Duchess lost her mother lately in Ireland, and has gone over to stay there.

Kiss the kids for their papa. Give my love to 'Liza. I'll write you next from Glasgow. God bless you all.

LIMICK

P.S. I add a line to tell you a bit of good news which I intended to keep until it was better. It has been suggested to me to publish a magazine here called 'Bret Harte's Monthly,' and, what is more to the purpose, certain printers and publishers have offered to bear the expense of it themselves. It would be *my own property*, the proceeds my own, deducting the expenses of publication. It will enable me to control my own publications and really profit by my own stories. It would enable me to turn my editorial faculty to count. I am at present working it up. If it can be done and made a success, I need not worry about the 4th of March, and I should arrange to stay here.

HÔTEL BELLEVUE
AVENUE DE L'OPÈRA
PARIS, *July* 28, 1880

MY DEAR ANNA,

I have just received yours of the 16th. I am utterly at a loss to know why you don't get my letters. After writing

to you from London on the 24th May — which letter you
say you received — I wrote twice from Crefeld before I
left there on the 17th June. I directed them to the care of
Houghton, Osgood & Co.

Had you not better write to Houghton, Mifflin & Co.
Boston (the new firm), and enquire if they know anything about them? I have sent you newspapers which
you have not acknowledged, and *music*. Did you ever
receive them?

As soon as I make arrangements with the bank in
Glasgow regarding your remittances, I will also arrange
to send my letters to you to their care. You can always
leave your address with them. Of course, this is only in
case you do not think it best to come to Glasgow this year.
I wrote you ten days ago, all about it, pro and con. I
hope you will let me know promptly when you receive it.
I shall not know otherwise whether to repeat what I said
then. I think, however, that I directed *that* letter to
Morristown.

I took charge in Glasgow on the 24th, although my
exequatur has not yet come from the Foreign Office. I
ran away here as soon as I could to get one ray of blessed
sunshine, for *it had rained every day for three weeks in
Scotland, and England too*, and my dreadful neuralgia was
returning. I cannot make you understand the terribly
depressing effect of that moist dull atmosphere and the
perpetual gloom of the sky. The rainy season in California is Paradise to it. There is no wind, there is no
downpour, there is only a thick, stifling, steamy muggi-
ness, everywhere. The contrast with this city is wonderful; to-day in this bright sunshine and dry warmth I feel
another man and my neuralgia vanishes. I *know* it is the
sunshine, for I don't otherwise like Paris. London is, but
for its damnable weather, much more attractive.

I saw Gerty and Jules and Dora last evening, and I am going to the concert at the Conservatoire to-morrow. I suppose you know that Gerty has got the first prize and is immensely praised by the critics, and is thought to be 'the coming American Prima donna.' I have not yet heard her sing publicly, and only once or twice privately, at a reception in Paris — and her voice seems to me exactly the same as it always was. I am, I suppose, no judge. But everybody goes into raptures over her. She is fine and *noble*-looking, and her face is full of melancholy intelligence.

When I passed through Paris coming from the R. A. Dinner in May, I received a letter from Mrs. Sherwood, of *San Francisco*, who was stopping at the Hotel D'Alma, inviting me to call and talk about old times. You remember her, of course, and how you used to say — most untruthfully — that she looked like you. I rushed off to the Hotel D'Alma, but the *concierge* said she was already *partie*. She has gone to Switzerland, but another Californian in London says she will be back soon, and I hope to see her. Her children have all grown up.

The world is very small, Anna! Every day I meet people we know or have met in California, in Boston, in New York, in Chicago even! Mrs. Starr — do you remember Mrs. Starr, of Starr and Marcus, the jewelers, who was at Eliza's in Morristown? She came up to me at the *Gare du Nord* as I stepped from the train yesterday, as if it might have been the station at Morristown. She is here in this little Paris hotel, where I always stop, with her husband and family.

I have a long letter from Franky. Tell him I'll write to him soon — meantime let him *study hard* and I will have something for him to do better than he proposes.

My friends are still talking about the magazine project. Everything promises well.

Kiss the children for me.

LIMICK

On July 24, 1880, Bret Harte entered into possession
of his new Consulate. He had taken up his quarters for
the time being, at Innellan, within a short distance of
Glasgow, and yet away from the air of the city, of which
he gives a graphic description in his letter to his wife,
written from a friend's house in the Lake District.

TULLICHEWAN CASTLE
DUNBARTONSHIRE
August 7, 1880

MY DEAR ANNA,

I've received no line from you since I wrote you from
Paris. I am still living 'in my trunks' at a hotel in Glasgow, not having found that home on the Clyde or even
lodgings yet. I am spending Sunday here with one of the
Campbells at his castle on Loch Lomond. It's a rather
famous place for scenery — but does not compare with
Lake George. The people are very kind, hospitable, and
intelligent — those that I have met. The general civility
is, of course, far superior to Germany, and the living
altogether more comfortable, but — the climate!

I don't know how to write about it! I am heartsick and
despairing. It is in the last degree depressing and ener-
vating. In Glasgow the vapours from chemical factories
and the thick mists make a compound that is simply
diabolical. I cough night and day — for night and day
are almost the same here — and suffer from neuralgia
between whiles. Even here there are only occasional
glimpses of the wet hills, when the mist rises, or the rain

does not hide them. I am writing this 7th August with a fire. It is called a warm 'soft' day.

My transfer from Crefeld here on account of my health resolves itself into a ghastly farce. I do not know how I can stand it. I am trying to think that I may become acclimatized, or I may be on the 4th March promoted, or — removed altogether.

Did Dana send you anything for the 'Gentleman of La Porte'?

I'll write as soon as I am settled — or anything but a weary wanderer on the face of the earth.

God bless you all.

LIMICK

Fortunately for Bret Harte, he was not disfigured by the serious accident related in the following letter. It is typical of his sense of humour that, in the midst of his anxiety as to the outcome of it, he thoroughly enjoyed the amusing little episode by which it was relieved.

INNELLAN, *September* 16, 1880

MY DEAR ANNA,

I met with a trifling accident a few days ago which I fear may get into the papers in a very exaggerated shape and might possibly frighten you. I was out shooting and my gun recoiled heavily, the hammer striking my mouth and cutting my upper lip very badly. I had the lip sewn up, and it is progressing favourably, but whether or not I shall be disfigured I cannot yet say. It was merciful that I got off so cheaply. Except that I am obliged to wear a bandage, cannot chew nor talk nor smoke, it does not trouble me. If I were quite sure that it would heal without a bad scar, I would not worry.

The gamekeeper had overloaded the gun. While I was

under the surgeon's hands and needles, the little son of my host came to the door of my room and asked to speak to me. In the confusion and excitement for some time, no one took any notice of him. At last he managed to say, 'Oh, I say, tell him he killed the hare after all.'

My birthday was honoured with great kindness from these Scotch people. In the little seaside hotel where I am staying (it is only an hour from Glasgow and I go to town every day), I found my table covered with bouquets. I received a handsome gold locket, cigar case, a telegraph portfolio, card case, etc., etc. I had forgotten the day. A lady in the house remembered it because I had given her an autograph for her birthday book. Then I had a lot of kind letters from my English cousins at Newstead Abbey — which I'll send you.

I shall know in a few days *positively* about the magazine, although it would be probably started on the 1st of January, 1881. One of the capitalists is coming from Edinburgh to see me.

I think the pictures of Tottie and Ethel awfully funny in their fancy dress. I wish you would send me a photograph of *yourself*, and of the boys. I must hurry this up to catch the mail. Kiss the children for me.

LIMICK

In his letter to his friend Pemberton, Bret Harte again refers to the incident of the previous letter, but is principally concerned with the future of 'Shem.'

INNELLAN, *September* 16, 1880

MY DEAR PEMBERTON,

When I took up the photograph of the noble Shem, and read the few gentle reproachful lines you had written on its back, I realized for the first time what a thoroughly abject villain I was. How could I have basely abandoned that beautiful and gifted creature? How could I oblige you to remind me of my duties during these long months? I stand powerless to excuse myself.

I am an unnatural parent — an ungrateful master, a fraudulent and hypocritical guardian. Can you forgive me? Do you think Shem can? Will he not secretly despise me? Will he not give me a bad character to other dogs?

When I left Crefeld three months ago, I thought of him and you, and said to my feeble soul: 'I will arise and go to Shem and those who abide with him, even at Birmingham, and take him to Glasgow with me and let him kill a fatted calf, etc., etc.,' but, alas, when I came to London, I fell into evil ways, and did nothing. Many times since then I have made good resolutions regarding Shem's future and forgotten them. I have talked about him, and what I was going to do with him, until I have become burdensome to my friends. I was about on the point of writing to you when my colleague, King, of Birmingham, wrote to me that he had seen and been nearly knocked down by Shem.

I was at the Queen's Hotel, Glasgow, one night last week, and left my card there for *two* Pembertons (thinking one of them might be you and possibly the other, Shem), whose names were on the register.

I have as yet no settled habitation, but have been staying at Innellan, a lovely little watering-place on the Clyde, an hour and a half from Glasgow, where I go every day. This fact, I suppose, is the potential reason why I don't send for Shem at once. I have been hoping that some of my relations would come to Glasgow this year, and justify my setting up a home. But as soon as I have a home, Shem must share it with me.

Will you send me a couple more photographs of Shem, at once? I want to send one to my family in America.

Don't be alarmed if you should hear of my having nearly blown the top of my head off. Last Monday, while out shooting at C—— House, I had my face badly cut by the recoil of an overloaded gun. I do not yet know, beneath these bandages, whether I shall be permanently marked. At present I am invisible, and have tried to keep the accident a secret. When the surgeon was stitching me together, the son of the house, a boy of twelve, came timidly to the door of my room, 'Tell Mr. Bret Harte it's all right,' he said; '*he killed the hare!*'

In haste.

Yours ever
BRET HARTE

Ill-health, disappointment, and homesickness are expressed in the gloomy outlook of the next two letters, to which the failure of the magazine enterprise and the after effects of his accident no doubt largely contributed.

GLASGOW, November 12, 1880

MY DEAR ANNA,

I telegraphed you a day or two ago — fearing that my long silence might give you anxiety. I have been almost *helplessly* ill for the last month, scarcely able to sign my name to official documents, going to my office in a cab, and often being able to stay there only an hour at a time. The doctors say my condition is owing to loss of blood, 'shock,' and, hardest of all, the attempt to acclimatize myself here in Glasgow. It is a hundred times worse than Crefeld — more *depressing*, and poisonous from chemical fumes from the factories. Even the Glasgow people tell me that, when they return after a temporary absence, they usually fall ill.

These are rather hard papers, Nan, but I hope I'll pull through. I went for a few days to Newstead Abbey — but returned no better. I may have to go farther and stay a longer time.

I do not know what to say about the boys. I hope to get a change with the new Administration, but at present things must remain as they are and the boys *must be patient.* The magazine enterprise, I fear, will have to be abandoned on account of the introduction of an English edition of 'Harper's.'

God bless you all. Don't worry about me. When I find myself very much worse, I'll still keep strength enough to come to New York if only for a few weeks.

Affectionately

LIMICK

BESTWOOD LODGE, ARNOLD, NOTTS
January 19, 1881

MY DEAR NAN,

I telegraphed you a few days ago not to draw again upon Schroeder. I have made other arrangements at last, and Schroeder was rather overcharging me here.

I was so ill again in Glasgow that I took the doctor's advice, and accepted the Duchess's invitation to come down here for a few days. To-day a fearful snowstorm — as bad as anything we have at home — is raging, and a little entertainment which the Duchess has been getting up for the benefit of the colliers, at which I was to try my 'prentice hand' at reading one of my own stories, will probably be stopped.

I began a letter to you the day I left Glasgow, but had to put it aside from the fact that at three o'clock in the afternoon the gas went out in consequence of the frost; — a fog, making the whole city as dark as midnight, prevailing at the same time. I do not know if I can make you understand the absolute mental and physical suffering I endure from this absence of sunshine. I suppose living so long in California made it a necessity of my existence. It is like living in a dark cellar.

I have letters from the boys. You must try and prevail upon them to wait until I get my leave of absence and come home before they commit themselves to anything. I would write this to them, but I have not the time. My other work takes all the very little energy I possess.

I expect to run down to London to-morrow to see finally about the magazine. If I *could* start it, it would solve so many problems in my future life here. Kiss the little girls for me and beg the boys to be patient.

LIMICK

Lest the foregoing letters should convey the impression of a perpetual absence from Glasgow, it should be pointed out that they are dated with several months' intervals, and that Bret Harte was, in between his short vacations, and in spite of his constant ill-health, very hard at work with his consular duties. His various communications to the Department of State testify to the thoroughness of his administration, and the statistics amply confirm the frank and honest statements contained in the next three letters.

GLASGOW, *April 22*, 1881

MY DEAR NAN,

I've received my leave of absence from Washington, but I've a letter from Mason, who says his wife, who is

visiting Washington, intimates that there are thousands
of people clamouring for Glasgow — that every little
mean paragraph about my being un-American (think of
ME *being un-American* when I get into quarrels every day
defending my country) is made capital of and poured into
the ears of the State Department and Congressmen and
Senators. Again, my alleged absences from my post are
brought to the fore, and Mason says his wife suggests
'that as a matter of selfish wisdom it might be well to
hang round there and kick up a dust for a while until the
pressure subsides.'

Hay is still in office — that is, was there on the 21st
March, when I received a letter from him, which I would
like to send you, but I keep it for reading when I am very
low in spirits, and am glad to think there are some two
or three men in America who are loyal to me. Speaking
of Clarence King, who has resigned his office, he says: 'I
do not know what Heaven meant by creating so few men
like King and you. The scarcity of you is an injury, not
only to us, but to yourselves. There are not enough of
you to go round, and the world pulls and hauls at you
until you are completely spoiled.

'Such times as I have seen since the 4th of March. You
would have got lots of fun out of it. I, only vexation of
spirit. They have even asked for Glasgow — never more
than once in my presence.'

It is the devotion of this dear little fellow, and the Masons, that keeps me here at my post. I am trying very
hard to do my duty as a Consul, but it is my luck that
a dozen different and difficult cases — for this seaport
Consulate is all new to me — have recently come up;
cases which my Vice-Consul says never occurred before
in the practice of my predecessors. I want to keep in or
go out with a clean record. So don't blame me, Nan, if

I don't write more often just now or if I can't take my leave just yet.

Love to the boys and girls.

Always

FRANK

CONSULATE OF THE

UNITED STATES OF AMERICA

GLASGOW, *May* 18, 1881

Miss Jeanette L. Gilder
    Office of 'The Critic'
        757 Broadway, New York City

MY DEAR MISS GILDER,

Pardon this monstrous delay in answering your letter. If I could have replied with an epigram or responded with a column sketch, I'd have done so *at once!* But the fact is that my consular duties are considerable here, *malgré* the newspaper squibs and sensibilities in this country, and as a *seaport* Consulate is a new thing to me, all my time, when I am not laid by my heels in this wretched climate, has been taken up by my official duties.

Forgive me — that's a good girl — and believe that when this right hand recovers its cunning, I'll do something for 'The Critic,' and won't I criticise! O. M.!

Love to your brother.

Yours ever

BRET HARTE

For six months we have no other letters, until the late autumn of 1881, in which he speaks of the seriousness of his sickness which made it almost impossible to do work of any kind.

LONDON, *November* 11, 1881

MY DEAR NAN,

I suppose you have been more or less alarmed at my silence, but I have been very ill, very uncertain *how* I should take my leave of absence, and I feared it would alarm you still more if I asked any one else to write for me. I have suffered terribly from rheumatism and dyspepsia, and have been quite unable to walk or write. I stayed with some kind foreign friends of mine — Count Van de Velde and his family — for over a month at Bournemouth — a little watering-place in the south of England, returned to Glasgow in company with one of my hosts, who thought me unfit to travel alone, and have again returned to London for treatment a week longer.

I do not know whether I told you in a previous letter that my Washington friends thought it better for me not to come to America after all that had been gossiped about my absences from Scotland. If I did not tell you this, I can add now that poor Garfield's assassination made it more imperative that I should remain in Great Britain until the new officers were appointed and that even my looked-for trip to the Continent was lost.

It seems a long time since I heard from you last. My hand is very stiff and cramped, and I must stop. I send you a telegram and some money — both, I hope, will relieve your anxiety — and I shall send again as soon as I can get my return of fees. God bless you, and love to the children.

Yours
FRANK

Address Glasgow as before.

Bret Harte's eldest son was destined for a literary career, which his premature death tragically cut short. His second son, Frank, wanted to go on the stage, in which line his father did not encourage him, as the following letter shows, although he did not refuse his consent, and later did all in his power to assist him, seeing that he was in earnest.

GLASGOW, *December 12, 1881*

MY DEAR ANNA,

The enclosed only reached me a few days ago, after I was better and able to return to Glasgow.

The writer, Lieutenant John A. Tobin, is an officer of the United States Navy, sent here on special duty by the Navy Department some six months ago to report upon iron ships, machinery, and other Clyde specialties. I was able to be of some little service to him officially and socially. We became fast friends and good Americans; and he lightened up my exile considerably. He returned home two months ago, and this is his parting blessing.

I think he means Frankie — he being the youngest, and Wodie being (I think) past the age for admission. I did not ask Tobin this favour; I had only spoken generally of the boys and said how I once hoped to get Wodie in the Hampshire Naval Academy.

What Tobin may be able to do, I cannot say. Whether Frankie would not think it beneath his dignity as an incipient tragedian to accept it, I don't know either. It is a scientific branch of the service and requires brains and cleverness. I think it a *safer* thing to be a Lieutenant of the Engineer Corps, U.S.N., than a clever stock actor. Tell Frankie this is a half answer to his letter.

Whatever you think or *he* thinks, let me know quickly that I may *first* communicate with Lieutenant Tobin.

No letters yet.

In haste

LIMICK

P.S. Don't laugh at the enclosed postscript of a photograph! I was asked to sit (or stand rather) for my portrait to be painted in a group of the prominent citizens of Glasgow in a painting of the Royal Exchange, and as I hadn't the patience to *sit* to the *painter*, I *stood* for a *photograph* on my last visit to London from which my figure was painted in the painting. That is the reason why you see me *with a tall hat on*. The photographer insisted upon giving me some three-quarters length copies — of which this is one. Can you conceive anything more unlike me as you remember me?

[Copy of letter enclosed in preceding letter]

IMPERIAL HOTEL
CORK, *October* 13, 1881

MY DEAR COLONEL,

When I saw you last, I intended to ask you if I could do anything toward getting your son appointed to Naval Academy as a Cadet Engineer. The term at the school is four years at a salary of six hundred dollars per annum. Two years are then spent at sea at a salary of one thousand dollars; at the expiration of six years he is appointed to the rank of Ensign at a salary of one thousand seven hundred dollars when at sea and one thousand four hundred dollars shore pay. If you wish to give me his address, i.e., if you think he would like to enter the Navy, I can assist in several ways and will only be too happy to send him the examination papers and circulars. I will also get the Chief of my Bureau interested. Let me know at once, please. Send letter, care United States Navy Department, Washington, D.C.

I enjoyed Dublin and the Lakes of Killarney very much. Yesterday I visited Blarney Castle with a party of Philadelphian young ladies, kissed the Blarney Stone, but as yet have not kissed any of the lips that kissed it. I do wish you were going over with me. What a good time we would have, crossing the raging Main in such a fine steamer as the 'City of Rome.'

With kindest regards and the happiest recollections of the many pleasant hours you gave me, I remain,

Most sincerely yours

JOHN A. TOBIN

As 'Shem' had by now grown into a full-sized Saint Bernard, his kind donators suggested that perhaps Bret Harte would prefer another prospective descendant, who would be of less bulky proportions. Bret Harte preferred, however, to keep 'Shem,' and has solved, through the kindness of Count Van de Velde's family of nine children, the housing problem.

15, UPPER HAMILTON TERRACE
December 1, 1881

MY DEAR PEMBERTON,

No, 'tis I who should do the apologetic thing to you, and be absolutely servile to Shem for my unnatural neglect of you both. Intercede for me with my noble enemy and nobler animal.

How good of you to be so patient with the foundling. Thoughtful and considerate as your suggestions are, I still think I must cling to Shem, my first love, though I have never seen him, and he might aggressively cling to me on our first meeting. Better is the adolescent Shem than a puppy *in futuro;* better a living dog than one *in utero.* Besides, the *Jungfrau* may, like other mountains, be delivered of a mouse.

I could not keep him in lodgings in Glasgow without armour-plating the furniture and enlarging the doors, but some kind friends with whom I am staying when in London are most anxious to keep him for me. They have a goodish-sized house, here in Saint John's Wood, and nine (9!) playful children who are ready to worship him. You may say to Shem that they are a genteel and even

a titled family; I would not introduce him to other, or
cast the slightest shadow on his brilliant London future.

Now, seriously, how could I get him here? — by express, or by parcel delivery, or freight? Nothing should I
like better than to bring him myself, but I have already
outstayed my 'leave' and must return to Glasgow in a
few days. I expect to come to London again to spend the
Christmas holidays. Could I take you *en route?* ...

With best regards to Mrs. Pemberton, and a shake of
Shem's paw, always

His and your friend
BRET HARTE

Bret Harte had always a desire to attain, in play-
writing, the perfection which he possessed as an author,
and this was to be his first attempt. The collaborator was
his friend Edgar Pemberton, who later worked with him
on several plays, one of which, 'Sue,' was a great success.
'Thankful Blossom,' a story of the Revolution, was written during Bret Harte's stay at Morristown. It is curious
to note that the name chosen was not imaginary, but
really that of one of his ancestors. There is an interesting
description of this story to be found later, in one of Bret
Harte's letters to a lady who had enquired into its origin.

QUEEN'S HOTEL
HARROGATE, YORKSHIRE
February 10, 1882

MY DEAR ANNA,

I telegraphed you a few days ago fifty-five pounds. I
should have sent it before, but I *did not have it* to send.
I was obliged to make up my accounts to the end of the
year and send off a heavy balance to Washington. My
silence so long was equally unpremeditated, but I hope

less unfortunate, for I have been hard at work. I have just written and forwarded a story for the 'Sun' and I have asked Dana to send you the money; it should bring from two hundred to three hundred dollars, but you must take what he gives. I hoped to have finished it on Christmas, so that you should have had a cheque from the 'Sun' before the 15th January.

After finishing my story, I began to *write a new play*. I have stuck at it, in spite of illness and interruptions, and last night at eleven o'clock I wrote the last words of the last act. I know not what it may produce; I have scarcely spoken to any one of it. I have made this time no contract with managers. I have written it in collaboration with a friend, whose name I have solemnly promised *not yet to give*, but who is, without being professional, thoroughly competent at play-writing. And what do you think is the subject? Think of it while you are in Morristown — think of it when you pass the headquarters. It is based on my little idyl 'Thankful Blossom.' It is wonderful how well and quickly it adapts itself to stage effect, and its dialogue keeps it *understandable* by all audiences, while all the old cant about my *coarseness* and slang certainly cannot be used against it. The idea first came to me from seeing 'Jeff Briggs's Love Story' made into a pretty little parlour piece for private theatricals, where *every word of the dialogue* was taken from my own writing and even the description of the book. It was so good that I began to think I would try once more to *adapt* my own items for the stage.

What it may be in action, whether I shall ever get a manager to take it, and when and where it will be performed, are all things yet profoundly vague. I only know I have finished the work, and written it all since the 1st of January. I have not worked at it regularly, except within the last fortnight, when I left Glasgow to come here, where I have done nothing else. Harrogate is a famous summer resort in Yorkshire — the highest table-land in England — which is not saying much — and has renowned sulphur baths. I took no baths, though I am suffering from rheumatism. I saw no sights — though Bolton Abbey and Fountains and Jerveaulx Abbeys are all near. I only *worked*. I have at least one satisfaction. During the last ten years I have done scarcely anything in the way of literary work. I began to fear that I had lost the power. It is with heartfelt gratitude that I find I can at least *seem* to do it. As I said before, I know not what *the play may be*. You must judge for yourself of the little story 'Found at Blazing Star,' which you will find in the 'Sun' about the 1st March.

All this must atone for my not answering your letters, and you must tell Frankie and Wodie why I have seemed to neglect them. Say to Eliza I will try to write her a few lines.

The trunk, I am told, arrived in New York and passed the customs safely. But there may have been some mistake in the directions. I am making enquiries now.

I am hoping to hear you are better of your rheumatism as the winter passes. Kiss the girls for Papa, cheer up the boys; always your

FRANK

Referring to Bret Harte's administration as Consul at Glasgow, and of his communications to the Department of State, Merwin quotes one of them which it is of interest to reproduce here in connection with the following letter. 'On a recent visit to the Island of Iona, within this Consular District, I found in the consecrated ground of the ruined Cathedral the graves of nineteen American seamen who had perished in the wreck of the 'Guy Mannering' on the evening of the 31st of December, 1865, on the north coast of the island. The place where they are interred is marked by two rows of low granite pediments at the head and feet of the dead, supporting, and connected by, an iron chain which encloses the whole space. This was done by the order and at the expense of the lord of the manor, the present Duke of Argyll. . . . I venture to make these facts known to the Department, satisfied that such recognition of the thoughtful courtesy of the Duke of Argyll as would seem most appropriate to the Department will be made, and that possibly a record of the names of the seamen will be placed upon some durable memorial erected upon the spot.' He goes on to say that, should the Department think fit, he would undertake to obtain, by private subscription, sufficient funds for that purpose. 'It is a pleasure to record,' Merwin adds, 'that these suggestions were adopted by the State Department. A letter of acknowledgement and thanks was sent to the Duke of Argyll, and a shaft or obelisk with the names of the seamen inscribed thereon was erected by the United States Government in the latter part of the year 1882.' It is a good example of Bret Harte's thoroughness and delicacy in the handling of his official duties.

LONDON, *February 28, 1882*

MY DEAR ANNA,

I wrote you from Harrogate about ten days ago. Since then I have been here revising my play and waiting overtures from managers. As *one*, only, has read it yet, I am still uncertain of its merits, its availability, or its prospects of success. I am keeping it quite a secret yet, as if I should find that the London managers are in doubt about it, I should quietly send it to America. I am unfortunate in the fact that McCullough, Booth, Barrett, and Boucicault are not in Europe *now*, and I have no one to consult with. The *one* manager I speak of is a Mr. Gunn, partner of my former agent D'Oyley Carte — in the Savoy Theatre here. Carte, you remember, brought out the 'Pinafore,' 'Pirates of Penzance,' and 'Patience.' Gunn thinks that the play will be more assured of success in America than here.

I am prepared for any disappointment, and should be willing even now to forego my work rather than have a public failure as far as *that* play is concerned. But I want you to try and think that I should not by any means be dependent on that particular result. The fact is, I have overcome all my difficulties regarding 'construction'; Mr. Gunn says, what I see plainly myself, that the action and movement and technical arrangement are particularly good — and that any failure must come from a want of interest in the *subject* here. Any ill-luck I might have with *this* play will be quite recompensed by my knowledge that I have greatly improved in 'dramatic construction.' I know now how to begin and how to end a play. *That* will satisfy me if my present venture fails. I shall try again. And select a better subject.

So much for discounting already a possible loss. For the rest I am, thank Heaven! still keeping up my old desire for work which I once feared I had lost. I can even forget my rheumatism and dyspepsia — which still 'go' for me at times — in work. I am hoping that I may make at least enough out of the play to justify me in beginning and giving myself up entirely to my American-English novel, which I am feverish to be at.

I have at times a certain flutter of anxiety over the new nominations for Consulship. Of course, I have no right to think myself secure in even my present berth, let alone any hope of promotion — and I may be at any moment removed to make a place for somebody. I do not think that Mr. Arthur would do it willingly, but I have no one to intercede for me nor have I even asked any one to use any influence to have me retained. While Hay was Assistant Secretary, of course I had a personal friend. On the other hand, the Department have treated me with what I am sometimes vain enough to think *peculiar consideration*. I have never asked for anything nor made a suggestion regarding my official business or the Service generally that has not been attended to. I have been repeatedly thanked by the Department, and only a day or two ago, for the performance of a thoughtful little diplomatic courtesy outside of my usual routine, I was not only thanked by the Department for my thoughtfulness, and all my suggestions accepted, but I was selected by the Secretary to carry the thanks of the President and the Department to the Duke of Argyll. Some particular attention to meteorological reports brought from the chief signal officer of the Tour Department a handsome letter. My office is capitally manned. My Vice-Consul is a hard-headed Scotch lawyer and devoted to my service. In fact, I'm *rather* a good Consul. All I believe they can say about me is that I don't go much into society, and that I escape the fogs of Glasgow whenever I can. But even when I am away, all my letters and documents pass under my eye, and I telegraph often twice a day.

I am writing all this, as I suppose you want to know what I am doing and what are my prospects. Of the latter you must judge. I keep nothing from you.

I wish, by the way, you would promptly inform me when and how much Mr. Dana sends you, and if you have received anything from Houghton, Mifflin and Company.

It is necessary I should know this, so as to be able to arrange the next draft I send you. Write me fully and frequently, and, above all, select *some permanent address*. Love to Eliza. Kiss the girls and give Papa's love to the boys.

Always
FRANK

P.S. I enclose two photographs, price 1/6 to the public generally; to myself nothing. They're not worth *that*, but you might as well know what can be bought for even that sum here.

Bret Harte was, as we see, taking very seriously to the theatre, and concentrating all his hopes into a successful play. His remarks upon certain characteristics of the English as they appeared to him have been written so long ago, and were so independent of any personal touch to them, that it is felt that they may be published without creating any prejudice toward him, from a people who showed him always the greatest courtesy, which was equalled only by his appreciation of it.

LONDON, *June* 7, 1882

MY DEAR NAN,

I have run down here for a few days to try for the last time to arrange my play for this season. But I find it will require so many alterations that I have quite concluded I had better spend that time and labour *in writing a new one* rather than risk more on the old. If this new one should be a success, it will help the other; if it should fail, the public will only know of my one defeat. In either case, I shall not worry much, and I hope you will not. I am only too thankful to be able to still keep the ear of the public in my old way. For, in spite of all the envious sneers and wicked prophecies that follow me, I find I still hold my old audience and that the publishers are quite ready for me when I have anything ready for them. It is quite wonderful also what a large and growing audience I have all over the Continent; anything I write is instantly translated. I should be, indeed, content if it were not that play-writing is so vastly more profitable, and that, with all my popularity as a *romancier*, I fear I could not more than make a scanty living.

I wonder if you will care for 'Flip.' It will remind you of 'M'liss.' It is odd that after it was finished I was visiting Tarbet on Loch Lomond, with a friend who was looking for a country house and a shooting-box. One of the estates was shown to us by a young Scotch girl — the 'daughter of the house' — who might have sat for a portrait of 'Flip.' Except her dialect she was a mixture of Lily Hatchard, Di Vernon, Bishop Odinheimer's daughter, and 'M'liss.' My friend, who had just read the proofs (and was in fact making the French translation for me), was as astonished as myself. It was a marvellous resemblance, for I had never seen the girl before.

I have not heard anything from Gerty Griswold lately, which is very singular. She was always a regular correspondent, writing often two letters to my one. I have no answer to three of my last letters. As I have not been to Paris since her *début*, last year, I have not seen her since.

Charles Watrous's son (Harry, I think), who has been painting in Paris, wrote to me the other day asking to meet me in London on his way home. I replied by inviting him to Scotland, as I could not leave at that time, but he wrote me since that he could not come, but that his father would be over this summer.

There have been so many changes in the Consular service that I do not know what will be done with me yet. I am trying hard to appear and to really be independent of the office, for this uncertainty is most trying. I fancy that I must have some *friends at court*, or I should have been changed about or removed with as good men as myself. I know that there are hundreds hungry for my place. But I hear nothing: the Department is kind and civil to me, and I remain. Dana offered to say a word for me in the right place.

I am here in the beginning of the London season, the city crowded over its vast proportions, and the weather abominable. The English come to town when we in America leave it for the country. I go out little, accept few invitations. I refused one for Ascot yesterday. Would you believe it? — I have never been to the Derby or Epsom. Of course, you would — for you know I don't like it.

The Americans are coming over this summer by thousands. It makes my heart sick to see so much money thrown away by these people — many of whom are merely vulgarians — upon things not so good as can be got at home, and upon a people as effete as these Europeans. Every American who comes to England helps to swell the inordinate conceit of the English; even the journals openly say that Americans cannot abide their own country and live only in the hope of coming abroad to really know what gentlemen and ladies use. You cannot conceive, until you have lived in England, the supreme contempt they have for all foreigners. They will flatter us occasionally to our faces, but let the slightest thing occur and they show their old hatred for us.

Where are you? I send this to Morristown believing you have not yet left for the Adirondacks. My love to the kids big and little. Always yours

LIMICK

P.S. I will try to write to Frankie and Wodie next week if I remain in London.

The visit which Bret Harte had planned for his son Frank to make him was only to be delayed by a few months, until it was possible for him to be more settled and less pressed for work than when the following letter was written.

LONDON, *July* 17, 1882

MY DEAR ANNA,

I telegraphed, in answer to your question, that Frankie must wait for my letter. There are two or three reasons why a visit as unprepared for and as unexpected as the one proposed would not be as pleasant to him or myself as it might be if made a matter of forethought and calculation. In the first place, I have no 'home' in this country beyond a hotel in Glasgow or the house of a friend in London. If I have a vacation, it is generally spent at some country house where I have been invited. My London friends, the Van de Veldes, who have been very kind to me, have a large family of nine children, but always keep a room for me. They have proposed to me to spend August with them at the seaside, and when I told Madame V. de V. that Frankie might possibly come, she of course offered him a room, which I of course declined, as it would be scarcely right to abuse their continuous hospitality. I have not the slightest doubt that he or *you* or *any of my family* that were with me would be promptly invited anywhere and everywhere I go, and most spontaneously, but it would take some time before people knew it, and most invitations, especially to country houses, are given months in advance. I know he would be a welcome guest at Newstead Abbey, but the Webbs are in Italy where two or three of the family are invalided. If he came to Glasgow at once, the only way I could amuse him would be to take him to the Western Highlands, for I have no acquaintances and there is nothing to do in Glasgow; but that would take me from the literary work I have cut out for this summer — the writing of two plays. This latter is really the strongest objection I see to Frankie's coming to me this summer. I shall be distracted and preoccupied in time and thought and could not do my duty to him here. I am determined to succeed with a play this season, and at Boucicault's suggestion I have begun to dramatize 'The Luck of Roaring Camp.' I have read him the first act and he gives me the greatest encouragement. Arthur Sullivan has proposed to me to write the theme and libretto of an opera on some Californian subject, and I have just sent him a sketch of one. You see how my hands will be full this summer and how I require perfect isolation. I have just declined an invitation from the Duchess because I could not work in the fashionable whirl of Bestwood. If I had my own house, Frankie and I might manage to get along; indeed, if I had my own house and a decent one in England or Scotland, we might all — but what's the use of dreaming? First let me get THE PLAY written!

I've gone into these details, that you may fully understand how I am situated and how your sudden and rather abrupt suggestion has put me into the ungracious position of declining a visit from Frankie. I don't think I am wanting in love for my children, and do not believe you will think it inconsistent with that affection if I hesitate about the expediency of their suddenly taking a trip of three thousand miles to find their father unprepared for them. I should be glad to have Frankie with me. I wrote to him to-day in reference to his desire to go on the stage, and what you call 'his disappointment' over McCullough's broken promises.

You have not yet acknowledged the receipt of my draft on Dana for two hundred and fifty dollars sent about June 23d. I enclose you another for the same amount, payable August 1st, making in all five hundred dollars, which will be due to me from him by the 1st August. I hope you are better. Try to go somewhere this summer where you can have complete change and rest, and do not mind a little extra expense.

I wrote to Frankie that I hope to arrange for his visit later on.

Love to all.

LIMICK

Although away from his country, he was yet in touch with his old friends, and such an occasion as the one he mentions in the next letter to his wife, was always a source of greatest joy to him, especially this time, as the meeting of his oldest friends took him back to two distinct periods of his life, to the West and the East.

BOURNEMOUTH PIER
September 9, 1882

MY DEAR NAN,

I received the pictures of the children (Ethel and Jessamy — why didn't you add yourself and the boys?) as a birthday gift. I dare say they are about as fraudulent as most likenesses, but I was struck with the fact that Totty was beginning to take a better likeness than Ethel, and was having more justice done to the delicacy of her face. Everybody thinks all the pictures *charming*, but I think they are most struck by those of Jessamy.

I have yours and the boys' two letters and very grateful

acknowledgement from 'Liza for her little birthday gift. I was very glad to find you were again in the Adirondacks; it may be dull, but I know it's better for you all than in New York in this weather. Don't come back too *soon*. I would rather you would give yourself more freedom in expense than run risks and have discomforts. I ran up to London for a day to dine with Osgood. Imagine *who* I found at dinner? Clarence King, Howells, Aldrich, Dr. Martin, John Hay, Booth, and Warner — of my dear old friends, and Henry James, Alma-Tadema, Conway, of the ones I knew here. It was a most wonderful coincidence to find all these men together in London — it would have been most remarkable for New York or Boston. In King and Dr. Martin I went back to the old San Francisco days. In Howells, Hay, and Aldrich to the first days of my arrival in the East.

I was relieved to find that, with one or two exceptions, all had grown *fat!* Howells is about as round as Jo. Marier and Shuter. I felt relieved.

I am steadily progressing with the play. One more act to finish only. I'll write again before the 15th. Love to all!

LIMICK

P.S. Address as usual to Glasgow.

Bret Harte was so keen upon his project of play-writing that the disappointment of being obliged to recommence a summer's hard work does not discourage him. The estimation of his limitations in regard to 'situations' and 'plots' as a playwright, as viewed by other men of that profession, is interesting in contrast to the dramatic power of his work as an author.

LONDON, *September 26, 1882*

MY DEAR NAN,

I've just finished two months work on 'The Luck,' and am somewhat disappointed to find from Boucicault, on submitting it to him, that the two last acts are radically wrong in structure — in other words, I must *begin it all over again*. You know how hard it is for me to write a play; imagine how provoked and exasperated I feel at having lost my holiday in such ungracious work only to find it futile. Of course, I shall not give it up — but it means that I must turn my leisure now to writing some little story *for money* to keep the pot boiling before I can go on with the larger work which is to pay me better in the end. I am haunted by the recollection that the time I have lost might have been worth so much to me in story-writing.

However, I have got stronger, I think, during my vacation and the disappointment has not damped my ardour. Still, I wish it hadn't happened.

It seems I can write dialogue like an angel, draw character like a heaven-born genius, but I can't make *situations* and *plots*.

I intended to write you a long letter about Bournemouth and other things. This disappointment has knocked it out of my mind.

I hope you have not hurried back from the Adirondacks too soon.

I enclose a letter from Gerty. It has the merit of answering every possible enquiry we might make regarding her affairs, plans, and ambitions — and I thought it might interest you. It is thoroughly characteristic in its frank egotism and independence, and is Gertyish throughout. I'm tired. Kiss the babies — if there are any and they have not all grown up. Write me soon.

FRANK

'I find I have been tempted,' Bret Harte writes, 'and led away by you into a long and egotistical account of myself and the way I live.' It is fortunate, for it makes this long and interesting letter to his wife a most valuable contribution to the story of his life at this period.

CONSULATE OF THE
UNITED STATES OF AMERICA
GLASGOW, *October* 11, 1882

MY DEAR ANNA,

I enclose a draft for two hundred and fifty dollars, which I send a few days earlier that you may certainly get it before the 1st November. I have heretofore been helped by that little balance in Dana's hands, due from my writings, but that is now exhausted, and until I have something more to send him I must draw from my salary here. I only tell you this, Nan, that in case I may not be able to send quite as much next month, you will understand it and not think it ungenerous or forgetfulness. You know I am only too happy when I can keep you and the children comfortably. I am trying to write a little Christmas story (a pot-boiler) between the acts of my play. I wrote you how disappointed I had been with 'The Luck' in its construction. I by no means despair, however.

My health is better, I think. I am stronger for my little change of air, for it is apparent, not only to myself, but to all who know me, that this climate (the climate of *Glasgow*) is most depressing to me. I think I have said the same, however, about any climate to which I have taken my blessed nerves, but even the Glasgow people tell me they can see the difference in me. I cannot get acclimated. I cannot help feeling that I am living by gaslight in a damp cellar with an occasional whiff from a drain, from a coal-heap, from a mouldy potato-bin, and from dirty washtubs. That is Glasgow to *me*, and that is all it has ever been since I have been here.

You ask me how I live. I thought I told you. The nearest approach I have to a home is, naturally, not where it ought to be — at Glasgow. I suppose I am most at ease with my friends the Van de Veldes in London. A friendship of four years has resulted in my making their comfortable London home my home when I am in London; their country home at Bournemouth my home whenever I can get a leave of absence for a few weeks in summer. I have a room there always known as mine, and always containing something of mine, summer or winter. I have surely told you all about this family in previous letters. There are nine children in all and nearly as many servants. It is the most refined, courteous, simple, elegant, and unaffected household that can be imagined. The father and mother are each foreigners of rank and title; Madame is the daughter of Count de Launey, the Italian Ambassador at Berlin. Arthur van de Velde is the Chancellor of the Belgian Legation. They have adopted me into their family — Heaven knows how or why — as simply as if I had known them for years. Perhaps there is a kind of sympathy in the fact that they are intensely *un-English*, and Madame as a girl thirty years ago visited America with her father and loved it.

When I first came to Glasgow I had 'lodgings' — an institution even drearier than the American boardinghouse. I had two rooms to myself, where my solitary breakfasts were eaten in a loneliness so intense that I now shudder to think of it. No wonder that at the beginning of my illness I gave up eating breakfasts at all. My dinners were taken at a lonelier club — where I sometimes was the only diner. I could not stand the dull, vulgar ostentation of the few people I met, who were mostly retired merchants; I only knew one family, and in this country of classes and divisions, they wanted me to take sides and participate in their prejudices, so I presently fell back into my first seclusion. I used to go to the theatre at nights; or visit one or two men friends. At times some of my London friends were visiting in the vicinity and I had a call from them, or some actors or actresses from America came here; Genevieve Ward was here a week or two, and Edwin Booth is here now. Black sometimes comes here. Such *was* my life here — such it *is* now, with slight changes; I live at a hotel and have made it my dreary lodgings. It is some one's 'folly' — a building too fine for this locality and is in bankruptcy — kept open by the creditors with a man in charge. Through this extravagance I am enabled to have two rooms handsomely furnished at a moderate sum, and the transient guests are company enough for me. I often wonder how many of the guests are creditors and whether the waiters are not bailiffs in disguise. As the hotel is run by a company of these creditors, there is not, of course, the unpleasant perennial spectacle of a ruined landlord before our eyes. One can be quite heartless over the wreck of a joint-stock company. The little entertaining I give in exchange for any hospitality thus becomes quite inexpensive. I can even offer some English or German friend a room for a night out of the dreary waste of unoccupied suites of apartments.

I have an odd idea I've told you all this before. But as you say I have not, I repeat myself. My friends of the past few years I keep still; the Webbs of Newstead Abbey, the Duchess of St. Albans, Froude — I visit them when I am very lonely. Only one friend I have been obliged to give up, Mr. ——. His wife got to quarrelling with my other friends because she and her husband could not 'run me' and keep me as their peculiar property

in society. I'm sorry — because I liked the husband.
But this is the only social disagreement I have had, and
even that matters little, as I do not go much into society.

I have written so much about myself to please you that
I have no time now to scold you about your own carelessness regarding your health. I am always hearing from
you that you are better and have been ill. Tell me all
your troubles. Kiss the children for Papa.

FRANK

P.S. I find I've been tempted and led away by you into
a long and egotistical account of myself and 'the way I
live,' but it is all your fault. I had many other things to
say — but it is too late now.

Bret Harte gives a description of 'The Luck' as he had
adapted it for the stage, but which was never produced.
His letter contains also some amusing impressions on
Holyrood and Versailles. In the second letter, to his son,
he gives him sound advice and help as well as affectionate
encouragement for the work he is interested in.

CONSULATE OF THE
UNITED STATES OF AMERICA
GLASGOW, November 3, 1882

MY DEAR ANNA,

Thanks for yours of the 19th and 20th, both received
the same day. The books were sent to you six months
ago; I cannot understand their delay; could it be in your
address? And will you not give me some permanent address in New York, where you can have anything sent
to you? I want to send you a box of clothes for the boys
and some trifles for yourself, but they must be addressed
to some one who can get them from the Custom House.

The etchings are here at last, and are capital. I shall have them framed for the office — until I have new permanent lodgings. Did I not write to you about the Morristown photograph, when I received those of the Adirondacks? I hardly think I shall publish 'Thankful Blossom' as a play, even if it should be ever theatrically represented. Whatever its fate, I shall try 'The Luck' first. Your criticism regarding the loss of the poetic element in a dramatization of 'The Luck' is true, but it is only used as a prologue to the play of the other acts, where 'The Luck' is a girl who has been sent to Paris and is educated by the wealthy members of the old Camp, who visit her occasionally. It is in this mingling and contact of these rough men with this high-super-civilized Old World and the love for their adopted daughter, 'The Luck,' that I hope to get dramatic as well as humorous effect. 'The Luck' is called 'Fortuna del Campo Clamoroso' (which is good Spanish as well as Italian) to the great mystification of the *noblesse* with historic names. When I finish my Christmas story, in a few days, I shall take up 'The Luck' again.

I have been several times to Edinburgh lately and think seriously of taking up my residence there; it would be but little farther from Glasgow than Düsseldorf lies from Crefeld. Although the climate is like all the Scotch weather, harsh and unkind, the city is beautiful and picturesque.

I was rambling over Holyrood the other day and was again struck, as I have always been in Europe, with a certain poverty of interior detail in all the palaces and castles of kings and barons of the old time. The audience chamber where Mary Stuart was obliged to listen to that horrid old bore and bigot John Knox is not as large as our parlour at 45 Fifth Avenue, and poorly lighted, while the famous supper-room where the poor Queen was having high jinks with Rizzio when he was slain is, upon my word, no larger than an ordinary hall bedroom in an ordinary New York house. The walls, however, are eight feet thick. Everywhere over Europe you see this extravagance of defence against the outer world of suffering and aggression, and this poverty of space for life and comfort within. In the Tower of London the actual living-rooms of kings, queens, and princes are smaller than those of a shopkeeper to-day. Even at Versailles, after you get through the great galleries where Royalty was always on exhibition, you come to the four little rooms where they slept. Marie Antoinette's pink suite of apartments (the one from which she attempted to escape) I am confident you would have rejected if offered to you at an American watering-place hotel. But would you like to have some photographs of Holyrood? You shall have them, anyway.

I had an invitation to Dalmeny Park, near Edinburgh, from the Countess of Rosebery (she that was Miss Rothschild, and presented her husband with a cheque for a million pounds sterling on her wedding day) for Saturday till Monday, but I must leave Glasgow Saturday morning for London to see about my play. D'Oyley Carte, my old lecture agent, is looking after it for me. Did you ever hear of him in America when he was managing the 'Pinafore'?

Tell Frankie I have received his impatient letter: I will answer it when I have seen Boucicault in London. Nothing can be done before.

Give my love to Liz and kiss my little girls for Papa. Tell Wodie I am waiting for a letter from him.

God bless you all.

FRANK

P.S. I shall not attempt to read this scrawl over again, written as it is with my clerk and Consular Agent in the room. Decipher it as you can.

Consulate of the
United States of America
Glasgow, 15th December, 1882

My dear Frankie,

Mr. Boucicault left or was to leave London on the 8th inst. for New York. I had another interview with him regarding your affairs a few days ago. He said he would see you whenever you could call or make an appointment with him, and that he would give you his advice frankly, and, in case he thought you were fit for an immediate engagement, would do all in his power to help you to it. Whether this means that he will be ready to take you *himself* in hand, I cannot say; he is a man immersed in his own business, but as that is dramatic, theatrical, and managerial, your interests may come together. Of one thing you can count surely; I believe he will be frank with you; not to discourage you solely, if you are not all that you think you are, but to show you what you can do in the way of a beginning. This is what McCullough said he would do for you, at my request — and *not*, as your mother writes to me that he said to you — 'be rude to you, if necessary, to keep you off the stage.' It is scarcely worth while repeating that I never *could* nor *did* say anything of the kind or write anything like it to McCullough. I told him that if it were true that you were physically not up to the active requirements of the stage, he ought to dissuade you from it.

As I wrote you before, if Boucicault cannot help you, either from want of confidence in your ability, or because he is too busy, and you feel you cannot wait any longer, it would be foolish for me to oppose what I cannot direct, and you must take what opportunity offers to you as best. I have no desire to keep you off the stage from principle or taste, but if you must go on I should prefer you to go on properly. I do not see any urgent necessity for the haste that may produce a failure. You must not forget, in the case of young Boucicault, that he lived in the atmosphere of the stage, and that he is the son and brother-in-law of actors, and he got a ready hearing and trial from a relation who was also a manager.

I enclose Boucicault's address. This will reach you about the time that he has got settled. See him at once.

With best love, my boy,

Your affectionate father

B. H.

The address is — 'Dion Boucicault, Victoria Hotel, New York,' until 24th December. After that, letters can be sent to care of Boston Museum, Boston.

Finally Bret Harte listened to the gentle advice of his friend, and agreed to renounce for ever 'Shem,' on the promise of receiving as compensation a puppy to take his place, making it the subject of his delightful reply.

CONSULATE OF THE
UNITED STATES OF AMERICA
GLASGOW, *February* 7, 1883

MY DEAR PEMBERTON,

I am heartbroken! What shall I say? What do *you* say? What, alas, will *Shem* say? Will he not be glad to get rid of such an unnatural master?

Perhaps it is for the best that he should abandon me. I never should have dared to look him in the face. As it is, I never have met a dog in the streets but I have been bathed in blushes. Whene'er I take my walks abroad, I tremble to meet him, and have him openly denounce and expose me to other dogs as a disgrace to my kind. I never hear a ring at the doorbell without expecting a servant to enter and say: 'Please, Sir, 'ere's a big dog a sittink and howlink on the doorstep with Mr. Pemberton's compliments, and what you're agoin' to do about it!'

And yet I have been base enough to be proud of him, to boast of him and magnify his proportions. If the conversation turned on big dogs, I always said, 'Ah! but you should see *mine!*' When pressed to exhibit this abnormal growth, I meekly said, 'He is staying with one of my most intimate friends, to whom he is deeply attached.'

And then the silent wings of disbelief would gradually enfold that company, and I would disappear.

Seriously, my dear fellow, I am such a homeless vagabond and wanderer myself that unless Shem actually did the Saint Bernard Hospice business for me, and carried me about with him — and a flask — I don't see what I could do with him just now. I couldn't carry *him* about, nor would he be content to live in the corridor of my hotel at Glasgow. My fond hope was to place him with some of my suburban friends, and visit him two or three times a week — but that is past, and I fear he is getting too old now to attach himself to me after that 'occasional' fashion. If you will keep your promise and give me a puppy to take his place, I promise to make amends by undertaking his early education *myself* this time.

I hope to come your way in a few weeks, and we will discuss this further. . . . Until then, give him my love and say, if needs be, 'Hail and Farewell' for me.

Always, my dear Pemberton,

Your friend

BRET HARTE

Little exchanges of gifts across the ocean to an absent family are the objects of the next two letters written in the spring of 1883.

LONDON, March 15, 1883

MY DEAR ANNA,

I enclose draft on Dana for two hundred and fifty dollars, which, with those already sent, make seven hundred and fifty dollars, or — including the telegraphic transfer for two hundred and fifty dollars — one thousand dollars I have sent you since the 1st January.

I also send you by Charley Watrous a few presents, viz. — a little watch for yourself, a locket for Ethel, and a bracelet for Jessamy. They are not much, but are good of their kind. It is not *the* watch I promised you some years ago, but I despair of being rich enough to get that and send this one, which will keep time until better days come. My own one is no better, nor more expensive, tho' a trifle larger. But they are both an improvement on the one I took away — was it Wodie's or Frankie's? The silver ornaments are *de rigueur* here — that's the best I can say of them.

I have met Watrous each time I have been in London, and as I wrote you before, I think, we ate our Christmas dinner together at the Van de Veldes. He can tell you how I am and what I do when I am in London; I am sorry he has not been able to come to Glasgow and see me in my 'native lair.' But he speaks of coming back with his wife in the spring and coming to Scotland then.

I am hurrying some manuscripts off with him, and have only time to send love to all.

LIMICK

London, *March* 28, 1883,

MY DEAR ANNA,

I should have thanked you ALL for the graceful presents which followed me from Glasgow nearly a week ago, but I have been so miserably ill with neuralgia. In spite of my pain, I think I thoroughly appreciated them — none the less that I heard for the first time that you had been a successful 'claimant,' and that I had been married many years to an *heiress*. I took a noble pride, too, in exhibiting them as real *American* products, and I think they were appreciated, although one gentleman — a distinguished statesman, by the way — said, 'Ah! rr! — O, yes! — then you find all that silver and copper at Washington's headquarters in — rr — New Jersey — great country yours, really — don't you know.' I thought the kerchief case awfully pretty and really artistic in painting. The 'crocodile' skin, as it is called here, made a beautiful and striking card-case — and, by one of those mere accidents, although I have had half-a-dozen card-cases on hand, I believe I have lost them all and was considering that very day that I must buy a new one. I think the copper match-box received the greatest praise from the men here on account of its novelty, in a country where the last thing, after dinner, is to pick up an old champagne cork from the table and light your cigar from the matches that are cunningly concealed inside its silver cavity. I think I must send the boys a couple. I am glad, however, that the few little trifles I *did* send you by Mr. Watrous really left before I *knew* you had sent yours. Nothing could be prettier than the painting of the paper-knife, but I grieve to say that Papa, having handsomely exerted himself to cut with it and having only gouged the inside out of a dozen magazines with it, has hung it up with a blue ribbon over his dressing-table. What shall I say of the pincushion? The pins take such a liking to it that they won't come out, and it hangs with a pink ribbon alongside of the knife.

Lest you should be worried over my unhappy neuralgia, let me say that it is a replica of my previous attack in Germany, only having for its base a *perfectly sound tooth* that has an inflammation of the bony socket, as nearly as I can understand. As I wrote you once before, I know how to pity you now. Only I have *begged* the dentist to pull all my teeth out, and he has turned me away from his door, telling me that I must wait the medication of time.

And all this while I am engaged to write a story for an English magazine!

God bless you all, and take my best and heartfelt thanks again. Kiss them all for their grateful papa. Always

LIMICK

LONDON, *March* 30, 1883

MY DEAR TOTTIE (I can't bring myself to say 'Jessamy' just yet).

Only a few days ago I wrote to your mamma about the nice presents you all sent me, and this morning, coming down to breakfast after a nasty night of cold and neuralgia, I find my heart lifted by your and Ethel's cards which had followed me here to London. I suppose yours is painted by yourself. It is capital. That *one* swallow is capable of making a summer all by himself among those roses — as he has in Papa's heart.

I opened the packet among nine children of different ages, and they were all most anxious to see what 'Mr. Bret Harte's little girls' had sent him. I have already told your mamma what nice good children they are, and I hope the day will come when you will see and know them. As they asked me to tell you about them, I do it —

confidentially. They are not like any children you know in America; indeed, I do not think the eldest, who is eighteen, knows as much of the world and things generally as *you* do, but — they speak four languages with fluency, and all play and sing. They have two governesses and a music-master and are the best educated (and *least informed*) children I ever knew. (The parenthesis is confidential.) They cannot believe that your mamma would allow you to walk half a square in the street without a footman or servant following. The eldest boy — who is as old as Frankie, is educated for diplomacy, has perfect manners, would not think of sitting down while an older person was standing, speaks and writes three languages perfectly — asked me quite seriously the other day if authors of plays stood at the box-office and took the money at the theatre when their plays were performed. For all that, they are very nice sweet children and make Papa's life — when he is here — less lonely, but they do not take the place of his own dear little ones at home, whom he wants to be true American girls always. And although Papa's proud of his little girls, he wants to tell them that they have much more freedom and pleasures generally than European children.

In this household they never appear (except as a special favour) at breakfast or dinner. They actually live in the nursery until they are eighteen; the young diplomat I spoke of actually prefers to take his bread and tea with his old nurse and the smaller children in the day nursery. They are all without exception up and dressed at seven in the morning and begin their studies at eight. Ten o'clock at night sees them all — even the eldest — in bed. They are practising the piano in a cold, fireless room when their parents are at breakfast. They are obliged to walk each day five or six miles (with their governess, of course);

they seldom are allowed to ride, although they keep a carriage: they are taught to help themselves in their rooms, although they have maids and a footman. The theatre is made a rare and occasional treat, and if I give them seats or a box at the pantomime they are absurdly grateful. (Imagine a young girl as big as Miss —— coming in and saying, 'Thank you very much, Mr. Bret Harte, for so kindly taking us to the theatre.') The eldest boy is quite content with one pound (five dollars) a year for pocket money. (Of course, he costs his father nearly one thousand dollars a year for education!) Yet, as I said before, they are very good and simple, and really childlike. The young diplomat is at this present moment having a pillow fight with his little brother in the room over my head. Except on State occasions the girls dress very simply — and their *full* dresses are always very *girlish*, and composed chiefly of enormous sashes.

There, I hope you know them a little now, and hope some day you will know them better. I'll try and send you their photographs.

30th April

I wrote this letter just a month ago, and put it aside unfinished only from illness. As it was an answer to your Easter cards, I send it, incomplete as it is. If you have seen Mr. Watrous, who dined here and visited the family I speak of, he can tell you more about them.

I'm much better now, but if I cannot get a leave of absence to come home to America, I shall have to go somewhere on the Continent to recruit. But I want very much to see my little girls again — and I shall try hard to come. Take good care of Mamma, and God bless you both.

Your loving papa   FRANK

P.S. This note is half for Miss Badness — i.e., Ethel.

GLASGOW, *June 5*, 1883

MY DEAR TOTTIE,

I was delighted to get your letter, and wrote to the Van de Veldes your message. The bracelet and locket I sent you and Ethel were hurriedly picked up when I found that Mr. Watrous would undertake to carry something for me, but I had hitherto found it *so* difficult to send anything — even the smallest trifle — to you, without imposing so much trouble on your mamma that I had quite given it up. The things that *are* pretty and characteristic of this country — the things Papa likes and he knows his little girls like — are things to be picked up on the spur of the moment, and ought to be brought home to you *that very evening*, as Papa hopes sometime to do again. When I was at Newhaven, near Edinboro', the other day, I saw some dolls — imitations of Newhaven 'fishwives' — in their actual picturesque dresses, made by the fishwives themselves. If I could have sent them in a letter to Ethel (you, you know, are too big for dolls!) — I would; but they would lie in the New York Custom House Heaven knows how long, if I sent them as a package, all because I *am* a Consul, and cannot ask favours of the Custom House authorities for myself. Anything that is really valuable — things that are made here, like shawls, etc. — can be bought as cheaply in New York, and I might as well send the money to Mamma at once and let *her* choose for you. As this doesn't occur when *you* send anything over here to *me*, you understand how thoroughly I enjoy all that you send me. This seems selfish, I know — but it's true.

I am afraid the time has come when you are too big to have the excuse of worrying Mamma with the task of teaching you, among her other duties. I know you couldn't have a kinder or more intelligent teacher, but for that very reason you must give Mamma some rest, and it is Papa's wish, remember, that she should put you to school. The French School is preferable for a knowledge of that language, which here is scarcely a foreign tongue, when you consider that the two capitals of London and Paris are only nine and a half hours apart, and people go to Paris *en route* to everywhere. Think how awkward it would be to you in New York if you didn't understand the language of Boston and Washington. (Papa doesn't understand the language of Boston yet, but Papa is peculiar.) As it is my great hope to have you all *come* to me in Europe or *go* with me there some day, I would like you to enjoy it, understandingly, which you could not do if you saw it only through an interpreter's eyes. The drawing school is also a wish of Papa's, if Mamma thinks you have a decided taste for it, and do not care for the drudgery it entails.

I wish I *could* go with you to the Adirondacks. I am longing — absolutely longing for some American scenery. I sometimes think that is the reason why I do not write more to you about the country here. I do not remember anything of Caldwell: ask Mamma to send me on a picture of it. I am glad you know those nice little girls; I hope you behave so nicely to *them* that *they* write to *their* father that *you* are nice, too.

I think I must stop soon. for I am feeling it difficult to write to a young lady nearly eleven years old when I only knew the dear little face that has looked up at me from the lions of the Sea Cliff House, in the photograph that stands in my album. Can it be nearly four years ago? Papa is getting old and foolish! Remember this letter is for Ethel, too: I don't know how to talk to her now. Will you introduce Papa to her? Would she let me take her on my lap and comb her hair down into her eyes? Did I ever use to do that to her, or was it the other little girl in my album standing upon a garden seat with feet exactly two and one quarter inches long?

I suppose one must *not* look a gift letter in the mouth or I might say that, before French and drawing lessons are commenced, some slight trifling or flirtation with a writing-master might be advantageous to Miss Tottie Harte. I know it is a *first* letter (I mean an *all* alone first letter), but it ought not to have been a first letter from a young lady of eleven. Now, you see, I am writing to you and not to the little girl of the album. Tell Ethel I don't count the little scraps she has sent me for letters — except of the alphabet. She must write me again. So must you. Tell Mamma I shall write to her before the 10th. With kisses and best love,

PAPA

P.S. It occurs to this same Papa that he ought not to say much about handwriting. But he has been signing his name all day — and writing a story all night.

PAPA

How faithfully Bret Harte adhered to the ideals of a free country is apparent from the many allusions he makes to them throughout his correspondence. His deeply patriotic sentiments seemed only to be increased by his stay in foreign lands, in spite of all around him that might have tended to modify his views. His son was about to make his first steps in his new career, which took him away from his mother and sisters, which the former laments in a letter to which the following is an answer.

CONSULATE OF THE
UNITED STATES OF AMERICA
GLASGOW, *July* 9, 1883

MY DEAR NAN,

Thank you very much for your full description of Caldwell. It must be a fascinating and charming place; my heart goes out toward it *in spite* of its one hundred years, which, I am afraid, have not quite the glamour they had over me formerly. I am longing for the freshness, newness, and youthfulness of my own country. Perhaps it's only because I'm getting old, and with my usual fickleness, instead of becoming conservative with years, I'm only getting more radical.

I don't like to destroy *your* illusions, but the longer I live *here* the more I appreciate the advantages we had at home of making our own history *ourselves*, instead of having it handed over to us greasy, dirty, and thumb-marked, and so blotted with years and stained with blood that half the time it is utterly illegible and unreliable. I don't think I ever before appreciated fully the importance of being a *first tenant*, hampered by no ideas, prejudices and belongings, and of getting things 'first hand' from Nature. I know you will smile when you remember how I used to howl and rave against new houses — do you remember the one near North Beach in San Francisco where Frankie, 'Peker, Peker!' was born — *the Frankie* whom you are now lamenting like Rachel?

Don't think I am not sympathizing with you, Nan, at his going away, but to me — *at this distance from you all* — Chicago or Cleveland does not seem so far from *you in New York*, and I do not think you are losing the dear boy in letting him go that far in his new career. Think how you would have felt had I sent for him to come to me. I won't say that I *did not* solely because of your loneliness;

I won't say I did not ask for one of the boys to relieve my own lonely life here *solely* because I would be taking him from you, for I do not think the country is fit for young Americans to try their callow wings in, and it might have been ruinous to them hereafter if anything happened to me and left them to their own resources, but the thought *did* have some influence with me, and I felt they were better in your hands and that you could help each other.

I shall not hear from my application for leave of absence for two weeks yet; I am also waiting anxiously to hear from Dana in regard to my new story. I hope to be able to draw upon him on the 15th July for your August money.

Mr. Watrous is here in Scotland with me — making his headquarters at my hotel in Glasgow. He gives a very *roseate and glowing* account of you all; says he never saw *you* looking better in any way, praises Frankie and Wodie, and of the latter suggests a hope that he may some day become a partner of his own boy in Paris in the picture-buying business — which seems to be the more profitable part of that young artist's career. It is vague, however. Indeed, I do not think Watrous — good fellow as he is — has ever troubled himself much of late years about any of us — although there is a slight 'Pumblechook' flavour about his reminiscences. He *poses* a little as a man of wild Californian experiences when he is in company here, and perhaps a little overdoes the story-telling ''49' business. I am expecting that Mrs. Watrous will join him shortly. Of course, he is continually seeing the 'most beautiful woman in the world,' and praising young girls in his husky piratical voice. His eyes are darker and more wicked for his grey hairs. I introduced him to the 'greatest ship-builder in the world' (Mr. Pearce, of Glasgow) and got him an invitation to a trip on the 'finest yacht in the world' (really true! for it is) belonging to my friend Mr. Pearce.

Love to all.

Yours

LIMICK

From the next letter we see that Bret Harte had already dramatized three plays, two of which, 'The Luck' and 'Thankful Blossom,' were adapted from his own stories, and the third an adaptation from a French novel in collaboration with the author.

CONSULATE OF THE
UNITED STATES OF AMERICA
GLASGOW, *July* 14, 1883

MY DEAR NAN,

I wrote to you a few days ago and now enclose a draft on Mr. Dana of the 'Sun' for two hundred and fifty dollars. Please acknowledge its receipt; I do not remember if you have acknowledged the last draft from Glasgow. Perhaps you had better send me a list of the amounts and dates up to July 1, 1883, from 1st January. I shall probably send you another draft on Dana next month.

Ask Frankie to see the Madison Square manager and find out if anything has been done with 'The Luck.' Let him also see Mr. Wallack — Lester Wallack — to whom I have written to-day — for information concerning 'Germaine' — another play which I adapted in collaboration from the French by Edmond About — which was given to him by Boucicault to read. I only want him to find out if Mr. Wallack has received my letter, as I simply addressed it to New York, not knowing his theatre or residence. Of course, Wallack will reply to *me*, and Frankie need not go beyond the simple enquiry. Should

I not hear from Wallack, I will give F. an order for the manuscript and other instructions.

I do not know if you remember About's novel of 'Germaine.' I thought it would make a good play, and Genevieve Ward, who read the manuscript, would have taken it here but for the sudden squeamishness of the 'Censor of Plays,' who had been lately hauled over the coals for permitting 'Odette' and who suggested alterations and difficulties. The bulk of the work was done by my collaborator.

It seems hard that I have three plays 'Thankful Blossom,' 'The Luck,' and 'Germaine' — the two former representing six months of hard work — lying idle as so much unemployed capital. Of course I would rather have them failures in manuscript than before the footlights.

We are looking for the arrival of Mrs. Watrous from Italy to-night. I have no news yet from Washington. The boys might write me a line during their vacation.

Love to all!

Yours
Limick

Much has been intimated concerning Bret Harte's separation from his family, with which even the most trustworthy of his admirers seem to have charged him, and of which these letters are the living denial. What this separation meant to a nature as sensitive as his own has been more than clearly seen from the past correspondence. In the following letter to his wife, he speaks of his plans for an American trip or a visit of his family to Europe, which he had been cherishing for so long. The perpetual financial strain imposed by the maintenance of his family was the necessary cause of this delay. He handed over for this purpose the entire amount derived from the Consulate, even to the exclusion of any share in it for himself, and frequently added to it, whenever possible, something from his literary work as well. The three letters that follow are proof of the perfect *entente* that existed between them, and the absolute frankness with which their absence from one another and their projected reunion were discussed. Bret Harte's kindness in assisting all members of his family who were in need, although he could ill afford to do so, is seen from one of them.

Consulate of the
United States of America
Glasgow, *September* 17, 1883

My dear Anna,

Since sending you a draft on the 18th, I have received your two letters of August 26th, September 5th, and Dana's letter. I am glad to have the *legal* aspect of that question settled, although, judging from the paragraph from the 'Tribune' which you send me, without comment, I do not think the social aspect much changed. If a paragraph that seems to be apparently written in *good-will* can contain a wanton fling at you, and an intimation that I do not live at Glasgow and have always been irregular there, what may not be said when the pen is sharpened by envy or malice?

I don't remember if I told you that the Department once wrote to me very kindly that they heard reports regarding my absences from Glasgow and asked me to write a denial, which I did, when they expressed their satisfaction. I was told privately that the reports were spread by people who wanted my place. The paragraph in question plays into their hands.

But I should not let this stand in the way of my contemplated visit, though the season is now so far gone that

I may take my leave a month or two later. Senator Cameron and one or two other Americans are in Scotland, and I should not like to be out of the country while they are here; and, more important, I may be able to finish a play I have in hand. I should not, of course, expect to do any writing in America.

In yours of the 26th, you speak, and so does Eliza, of some picture you are to send me of yourself and Frankie. Up to this date nothing has come. I suppose you know that I have no photograph of you or either of the boys. I have written to Frankie and shall send a few lines to-day to Wodie. I will write more fully of my plans in a few days. Unless Eliza were so situated that you could be with her and have room for us all when I come, without crowding, etc., etc., I think we had better go to a hotel. I would not say anything of it yet to Eliza — but wait for further advices from me. Do you not, yourself, think we would be better at a hotel? Only the thought that by coming to her I might help her in her affairs makes me hesitate. Perhaps you might enquire what it would cost for our family at a good hotel like the New York (as it was when I was there) or some other. The question would have been settled if I had been able to come in the height of summer, for we might have all gone to a watering-place where I could have spent the whole of my stay. It will be autumn before I come now.

Nevertheless, I wish you would still consider if it would be pleasant, *looking at all things*, if you all came *here* to me — instead of my going to you for the *visit*. Perhaps you will smile at what I am about to say; it may be the weakest superstition, but I have a strange feeling about returning to America, that runs through all my longings and all my desires to return. I cannot call it a dread; the word is too large to express my meaning; it is not a *pre-*

sentiment, exactly. Perhaps it is because I have been *singularly lucky while I have been here in Europe.* My affairs have prospered; I have a market for my wares; I am not dependent upon publishers' whims or caprices; I have had no extraordinary expenses; I have been kept in my official position without any effort on my part and against outside influence. I have for the first time in my life known what it is to be independent. I dread one step — one unconscious act, that may change the luck.

I dare say it is foolish, so I merely reiterate to you that, if you proposed to come to Europe for the visit, there would be more substantial reasons for that preference than my silly fancies. We could spend a month or so in the South of France or Italy if you liked in the autumn, when England is unendurable. But if you think the other course advisable — and the visit to America better in all ways — I am quite willing to laugh at my fancies. I suppose *that paragraph* has not made me very hopeful. It is hard, is it not? that, when I found that the American papers 'were going for me' because I was being 'lionized' in England and 'becoming snobbish' and 'un-American,' and I gave up going into society because I feared that my name being in the papers with other visitors might give a colour to these reports, the only satisfaction I got from it is the suggestion that I stopped it because I could not work and do it, or rather that my friends had to drag me from it!

I shall write a few lines to Wodie — although I have written to him since he wrote to me.

Much love to all.

Yours
Limick

CONSULATE OF THE
UNITED STATES OF AMERICA
GLASGOW, *September 27, 1883*

MY DEAR NAN,

I have received a letter from Eliza asking me to give her an advance of from two hundred and fifty to three hundred dollars to be repaid in board for you and the children. She wants it on account of her usual troubles and chiefly to enable her to get a house in New York. I cannot say the letter was unexpected. Since I have been able to do a *little* for her, I knew she would—I say it not unkindly — turn to me in her troubles for increased assistance, with more confidence each time. I always calculated upon that peril in giving her what I could. I *could* give it at the moment, fully aware that she would eventually expect it when I could not.

I have sent her two hundred dollars, by taking the greater part of sixty pounds I had put by for my proposed 'outing' to America or the expenses of your coming over for the Continental trip. But I positively declined giving it to her as an *advance*, or having your relations with her in any way hampered by being obliged to board it out. I do not quite know if it is *just* in me to give her the two hundred dollars at all, when I have so little for myself and others, but I do know that it would be very unjust to you to handicap you with the recovery of that advance if *I* came later, and it would be equally a gift to her if you came here this autumn or winter. So I shall send you your draft for two hundred and fifty dollars the same as before, on the 15th October, and if you choose, of your own free will and out of your own kindness or judgment, to advance her a little more to make up the two hundred and fifty dollars she asks for, of course, I shall not say nay. But of that you are the best judge.

Meanwhile I shall withhold my leave a little longer until I can write something to bring me in some more money. (I had been giving myself a rest lately.) Eliza should know that I am far from being prosperous yet, and that I have been much disappointed in the results of my last story. I fear the play will not amount to much in America — here it is at present unmarketable. I intended that you should get my share of it there, and hoped that you would be drawing it before now, but I must send you a draft again on the 15th out of my salary account here.

The photograph of you and Frankie arrived only yesterday. It is worthy of your praise. You are looking exceedingly well — more so than I think I ever saw you look but once — and wonderfully young and unworn and untroubled, while your evident *embonpoint* is not unbecoming. I beg you to remember that *I* am getting fat and the combined avoirdupois is to be avoided. Of Frankie I can only say that, if he looks like that, I should not recognize him again. It seems to be another face than the one I left six years ago — not only in years, but *outline*. Of course, it is a fine, manly, determined face, one that no father need be ashamed of — a face admirably suited for his profession — and in fact one that reconciles me more to a belief in his 'stage capacity' — but it isn't the face of 'Peeker'! I make all allowance for the change from the boy to manhood — but still there is something strangely absent.

Please send me another one of each of you, separately if you have it, or together if you have not, and don't forget to have one taken of Wodie — if he has not one ready. I am very anxious to know if he has changed, too.

I shall write you again before the 15th. Love to all.

Limick

CONSULATE OF THE
UNITED STATES OF AMERICA
GLASGOW, *November* 8, 1883

MY DEAR ANNA,

I have been waiting and hoping to arrange my affairs so that I might make it not only possible, but *best* to visit home this autumn, as I proposed to do, but it is still so doubtful that it would be cruel to keep you longer in suspense, and it is better for us both to look upon it now as *postponed* until the spring. I say *postponed*, because the same leave of absence will do and need not be applied for again.

My most urgent reason, of course, was the financial one. Besides the Christmas story I am writing *now*, I have an offer for another this winter to make up another volume for the spring. Although I might, and it is possible *could*, raise enough money now for my visit, I know my own unfortunate self too well to believe that I would be as able to work and complete this volume by spring if I came to you as late as this. The offer is a *good one*, and if I took it, I should be able to come home in the spring that much *richer*, and of course much easier in my mind and more able to fully enjoy my visit.

My next reason is that Frohman, of the Madison Square Theatre, is to bring out my play in the spring, and as it is to be altered and revised I should like to be there at the time and possibly oversee one or two rehearsals.

Another reason is that the State Department have in consideration a proposal to elevate my Consulate at Glasgow another step in rank, with an advance of one thousand dollars on the salary. This has not been suggested by me, and may be only to prepare a more profitable berth for some one to succeed me, but, as it has to go before Congress this winter, in either event it would not look well for me to be present.

I do not think you can be more disappointed than myself and I have tried to look at the whole matter calmly — but I still want you to write freely to me about it and point out any fallacy you may see in my reasoning. Your suggestion in your last letter to sacrifice yourself by letting the money I gave Eliza go as an advance on what I send you is kind and good, Nan, but you know as well as I that it would not solve the problem. I should eventually, and perhaps the more certainly if I were in America, have to assist Eliza in her present trouble. It would be doubly difficult to refuse then, or even to refuse *more* if she asked it — as she probably would do, poor child. That is why I wished you need not be mixed up in it. It goes to my heart to disappoint you all — to disappoint the poor children. I almost wish I had not asked for the 'leave of absence' or told you of my intention. God bless you all. I'm too full of this to write much on any other subject, and must write you again.

LIMICK

The month of December approached, and Bret Harte was not able to go to America, nor was his family able to join him. He sends his little Christmas offerings instead with the kind little note that follows. The second letter, written a week later, speaks of his niece Miss Griswold, for whom Bret Harte had a great affection, and for whom he used his influence in endeavouring to assure her success.

CONSULATE OF THE
UNITED STATES OF AMERICA
GLASGOW, December 7, 1883

MY DEAR NAN,

I enclose a draft for one hundred dollars for Christmas presents for yourself and the children. I had set my heart upon making the presents this time, myself, but I must again ask you to do it for me. *First,* you are to expend the half, fifty dollars, on your own self — *your very own self!* — and then see that the boys, both Frankie and Wodie, and my girls, both Jessamy and Ethel, have something each for their own selves, to remember Papa by on Christmas morning. I wish it were possible *to send something* from here — something local and peculiar, but, as I once explained to you, it is more than difficult — it is uncertain.

I have finished my story. I fear it will not be as profitable here as I expected, but I hope to get good news from Dana. I will send you the usual draft on the 15th, and write. Meantime, God bless you all and may you have a merry Christmas. I had intended to write you a long letter at about this time, but I must put it off; I have not been very well lately and am yet not quite strong. God bless you again, one and all.

Yours
LIMICK

P.S. I have yours of the 23d. I send a draft for fifty dollars to Eliza.

CONSULATE OF THE
UNITED STATES OF AMERICA
GLASGOW, *December* 15, 1883

MY DEAR ANNA,

I wrote you on the 6th, enclosing a draft for one hundred dollars for Christmas. I sent to-day your regular remittance of two hundred and fifty dollars — for January. I say 'regular' remittance, Nan — and I hope it may always be *regularly* two hundred and fifty dollars — but I hope at the same time that you are able to put a trifle by from that two hundred and fifty dollars occasionally, so that if I should sometimes fall short of that amount *monthly*, you would not be inconvenienced.

On the 4th inst. Gerty Griswold was here in Glasgow and sang at one of the great public concerts. She and her travelling companion — for her mother was not able to come with her — were my guests at my hotel during their stay. I did everything I could to make their three or four days pleasant to them.

About two months ago, they — Gerty, her mother, and their companion Miss Melville — came to London, having shaken the dust of the Continent from their shoes. I knew nothing of their coming until I received a note from Gerty that they were here; but from all I hear and all they tell me I fear that Gerty *has not made a success* on the Continent and that England — or America perhaps eventually — is their *dernier ressort*. As they did not bring much money with them, I suppose, and as their expenses were considerable and they were quite strangers here, I naturally put aside all my past grievances — particularly Mrs. Griswold's letter to me — and did all I could for them, the more particularly as I saw that Gerty was, for the first time in my experience of her, disheartened and broken. I introduced them to all the managers and critics of note in London and *almost* secured for Gerty the principal rôle in Gilbert and Sullivan's new opera of the 'Princess' — the manager D'Oyley Carte and Sir Arthur Sullivan being friends of mine; but Gerty did not quite come up to their requirements as an actress, though Sir Arthur praised her voice and liked her — and that plan failed, although the idea of it at first seemed *infra dig.* for the prima donna of the Grand Opéra at Paris. She then sang at a Crystal Palace Concert — it was a 'success' in the eyes of the critics and her own, I suppose, but, candidly, I did not think it a *hit*. She got an invitation to sing here at the Glasgow Concert — but again it was not a great success — that is, it was not up to her reputation or the public expectation, I fear. I like the dominant quality of her voice which to my unmusical ear is freshness and purity — it is a fine *young* voice, but her *tremolo* does not please. She is now looking out for an engagement — and expects to sing again at Manchester. But meantime — the expenses, of course, go on.

I am very sorry for them, and shall do all I can for them. Outside of Gerty, and even with her, they are a helpless party. The mother's health renders it impossible for her to be without a companion constantly, so that they move around with a larger *ménage* than is economical. My friends the Van de Veldes have been very kind to them — on my account, perhaps. Charley Watrous knows something of their Continental troubles. If you see him you might learn more.

Watrous has been kind and thoughtful in managing the play business for me, although there are some difficulties still in the way of the reproduction of 'The Luck.' I have never heard from Frankie, since I wrote him about it; nor did Frankie ever answer Madame Van de Velde's letter to him; she is a great admirer of his, and I think feels a little hurt at his inattention. I write a few lines to Wodie by this steamer. God bless you all.

LIMICK

The next letter, to the Duchess of St. Albans, written during one of Bret Harte's brief visits to London, speaks of the little book of fables which he is sending her. Three of them were from his own pen, and have been published by C. M. Kozlay, together with the lectures, in the book already mentioned.

15, Upper Hamilton Terrace, N.W.
January 4, 1884

The Duchess of St. Albans.

MY DEAR DUCHESS,

Many thanks for the lost lamp, which reached its proper address safely.

Some day, when the fog is particularly depressing, you might look into a little book which I send you to-day, in the faint hope that you may not have seen it before. It is a book of 'Fables,' retold for American children; has a half Californian origin, and one or two of the least amusing ones were written by me, in my younger days. If you are very low-spirited, they may exasperate you, by their absurdity, into a healthy reaction. I would especially commend 'The Kind-Hearted She Elephant,' and gently draw your attention to the illustration of 'The Intruding Camel' — which are not *my* work.

I hovered over a book-stall in the fog, to-day, thinking of you, and wondering if you had ever read 'English as She is Spoke,' and how you would have enjoyed the *bona-fide* edition — a big book which was given to me by a traveller, fifteen years ago. I need not ask you if you love 'Uncle Remus'; of course you do — but have you read the latest? They are more like 'Reinecke Fuchs' than ever.

But be thankful that the fog brings you, at Bestwood, only the honest country moisture and the *flair* of the soil. Here it means liquefied London — a subtle deliquescence of all the grime of three million people! It's something awful to look at, on the pavement, terrible to touch! A foreigner appreciates the magnitude of London by what it casts off.

I enclose a copy of 'Longman's' also and will be glad

to send you any of the books I spoke of to lighten a half-hour.

Always, dear Duchess

Yours

BRET HARTE

Similar to the piracy of 'M'liss' and its conversion into a variety entertainment which has been mentioned earlier in this volume, an adaptation of 'Gabriel Conroy' was also produced upon the stage, in New York. The circumstances were all the more exasperating, inasmuch as Bret Harte had made no previous dramatization of this story, and the man who had made a very inferior version of it was using the author's name to cover it. All the steps, moreover, that were taken to protect his rights, and of which he speaks in the following letters, were powerless to prevent the production, to Bret Harte's great annoyance.

GLASGOW, *February 5*, 1884

MY DEAR ANNA,

I have yours (not dated) enclosing the newspaper slips about 'Gabriel Conroy.' But I had already (on the 21st January) a note of warning from Joaquin Miller, who wrote that McKee Rankin was using my *name* as well as my material, and I at once telegraphed to Watrous that 'Gabriel Conroy' was *dramatic* copyright of mine, and to notify Rankin of the fact. To-day I have a note from Watrous to the effect that a Mr. Andrews, the adapter, says that the American Publishing Company of Hartford *sold* him the dramatic copyright, alleging that they had advanced me one thousand dollars on account of it!

I send you a copy of the letter I have written Watrous. I do not honestly *believe* that I ever parted with my dramatic copyright to the Publishing Company in any way — or particularly in the way indicated. But, unfortunately, my memory of that particular advance is somewhat confused. Although I do not doubt that it is as I have related it, I cannot *swear* to it, and I beg you to recall, if you can, all the circumstances of the transaction. It must have been while we were at Lenox — after Cohasset; and you will probably remember the worry and anxiety I had at that time for money and my journeys from Lenox to New York and Hartford to get the advance. I cannot just now remember the name of the President of the Company — the man with whom I always dealt; but I remember that Mark Twain used his influence as director in my favour, but I am quite oblivious of there being any other security than the sales of the book itself. If I had been tempted to give my dramatic copyright as security, I certainly should have *told you at the time.* And as the actors always wanted *me* to dramatize the novel — and no other person — I don't see what value the copyright would be to the Company — if I didn't covenant to dramatize the novel for them at the same time.

I think that Mr. Walker, my legal friend, has the contract with the American Publishing Company in his safe. I know I once consulted him upon the advisability of forcing the Company to give me a statement of account. If you remember anything of the transaction, you might communicate to Mr. Watrous.

But, in any event, neither Mr. Andrews nor McKee Rankin has any right to use my name as countenancing this dramatization of the novel.

I had Frankie's letter and the notice from the Georgia paper. I was, I need hardly say, delighted with his making himself equal to an emergency — which I hold is the greatest element of success in everything. I was rather proud of my boy, and read the paragraph to my friends here. I liked the letter which accompanied it — which was *modest* and *strong*, and as promising as the paragraph. But more of this and his future another time.

I have begun my new story for 'Longmans,' which will complete a volume to be published in July. I have not been very strong in health this winter, and, if I had not been afraid of anticipating my leave of absence in the spring, I should have gone to the South of France or Italy for a few weeks. But I must wait now for the tonic and stimulation of my visit home. (Apropos of stimulation, I am quite a blue-ribbon man. I have not touched any alcohol of any kind for a year. I am none the worse for it — nor much better!)

I spent part of the Christmas holidays at Bestwood Lodge with the St. Albans. The Duchess's sister goes to America *en route* to the Bahamas, where her husband has been made Governor-General. I have half promised to run over with some of you when I come to America.

I'll write again on the 15th. I sent you on the 15th of last month a draft on Dana for two hundred and fifty dollars.

With love to all and a kiss for the little ones

LIMICK

GLASGOW, *February 5*, 1884

MY DEAR WATROUS,

I have yours of the 22d, enclosing Judge Dittenhoefer's letter.

I am amazed. The American Publishing Company of Hartford contracted with me for the publication of my novel of 'Gabriel Conroy' in book form, on payment of a royalty — advanced in certain sums on certain dates — upon the sale of the volume, but to the best of my recollection at no time did they ever contract for or pay anything on account of my dramatic copyright. An advance over and above the advance stipulated for in the contract was made by them some time after the book was published, but it was solely on account of royalties to accrue hereafter, and if I mistake not Mr. Clemens [Mark Twain], who was then a shareholder or director in the Company, became personally responsible for the amount advanced in event of the royalties not being sufficient to repay it. As the American Publishing Company have never given me an account of sales, but simply contented themselves with saying there was nothing due to me, I am unable to say whether the amount was ever realized.

The dramatic copyright was an afterthought of my own, taken out at my own request during the publication of the story (in reference to offers I had to dramatize the story) for my better security. I asked the President of the Publishing Company to attend to it for me, and he agreed to do so. But neither he nor the American Publishing Company ever preferred any claim to it whatever; in fact, as the only value a dramatization of the novel then had in the eyes of purchasers was because *it was my dramatization*, I cannot conceive what value the dramatic copyright would have been to the American Publishing Company, unless I had contracted to make the play for them, which certainly was not contemplated. If, however, my memory is at fault, and there was at one time a *bona-fide* transfer of the dramatic copyright to the American Publishing Company, they must have some document — if it be only a receipt — to show for it.

If they will exhibit it to you or Judge Dittenhoefer, I will be satisfied; if they cannot and rest upon some *implied* right in the property, I will try to find out what legal remedy I have. Perhaps Judge Dittenhoefer will know.

In no case am I in any way connected with McKee Rankin's present play nor has he any right to use my name as a consenting party.

I will have a power of attorney prepared and sent to you to enable you *to protect* all my dramatic compositions. But I will have to ask you to find out the *modus operandi*.

Our laws and the English laws are different as regards what constitutes a dramatic right.

I believe that here you are obliged to actually *draft the dramatization yourself*.

Very truly yours
(Signed)   Bret Harte

Bret Harte did not go over in the summer of 1884, for political reasons, and again urged his wife to join him in Europe, which, however, she did not see fit to do.

Consulate of the
United States of America
Glasgow, June 15, 1884

My dear Nan,

I enclose the draft for two hundred and fifty dollars.

I have not heard from you since the 19th ult., but I suppose you are waiting to hear from me about my coming home — perhaps even waiting my arrival. But my coming to America this summer seems to be now even a more difficult question than before. I can only make amends for your disappointment and my own by telling you that, after you read this letter and consider it carefully, if you think it better, I will come, or if you believe it better to come over yourself this summer, with the children, and *pay me a visit*, I will arrange it.

The difficulty is no longer the one I spoke to Watrous about: *that* he thinks will be trifling. The question now is only the advisability of my going over *before the election*. I have seen much of Colonel John Hay while he has been here this summer; he is quite *au fait* on the question, has great influence in Washington, and you will remember is the man to whom I entirely owe my promotion from Crefeld to Glasgow. I think he is a true, disinterested friend of mine; he advises me strongly *to wait until after the election* solely in reference to the possibility of my bettering my condition, or *retaining it* through another Administration. In the meantime he will do all he can to help me with the 'power that is to be.' His advice seems the more reasonable as *in any event* I should come to America after the election — either on a leave of absence if I still retained my place after the 4th November or as a matter of necessity if I lost my position. If I came in the present uncertainty as to whether I should not be *obliged* to come over again in the spring, I would also lose the credit I got from the Department during the last campaign by being (with Captain Mason) the only Consul who didn't ask for leave to come over and 'help the election.' This Hay used to quote in my favour; while even if I came over quietly, and didn't at once go to Washington, the fact would still go against me. The possibility that the Democrats may succeed also makes it advisable *that I should wait*, and not appear there as '*affiché*' to any candidate, as Dana, who has always promised me his assistance, and Barlow, who is my friend, could both help me better.

I have considered the matter with great care and anxiety and after serious consultation with Hay and Clarence King — who is also here. It would be foolish of me to undervalue the importance of my keeping my consular position — I might almost say the *necessity* of it. Three thousand dollars a year could not be gained by me by the extra time I could give to my literary work in losing my official position.

Again I have before me a summer of hard literary work. I have concluded my story and Christmas story for 'Longmans,' but no sooner is it done than Mr. Frohman, the manager of the Madison Square Theatre, comes over here with the manuscript of my play, and the unpleasant information that it must be almost entirely rearranged and rewritten before it can appear. This was the play that I expected would be paying me a royalty this autumn! The work must be done at once — it will take the better part of two months to complete. I have also just concluded the rough draft of another play which I may substitute for 'The Luck,' but this will take almost as much time to complete.

You may wonder why I work so hard at a thing thus far so unprofitable. I do so only because, if I write a good popular play, it would take the place of my Consulate in eking out my income. A good play ought to give me certainly three thousand dollars a year for a year or two.

I have no time to write on any other subject except to say that you may tell Frankie that Barrett — Lawrence Barrett — has offered to take him into his company, immediately on his return to America, next month, and that I have not yet consulted Irving (except to learn that his company is full). I will try to see him, but I should advise Frankie not to undervalue Barrett's offer, which will give him all the experience he asks for, and I think the best salary he can expect.

Write me at once, and write freely, dear Nan. And with my love to all of you, always

LIMICK

It was at last arranged that, since it was not possible for the whole family to join him, Bret Harte's two sons should come first instead. He was delighted at the prospect of seeing his two boys again, after six years' separation, and in his letters he explains all the plans he has been making for this great holiday they are to take together.

Consulate of the
United States of America
Glasgow, July 31, 1884

Your letter of the 16th inst. has just come and explains much I could not understand. I received your cable message, but, as it said so little that seemed to justify your telegraphing, I concluded there must be some other explanation and could only reply by asking you to tell the boys to wait for my answer to your letter. I got Frankie's letter first, which partly confirmed my suspicions that the whole thing, with its sudden energy and impatience of delay, was a caprice of *his own*. I tell you this to explain my cautious answer, which might have been disappointing to you, and because, when I received your letter of the 2d July in which you declined the invitation to make me a visit, I made my plans of summer work, vacation, and leave of absence to my Vice-Consul and employees. All this must be reorganized now and *can* be, and shall be *joyfully*, I need not say, but it is incompatible, I fear, with the boys coming as soon as you, or they, or I could wish.

In the first place, I want to give them a clear five weeks here (and on the Continent). It is hardly worth while their coming three thousand miles for less, or to be shut up a part of the time in the most uninteresting city in Europe, Glasgow, where they might as well be in Pittsburgh. I want to take them to the Scotch Highlands, to

London, to Stratford, to Paris, to the Rhine. I want to bring them with me to the English country house in Surrey where the Van de Veldes, my great friends, are, who have extended an invitation to them, and where they can rest a while quietly.

All this cannot be done now, or *before the tenth or fifteenth of September*. At present, owing to the cholera panic, the quarantine regulations make the Continent almost inaccessible and entirely unpleasant. By the first of September, it will all be over probably. By that time I shall be quite free: my Vice-Consul's leave will be over, my work on the play (I forgot to say I am dramatizing 'A Blue Grass Penelope' to take the place of 'The Luck,' possibly at the Madison Square Theatre) will be completed, and I can have fairly earned my holiday with the boys. The two or three friends I want them to know will be accessible, and they will see London under better auspices than now — when the season is over, the theatres closed, and the large city deserted by every one. The early autumn is the time for Scotland also. Last, and not least, the expense of their outing will be considerably less, under these conditions.

I propose, therefore, to have them leave about the second or fifth of September, so as to be here on the eighteenth. I will make arrangements for them to come by either the White Star to Liverpool, or Germanic (Hamburg or Lloyd's) steamers, landing at Southampton or Plymouth, where I would meet them, and where their first glimpse of England would be as charming as it was to me, or they could come to Glasgow by the Allan or State Line as they preferred — but I fear they would find the voyage slow and uninteresting. I could make equally good arrangements by the other lines, I think, and I would prefer to, as I already use the Glasgow lines to send home impoverished and vagabond Americans, and have almost trespassed upon their generosity in my half-official capacity. In fact, I don't think I should ask them a favour for myself or my own family.

Let the boys, therefore, join you in your country vacation now in some pleasant place, even if it costs you a little more, which I will make up in my draft on the 10th of next month, and wait until a month later. They need not make any expense of preparation and can bring but few clothes, and only their *best*, as their wardrobe can be easily refitted here.

That is all I can say now. I hope you will not be disappointed by their not coming as soon as you expected, but I hope you will admit, on reflection, that a visit like theirs cannot be arranged by telegraph entirely or without some little delay, to enable them to make the most of it, nor can their merely crossing the ocean to wait in the hotel of a dull town like Glasgow — duller than usual in mid-summer when every one is away — until I am at leisure to go with them, be called a pleasure visit. If it were a question of their health or business, it would be different. I should say come at once.

Write me fully when you receive this. You say nothing of yourself — of your own hopes or disappointments. What can I say but to repeat the old song — 'Wait and hope.' I don't know anything has been gained by hoping, but I do know nothing has been *lost* by waiting. Kiss the girls for Papa and read the boys this letter.

Always, dear Nan

LIMICK

LONDON, *July* 31, 1884

MY DEAR NAN,
Coming up to London to-day I despatched a long letter to you which I had previously written, but, for fear lest

my suggestions should be not explicit enough, I add this to say that if Frankie and Wodie left at any *time after the fifth of September* (so that they would arrive here about the fifteenth), it would suit me. I have been to make some enquiries about steamers and will write you again as soon as I have got the information I require. I want to have Frankie see Mr. Irving, who also returns to America this winter, if possible.

I have also telegraphed to you that I have answered your letter — which answer you should receive within ten days from to-day, as the post gains a day over Glasgow, from London. I hoped to be able to send information about the passage in my letter this morning, but I feared to miss the post.

In great haste but with much love to all

LIMICK

This visit of his boys was now the principal subject of his thoughts, and he speaks of it proudly and fondly in all his letters to his friends. To the Duchess of St. Albans, who had invited him to her home in Ireland, he mentions their 'projected visit,' and asks her to delay the date until he knows when they are coming, 'if they are coming,' not daring yet to believe too implicitly in his good fortune.

CONSULATE OF THE
UNITED STATES OF AMERICA
GLASGOW, *August* 15, 1884

The Duchess of St. Albans.

MY DEAR DUCHESS,

Yours of the 9th came while I was out of town. I hasten to say I am as eager as ever to make the promised visit, and to come as early in September as possible, but I must crave your indulgence a few days longer, before arranging the date, as I am waiting letters from America regarding a projected visit from my two boys this autumn. The friends I spoke of also, to arrive on the 13th August, are already here, so that I shall be quite free as regards my duty to *them*. I only wait now to learn when the boys will come, if they are coming at all, to give you a positive date, when I shall be at your service.

Pray don't scent in this an impending repetition of former feeble failures. I am coming despite my promises.

Is Ireland as mellow as England in this weather? During the intense heat of the last week I was in an old country house that had, in fact, almost passed its maturity, and was exhaling itself in a *pot-pourri* odour of desiccation. The unwonted heat had taken away that treacherous damp which is to me an unpleasant reserve of the English climate, and always suggests the *deliquescence* of decay, but here was a fine mummified spice of Old England that quite interested me. I sat in an old church (tempus Edward III) redolent with the fragrant dust of somebody's ancestors, and sneezed, not unkindly, at one of their early parliaments. The past was in the sluggish, heated air, everywhere; it escaped under the effaced brasses of old tombs in the church, shook out of the tapestry and the walls of the old Manor House, and rose from the dust of oaken floors. Heaven knows how much of Conservatism I have inhaled during the past week.

I am waiting to get an American copy of 'On the Frontier' to send you. The English copies are in paper covers.

Always yours
Bret Harte

Three weeks later, all was definitely settled and the joy and excitement of their near meeting fills the next letter to his wife, in which all arrangements for their journey across are made. Bret Harte's dear friends Monsieur and Madame Van de Velde had invited them on a visit before they should go farther and everything seemed for the best.

CONSULATE OF THE
UNITED STATES OF AMERICA
GLASGOW, *September 5,* 1884

MY DEAR NAN,

I telegraphed you yesterday that I had paid the boys' passages to Southampton by the North-German Lloyd steamer Enis that leaves New York on the 17th September. I paid eighty dollars each, which was a reduction in the usual fare, but not as much as I could have got from the White Star Line. I preferred the German Line because the steamers are uniformly good, and the landing at Southampton (where I shall await the boys) will give them a view of the south of England on their way to London, and economy of *time* — as their stay is limited — is almost as much as economy of *money.* I enclose two five-pound notes (equal to fifty dollars) which they can turn into English gold to have with them on the passage. Let them bring only their *best* clothes, besides what they will wear on the steamer. You can telegraph me a single word, 'Left,' when they sail, and I will arrange with the agent at Southampton to telegraph me when the vessel is signalled off the Lizards. I shall probably bring them both at once to the Van de Veldes' country house in Surrey, near London, and on the way from Southampton, where they can rest for a few days and recruit, until we return north to Scotland.

It is only within the past ten days that I have been able to thoroughly compass their coming and arrange for them. It will be a trifle more expensive than I thought, but *we will make the best of it.* The passages, both ways,

will alone cost three hundred and twenty dollars. This
has occasioned the delay, and is the reason why I had to
telegraph yesterday and why you will have barely time
to receive this in season.

I have yours of the 1st and 19th. I will answer them —
particularly the latter — as soon as this hurry is over.

Love to all — in the greatest haste, but the fullest
heart.

LIMICK

P.S. Say to Frankie that *of course* I am satisfied with
his engagement with Barrett. He must not let it slip in
any case.

LIMICK

It was a great disappointment, therefore, when at the
last moment his eldest son was prevented from coming.
The uncertainty and fear of any injustice of which he
might involuntarily have been the cause, and to which
he was very sensitive, came in addition to the sincere
regret at the absence of one of them.

CONSULATE OF THE
UNITED STATES OF AMERICA
GLASGOW, *September* 16, 1884

MY DEAR NAN,

I have just received your cable despatch that Wodie
could not come with Frankie. It has worried me not a
little, since, in spite of the word 'business,' which I suppose is explanatory of his not coming, I fear you may have
imagined I was beginning to be troubled by the prospect
of their *joint* expenses. This would have been exceedingly
foolish, as the differences would have been slight, and
scarcely enough to justify either to make a sacrifice of
himself for his brother's sake, if you construed my state-

ment of the cost of passages as a desire to reduce it by one. It was farthest from my thoughts, Nan, and, if I had been forced to limit the visit to either one, I should, in the first place, have said so *frankly*, and then have considered, perhaps, that Wodie had the better right. But I try to believe that my loss is offset by some advantage to him. At any rate, tell him how Papa is disappointed by the absence of the 'Malignant' and that 'Peeker' will not seem entirely like himself without his brother.

I have Frankie's letter informing me of the failure of his Barrett engagement. I am very much disappointed, as I hoped for some good experience for him in that engagement and these chances are rare in his profession just now — in the opinion of the actors to whom I have spoken here. I shall try to see Irving before he leaves for America, day after to-morrow — and regret he could not see Frankie *here*, as, of course, he could not engage him, however favourable his prejudice might be, until Frankie returned to America. I do not know what are F.'s ideas, *but I do not think there is the slightest chance of an opening for him in England.* His only advantage in coming will be to see the best English and French acting — and profit by it — *in America!*

I enclose you a draft for two hundred dollars on Dana, and will try to send you fifty dollars more in a few days, but I have been short of ready money by reason of paying these passages *in advance*. Tell Eliza I have received her last letter and shall write a line to Murat Halstead regarding Ernest. I thought the Customs very clever.

With love to all.

LIMICK

The next letter is written a month after the arrival of his son in England, and is characteristic of Bret Harte's faculty of independent judgment even as regards his children.

CONSULATE OF THE
UNITED STATES OF AMERICA
GLASGOW, *October* 30, 1884

MY DEAR ANNA,

We are still in Scotland, but, as the weather is very unpropitious for sight-seeing, I shall, as soon as I have made my monthly accounts at the Consulate, go to London with Frank and thence to Paris. It is a pity that he has not been able to 'do' the Scotch lakes, but the season is fully a month too late, and Scotch lakes and mountains in a perpetual drizzle and mist are neither picturesque nor cheerful. I think he is getting a little bored here, with no company to speak of, and only the range of my lodgings at the hotel and the Consulate. He is very fond of ladies' society, but, as I know very few families here and they are old-fashioned people, I dare say he finds it dull. ... Madame Van de Velde is away in Switzerland with her mother, but should she bring the old Countess back with her to Paris, I hope to introduce him to this specimen of the *old French noblesse* before he goes back. The Duchess of St. Albans has written to me to bring 'my boy' with me to Bestwood Lodge, and although I was obliged to postpone the visit this week, I hope to take him up there with me next week. Dr. Hendry, my Scotch physician and friend, says he has not got 'clergyman's sore throat,' but that he has weakness of the vocal cords from general weakness and depression, and advises strongly 'cod-liver oil' (with Extract of Malt) for regular treatment, and *Belladonna* (homœopathic, of course) for a direct medicine at all times.

Dr. Hendry says, and your opinion evidently agrees with the fact, that his dyspepsia is his *dominant* source of weakness. I have watched him closely and *sympathetically*, for I know what the disease is myself; but I am pained often to see how his want of self-control and his habitual intolerance of any restraint works against his cure, and keeps up a chronic state of irritation. Without saying that he stimulates too much, or that he at all *over-indulges* in liquor of any kind, he has learned to depend upon its effect too much at his meals, and, when he is not feeling well — to keep up an appetite. I do not mean to say that he drinks between meals *or drinks too much at meals*, but I know that he would often *be unable to eat at all without wine or beer*, and this condition of his stomach is not right *at his age*. I observe, too, that he uses such things as *spirits of ammonia*, and *spirits of camphor injudiciously* — and certainly to the point of utterly weakening the effect of homœopathic medicines. He meets my objections by saying that the doctor — Gilbert — advised them. Dr. Ayert — the London physician — of his own intuition told him to avoid the use of stimulants. My idea in telling you this is not that there is a necessity for guarding him from *dissipation*, but from increasing his stomach trouble until liquor will affect him badly. You can do more than I can to correct this; my voice will be quickly forgotten when he returns; my influence — of which I doubt — is only an episode. I have talked to him about it — and continue to do so — I know not with what effect. He wants a health *discipline*. He is a most singular mixture of a man and boy; with the thoughtlessness of the one and the independence of the other, and a perfect satisfaction in both.

He applies himself very assiduously to his idea of work, writing in his diary, making French translations, corresponding, etc., etc. — which certainly is not wasting his time, even if the result is not always brilliant. Maurice

Van de Velde, who is a year younger, helps him with his French, and, as they are both equally good at music, they are at the piano in my sitting-room all the time. Frank's proficiency in playing so well by ear is a pleasant accomplishment, and by no means an inconsiderable one.

I will write a few lines to Ethel by this post if I can; if not, the next. Give my love to them all and say that Papa often finds himself talking to their mother, and thinking of them.

Always

FRANK

The short vacation was now up, and the return of his son to America left him again alone. Monsieur and Madame Van de Velde had become intimate friends of Bret Harte, and to their kindness and hospitality he owed the pleasantest part of his life abroad. That they extended to his son the same courtesy is seen from Bret Harte's next letter to his wife.

LONDON, *November* 14, 1884

MY DEAR NAN,

Frank sailed yesterday from Southampton on the W—— for New York. I telegraphed to you (in his name to save superfluous words) as he was about to embark, and you have probably seen him before this reaches you. He will tell you how Monsieur and Madame Van de Velde and his friend Maurice came down from London to see him off, and I can add that they all seemed to miss him greatly. I think he liked these people, who gave him the nearest approach to a home that he could have in a foreign country during his stay, and I think he allowed Madame Van de Velde, whom he evidently admired, to control him with good-humoured advice more than he did me. Indeed, I may confess frankly that Monsieur's gallant politeness and unfailing good-humour, Maurice's breeding in fellowship, and the young girls' unaffected naïveté influenced him more in its way than his companionship with *me*. I am afraid he found it dull with me in Scotland, although *I* did not find it dull with him. He kept me very wide awake with his impatience, in fact, and I suppose our combined dyspepsias helped it along.

It will be for you to say and judge if his two months' visit has been of any benefit to him and in what way.

I have your letter of October 28th. You can easily imagine that the ill-luck of Wodie's enterprise (though I cannot conscientiously say that I was sanguine of it) adds no little to my embarrassment in looking ahead to the changes that the few next months may bring. I have not yet been able to form my plans, but I will write to you as soon as I do. Meantime, 'don't worrit' and keep up your courage, Nan. Love to Wodie and all.

FRANK

P.S. I enclose in another envelope a draft for two hundred and fifty dollars. I need not say be careful, but be as careful of its use as you can. They might not be as frequent hereafter.

'The year 1885, an eventful one for Bret Harte, was to mark the beginning of a new era in his life. The first letter, written home, was in reply to the exchange of little Christmas gifts, which was the tie, broken only by death, which kept them united in their separation. The portrait by John R. Pettie, to which reference is made in other parts of this volume, is the one which illustrates, in frontispiece, the present collection of letters.

15, UPPER HAMILTON TERRACE, N.W.
January 16, 1885

MY DEAR NAN,

Since I wrote you acknowledging the receipt of the
pretty Christmas box, I have received the second, or
encore, parcel with the shirt-case and photograph! I
have just written to Frank about the latter, which is most
clever in treatment and very, very charming in subject!
and I have only to thank you, my dear Nan, for the beautiful and tasteful work of your own hands, whose elegance
filled the eye, and whose perfume filled my nose for several days. Where on earth — or in Paradise — do you get
your scents? There is a decided freshness and originality
about the aroma of everything that you send me which
makes even the children of the house sniff on the staircase
and say, 'Mr. Bret Harte has got something from his
family in America!' I confess the shirt-case — admirable
as a thing of beauty — puzzled me as to its *practical* use.
I had to struggle hard against a disposition to *wear* it over
my shirt, as a kind of delicately-flannel waistcoat (that
would be a *shirt-case* naturally) and to put it on my pillow
as a night-shirt-case. I have finally folded it around two
of my 'smallest' two-buttoned dress shirts and laid it
atop of my drawer — which I carelessly leave open to
dazzle the housemaids.

How very charming is Tottie's picture! I have begged
Frank to send me one of *yourself* and Ethel, and if he does
not, I entreat you to have a good one taken and sent to
me — even if I am able to come to America and compare
it with the original not long after I receive it. I think
Jessamy has your eyes — or rather your eyelids — has
she not? In this photograph the resemblance is remarkable. I shall try to get you a photogravure of Pettie's,
R.A., picture of myself; you know he presented me with

the original. Eliza's photograph was capital, and every one admired it.

Although my year of hard work has barely closed, I have begun the New Year with another task, but I am quite confident of completing it — unless my health fails again — by the end of February or the middle of March, at the latest. Then I shall be quite free for a while — and then? — but I shall not plan or prophesy — at least to-day.

I hope you are better of the cold you had when you wrote last, and that Tottie continues to improve. Her portrait does not look *delicate*, though I should not call her buxom! Make Wodie send me his portrait — I am weary of asking for it! As weary as I am of asking him to write to me. I have had *two* letters from him in *five* years. You speak of Ethel's and Tottie's letters. I have Ethel's, which I shall try to answer by this post, but nothing from Tottie.

I send enclosed the usual draft. May God bless you all, dear Nan, and with kisses to the girls

Ever

FRANK

CONSULATE OF THE
UNITED STATES OF AMERICA
GLASGOW, *February* 14, 1885

MY DEAR NAN,

I have been suffering from a heavy cold which has 'rampaged' my jaws with neuralgia and my ankles with rheumatism, and sent me to the South coast for a few days to recover. I am not over-bright and I send off the monthly draft for fifty pounds to-day, and I can do little more than ask you to forgive a short letter. There is really no news to write: I have just finished a long story, and am to-day trying to begin a short one that will be enough to make a volume for the early summer. It's a 'demnition grind' as Mr. Mantalini says, and my hopes of getting a little relief out of the royalty of a play seems as far off as ever. I have been — in spite of this — working over a dramatization of 'Penelope,' so my 'gouty' hands are full. I am not joking when I say 'gouty,' for there is little doubt there is *that* tendency in my blood, say the doctors. Think of it! — I who am an anchorite, and for the last two years almost a teetotaller — a subject for gout! It is the climate.

I hope you are better, and I wish I had prevailed upon you to go south to Florida this winter, with the family. I don't think it would have cost you much more than staying in Plainfield for the three months. It is provoking that I had not thought of it sooner. But I'll keep it for the time when we can all go together.

I will answer Tottie's little note in a day or two. It's a dear little baby-like note, but isn't it a trifle infantile in calligraphy for her actual years? I am not cavilling; I'm only wondering! Bless her — anyway. Kiss them both; give my love to the boys.   Always

LIMICK

P.S. I don't like to be importunate or indelicate or greedy or indiscreet — but *where* is that Christmas box? Was it for next Christmas?

Bret Harte was always considering the possibility of a change of office with the new Administration, and was fully cognizant of the effects which his departure from the Service would have upon his financial situation. In his indefatigable and courageous manner he was striving, therefore, by his literary work — to shield his family against such an eventuality.

CONSULATE OF THE
UNITED STATES OF AMERICA
GLASGOW, *March* 13, 1885

MY DEAR NAN,

I'm shocked to find it is a month since I have written, but nearly every hour of the time has been passed in work. I have finished another short story since I wrote you on the 14th, and to-day I have just concluded a contract with the 'Illustrated London News' for another longer tale for their summer number, which must be ready by the 15th of May. I am working thus breathlessly to make the most of advantageous offers that do not occur every day, and to avoid being stranded hopelessly here, in case I shall not be able to keep my office. Philosophical as I may try to be, it is not a pleasant thing to lose three thousand dollars a year, and although I ought to be thankful that I could earn a living by my pen, I doubt if I could do it long, or work as well as I do (by 'well' I mean with less strain and feverishness), with the consciousness that *your actual sustenance and that of the children* depends upon my hourly labours. I do not know how long my popularity will last with the public, and I must make the most of it now. I hear nothing further of any efforts to have me retained, although I learn that Bayard, the new Secretary of State, is Mr. Barlow's great friend. I wonder whether it would be worth your while to see Mr. Barlow. Dana has spoken to him for me.

I do not know if you will like the 'Ship of '49,' which Dana must be now publishing, but I think you will like the little story I have just finished called 'An Apostle of the Tules.' I have not yet determined what I shall write for the 'Illustrated News.' Everybody tells me here that it will be a great advertisement for me with the English people, even if it does not pay after the American scale of prices. But even that has lately fallen off. Dana pays me now about half as much as he did two years ago. Another cause why I must work harder and quicker. Unfortunately, though I spend more time in writing than formerly, I fear I do not produce any the more easily.

I send you your draft for two hundred and fifty dollars for the next month. I don't ask you to be more economical, but I beg you to reflect that I may not be able to keep up that amount long. Watrous has got a small forfeiture from Frohman for 'The Luck' — but there may be some New York debts to pay with my share of the sum.

I shall write a few lines to Frank by this mail. I am sorry to hear you have all had sickness lately, but I trust that with the coming of spring you will be better. God bless you all. I'll write again in a few days.

Kiss the children for

LIMICK

Bret Harte and William Black, to whom the amusing letter republished here was written, met as guests of Sir George Wombwell, a few years previously, and had become very good friends. Many references to him are found in the biography of William Black, by Sir Wemyss Reid, who was also a personal friend of Bret Harte.

GLASGOW, *March 15*, 1885

William Black, Esq.

MY DEAR BLACK,

I was in the far south, trying to get rid of an obstinate cold, when your note reached me, and haven't been in London for some time. I expected you to drop in here on your way 'to Balnagownie's Arms' — whoever she may be. I'm afraid I don't want any 'Ardgay' in mine, thank you. Why any man in this damp climate should want to make himself wetter by salmon-fishing passes my comprehension. Is there no drier spot to be had in all Great Britain? I shudder at the name of a river, and shiver at the sight of any fish that isn't dried. I hear, too, that you are in the habit of making poetry on these occasions, and that you are dropping lines all over the place. How far is that place — anyway?

I shall be in Glasgow until the end of March, and if you'll dry yourself thoroughly and come in and dine with me at that time, I'll show you how 'the labouring poor' of Glasgow live.

Yours always
Bret Harte

The two following letters are of particular interest in the light they throw upon the extreme integrity and cleanliness of Bret Harte's administration of his consular duties, and contain also comments connected with his literary work, showing how hard at work he was, in prevision of a change in his post.

Consulate of the
United States of America
Glasgow, April 4, 1885

My dear Nan,

I'm ashamed not to have acknowledged before your Christmas box which arrived in perfect good order about ten days ago. But as you can imagine I have been very busy. I have been writing about seven hundred words a day on my new story for the summer number of the 'Illustrated London News,' besides my consular work. Except when I was in the Mint in San Francisco and edited the 'Overland' at the same time, I do not think I ever worked so hard.

But to return to the Christmas box. The smokers'

service was lovely; so unique and so unlike anything to be seen in Great Britain. The copper ornamentation is unknown here and I should think would be quite 'the craze' if it were. Tell Frank I have put it out on the sideboard in my sitting-room at the Grand Hotel; he will remember it.

They are beginning to make the Consular changes — in spite of a paragraph published in the telegraphic news to the London papers that there would be none. I sit here and work and calmly wait! Watrous says he spoke to Secretary Whitney; Dana says he asked Barlow to speak to Bayard — but as yet I see no result except that no news is good news.

My Vice-Consul, who had served under four of my predecessors, told me, very quietly, the other day, that the office had never been as purely administered as under me. I 'fished' to know why, and it appeared that all the other Consuls used to cheat the Government in small ways by taking certain fees that were 'official' and calling them 'unofficial.' I was surprised at Mr. Gibson (my V.-C.) telling me this. He is a cautious, careful Scotchman, who would almost die rather than flatter or compliment you to your face.

And — of course! — this is a kind of thing the Government cannot know, so, except for the knowledge that my V.-C. respects me — I am none the better for it. I take no especial credit for it, as I have no temptations. I hate pecuniary meanness, and I think I am loyal to my trust by nature. I spend all that the Government allows me for office rent and clerk hire on the things themselves and not *on myself*, with the result that my office is better equipped than some of the better-paid Consuls — and I should go out of it poorer than the least paid. But here I have no reason to complain, for I prefer it. I should not like any one to think of me — what *I* have thought of some of my colleagues.

Pardon this frank hint of egotism! To come back to the box. I was greatly pleased and surprised with the *sachet* Tottie painted for me. It was admirably done; did she design it herself?

I wrote to Frank; I wish you would ask Wodie to write to me once in a while. He might in that way suggest something by writing frankly and regularly where and how I could help him. At present I know of his affairs only through your occasional records of his hopes and his disappointments. Watrous is, I think, a good friend of mine, and of the family, and I think if he could help Wodie he would do so gladly in his practical way, by recommending some particular employment and perhaps assisting him to procure it. You must remember that Charley Watrous is really the only link I have with you all — as being a person to whom I can talk about you all, and who, I think, likes you all. Hay and Clarence King haven't even seen you for years; and Watrous is the only man I habitually meet who knows my family.

Your idea of the bear — the *Overland Bear* — was capital; but you did well in not spending all that money, especially at this moment. I should have kept the dear old bear, for my note-paper, but the English people are so pleased when an American puts on anything like a 'crest' that, except the Scotch note-paper with the stamp, I have avoided anything like pandering to their prejudices. Every Englishman believes in the bottom of his heart that Americans long for an aristocracy of birth and try to imitate it, and I am sorry to say they often have reason to think so, from some of the men — and nearly all the women — who come over here. Lowell made himself vastly popular here by doing the Boston-English style, and by judicious truckling, and I am not sorry he was recalled.

My new story is a glimpse of the better class of Californian-Spanish life, and I have naturally to introduce a heightened portrait of Majendra Atherton — do you remember that awful flirt! Of course, it is only a suggestion and the incidents are imaginary. The story is to be illustrated by one of the 'swellest' English artists of that kind — 'R. Caton Woodville.' It is considered a great honour to me to write for the summer number of the 'Illustrated London News,' and have such an illustrator.

Unfortunately, while my stuff is held at a premium here, it is falling off in America. Dana gives *less than half* what he gave me at first; my publishers, Houghton, Mifflin and Company, scarcely anything. This is not a pleasant prospect in case of a Consular change!

Did you read 'The Ship of '49'? If not, read 'The Apostle of the Tules' — it's said to be in my old shorter and more condensed style.

I got a note from Eliza a few days before the 13th March, asking me to send her some money for a specific purpose before that day. It was simply impossible for me to do so. What could I do? There was no use to write to her — to telegraph would have been an unnecessary expense. I will write soon to her and if I can send her a little, I will.

I heard the other day that it was stated in a Brooklyn paper that Wallack had paid me one thousand dollars. It won't hurt me to let people *think* so — but I wish I had the money!

God bless you all and keep you safely.

Good-bye till the 15th.

Affectionately

Limick

LONDON, *April 15*, 1885

MY DEAR NAN,

Just a hurried line to thank you for yours of the 1st and to enclose a draft on Dana for two hundred and fifty dollars.

I am very glad you saw Dana and Barlow; indeed, it is the first I have really known of what they were doing, and the prospects of success.

Thanks for your defence of my absences from Glasgow. But isn't it hard! There are no *complaints!* — there cannot be; there may have been 'reports' and jokes — but there is no 'inattention' — and nothing to complain of at the Consulate. I am always there when wanted. No Americans come to Glasgow to *complain*. In fact, it is this utter desolation and loneliness which often makes me run down to London to see the face of a fellow-countryman. There is but one American resident in Glasgow besides myself, and I am told he wants my place! I have never seen him! The merchants here naturally prefer to do their purely clerical business with my Vice-Consul — their own countryman, who is one of the best and most efficient lawyers in Glasgow. *They* don't complain. *The Department* don't complain of inattention. Who does?

I have just now run down to London to read proofs and see the artist who is illustrating my new thing for the summer number of the 'Illustrated London News.' The drawings are perfectly charming. I have never had anything like them before.

I am still hard at work, grinding out my six hundred words a day, Sundays and holidays, sick or well.

Apropos of my *absences* again! Regularly every year I have always received an invitation from Berlin to the Court Ball given by the Italian Ambassador (Madame Van de Velde's father) to the Emperor William. I never dared to go on account of the possible criticism there might be of my absence from Great Britain on the occasion — as it is an affair of public ceremony. Only a few days ago I declined to accompany the Van de Veldes — who had gone on there for the Ball of this year — for the same reason. And now I hear that there are 'complaints' made of my absences at London! It is a little too hard! Young Bismarck gave me an invitation to come to his father's house and stay; it would have been an affair of only two days, but — you can imagine what would have been said in America! And yet I have taken no leave of absence since I came here.

I wrote you how pleased I was with the Christmas box. Tell Frank I'll answer his last letter soon. God bless you all.

LIMICK

Messrs. A. P. Watt and Sons had been for some years past, and were, until the time of his death, Bret Harte's literary agents. To their skillful administration he owed much of the financial success of his works, and he was relieved by them of all the business connected with them. There are a great many letters of interest from Bret Harte to them, which, unfortunately, lack of space does not permit to be included in the present volume. Bret Harte's following letter, showing his appreciation for their services, has already been published.

CONSULATE OF THE
UNITED STATES OF AMERICA
GLASGOW, May 21, 1885

MY DEAR MR. WATT,

I am sending you back the last proofs of 'Maruja' to transmit to the publishers. I want to thank you for the trouble you have taken in connection with this part of your service to me as my agent — not the least of your valuable help to the literary man in his relations with his publishers. It is hardly necessary for me to repeat what I have already told you of my satisfaction with the financial result of your business arrangements with the publishers, both here and in America. Your disposal of 'Maruja' to the two largest illustrated weeklies in Great Britain and America was managed with great tact, delicacy, and patience, and I can believe that you have pleased the publishers as much as the author. No recommendations from me to my brother authors can be as potent as a recapitulation of these facts, and I doubt if you require anything more.

Until authors know a little more about business, and are less likely to feel that it interferes with that perfect freedom essential to literary composition, it seems better that they should employ a business man to represent them with those other business men, the publishers. And I hope I won't shock your modesty by adding that I don't think they can find a better man for that purpose than yourself.

For myself I am quite convinced that the commission I pay you has been fully returned by the appreciation of the market value of my work through your efforts, to say nothing of the saving of time and trouble to me during the progress of that work.

I am, dear Mr. Watt

Very truly yours

BRET HARTE

The scathing comments of the following letter to his wife are not without a singular force, coming from a man who knew and appreciated England as he did, and whose association with the most distinguished representatives

of her aristocracy was powerless even to modify the belief
he held in the ideals of his country.

CONSULATE OF THE
UNITED STATES OF AMERICA
GLASGOW, *July* 13, 1885

MY DEAR NAN,

I enclose with this a draft for four hundred and fifty
dollars — being two hundred dollars more than your usual
monthly draft, which I wish you would apply to the expenses of some summer recreation for yourself and the
children, either in the Adirondacks or the seaside, which-
ever may be most pleasant and beneficial to you all. I
beg you not to use it for any purpose other than this
change — which I think will do you all good. I only wish
I could go with you, but there seems to be no chance of
my coming over until something is definitely settled about
my continuing in Glasgow. I may go over to Ireland
about the 1st of August to visit the Duchess of St.
Albans for a week or ten days, but I shall not be able to
take any extended recreation or rest at present.

Do you see 'Harper's' with the reprint of 'Maruja'? I
will send you a copy of the English one. I will ask you in
return to send me any notices you may find of it or of
'Shore and Sedge' in the reviews or newspapers. I never
see *any* American critics. I wonder if they are any kinder
to me — those critics — than they were.

Apropos, whenever I read the New York papers or
hear from my countrymen socially, I am heartsick and
consumed with shame to observe how despicably and
shamelessly 'English' we are becoming in American
society. When I think of how much we have that is real
and true and refined and original, the thought that *we*
should ape the customs and manners and follies that the

best Englishmen are ashamed and sick for — I am lost in mortification and sorrow. Englishmen have the excuse of a climate, of a certain education and a certain conservative habit which make them what they are; we have no excuse for slavishly imitating them in everything, as I hear we do. With all the talk of international good feeling, etc., etc. — of which so much is due to Mr. Lowell's Britannia — New *England* predilections, if people like Curtis and others could see, as I do, the amused and self-satisfied contempt for these feeble Americans who are trying to ingratiate themselves by their ludicrous imitation of small things, they would change their belief and stiffen themselves into something like manhood. I really believe that the American reverence for the aristocracy and their habits is greater than it is among those to the manner born, and it is most humiliating to think that at a time when the best of England is seriously skeptical of the old and conservative, or honestly striving toward the new and democratic, American flunkeyism, in borrowed plumes, and ill-fitting cut-off clothes, swaggers into the road before it. Real Americans think it their first duty to impress Englishmen with the fact that they are still as English as they are, and ignore the fact that a hundred and fifty years of isolation and independence have made us a new and distinct people. With much that I honestly like in the English character, I cannot help seeing how great is the difference between us, and, apart from any patriotic feeling, how far we have left them behind in all things that tend to make humanity better and broader. I think this would be my belief if I were a foreigner to both nations. And yet we are always striving for the good-will of only one nation — the English!

Heaven knows how I have come to write all this to

you instead of writing more about myself and you and the children. I suppose the fact that my official position stays my pen at all times and with all others makes me pour out all this stuff on poor, unoffending, helpless Nan! Put it aside to read some day when you are a little discontented with your life *at home*, and when you think *I* am quite contented with my life here.

I hope to get some more work done this autumn, to be able to put a little money 'by.' I am fairly well, except that some of my complaints have become chronic with my age (I scarcely dare to think *how old* I am, although my white hair certainly obtrudes the fact upon me), and I regularly look for a return of my rheumatism any spring and autumn. Yet I believe I am still able to do good work; God grant I may continue so, a little longer, for the sake of you and the children.

Write me as soon as you get this. And give me all the family news. Make Frank and Wodie go with you on your 'outing.' Tell Eliza I'll write to her before her birthday.

God bless you all — always

LIMICK

PART IV
LONDON: 1885-1902

PART IV
LONDON, 1860–1862

PART IV

LONDON: 1885–1902

AT last with the new Administration came the change which he had, for so long, half anticipated, and when the following letter was written his duties as Consul had already ceased. That it found him not unprepared can be seen from the foregoing correspondence, but it was nevertheless a severe blow to him, inasmuch as it swept away that freedom from financial worry which he had known for the past eight years. Now, once more, Bret Harte, at the age of fifty, was again to be dependent on the resources of his pen for the maintenance of a family of which he was the sole support.

GLASGOW, *August 3*, 1885

MY DEAR NAN,

Since I read in the London 'Times' telegraphic news on the 18th July that a new consul was appointed to Glasgow, I have been daily and hourly expecting a telegram or letter from you. Now that I have official notice from the Department that my successor *is really appointed*, it matters little, but it would have been some satisfaction for the last two weeks to have had a line from you of explanation or sympathy. Everybody here was asking me, 'But what do *you* hear from America and what do your friends say?' I was ashamed to tell them that my friends did not seem to concern themselves much about it in any way, and I said nothing. I was so certain that some cable despatch would come from you or Dana or Watrous, that I was inclined to doubt if the news had been made public in America. Since then I have seen in the 'Sun' the full details of my removal (and not couched in the most complimentary or kindly sense), but I have no letter from any one.

It is fortunate that I have been always, to a certain extent, prepared for this change, and never, as I have written you, really believed the easy assurances of my friends that I was sure to retain my position. I was quite unprepared, however, for the excuse that I was removed for 'inattention to duty,' and this gratuitous insult galls me. I never should have blamed the present administration for removing me, but I do not think it necessary for them to anticipate criticism by reviving a wretched newspaper squib as an excuse for getting my place.

I have made no plans yet — except that I shall remain here long enough, at least, to finish some more literary work. While I am expecting my successor I shall go to visit the Duke of St. Albans in Ireland for a week or ten days in fulfilment of an old promise. When I leave Glasgow finally, I shall probably accept the Van de Veldes' invitation to their country house 'to do my work' there, and make the most I can of the English demand for my work just now. I hope to make enough to cover the loss to my income of the half-year's salary. This will bring me to the middle of October. After that — we shall see. Frank made a suggestion (that was somewhat of a presentiment) in his last letter, that I should, if I returned, 'lecture' again. It is something to consider.

In great haste, but with love to all, and anxiously expecting a letter.

LIMICK

He was, nevertheless, quick to react, and had already several projects by which he hoped to recuperate, through his literary work, the depreciation caused in his income by the cessation of his consular duties. The lecturing field, however, was not attempted again.

GLASGOW, *August* 17, 1885

MY DEAR NAN,

I got your good sympathizing letter in Ireland during my visit to the Duke of St. Albans. It relieved me greatly to hear from you, for I was much depressed in spirits, with a severe cold that continued throughout my stay, and although my friends and entertainers were as good and sweet as they always are, I had somehow lost my capacity for enjoyment. I was glad to find you still hopeful and confident; it gave me courage to go on and try to make up the palpable loss to my income of three thousand dollars a year — by extra work — perhaps by some position in which I could use my *editorial faculty*, which is a capital I have not drawn upon for years and has always seemed to me a pity to allow to remain idle. This is something to be considered. There is also the chance of lecturing here; I have not lectured since I first arrived, and I have had many invitations which I have declined hitherto.

As far as I can judge hastily, my chances, for the present at least, are better *here*. I have never stood so well in regard to the *market value* of my works in any other country as here; with all my patriotism I am forced to confess that I do not stand as high in my own country; indeed, not a few Americans are kind enough to intimate to my friends here that I am no longer a popular visitor in America and have done nothing since the days of 'The Luck of Roaring Camp' and 'The Heathen Chinee,' etc., etc., etc.; and I was told that Mr. Sargent, of California, while Minister to Germany, intimated to the Countess de Launay in Berlin that he was surprised at my German reputation, as I was completely 'played out' in America. The attitude of the press in my own country shows me very plainly that there is no personal sympathy whatever for me there, and I think — indeed, I *fear* — that, if I returned, as if to earn my bread among them once more, the value of my work would be lessened because the publishers would think I was *dependent* upon them. With the solitary exception of the 'lecture field,' which might be open to me as an American fresh from abroad (as Frank has nicely suggested), I see nothing for me to do there. But *that will always be open when I return*, and can be used as a *dernier ressort*, while the demand for my work here must be met while it is good and profitable. Summarizing my reflections thus hastily, it would seem wiser if I did not return at once. If I found it better after experience to stay here permanently, we could next consider the question *of our all living here*. For the next two months, at least, I shall quietly continue my literary work. I am afraid, however, you are wrong as to the time when my successor takes possession. By the statute he can take office *temporarily* until Congress meets, and from the action of the Department and their instructions to me, I judge that this is the case. So he may arrive at any moment.

Console yourself, my dear Nan, that with the sole (and I admit the *important*) question of income, my removal from Glasgow in no way else affects me here. None of my best and most influential friends here *care* if I am Consul or not; many of them did not at first know that I was — some do not yet know it! I can fairly say, without the least vanity, that my present position in Europe is not only independent of my consular position — but immeasurably above it. In fact, it has somewhat humorously perplexed some of my official friends in matters of etiquette and procedure, at dinners and social gatherings when I *personally* 'ranked' those officially above me, even of my own countrymen, and yet was a plain United States Consul. I know that my removal from a subordinate official position was by no means *devised* by any United States Minister, including even Mr. Lowell, who was himself a great *personal* favourite, but who unfortunately valued *his* official position more than I did *mine*.

I am sorry I could not send Eliza anything for her birthday this year. But you will comprehend that just now I must be careful of my smallest expenditure. I send you, however, the usual monthly draft for two hundred and fifty dollars. Make it go as far as you can, Nan, in case it may not be followed next month by a sum quite as large. Believe, however, that I am doing my best for you and *ours*. God bless you and the children.

Always
FRANK

P.S. In some other letter I will tell you all about Ireland. Enough that one never can understand the Irish people without first seeing them at home and under their own conditions of life. A more hopeless outlook to a political question I never saw before; nor a more utterly helpless, *unhelpable*, and weakly incorrigible *nation!* They are a race of badly brought-up children — whom one can only hope *will never grow up!* God help them; no one else can; least of all *themselves!* Yours

FRANK

It was during his stay in Ireland that Bret Harte wrote for the Duchess the following little poem. Sir Charles Dilke was at the time also a guest of the St.

Albanses at Newtown Anner, which explains the amusing reference to him in the title.

A DAMP DAY AT NEWTOWN ANNER

From the French of Sir C——s D——ke

When the skies are full of feeling
Mud, like plaster from the ceiling
Drop the loosened clouds revealing
Airy rafters shining through.
'Twixt that rifted space one catches
Sweetly inconsistent snatches
Of the eyes of Heaven — so Irish
And so very very blue!
Now in tears and now in laughter
Till you wonder what they're after.
Are they smiling for the future;
Is it sorrow for the past?
No, it simply is the manner
Of the sky at Newtown Anner
Most capricious — most delicious —
And like woman till the last.

BRET HARTE

A. S. Boyd, the well-known artist, who illustrated several of Bret Harte's works, was, with Mrs. Boyd, a faithful correspondent of his, and the following letter is the first of many delightful ones which find their place in this volume. Mr. and Mrs. Boyd became intimate friends of Bret Harte later, in London, where they both took up their residence.

LONDON
15, UPPER HAMILTON TERRACE, N.W.
October 12, 1885

MY DEAR MR. BOYD,

I found *the* portrait and your charming letter here when I arrived from the south coast last Friday. I am almost ashamed to accept this result of our pleasant *tête-à-tête* in your studio, to which you contributed so much honest and good work and I so little of anything. But I shall keep it

MR. AND MRS. A. S. BOYD

as a memento of our friendship, frame it as it deserves, and hang it where it shall be 'seen of men' and admired.

The photograph is Mrs. Boyd's, if she will kindly keep it until I can send her a better one. I am sorry I have not a happier way of assuring her that the original is at her service always, and does not forget her gentle kindnesses.

Thanks for the newspaper cutting. I need not say that there is no foundation in the story except that I was at Newstead Abbey when Mr. Miller was there, and that I met him once in Westminster Abbey. But really *this* is so much more truthful than most of the 'characteristic' stories that I suppose I ought not to complain.

Very different are the few verses in 'Luiz' which Maurice showed me yesterday, but which had been overlooked, as he will explain. They struck me as being *very graceful and kindly*. Even when one does not complain, it is always very nice and soothing to be told that one's not appreciated as one deserves.

I cannot tell when I may be in Glasgow again, but when I am there I hope to find you.

With best regards to Mrs. Boyd, believe me, always yours

BRET HARTE

Monsieur and Madame Van de Velde, to whom Bret Harte so often refers in his letters, were his closest and most devoted friends. He met them during the time he was in Glasgow, and had known them for over five years when he came to stay with them in London. Monsieur Van de Velde was the Belgian Minister Plenipotentiary to Great Britain, and his wife, who was the daughter of Count de Launay, the Italian Ambassador to Germany, was a woman of great distinction and remarkable personality. Both understood the need that Bret Harte had for friendship and congenial surroundings, and their home, as long as Monsieur Van de Velde was alive, was the refuge to which he always turned when in need of comprehension. After his departure from Glasgow, he came to London, and for some time was an inmate of their house, from which the next few letters are written.

LONDON
15, UPPER HAMILTON TERRACE, N.W.
November 16, 1885

MY DEAR ANNA,

I wrote you yesterday enclosing the draft for two hundred and fifty dollars, and write again to-day to thank you for yours of the 6th inst. which has just come, and generally to mitigate the grumbling of my last two letters. I am really delighted to hear that Dora is teaching the girls, and particularly that there is a possibility of their having a good foundation in German and French, which may be of great importance to them in the future. Music they cannot help but learn from *you*, and I have no anxiety on that score, but I am convinced that a knowledge of German and French is an equipment for life *anywhere*, and of course the most indispensable European outfit. You might get them to write me a letter in German or French — no matter how they do it at first — and I will answer. I know that the Van de Velde children would be delighted to correspond with them.

I hope Wodie will have returned from the Catskills stronger in health; I am worried about what you tell me — his blood must be much deteriorated. I wish you would see that he has some general treatment. I read the cutting you sent me from the Plainfield paper. I take it rather for what it does *not* say than for what it *says* — reticence and good taste are rare in youthful reporting, and I am glad to see that he doesn't quote or report others. Frank has already written to me about himself (he seldom tells much about the others), so that I know enough to satisfy me that he is with Barrett, with whom *I* think he should have engaged before in preference to Boucicault.

I don't think I had given a title to my Christmas story when I wrote to you about it. As you have probably seen in the 'Sun's' advertisement it is called 'Snowbound at Eagle's'; I think the idea of the story is quite unique and original, but that perhaps is all there is to it. The 'Sun' has probably bought it from the syndicate to whom I sold it here; if there is any money made out of it, at least it will *not* be made by me. It is the *worst paid* of all my performances, and has been the hardest and most continuous work I have done: — but I'll stop grumbling and go to work.

Love to you all.   Always

FRANK

The next four letters mark the closing of the year 1885. They accompany and acknowledge that little exchange of gifts that was never forgotten, and some interesting comments concerning his son's career, the stage, and his own plays.

LONDON
15, UPPER HAMILTON TERRACE, N.W.
December 9, 1885

MY DEAR NAN,

Just a line, a little money, and a hope that they will reach you before the 25th. They aren't much, altogether, but they go, dear Nan, with the fullest heart to you and *ours* for a Merry Christmas and a Happy New Year. God bless you all, and don't forget the absent but not forgetful

PAPA!

This Indenture made this ye twentie-fourth daye of Decembere in this ye yere of grace One Thousande eighte hundrede and eightie five Witnesseth that it is ye true and heartfelte wishe of Bret Harte that his son Francis King Harte may passe a righte merrie and joyous Yuletide, and that ye yeare next followinge may proven to him riche in every blessynge of healthe, happinesse and prosperitie. In Witnesse Whereof, I to this Indenture have putte my Hand and Seale.

Bret Harte

London
15, Upper Hamilton Terrace, N.W.
Christmas Day, 1885

My dear Nan,

I feel I must thank you for the Christmas box while the Christmas halo is still over it and the Christmas flavor still fresh. It arrived only last evening — Christmas Eve — about half an hour before Christmas and might have been put in my stocking! I showed it to the Van de Velde family amidst the Christmas felicitations to-day and I assure you I was very proud of it.

The glove-case must have *first* mention, not only because it was the work of my dear Tottie's hands and made for her Papa, but because it was a neat, artistic piece of work and showed the greatest progress. The painting is admirable; I only learned from your letter (which came this morning as another Christmas gift) that she made the study herself from Nature — and it adds to my conviction that she has the real artistic spirit. I hope to see something more of her work — apart from its being the embellishment of any souvenir. Can you send me one of her first sketches? The Candlestick was perfect and original; I, who have been through all the great bazaars and celebrated shops of this metropolis 'doing commis-

sions' and Christmas shopping for others, have seen
nothing I liked as well! What you call the 'ashes cup'
or paper-weight, but which in my ignorance I believed
to be a spirit lamp for cigar lighting! — was also most
beautiful and equally unique. They stand, and challenge
admiration, on the shelves of my mantel mirror in my
bedroom; the paper-knife, which is simple and elegant,
and *genuine*, exactly matches the brass furniture of my
writing-table — except that it's a better quality! I shall
have my old Bear cut as a seal on the handle.

By the way, what delicious perfume was the glove-case
scented with? It filled my bedroom with its fragrance,
and when I showed the case in the drawing-room the next
morning, everybody was struck with its penetrating
delicacy, and was anxious to know if it was something
peculiarly *American* too!

I was doubly proud of my American presents, for I had
some pretty gifts from the V. de V.'s; a charming 'map'-
case or 'hold-all' from Monsieur; a fine 'platinum and
gold' evening-dress watch-chain, like a fine thread; and
pictures from the children; and a very wonderful critique
and review scrapbook from Madame which she sent to
Berlin to have enamelled and hand-painted with my name
illumined on it and the donor's crest on one side — a very
striking affair, as quaint as old French 'marquetrie.'
They were very nice, but the American box held its own
against them all.

I have been at home all day at work. It is the usual
English Christmas weather — dull and dispiriting beyond
belief. A cold fog hides the houses opposite; it has been
necessary to keep the gas lit all day. When you read in
the books about the 'snowy Christmas' of England and
the frost and ice of the season — it's all a fraud! It is the
most disagreeable and gloomy season of the year, and as

unlike the crisp heartiness and sincerity of an American winter as you can conceive. They make it naturally a holiday of *eating* and *drinking*, and in the latter — forget themselves and their weather. The streets have the appearance of an intensified British Sabbath; whatever there is of cheer and jollity lies behind those heavy, gloomy walls, and never shines or glitters from the windows.

Every Christmas I have always given some presents to the Griswolds, and this one I gave Gerty a small 'desk' or 'secretary' and some gloves and ornaments to Dora with the usual Christmas 'hamper' of eatables and 'drinkables' for the dinner, as they are in lodgings. The first year they were here, Madame V. de V. invited them to have Christmas dinner.

They go out a good deal in society, and have many influential friends.

I find I am at the end of my page and must break off. This is not a regular letter, but a kind of 'voluntary.' God bless you all to-day and all days is the wish of one who is with you in spirit! Always, dear Nan,

FRANK

LONDON
15, UPPER HAMILTON TERRACE, N.W.
December 28, 1885

MY DEAR FRANK,

I must answer your two last letters together. I suppose that your mother, who was expecting you at Christmas, has told you that I duly received them. I acknowledged them to her in the only letter I had time at the moment to write.

I am glad you liked the clothes I sent you, for I fear it may be difficult to send you more. Through some stupidity of the steamship offices I was obliged to pay the *full* duty for new clothes upon them which did not make

the transaction a very profitable one. Unless you wish
to have my clothes altered to fit you, merely from a
touching sentiment of wearing 'Papa's things,' it would
be much more economical hereafter to send you their
value, with the duty added, and let you buy them in
America. I might get some obliging passenger to adopt
them as part of his luggage, but it would be difficult to
get obliging people of the proper size to make the suppo-
sition tenable. Seriously, except in the question of cheapness I find that you can get better fitting clothes in America and of equally good material. So the best American
tourists tell me, and I have long had my suspicions that
the American craze for English clothing was only a part
of our detestable snobbishness. I know that Poole is a
fraud, and I believe there are a dozen good tailors in New
York that surpass any here. The only difference is that
Americans usually pay their tailors promptly, and Englishmen *don't* — and often (as with Poole) borrow money
from them. Which isn't conducive to economy or a good
fit.

I am glad you are with Barrett, for in spite of your
intimacy with Boucicault, I think you will get along better with Barrett permanently. I dare say it *is* hard to be
condemned to unimportant rôles and small pay. But
there are compensations — and opportunities.

For instance: I am told that the great character success of Irving's late spectacular 'Faust' is not his own
acting as 'Mephistopheles' nor Conway's 'Faust' (can
you think of it!), but is a certain Mr. Alexander's 'Valentine,' who has only a few weak lines to *speak*, but who
acts so genuinely good, that I am told (for I have not yet
seen the play) that the audience gave him the most sincere and unexpected applause — completely astounding
Irving, and taking the whole scene (the duel scene) away

from him and 'Faust.' I don't like the play; it's an outrageous tergiversation of a great poet's work by a man who is not a poet; it's an attempt to put a modern, domestic, and melodramatic interest in a poem that is purely philosophical and imaginative, but I was intensely amused that after all that had been done really for Mr. Irving and the superior members of his company, and according to the sacred canons of the Lyceum stage, with scenery and costumes that cost extravagantly, the one solitary legitimate success of the performance should come from an accident of histrionic ability in a subordinate actor!

I submitted the *scenario* or part of the adaptation of 'The Luck' which I spoke of to you to Toole as I promised, and he was good enough to praise it and accept it. *But*, after thinking it over and beginning the serious work of it, I found it would be too complete and violent a change from what the public had always accepted as the *sentiment* of the story — its serious and pathetic interest. Unfortunately, the people who liked 'The Luck' as a story would be the ones who would go to see it as a play — and I know would be disappointed, even if it were successful as a farce, with a dash of seriousness. As I wrote, I found that either the pathetic or the farcical interest must be dominant; that I could not blend them, and that either Toole or the audience must be disappointed. I finally admitted this to Toole, who understood it, and I finally agreed with him to attempt a purely original comic piece — based upon some one of my Californian characters that would fit Toole, but with a perfectly new situation and plot.

I intend to do it, as I really believe from a study of Toole's quality that he could embody a character like Tennessee's Partner — in a different setting or with the humour more strongly accented. This is all he wants, if the situation is a little more fresh and novel than the old farces he plays. I have seen him, in an old English farce, play *exactly* the character of the 'Old Man' in my story of 'How Santa Claus Came to Simpson's Bar,' and I know what he can do. As soon as I get rid of the work I have on hand, I shall go at the play. There is no hurry. Whenever I can get something good, he will produce it. Meantime, you need not say anything about it. 'The Luck' — that long-travailing infant — must postpone its birth — if indeed its existence is at all required. At times I doubt it.

Toole asks after you always with kindly and sincere interest. I wish you could give me some particulars of the rôles you are playing — however unimportant they may seem to you.

I am still with the V. de V.'s, at No. 15, Upper Hamilton Terrace, and shall remain as long as I have work to do in London. I spent Christmas very quietly — and — I believe — did not work at all on that day! The weather, which was hideously gloomy — as only England can be at Christmas-time — put all merriment and joyousness out of the question. One only attempts to eat and drink on that day — but always with the sense of being underground, for all that the skies participate. It is the British Sabbath decorated with holly and ponderous with plum pudding.

Maurice often talks of you and would be transported with a letter. Write to him sometimes instead of Madame V. de V. if you can't compass both letters. I suppose she tells you all the other gossip of the household.

I find I have written a long letter — probably not touching any topic I intended to write you about or that would interest you. I meant well, however!

Be a good boy, old fellow, and at this season, thank God

particularly for the one purely accidental blessing that you have — youth! With lots of love, and fond prophecies for the New Year for you, my dear boy, always your loving father

B. H.

LONDON
15, UPPER HAMILTON TERRACE, N.W.
January 1, 1886

DEAR MR. WATT,

I hoped to wish you a Happy New Year under better auspices for your happiness, but I send a line to assure you of my sympathy with your boy's illness, to wish for a speedy recovery, and to beg you not to concern yourself at present with any idea that any business of mine is suffering from your preoccupation. I will promptly inform you when there is anything that requires your attention especially.

Yours very truly
BRET HARTE

LONDON
15, UPPER HAMILTON TERRACE, N.W.
January 17, 1886

MY DEAR NAN,

Although the enclosed draft for two hundred and fifty dollars leaves here two days later than the last, I hope it will reach you before the 1st February. I have nothing from you since the 14th December (the Christmas letter), and that I have answered besides writing to the children. You ask me if I received yours of the 30th October and November 10th. I *most generally* keep all your letters, and *invariably keep them until I acknowledge* their receipt or answer them, so I cannot positively say I have received yours of the 30th October unless I have acknowledged it. I have one of the 6th November, but none of the

10th. I have not heard from poor Eliza for many months.
I expected, however, you would remember her in some
little offering from me at Christmas-tide. Did I suggest
it? I meant to, and would have written to her in the New
Year had I heard from her. She must not wait for letters
from me; my pen, nowadays, soon gets weary, and when
my actual work is done, I cannot bear to take it up again
for pleasure — and with difficulty even for duty. Tell
Wodie I thank him for the 'Town Topics,' which is coming
to me regularly. I like it as well as I can like any penny
society journal, but it strikes me as being more *refined* and
quiet than most of them. I hope this venture will be a
successful one, and that he will share in its success.

I have been using my brief holiday with trying to make
some verses like my earlier poems. I do not quite know
whether, after these years, the gentle muse will again
visit me, for I fear I have let her know that she is too
expensive and exacting a flame for my old age, and that
prose is a better housekeeper and more profitable. I have,
however, made some negotiations with the 'Illustrated
London News' for any occasional poems I might write,
and which would be prettily illustrated — and if I can suc-
cessfully move the muse again it might pay me — but
never as well as prose. I only thought of it as a *change* to
my monotonous romances. Perhaps it is very *little change*,
for my poetry, I fear, is coming from the same spring as
my prose, only the tap is nearer the fountain — and
filtered.

Have you seen Mr. Watrous since his return? He was
to write to me — but I have not heard from him. Frank
has lately written to Madame Van de Velde (so she tells
me), so that I know he is well and at work. I am glad he
is with Barrett.

As soon as I get your next letter I will write again, and

try to formulate some ideas I have of our prospects for the coming spring and summer. God bless you all.

With kisses for the girls, always, dear Nan, yours

FRANK

The next few letters are principally with his plans for play-writing, to which he always looked for a rest from his usual work, but which, with the exception of 'Sue,' was never to be the financial success for which he hoped.

LONDON
15, UPPER HAMILTON TERRACE, N.W.
February 15, 1886

MY DEAR NAN,

I suppose you were startled at receiving a large 'panel' photograph of me without a line of inscription. So I hasten to explain to you that under the post-office rules here, a single word of *writing* on the back or the face of the photograph would have debarred me from sending it in that neat 'professional' way with the photographer's original box-like envelope, and it would have cost several times its value as a *letter*. You must try to imagine your name written on it, dear Nan, with a benediction — which I fear, however, is not at all suggested in the expressionless face of the photo. However, it is considered very fine by the great Court photographers, who made it in a leisure moment when they were not photographing the numerous Royal Family, Prime Ministers, or latest 'Society beauty.' It's younger-looking than I am, but people think the attitude and figure less affected than the usual photographs. It was done at the request of Harper and Brothers of New York, who want it for engraving — and I sent you the one they selected. There are two or three others from which I will select another hereafter. The Harpers paid for the original 'sitting.'

I have Ethel's group of herself and 'Worldly' and wrote her to-day a little note thanking her for it. But I would like to have a *larger* picture of her alone, and also one of Jessamy. But what I want more than this is a good coloured picture of *yourself* — to take the place of the one you sent me (the one taken with Frank) which was stolen from my room in Glasgow a few weeks after I received it. Make a special occasion of it, and go to some good photographer and have taken one of *yourself*, one of *Jessamy*, one of *Ethel*, and one of *Wodie*. I have already a good one of Frank — at the same time, if he will send me another, taken by some of those photographers who 'do' the profession and to whom he has frequent access, I shall be delighted. I will send you the money for it.

I have answered Jessamy's letter and shall write to Wodie by this post. I shall try to write to Frank — but if I have not time, tell him that the Consul at Liverpool promised to forward his clothing and that I have sent it to Liverpool, but have not yet received his intimation when and by whom it has been or will be sent. He promised to write me the particulars when he had the chance to 'ship' it off. I have yours of the 3d February this morning; yours of the 21st January came about ten days ago, and I have Tottie's, Ethel's, and Frank's letters. I believe I have acknowledged them all.

I quite agree with you that Frank is *morally* better off with Barrett than Boucicault, although I perfectly understand his fascination with the latter, who is far cleverer than Barrett. The little *repression* Frank gets from Barrett's 'vastly genteel' manner and respectable snobbishness will not hurt him, and F. is clever enough not to *require* the contact of Boucicault's brightness. I am very glad Frank has abandoned the stimulants which his digestion could not stand, and is getting quite out of the atmos-

phere or inclination to artificial excitement, which I think
he would be exposed to more with Boucicault than Barrett.

You tell me I wrote that I intended 'to *formulate* some
ideas for the spring' — Good Heavens! Did I ever write
such a gorgeous sentence! — in another letter. What I
was trying to say was that I had some vague plans I hoped
to put into shape to lay before you soon. But this was a
good deal dependent upon the passage of the copyright
bill, which would enable me to hold *in America* some of
the advantages I have *here*. That bill hangs fire, I see —
indeed, I fear if it will ever pass. Another contingency —
which would include your coming over here with the
family — is my connection with a magazine. But here
again, the political excitement, the depression of business,
and last of all the rioting of those poor starving devils of
unemployed labourers, stops for the present any negotiations of that kind. '*Punch*' and the 'Illustrated News'
have both talked with me about contributions; I see my
way to a reasonable certainty of always *disposing of my
work* here — but as yet I don't see the *fixed salaried position.* Hence I can't 'formulate' (I like that word!) just
yet. It would cost too much to live in England — although we could live *better* for the same sum — unless one
was *secured*. But we might live in Germany.

For once I have seen the English upper classes shaken
in their firm belief in their own superiority and eternal
power. I have seen them brought face to face, though
through plate-glass windows, with the howling, starving
mob they and their fathers have trodden upon and de-
spised for all these years, and they have grown pale, as
the plate glass shattered around them. For once their
sacred police could do nothing! For once they saw these
terribly famished creatures, whom they had patronized
in workhouses, petted in hospitals, and kept at a dis-

tance generally with good-humoured tolerance, absolutely breaking their bounds and clamouring for Heaven knows what! You will read all these accounts in the papers — but you will never understand it until you see these people as I have seen them — of both classes! — and learn how hopeless is the ditch that has been dug between them by centuries of class government. God knows whose bodies will fill this ditch that better things may walk over! If the poor devils themselves — I don't think they care much. As one of their speakers said — a kind of English Danton — 'I suppose they will kill us — but it's better than sheer starving.'

I have nothing from America except the family letters. W. hasn't written to me for a long time. Hay neither. Do you ever hear of him or Clarence King? Or Musgrave?

I enclose the draft for two hundred and fifty dollars. God bless you all!

FRANK

P.S. I forgot to tell you how marvellously like *you* Ethel's picture is — but is not this the general criticism at home? and so common a remark to your ears that you did not think it of interest enough to tell me. Or were you waiting for me to discover the extraordinary likeness? I detect the resemblance even in the figure and attitude.

BOURNEMOUTH, May 15, 1886

MY DEAR NAN,

I had been so run down by worry and work this winter that I was obliged to come down here in the hope of driving away my persistent headaches and being strengthened by the salt air. I have been here two weeks and am already sleeping and eating better, though my return to work — even writing a long letter — brings back the old symptoms. I expect to be here a week longer, although I would require at least a month of this Channel air to blow out of my wretched carcase the accretion and deposits of last winter's work and confinement. This is, unfortunately, an expensive watering-place — and, as you nicely suggest, I have an expensive predilection — so I cannot afford to stay here long. The cheaper places are farther from London, and my ideal of a French fishing village, or a quiet Dutch seaport, are impossible with my working connections with London.

I have a very sad but very grateful letter from Eliza, thanking me for the money I sent her. I am myself very thankful that I was able by my means to help her — though I still don't quite understand from her letter *how* I have helped her. She seems to be with Fred and yet in Plainfield, and she says nothing of the home — or of you and the children who occupied it with her. Your letter of the 15th April does not tell me whether you are leaving her, or, if so, when.

I shall only speak of that letter, Nan, as something you have written hurriedly, under a strong misconstruction of the meaning of my few words of caution to you for your own sake and that of the children. I have never asked you for an account of your stewardship; I have only tried to make you understand, ever since I have been away from you, that my income, though better than in America, was not permanent, and that consequently it could not indicate what we could afford to spend. I think you will remember that I only spoke of it seriously after I had lost the fixed income I had from the Consulate. You quite frighten me, however, when you tell me that during the first three years of my absence the income of one hundred and fifty dollars a month 'did not cover the expenses of your living.' If I had not been *promoted to a larger salary*,

I tremble to think what would be your condition now. I would rather have you generous and uncalculating than selfish and exact, as you well know, and I do not question your bounty or necessary charities, but I only spoke to warn you of the possibility when there was not enough to divide. And now let this talk pass, Nan; there is no one but yourself to whom I should, could, or *would* trust these matters, and whether you like it or not, you must continue to act for yourself and the children and me equally as steward of what I gain in this world. And you must not be angry nor hurt when I venture to hint that the income is *uncertain*. It is the least I can do as the one who creates it.

I hope Frank has received the play I sent him. I have lately made another venture *in collaboration*, this time with a well-known English dramatist, but I don't know yet what success will attend our efforts. It is still a secret, and I hope you will not repeat even this much to any one. God bless you all.

FRANK

P.S. I enclose draft for two hundred and fifty dollars which I have just passed for London.

LONDON
15, UPPER HAMILTON TERRACE, N.W.
July 15, 1886

MY DEAR NAN,

Since I received yours of the 23d June, I have been greatly worried about your health. Madame Van de Velde tells me that Frank has written to her from Cairo (where you were to go — or *said* you were going in a previous letter), but does not speak of your illness, which he would be likely to do if you were worse. I am hoping, therefore, in the absence of direct news, that you are bet-

ter, and that the change is doing you good. But I hope
you will take more care of yourself than you evidently
do, and think of nothing at present but getting well. I
am not alarmed for your actual physical danger, but,
knowing as I do how large a factor your nerves are in your
well-being, and how they react on your general health, I
do hope you will try to *rest* this summer — and 'don't
worrit.' If the sea air still affects you badly as it did formerly (and it is a pity, for it is such a sedative and restorer
to most people), I wish you would try the mountains.
When I *do* see you again, I want to find you looking as
well as you did in your photograph, or as well as Watrous
declared you were looking. *Please* send me another photograph, not only to take the place of the one that was
stolen from my rooms in Glasgow — but to let me see
that you are better. And 'don't worrit' — especially
about me. I am trying very hard to finish a little two-act
farce for Toole (he has read the first act and likes it), and
I hope to do it before I leave London for the country,
where I must write *two stories* to make up my year's income. For unfortunately this play-writing is the one
thing yet that doesn't pay — more than that, it prevents
me from writing that which *does* pay. But there is always
the hope that it *will* pay, and give me that little rest from
other creative work which I need. People are kind enough
to say now that I am writing as well and even better than
in the heyday of my youth and reputation — and Heaven
knows! I want them still to believe it. But it is hard to
always write in *unity* with one's self!

Apropos, John Hay wrote me a charming letter saying
he thought from my last stories I was only now in the real
maturity of my powers. Heaven send it may last! I have
little else to live for now but to leave a name, and I hope
a little something more tangible to you and the children,

and I only ask for health and strength to do that. Everything else will come.

I am glad to hear what you say of Wodie; I still think he might find time to write to me, and tell his father frankly all his hopes and prospects. I have had only the one copy of his paper. I will gladly subscribe to it, if he will let me order it from the office.

Tell the girls that Papa would write, but he has been *so* busy, and that must not keep them from writing.

I cannot understand what you tell me of Eliza. I do not see what any of her family could say to you that was unpleasant or why they should have any other feeling but gratitude toward you and yours. And I do not see why you should tolerate it for one instant. I am sorry, very sorry, for Eliza and her troubles, and even for the man who has been the cause of them, but I do not see why *you* should suffer for them — and I beg you, hereafter, to order your life without reference to her family, or any claims they may think they have upon you. What I can do for Eliza I will do as I have done gladly, but your duty is to your children and yourself first of all.

I am a little better than when I wrote last, but I am waiting until I go to the country to get the change and strength I need to write.

God bless you all, with love from

FRANK

The next few letters are dated already in the autumn of 1886. Bret Harte still plans a visit to America, the accomplishment of which, alas, seemed only to be possible as the reward of work always remaining to be done. This time, however, it would be only a visit, for Bret Harte fully realized that he could no longer earn in his own country what he was able to obtain abroad.

LONDON
15, UPPER HAMILTON TERRACE, N.W.
October 16, 1886

MY DEAR NAN,

I have nothing from you later than the 6th of September, and now Jessamy's letter, which I received only yesterday, was dated the 17th September.

I returned to London on the 13th after having been ten weeks in the country. As I wrote to you, all but the few last days of that vacation were spent in work, but I must have been kept up and invigorated by the fresh air and simple life of the country during that time, since I find London on my return so depressing and so unbearable. I may be obliged to go away again for a few days to the seaside while I am arranging proofs for my new volume.

I have heard nothing more from Toole about my play: it is very evident, however, that it must go over for this season. It is a great disappointment, and I beg you not to be discouraged if you will be called upon to share that disappointment with me — for it will *delay my leaving for America!* I cannot go now until I have done some more work and made some more money. It may not be until Christmas — it may not be until early spring. But it cannot be later — of that I am at least certain.

It is simply a question of *money*, and I scarcely dare to confess to you how, as I grow older, and my best days are behind me, *that* assumes a paramount importance. I could not, and *would not under any circumstances*, again go through what I did in New York the last two years and particularly the last winter I passed there. And from all that I *have* experienced there, from all that I hear now from there, there is not the least chance of my doing any better now. I am paid in America less than half what I get here, and while I am there I should lose *all* that I am able to get here. If I could even have the three thousand dollars a year which I send you now, assured to me, I should not hesitate.

Our old friend Dana of the 'Sun' was here in England a few weeks ago, and, on the invitation of my host, came down to the country and spent two days with me. But even he offered me no encouragement to return.

My visit, therefore, to you must be first *earned* here, and I must have a little money, *over and above my actual expenses while there*, in my pocket, when I come. I presume that is only a question of time now, but I must make the most of my opportunities while I can. Just now in England there is no one who can fill a certain want as I can — or as the English publishers *think* I can. I dread, by my absence at the exact moment they might want me, to have them find out that they *could* do without me. I would like to *fill* the market for a few months, by work ahead, and then take that opportunity to make my visit — and return before they know I am gone. If I lose the hold I have upon them here, Heaven knows what would support me. America alone would *not!*

I want you to think over these things when you are getting disappointed and discouraged, though I know you count on them as closely as I do. I have put early spring as my limit; if I dare not leave then, you must come over here, and I must make a home for you as best I can in England or Germany. You must look at *that* contingency with the rest.

I enclose the draft. God bless you all; I will try to write a few lines to Tottie. Always

FRANK

LONDON
15, UPPER HAMILTON TERRACE, N.W.
November 16, 1886

MY DEAR NAN,

I am afraid I can send only a few lines with the draft to-day. I have received an order for *another* novel for the 'Illustrated London News' — of nearly double the length of the Christmas story — and I am already hard at work on it. It must be ready by the 1st January — that is my extreme limit. Of course, I am trying to finish it much before that time, and naturally *before* Christmas.

I write this, knowing that you will not be able to look at this *possibility* of delay beyond Christmas, in anything but the light of another disappointment, but I wish, my dear Nan, you could see it as *I* do. Before accepting the offer, I looked at it in every light, and I came to the conclusion that I ought not, on your account and the children's, lose the opportunity of securing them a few more months' income, merely to gratify myself by making my coming at Christmas a *certainty*. I may still finish the story in time to do it.

I had a foolish idea, which I quickly abandoned, of beginning the story here and taking it with me to finish in America. But I know my own weakness too well and remembered my old attempts to finish a story when I was on my lecturing tour. I had either to give up the story, or do it at once.

I did not expect this offer — following so quickly on the heels of the other — and from the same people. But I have a very good agent here, who looks after my interest, and to whom I pay a percentage, and who relieves me from all the horrible torments of being obliged to offer my manuscripts personally to publishers, as I used to do in America. It takes away half the pains of authorship. I generally know before I trust pen to paper that my work will be disposed of and the amount it will bring. You can imagine how I dread to lose this great relief — and the terror with which I look upon the prospect of heavily going the rounds of New York publishers with my manuscripts in hand. When I have finished this work, I shall have earned two months' holiday when I need not think of publishers and work.

Forgive my taking so much space with my business, solely. I am afraid I am thinking of nothing else — but I have some excuse, as this affects *you*. Cheer up, Nan, and if you are disappointed again — think it is because I am working hard for you and yours. Tell Wodie I will answer his letter soon. I shall try to write to you next Sunday. God bless you all, dear Nan. Always

FRANK

There is a touch of the old loneliness that seems to have crept into the tender and pathetic letter to his wife accompanying the little Christmas offerings which closes his correspondence for 1886.

LONDON
15, UPPER HAMILTON TERRACE, N.W.
December 14, 1886

MY DEAR NAN,

This is my last day of grace to send you *anything* — even these few inefficient lines — that will be sure to reach you by Christmas! It must be a short note, for I have lost three whole days through a cold and neuralgic toothache, and I must make up the time taken from that promised work — which for three weeks yet claims my time. So I hurriedly enclose the usual draft, and an additional one hundred dollars for Christmas. I beg you will keep at least half the sum and buy yourself a present from

me — such a one as I should send you from London if I
could find the means of getting it to you. I have sent
Liza a few lines and a draft for fifty dollars. If I do not
find time to write to Frank in a day or two, explain to him
that it would be too *expensive,* if *not impossible,* to send
him the things he wants *from England.* I will try to send
him the money. Select some little thing for Wodie from
me, and tell him I will write him soon.

God bless you all, dear Nan! and give you a happy
Christmas even without Papa, who tries to make himself feel grateful that even his disappointment is the means
of giving a little more material comfort and security to
them he loves so well, and with whom he will be in spirit
on Christmas Day. Cheer up, Nan, on that day, and
believe still in

FRANK

The next three letters representing Bret Harte's correspondence for the first four months of 1887 are not very
hopeful. His constant ill-health and the strain of perpetual and ever-increasing work, together with his worries
and the uncertainty of the future were making him lose
faith, at moments of depression, in his energy to work,
and account for the pessimistic note which finds its way,
more and more frequently, into his letters to his wife.

LONDON
15, UPPER HAMILTON TERRACE, N.W.
January 15, 1887

MY DEAR NAN,

First let me thank you all for those dear Christmas
gifts, which arrived here only a day or two late. But as I
had received your letter about them, it only lent a pleasant anticipation to the delay. They were all charming.
... If I dared to look into the mouth of the 'gift horse,'

I should confess I was a little disappointed that only two of the photographic frames are filled. I *did hope* for a good picture of *you* and *one* of Wodie. Tottie's and Ethel's pictures are very fair, but I *know* they might be better, and I do hope you will make a point of sending me a *complete* set of your photographs as soon as you get this. I have a fair one of Frank, but, as I told you before, I think the only picture I have of you — the one taken with him — disappeared from the mantelpiece of my sitting-room at Glasgow one week when I was about in London and has never been heard from since.

I had a nice Christmas letter from my sister Maggie, enclosing a photograph of her daughter *Maud* — a pretty likeness of Maggie, at her youngest and best — and another photo of her from 'Ben.' Her letter, which was full of news to me, was charming, but made me realize that I was frightfully old. Think of Maggie being a grandmother — frequently — and talking to me of Floy's *seven* years of wifehood. It was a terrible revelation to me — who am inclined to let the years go by with idiotic complacency! I don't know but it is worse to be old without feeling it than to feel it without being it.

I feel it particularly *just now*, for I fear I have lost my energy. My story is dragging frightfully on my hands — it is only a little more than *half done;* and I am beginning to be worried by Harper's in New York cabling here for greater despatch. My illness about Christmas-time threw me back, and it is doubtful now if I can finish before a month's time. My reputation is too much at stake for me to slur my work, or give any sign of the haste that pursues me, so I am obliged to write slowly. I say *slowly* — but you must remember, even then, that I am writing nearly a thousand words a day (Sundays included), a thing I never did until this last year. The story (you can begin to read it in 'Harper's Weekly') is on new ground and has an original idea as its foundation which consequently gives me more trouble and anxiety.

I would not bother you with all this, but it concerns us both in its effect upon my coming — or rather the time of my coming — for, as I promised you, I shall come to you or you to me during the spring; that promise I shall keep, despite everything.

I have your letters of July 4th and, a few days ago, a very kind one from Eliza. If my answers must be short, it is because my pen is weary after my day's work. I send you your draft for two hundred and fifty dollars — enclosed. Tell the children they must wait until I am less hurried for a letter from me.

It was quite a Christmas gift to me to hear that Wodie has a chance to do something in the 'World.' Heaven grant that it may be a permanency! God bless you all, and write to me regularly. Always

FRANK

NEWLYN'S, ROYAL EXETER HOTEL
BOURNEMOUTH, *April 2*, 1887

MY DEAR NAN,

Just a line from the seaside, where I am finishing the last pages of the 'Crusade.' I was relieved to get yours of the 18th soon after yours of the 4th, and to find you were at Plainfield with Tottie. I had begun to be anxious about her and yourself, and I hope you are both recuperating in the country air. I also am simply overworked, have been at last driven to make this change, but, as is often the case at the seaside and *after* a long strain of mental and physical work, I do not find myself getting as strong as I expected. In the case of yourself and Jessamy, I do hope you will have picked up more decidedly — one gets over physical weakness quicker than nervous depression. I believe you will be wise enough not to hurry back to town while the weather is treacherous and uncertain; I have a very vivid and unpleasant recollection of an American spring.

I shall stay here after my work is done, until I am a little stronger, reading proofs, and getting up the outlines of a little story I have engaged to do for the great Parisian art journal — 'Lettres et Arts'! — the finest and most expensive pictorial magazine in the world! Each copy costs about seven hundred dollars! My story — a small affair of six thousand words — will be published in French before it ever appears in English.

I have been wondering whether it would not be better to bring you and the children *over here* (for a trip to Switzerland) this early summer — instead of coming over myself to America. It is, of course, only a question of *your* choice, and the relative cost I don't think would be greater. *I* would, of course, prefer to come *home* — but the other plan would enable me to keep my hold on the publishers here a little longer. But there is still time to settle all that. . . . I did think I could get away before the end of May, so that whatever we did would be for the *summer!* I will write again when I send you the draft, on the 15th, and tell you what I think of it.

I am trusting to hear that Tottie and you have greatly benefited by the change to Plainfield. Ask Wodie to write me again; I know I owe him a letter — but I have had so little time to write. With love to all the others and yourself, always

FRANK

NEWLYN'S, ROYAL EXETER HOTEL
BOURNEMOUTH, *April* 17, 1887

MY DEAR NAN,

I send you the draft to-day from Bournemouth, although I shall not have any news for you until I return to London next week. I am getting a little better, and have been lingering here in the hope of more decided improvement than I have yet experienced. I was very much below par when I came — more than I imagined; and as I grow older I fear I recuperate less and less quickly.

Apart from your letters and those of the children, the tidings I get from America are seldom promising, hopeful, or calculated to make me anticipate much pleasure from anything there — out of my own family. I am either written to about old obligations or indeed to grant favours to strangers, or informed that my literary work is of no value intrinsically and commercially there, anyway. . . . I can readily believe that I am not as popular as formerly — but I cannot think the change is so great.

I will write as soon as I get back to London and have time to make my calculations for next month. Until then, dear Nan, with love to all, always

FRANK

The following is Bret Harte's charming congratulation to his friend Boyd on the birth of his son Stuart, who is frequently mentioned in his letters to them.

LONDON
15, UPPER HAMILTON TERRACE, N.W.
June 9, 1887

DEAR MR. BOYD,

I hasten to congratulate you and your wife, while there is yet time, and before the artful stranger, introduced into your peaceful home, shall have revealed himself in all the plenitude of his despotic power! When you two find yourselves rotating on his powerful axis; when this gentle and ineffable tyrant pinions you both in the feeble clutch of his fat and ineffectual fingers, and 'crows' over you in your utter helplessness, then I'll be happy to hear from you again! Meantime, I extend my heartfelt sympathy and compliments to Madame.

Your letter reminded me that I should have acknowledged your friend's charming book before this, and it is too worthy of careful praise for me to hurriedly commend it at the end of this scrawl. I can only say that what I have yet had time to read of it, has touched me very genuinely with its grace, true poetic feeling, and distinctness of individuality and atmosphere. I have not much belief in the efficacy of criticism, but I wish I knew some good critic who could get the ear of the public with a translation of the pleasure which the perusal of Mr. Canton's book must give him.

Yours always
BRET HARTE

LONDON
15, UPPER HAMILTON TERRACE, N.W.
July 15, 1887

MY DEAR NAN,

I have been daily looking for a reply to my last, but I conclude to send the draft for this month without further delay and write again as soon as I hear from you.

The 'Jubilee' craze has disorganized everything and everybody and rendered it almost impossible for me to secure my contracts for the year, and settle my work ahead so that I could leave here with safety for the summer. If I had imagined any such difficulty, or have known what I now know — I should have unhesitatingly decided upon your *coming here*, in spite of the fact that the Jubilee has spoiled everything for strangers in the way of *real* sight-seeing and the enjoyment of all that is characteristic in England. You would have found almost as many foreigners as English people in London and have met — as I have met — all New York and Boston on the London streets. Mrs. Sherwood, Mrs. Hitchcock, Mrs. Courtlandt Palmer (you remember her in New London the summer we spent there!) and Mr. and Mrs. Dana. Dana has dined here — at the Van de Veldes' — several times and Mrs. Sherwood has been calling, so that with the Rogerses and Osgood this quiet foreign household has become quite an American ranch. This would be newer and fresher to *me* than to you, of course, but it doesn't compensate for my lost 'outing' and the upsetting of all business, and the fact that this wretched Jubilee has put back my work nearly two months.

Tell Frank that I have tried hard to see Abbey without actually running him down, and going to see him ostensibly on his (Frank's) business. Experience has taught me that theatrical managers — especially some American ones — are apt to be very uncivil and ungracious if they think you are dependent upon their kindness — and the reverse; and I don't believe I would have helped Frank's suit by showing my or *his* anxiety. I have gone regularly when I have expected to meet Mr. A., and have asked some theatrical people to bring us naturally together. I have confidentially asked Jules's assistance, but as yet I haven't had the opportunity I wanted — and which I believe might help Frank.

I wish Frank could be made to believe that he has done very well for one who has yet to really 'win his spurs' before the public, and that there are lots of young fellows here who would have been glad to have graduated as he has, under such men as Boucicault, Barrett, and Booth — and have had them for personal friends! Everybody here

thinks him intensely lucky. You may tell him that in one
of my essays on his behalf I met Mrs. Boucicault (No. 1),
and she spoke very highly of him (Frank) as a friend, but
did not seem to have ever seen him act.

Waiting your letter, dear Nan, when I will write again,
always

Frank

Since the early California days, Bret Harte had not
worked so hard as he was now obliged to do in order to
meet his contracts and, in the new state of things, make up
the deficiency of his income. The next letter gives a good
description of an old country seat in England, and certain
aspects of its life.

Buckenham Hall
Mundford, Norfolk
September 15, 1887

My dear Nan,

I got your pretty birthday gift soon after I arrived here.
The views of the hotel and lake were very charming, and
very comforting to me, as they give me some idea of the
place where you and the children were enjoying yourselves, but I think I would have preferred those promised
photographs of *yourselves*. You know I have no picture of
you now, since the singular disappearance of the photo
you sent me in Scotland, during my absence. I also want
to see Jessamy as 'grown up' — so as not to be *too much
surprised*, when I see her in the flesh again.

It will be rather monotonous for you to hear that *my*
vacation was spent in the same unrestful way that it was
last year, in Staffordshire. I came here a month ago to
work. Since then I have written twenty-nine thousand
words, or nearly one thousand words a day — to have my
Christmas story for the 'Illustrated London News' fin-

ished in season. It will weary you to hear me repeat, as I did last year, that I will never do it again! But I *did* do it — going out a little in the morning before I began my work, and in the afternoon, after it was finished — but making no excursion and giving myself no holiday. My writing-room overlooked a beautiful park through a large open window and over a stone balcony — and this was my only extended view of the country. The house itself, one of the old Norfolk country seats, was nearly as large as your hotel. The Van de Veldes, who, with their servants, number eighteen, were quite lost in this great English country house which, you can tell Frank, is much larger than Oakham Park. The length of the library and drawing-room, communicating, is one hundred and twenty-four feet; it is quite a walk from the central hall through one of the wings to the stables, whose courtyard would comfortably enclose Eliza's old country house at Morristown. This estate and the adjoining one five miles away belong to one man — a Member of Parliament — whose income is over five hundred thousand dollars a year. Near at hand is Lynnfield Park, belonging to an old lady who has eighty thousand pounds, or four hundred thousand dollars a year to spend on it. And all these vast properties are simply kept as *sporting* estates — Norfolk is a great shooting country — where partridges and pheasants, fed and preserved like domestic fowl — are kept for a *two weeks' battue* or shooting-party of the proprietor and his friends in one month of the whole year. In plain English, about twenty square miles in the middle of this densely populated country is turned into one vast game park, where nothing is cultivated but game, where the birds are so many and so tame that they have to be driven away from under your carriage wheels in the mud, where not a shot is allowed to be fired until a few weeks in the year when the proprietor and his friends engage in — not sport, but wholesale *butchery*. One of the keepers told me that it took a van with four horses to carry the game away after one of these battues. All this wild extravagance and waste — for the delectation of a *few* — is a story repeated in most of the English counties.

I am an earnest Republican — and I think a *just* one; but I can understand how a man feels when he is a Communist and a Socialist — and what makes him one! I like these people very well — but Heaven help them when the day of reckoning comes!

I have in my Christmas story touched lightly upon English country life — putting the last chapter here in England, and describing an old English country house. I don't know how it will be liked. Did you read the 'Crusade of the Excelsior'? I am rather disappointed in it, myself. I had really only one strong character on which to base a long story — the character of the wild filibuster. The wife of Hurlstone was a study from some of my recollections of Ada ——, in the old Californian days. But I fear they were each not sufficiently treated to make the story interesting.

Since writing you last month, I have seen and known nothing but my work. I know nothing yet of my prospects for the autumn. I enclose the usual draft. God bless you all and don't forget

FRANK

Bret Harte was feeling the struggle for financial freedom a very difficult one with his increasing years, and it was not without its effect upon his health and spirits. His warning, unfortunately, was not so often heeded, and was to be, as time went on, one of the great disappointments in his life.

LONDON
15, UPPER HAMILTON TERRACE, N.W.
November 28, 1887

MY DEAR NAN,

Your letter acknowledging the receipt of the money I cabled to you nearly a month ago only reached me a few days ago. It relieved me of great anxiety. I was fearful of some sudden illness, accident, or unexpected trouble, but never, for a moment, thought it could be on account of the Adirondack trip. I am most thankful, dear Nan, I could get it for you, and I do not regret the pleasure it paid for — of which you haven't too much! — but it seemed to me, for people in our circumstances, a rather large *extra* taken in account with the other *extras* I added to the regular draft in view of the summer trip. I thoroughly understand your explanation — but no explanation would have got the money if I hadn't had it or was able to get it — even the sacrifice of your Christmas box, which I hope may not be necessary. I don't want to use it to hang any moral upon, but sometimes when you are naturally impatient of my putting my work — the making of money to support us and keep us out of debt, and perhaps provide for an emergency like this — above *everything else*, you will admit I am not far wrong. God knows I should not be an exile here if it were not for fear of the poverty and struggling that I am getting too old to fight against, single-handed, and which would ruin even the power of work in me. I do not believe I could do the amount of actual labour I perform now if I were, on two thirds of my present income, competing in New York with other writers, at the mercy of publishers who knew of my precarious income and availed themselves of it. The half of my success here — in fact, the whole reason why I am able to keep up my prices — is because my publishers think I am independent, and as a distinguished foreigner I have a peculiar position which my agent makes the most of in dealing with them. These are the selfish considerations that are keeping me here, in spite of estranging years that are ageing *both of us*, apart from each other, and adding an unnatural loneliness to our lives. These are the things that make me ever tremulous and fearful of leaving here, at present, even on a visit home, lest I find my place occupied when I return, and the harvest gleaned by some one else. That is why, when I have promised myself that I should go over to you at some stated time, and my agent has come to me with new work, and the suggestion that I had better not let the offer pass, I have hesitated and yielded at last. All my efforts to get some independence, by means of other work — such as a play, or a position as editor, which would even allow me a leave of absence — have failed. I see nothing ahead of me but my habitual work — as long as opportunity and strength suffice.

I would not go over all this, which I have written to you from time to time since I first thought of returning to America — but it comes back to me — and I dare say it will to you — when I see that the passing years bring no decrease in our expenses or the apparent ability to reduce them. And I would not repeat it if I didn't still live in the hope that, failing to live on less, and put money by for emergencies, I still may be able to save something out of my income, by running no risks and taking every opportunity of increasing it. *I* haven't lost heart yet — if *you* have — I haven't yet given up the hope of being with you all again — and without the precariousness and anxiety that would embitter it for us all.

I haven't been very well lately, and I suppose you must put this gloomy letter to that account. I dare say it's the reaction from the work that has kept me so incessantly occupied for the last month, that I have had no time to write even a letter. I sent you a copy of 'Les Lettres et les Arts' with a story of mine, *first* published in French — and translated directly from my manuscript. It is something quite unknown, methinks, in literature. I'll write you again on the fifteenth of December. Meanwhile, give my love to the children and tell them Papa is too tired to write to them now, but will do so soon. God bless and keep you, Nan, always.

FRANK

The incident referred to below was caused by a mistake made by Mrs. Bret Harte, who administered a bottle of laudanum to her son, through a most unfortunate error. He was saved from death by noticing on the bottle the death's head indicative of poison, and was able to call in medical aid while there was still time.

LONDON
15, UPPER HAMILTON TERRACE, N.W.
December 20, 1887

MY DEAR NAN,

I read the account of Frank's accident in a Glasgow paper nearly *three* weeks before your letter came with an allusion to it. I had treated it as a gross fabrication — based upon the fact that I had heard personally nothing about it, and told every one so. I am still at a loss to understand why you kept silent about it, after it had appeared in the New York papers, as, unless it was telegraphed directly to the Glasgow papers — which is most improbable — it must have been known to you three weeks before I saw it. You may be certain that it appeared here in its most exaggerated form — of Frank's *fainting from fright* — of your own carelessness which

even kept *you* from discerning your own mistake, and of
the *twelve* hours' incessant labour to save Frank from
death. I confess, therefore, I was more alarmed and indignant when I found that *something had* happened unknown to me, than when I believed it an utter falsehood.
I had poo-poohed the whole thing, and told my doctor
that it was ridiculous from the fact alone that you were
not only excessively careful and chary of drugs, but that
you were a homœopath and never had laudanum in your
house. I had thought so little of it that I did not mention
it to you in my last letter. Of course, I am deeply thankful it was no worse; the only unpleasant suggestion left
behind is that Frank is obliged to take such sedatives as
'hips,' etc., etc. I am worried about his state of health
and his impatience of illness and discomfort which obliges
him too often to seek relief in anodynes.

I generally pay little heed to rumours from America
concerning myself or family, and I have learned by sad
experience not to look for anything kindly or truthful.
But I was a little surprised the other day to hear that some
Americans had gossiped at the hotel, and at the United
States Legation here, to the effect that you were left in
such poverty by me that you were obliged to borrow
money to keep yourself and children from want. Luckily,
one of the Englishmen present happened to be connected
with the bank here which draws on the Bank of British
North America, through which my monthly drafts to you
pass, and he expressed his surprise pretty freely, and
thought it strange that six hundred pounds a year —
which he knew was *more than the income* of even families
of officers, and even of younger sons of the nobility here
— was not enough to keep mine 'from want.' I wish you
would try to trace the origin of that story in New York.
It seems hard to exile myself here at hard work in order

that my family may live *comfortably*, and be met by such gratuitous falsehoods.

Watrous and his wife have been here two weeks on their way to the Continent. Charley and I have been discussing my affairs, and I think he understands exactly the value and importance of my *practical* position here. We have been discussing also the probability and the *possibility* of my arranging my business so that I can return *with him and his wife* to New York in the early spring — if only a visit. I'll write you again about it, when my present work is off my hands. I have had a year of very hard labour. I cannot yet say what the next may bring forth.

I enclose the usual draft. I don't want you to live meanly or stingily — but *I wish* you could put by a little something — against the next year. You do not seem to care particularly for society or the city — could you not find some little country place, where you could begin in a small house to make the nucleus of a home for us? There are cheaper places than Plainfield: are there not? And more independent homes than a boarding-house offers. Try and look about you, Nan, and write to me what you think.

God bless you all.   FRANK

P.S. I sent you fifty dollars on the 10th, which I hope came safely to hand for Christmas.

Two letters to friends, the first to Mr. Albert Rhodes, who, hearing of Bret Harte's intention of spending the winter in the South of France, sends him an introduction, the second to Edmund Clarence Stedman, who was then preparing his Library of American Literature, break the chain of his letters home.

LONDON
15, UPPER HAMILTON TERRACE, N.W.
December 25, 1887

MY DEAR RHODES,

I am surprised that an old literary man like you should be led away by a newspaper paragraph about another. But it has given me a pleasant letter from you, and has served a good purpose, even if I haven't the slightest prospect of going to the South of France — and never had any to speak of, or to be written of. I may have said in somebody's hearing that I should like to go, but if wishes made an accomplished fact, I should, at the present moment, be a millionaire — in America!

I should be delighted to see your friend Mr. McCreary, and, if I go South, should do my best to make his acquaintance. I say 'if' — such is the baleful influence of your letter, which has reawakened my desire to go, and I am thinking that, at least, it may be possible this winter for me to get as far as Paris, when we will talk it over.

What are you doing in a literary way? Have you anything in prospect as good as your book on the French? Madame V. de V. always declared it one of the finest criticisms on French life and character she had read.

I am Christmasing with the V. de V. family as usual. I gave them your polite messages, and they were all delighted to hear from you again. Madame begged me to tell you that she bears your visit in the kindest remembrance, and Monsieur was charmed. I suppose you have read the outcome of your kindly introduction to 'Les Lettres et les Arts' in the November number, as well as in 'Scribner's.' The illustrations in 'Les Lettres' were admirably done, in spite of the amusing idea of California costumes!

Wishing you a Merry Christmas, and a most prosperous New Year, believe me, always yours

BRET HARTE

LONDON
15, UPPER HAMILTON TERRACE, N.W.
January 14, 1888

MY DEAR STEDMAN,

Many thanks for your India proofs of the engraving. They were admirable; equally so is the naïve simplicity of your using a *typewriter* to ask me to *copy* out for you a whole sixty-line poem, in return!

Be thankful that I have found time to copy the enclosed. It is, at once, chaste, non-committal, and brief — and lends itself beautifully to chirographical illustration. Be satisfied with it, my dear Stedman, and believe me yours always

BRET HARTE

FATE

The sky is clouded, the rocks are bare,
The spray of the tempest is white in air;
The winds are out with the waves at play,
And I shall not tempt the sea to-day.

The trail is narrow, the wood is dim,
The panther clings to the arching limb;
And the lion's whelps are abroad at play,
And I shall not join in the chase to-day.

But the ship sailed safely over the sea,
And the hunters came from the chase in glee;
And the town that was builded upon a rock
Was swallowed up in the earthquake's shock.

BRET HARTE

Bret Harte, as one sees, had placed great hopes in the success of one of his plays, and his disappointment represented, in addition to its financial failure, the loss of a great deal of valuable work and time. The next two letters are not very cheerful in their accounts of this period of his life.

LONDON
15, UPPER HAMILTON TERRACE, N.W.
July 18, 1888

MY DEAR NAN,

Since I wrote you last, I have been having great annoyance and greater disappointment with the dramatization of 'Gabriel Conroy,' which seems to be going the way of all my dramatic ventures. The man who undertook to make all the preliminary arrangements for me — as my other literary work prevented my doing it myself — has bungled so frightfully that I fear the scheme is not only ruined for the present, but that he has got himself in the hands of some of the literary thieves that hang about the theatres and so spoiled the prospect for the future. He was a young man accustomed to do certain work for actors and managers, had that access to the coterie who surround the stage in London which I have not the time nor disposition to cultivate, and seemed to me trustworthy and competent. In the present state of literary property in novels, I had only the choice of selecting a man who would steal from me and pay me part of the profits, among others who would steal from me and pay me nothing. It would be unfair yet to say that *he* has helped to deceive me— but there is little doubt in my mind that he has been deceived. The annoyance and worry that the affair has cost me is worse than any actual loss I have yet sustained. I have just finished the last proofs of 'Cressy,' my latest story, and am trying now — in the few days of leisure left me before I begin again my mere bread-and-butter work — to learn how the matter stands and what hope, if any, remains.

I'll write you again the result. I am anxiously waiting now to hear when you are beginning your summering. God bless you all.

LIMICK

P.S. I enclose the draft for two hundred and fifty dollars.

LONDON
15, UPPER HAMILTON TERRACE, N.W.
August 15, 1888

MY DEAR NAN,

I have not been away from London myself yet. The Van de Veldes, owing to the dreadfully cold and unseasonable weather, have not yet got their country house, and the same necessity of work and of being *near my work*, which keeps me from coming to America, has kept me from going on the Continent for recreation — as everybody else does. In five years I have not crossed the Channel, and if I should return to America to-morrow, I should have seen less of Europe than most Americans who have come here for a summer trip. My two years in Germany enabled me to go to Paris and Switzerland, but I have never been to any of the baths or health resorts, although my doctor has repeatedly advised me to go. I have always felt that my one *vacation* — when I can get it — could be spent with more benefit in my own country.

I *did not* receive either Wodie's letter or 'his picture of himself' which you say he sent me. I have nothing later than yours of July 11th from Block Island.

The Watrouses are in London, but sail for New York on the 27th. It was part of my plan to sail with them, and we had even arranged to secure a stateroom for me on their ship. I suppose it was this that started the various rumours I have seen in the American and English papers that I was already in New York. It is part of the same gossip, I suppose, that I was leaving England because I was so 'greatly lionized' that I had no time to myself. This — to all who know my quiet life here — is exquisitely absurd! A half-dozen nice people — or, as they call them here, 'smart people' — have always been very polite to me. As they all happen to be 'titled' folk, it is quite enough for the average American to assume that I am a 'lion' in consequence and in fashionable society. There is no flunky anywhere so atrociously servile and mean as the average American who haunts London society. And I am sorry to say that the American *woman* is even worse than the American man. It is rare, indeed, to meet one — the most simple — who is unspoiled, or who does not 'give herself' and her country 'away' to the first title she meets.

As soon as I go into the country, I'll write you again without fail. Let me know how Frank is progressing in his play-writing. Try and have Wodie come to you out of the city. Tell Tottie and Ethel to write to me, and keep your health and strength, dear Nan, for them and your

LIMICK

That, away from the earnestness of his everyday preoccupations, Bret Harte could be a delightful correspondent, is seen from the amusing and charming letter written to Mrs. Boyd from Windsor Forest.

CRANBOURNE COURT, WINDSOR FOREST
September 20, 1888

DEAR MRS. BOYD,

Thank you so very much for the lovely flowers you sent me. What floral opulence there must be at Kilconquhar to enable you to grant so much from your abundance, and all of a kind! You ought to be, and I dare say you are, very happy in your 'flitting' from Glasgow this year, even with the Exhibition and Royalties to the fore.

I am here with my old friends the Van de Veldes for a couple of months. We are only three miles from Windsor Castle, and not half a mile from the wildest woodland, penetrated only by 'flys' from Windsor at 2/6 per hour; — where there are deer whose 'tameness' is as 'shocking to me' as the 'owls and brutes' were to that most truthful of Scotchmen, Alexander Selkirk, on his desert island. Then we have the contiguity of absent Royalty, and, moving in a kind of *pot-pourri* dust of their vanished presence, we have really nothing more to desire!

I had the honour yesterday of speaking to a man who had been in personal attendance on the Queen for fifty years. He was naturally very near the point of translation, and gave a vague impression that he did not require to be born again, but remained on earth for the benefit of American tourists. He only cost me five shillings and was cheap at the money. .   '

I send in return for your flowers two leaves of ivy from Stoke Poges, 'The Country Churchyard' of Gray's 'Elegy.' I took them from the green shoots at the base of the 'ivy-mantled tower,' now, alas, crowned with a hideous 'meeting-house' spire! I had my doubts about the 'yew tree's shade,' and am not sure that this ivy is in direct succession to what Gray saw and sang about. In fact, I am not quite certain that I got it there, or elsewhere, but it's from some equally blessed source. The poet Gray nestles with his mother, near the church that he consecrated. His monument, on an eminence beyond the churchyard, is a heavy affair in the most relentless form of British art, but is redeemed by a dozen of the noblest lines of the 'Elegy.' The whole thing looked quite new,

and I was a little disappointed; but it was a perfect day:
a few bees were humming around the tower, as if they
were chanting the 'Elegy' and were half-drunken with
its sweets.

Give my kindest regards to your husband. The V. de
V.'s all send their compliments, Maurice in particular,
who is now 'in business' with a firm of stock-brokers in
the city, and Madame V. de V., who wishes to be kindly
remembered. Always yours

Bret Harte

With the failure of his schemes for the stage, Bret Harte
found it more and more difficult to make up for his now
considerably reduced income, so that in spite of the enormous output of work and unceasing labour, he realized
that it would not be possible to carry out the plans he had
made.

15, Upper Hamilton Terrace, N.W.

November 20, 1888

My dear Nan,

. . . I was startled out of my usual patience a few weeks
ago to find an article in an American paper (twice copied)
alleging that I was a ruined spendthrift living in England
'on money I borrowed from my English friends,' and that
I would probably stay almost as long as I could borrow
money from them. To make it appear more plausible,
the article was written with an air of affected regret and
commiseration on the decadence of a once brilliant, 'over-
praised,' but now 'played-out' and 'broken-down' hack.

I was so angry that I was foolish enough to write to
Dana begging him to advise me whether to sue the newspaper proprietors, or if he could point out the outrageous
falsehoods in his own paper, the 'Sun' — which he could

do of his own knowledge — as he has seen me here, living in my almost *too*-methodical, business-like fashion, and was fully aware of my position in every respect. He has since written to me and I find a denial of the slanders in his paper of the 8th November. Perhaps you have already seen it; perhaps you have seen the poison, too, as well as the antidote.

Since I wrote you last, I have yours of 26th October, and this morning yours of the 9th. What I meant, in speaking of the effect of the Newport air upon your health primarily, was your own statement that I remembered that it made you *sleepless* and *intensely nervous* — in which the doctor agreed with you, I think. I was very much worried over your illness, and in the belief that you might require to stay at Pittsfield longer than you thought you could afford to, and in order that you should want for nothing, I sent all I could get — one hundred and fifty dollars — by cable (as you requested). The fifty dollars I sent the boys was a precious present for themselves — before I knew of your illness — to mitigate Frank's disappointment over the clothes I couldn't send him, and to help Wodie in his summer 'outing.' *He has not*, however, written to me, and except from your letter I should not know that he had received it. I read the newspaper extract of his 'correspondence' which you enclosed. He writes well enough for the *papers* (if he doesn't often give his *father* a taste of his quality) and I liked the extract you sent me — because it was simple, and without any 'attitude' — or affectation.

I am greatly pleased with Jessamy's photograph. Tell her so and say I will thank her later. Everybody here who has seen Frank says she looks like him. I *do wish* you would send me *yours*. Make a *duty* of going and having it done — if you do not find it a pleasure!

My work is waiting me and I must halt at the end of this page. I'll manage to write again before the end of the month. God bless you all.

FRANK

15, UPPER HAMILTON TERRACE, N.W.
March 19, 1889

MY DEAR NAN,

I enclose the usual draft for two hundred and fifty dollars.

I have just got your letter of March 8th. At another time I will answer it at length. I can only say now that I am grieved that you should misunderstand the object of my last letter, or believe that I do not perfectly understand that you are no more happy than I am in the position we are placed. That is the reason why I beg you to give me some reason at least to *hope* from something you are doing and the children are doing, or, better still, the practice of some trifling economy in our expenses, that this position may be changed, and that I can support myself and you and the children as well living together in America, as I am doing, in the lonely and not very happy life *I* am living here. If any of my friends speak to you of my life here, that is what they mean — at least, that is what they say to *me*. And I do not know one of them who would raise a hand to help me in America — or who is willing, even now, in the mere matter of assisting me to secure some position under the Government that would increase my income and enable me to return there — to take the least trouble in my behalf. They believe that I am doing better here than there, and would be the first to exclaim against our improvidence. And they know — as well as I do, if not *better* — that we could not afford to move, and live in London all together as a family, keeping our own house and servants in the most simple manner. It would cost us double; to say nothing of the hopeless outlook for the boys, and the still more hopeless chances for the girls.

I do not complain about my work as long as I am able to do it, but when you say you are sorry that I have no recreation or rest, you should remember that, if through an extra expense, I am unable to take even a few weeks' recreation out of London, how hopeless becomes the prospect of my making a visit for two or three months to America, to say nothing of the risks I run of losing an order, while I am away.

I have not heard from Wodie, as I suppose the poor boy has again been disappointed. God help him, and help us all.

FRANK

Although 'Cressy' had only just been published, Bret Harte was still so deeply steeped in work that he was not able to take the brief holiday of which he speaks in his next two letters to Mr. and Mrs. Boyd.

15, UPPER HAMILTON TERRACE, N.W.
April 11, 1889

DEAR MRS. BOYD,

Through one of the yellowest blights and fogs we have ever had in London, your letter and flowers burst upon me just like a ray of sunshine! The footman did not exactly say, 'The Spring — with Mrs. Boyd's compliments, Sir,' but I know that was what he meant.

How can I thank you! And are you not to be envied — I had almost written *hated* — for being where such things are possible, and not here under the flaming gas, at 11 A.M., with a chill and hopelessness of November in the air;

and this sheet of paper before you, trying to realize it! How nice and clever of your husband to bring you out of Glasgow at this season, and how lucky he is that his work can take him to such places, and allow him to revel among things that do not still have to be boiled! Perhaps it's the fog, but I feel myself turning blue and yellow with envy.

I feel it the more keenly, as I have been trying to get away for a fortnight to the seaside. A frenzied desire to go to Guernsey seizes me at this moment; if it were not so far from printers and proofs, I really believe I should start to-morrow! At any rate, tell me more about it; how far is it, in hours, from London? Is there a good hotel? Can one smoke and break the Sabbath? I have a vague idea that the boat only stops there in certain weathers, and under certain contingencies. Would you object to your husband and myself going 'devil-fishing' among the rocks, and bringing home a small one? Or does the fiend exist only in Victor Hugo's pages? Have you seen any one like 'Derrichette'?

Madame V. de V. and Maurice are in Paris. I do not know if you have heard that Sarah Bernhardt is trying to bring out a play adapted by Madame V. de V. and Mr. Bertin. Madame is there attending the rehearsals. It is a brilliant literary feather in Madame's cap.

I do not know if you have read 'Cressy,' but I send it to you, in case you have not. I think it will suit you there, for it is as far away from Glasgow in colour and atmosphere as you are now.

I hope you are getting strong again. With pleasantest remembrances to your husband, always yours

BRET HARTE

15, UPPER HAMILTON TERRACE, N.W. ~
Good Friday, April, 1889

MY DEAR BOYD,

I ought to have acknowledged, before, your full response to my lazy enquiries about the Guernsey accom-
modations. Certainly nothing could be more satisfying
than the noble, not to say, *seigneurial* aspect of the 'Old
Government House' Hotel. Life there, as per advertisement, filled with such figures in admirable tourist suits,
as are represented in the glowing picture, etched upon its
tranquil surface, the blue sea beyond (which you can't
see in the picture), and La Bruyère not far away, would
be perfect.

But how long do *you* expect to stay there? You rightly
guess that the Bank Holiday engages and congests all
traffic, and it would be a very unpleasant process to get
there from London or *anywhere* for the next five or six
days. At present I shall stay here, but I will forewarn you
duly, if I can come. The *postal* distance is the great
draw-back.

The household here expect you both to stop and see
us, in London, on your way back, if only long enough to
dine or luncheon. Madame will write you when she returns, if the young ladies have not already written. They
are very anxious to see Mrs. Boyd again, especially Marguerite, who hopes Mrs. Boyd hasn't forgotten her.

Many thanks for your kindly appreciation of 'Cressy.'
Hastily but very heartily yours

BRET HARTE

The next three letters to his wife cover the summer
months of 1889, and have to do, among other things,
with the centennial celebrations and an introduction to
the Dowager Lady Shrewsbury, and the last, a very long

one, contains curious observations on English life, as he saw it in his day.

15, UPPER HAMILTON TERRACE, N.W.
May 18, 1889

MY DEAR NAN,

I hope this will find you better than when you wrote on the 7th. I fancy that the same luck that produced your bronchial irritation sent a wave of sickness across the Atlantic, for this whole household is down with colds and coughs, and I, who was free from even the slightest influenza during the severe weather, have been of late quite upset with a most refractory and protracted attack. I haven't yet been able to get a change of air.

I think the 'Oyster Bay' idea is a great one. I believe Long Island is healthy, and it used to be inexpensive and accessible. I only fear it may be dull to you all, after your more fashionable watering-place experiences. But try to pull through it this summer with little expense; if I came, it would be an excuse for a change if you didn't like it — but I fancy that I should like almost any *quiet* place. My idea of your looking for a house, was of course a reference to your finding something that would be a '*home*,' summer or winter, and could be bought on easy terms. If you found that Long Island was only fit for a summer place — you could look elsewhere.

I have written to Frank in reference to his play, and shall write to poor Wodie to-morrow, as I must get this off with the draft (which I enclose) by to-day's post. Thank you, Nan, for the pretty Centennial gifts. The celebrations must, from all accounts, have been an unequalled spectacle. The European press was full of it and I felt, you may imagine, exceedingly proud of my country. I wish I could always feel as proud of some of my degenerate countrymen and countrywomen, who come here only apparently to show how little they revere their own country and its institutions, and how much they meanly admire this and its Court!

It is too bad that *you* didn't see the celebrations. But I don't think you needed it to be a true American woman!

With best love to all the children, dear Nan, always

LIMICK

15, UPPER HAMILTON TERRACE, N.W.
August 6, 1889

MY DEAR NAN,

The Dowager Lady Shrewsbury, one of my oldest London acquaintances, is sailing for America to-morrow, on a three months' tour, and will be at the Brunswick Hotel, New York, at about the time this reaches you. If you happen to be in town and could call with one of the girls, I should like it, as she has always been very polite to me during the five or six years I have known her. I have told her that we live very plainly, and of course cannot expect you to do any more than call. Even that, I have explained, may not be within your power if you are in the country during the short time she will be in New York on her first arrival. I have written to Dana to show her some civility — which he can do more easily at his big house — and I introduced her to John Hay, while he was here.

She is Theresa, Countess of Shrewsbury, the mother of Lady Londonderry and the Earl of Shrewsbury, a very clever and good woman — and one of the most popular hostesses in London. Even if you do not see her — and she may have many engagements — there will be no harm in leaving your card, and I think it will please her.

In haste, but with love to all, yours

LIMICK

Trewsbury,Cirencester
September 15,1889.

My DEAR NAN,

First let me thank you for the Christmas
and birthday combination presents. They were
beautiful - almost too good for daily wear on
my modest work-table - but I wish, dear Nan,
that you would not buy me expensive presents;
any trifle you or the girls might make or pick
up would amply suffice me for remembrance. I
value for this reason Jessamy's sketches in
the album for autographs, the shirt-case you
made for me the year before, and all the little
things the girls worked and painted for me
from time to time.

I have been here four weeks now, but during
that time until the last three or four days
have been steadily at work and have really seen
but little of the country. I have written to
the girls some descriptions of certain things
which I thought might interest them. I can add
very little for you, I fear. This is the usual
English country house like the others I have
described and the impression one gets is nearly
the same that was very truthfully and characteristically expressed by one of our countrymen to an Englishman, 'You're to d-d comfortable
over here.' Nothing can be truer. The
spectacle one ever has of a privileged class
with nothing to think about but their own amuse-
ment, who apportion their lives with a certain
kind of ridiculous formality to the regular
habit of hunting, shooting, and race-going, who
even arrange the meetings of Parliament so that
the duty of governing the country shall not
disturb their sacred institutions - is a little
to d-d comfortable - to be even manly. There
is no ambition - no endeavour - but of the most
pitiable, trivial kind. Nowhere, I believe, in
the whole world can you find a class living

so entirely for themselves and in themselves
as the English better class. Of course, there
are some exceptions - men who travel about, men
who devote themselves to higher pursuits; but
never entirely break away from their habits;
the Prime Minister, the great politician, the
great lawyer, must have his shootings, his
game preserves, with all the costly wasteful
accessories and paraphernalia. For it is a
most singular thing that that simplicity which
is the hall mark - the distinguishing trait -
of the aristocracy is utterly wanting in their
peculiarly English sports. They not only go
about them 'sadly,' as Froissart said, but with
a ridiculous show and even vulgar ostentation;
they cannot shoot over these great preserves
except in great parties, specially invited,
and their proceedings are as vulgarly published
as the Court Circular, not only how many brace
they shot but who shot and what Lord So-and-So
did; their costume is extravagantly ridiculous,
their luncheons are feasts and as much of a
feature of this 'manly exercise' as their game-
keepers and beaters. Once a year all England -
I mean all fashionable society - flock to see
their schoolboys - not rehearse their studies,
oh, no! - but play their games! The Eton and
Harrow cricket matches thrill the fashionable
parents as no examination of studies ever could
or would do - for there are no public examina-
tions that are fashionable; to be the mother
or father or sister of a great cricketer or
football player is a prouder distinction than
to be related to a prize scholar. This is
tacitly impressed upon them in their childhood;
in their adolescence at Oxford and Cambridge
they are as tacitly taughet that it is 'better
form' to be good oarsmen at a regatta to which
all fashionable society flock, than to win
prizes or take degrees at college, honours which
fashionable society coldly ignores. What wonder
that the

average Eton or Harrow boy can't write a decent English
letter! But what can one think of Americans who worship this sort of thing — and send their children here to
have an English education!

There has been a good deal of visiting from the neighbours, who have very beautiful seats (not the only ones
they have — for there is one family of three who have as
many places in other counties) and they are very hospitable. Our nearest neighbour is a Lady Elizabeth
Biddulph, of very old family, whose daughter is a 'Maid
of Honour' to the Queen. She is plain, but very well educated; talks well and plays and sings well — which I am
told is essential to those who 'wait' on royalty. One
thing strikes me about these people — and my knowledge
of them is gathered from another 'Maid of Honour' I
know, and an 'Equerry,' who is a very charming 'War-
rington' sort of fellow, and also is one of my London
friends — and that is, that they are one and all exceedingly gentle and singularly diffident in their opinions;
sympathetic without being at all excited about anything
and certainly never visibly *astonished* at anything. It may
seem a dreadful thing to say, but their manner is that of
persons who might be in the habit *of living with mad
people*, or attending some kind of a reformatory. Of
course, I don't dare to say such a thing 'out loud' to any
one; although these very people are themselves by no
means always reverent or subdued in their own passing
allusions to their duties.

This reminds me of another queer thing I have noticed
among the best society people, which I do not remember
to have heard spoken of before. They recognize and put
up with a certain degree of eccentricity of conduct, dress,
or behaviour among themselves that is simply astounding
and seems utterly inconsistent with not only any sense of

the hideous or annoying, but utterly inconsistent with their own canons of 'form.'

I have met people who acted like lunatics or idiots — and who indeed *were* in all but legal restraint and harmfulness. I have met people in drawing-rooms who were so outrageously absurd that I pitied their host and hostess until I saw that *they never seemed to notice it.* Once when I ventured to say to a lady, whom I know very well, that it was rather strange — she said simply, 'Oh, it's only Lord A,' or 'Lady B,' or 'Sir So-and-So — *we all know him!*' — as if it were all-sufficient — as indeed it seemed to be. I once dined at a table of distinguished people, when our host, half through dinner, calmly went to sleep and *snored* — and, what was sublimer still, was not awakened by his brother peer at his side! I sat next to a man at another dinner, who wore a star, and who only had three words, 'Ah! Ho! Hum!' The 'Ah' was interrogative, the 'Ho' confidential, the 'Hum' contemplative. He said these three words continually through dinner — *and never said anything else!* Again, we were all assembled in a certain drawing-room before dinner, when there glided into the room, unannounced by the footman, the most extraordinary apparition I ever beheld in a dream or on the stage. She was hideously painted in pink and *yellow*, like a waxen mask; she had bright yellow ringlets, like golden sausages clustered round her forehead, and larger ones that depended nearly to her waist; a woman evidently of *sixty*, she had a baby waist and sash to her brocade dress, and the whole of this astounding figure was covered by a lofty headdress of ribbons and lace and tinsel like a grate ornament. I was speechless with alarm. I thought she was a family lunatic who had escaped from her room. I felt myself blushing for our hostess. But no one seemed concerned. The next moment she was introduced to me by a name and title that I had often heard and saw continually in the society news. Everybody knew her, everybody was accustomed to these vagaries; the mere possibility of her appalling anybody outside that sacred circle never occurred to them, and they *didn't care!*

I find I have wandered on to another sheet, and I must keep the rest of what I have to say on some other things for a separate letter, which I will send with the draft.

Good-night, Nan. Always

LIMICK

James Anthony Froude, the celebrated historian, was one of Bret Harte's oldest European friends. Many references to him are found in the earlier letters, and it was to his home that Bret Harte made his first visit in England. Unfortunately, one letter only has been preserved of their correspondence, but it is a charming and characteristic example of the writer's whimsical pen.

15, UPPER HAMILTON TERRACE, N.W.
November 7, 1889

MY DEAR FROUDE,

My concern on reading your account of your illness I confess was mitigated by envy! To be a sweet and gracious cynic, a fascinating historian, a perfect Master of Style, and the idol of British Imperialism — was that not enough for you, but you must go and develop a rare and 'typical' complaint that leaves even dispassionate Science regarding you with admiration! *I* only have 'vulgar neuralgia' which my doctor contemptuously refers to my teeth, a fit of indigestion, or excessive smoking. I quiver with jealousy!

What a treasure you must have been to that local practitioner! I can fancy his entry in his notebook for the benefit of his medical journal: 'Called to see J. A. F., gentleman of independent means, of literary tastes, a great traveller, and, I am told, a special correspondent of the "Daily Telegraph." Pulse of patient, normal, rising to 125 on mention of the name of Gladstone, with symptoms of irritation and slight eruption. Evidently a rare and beautiful case of *Prim-roseola.*'

Nevertheless, my dear Froude, I *am* concerned for you! Will that doctor willingly part from his one rare 'typical' case, this blessed opportunity that South Devon offers him? Will he not do all he can to keep you there until your eruption comes out perfectly, with the spring flowers? Is there a special season for that sort of thing? Don't trust him. The temptation is too great!

So hurry back here, my dear Froude, and if *I* have to stay here the whole winter, we will meet together often and 'rail against the first born of Egypt' and the darkness. Always yours

BRET HARTE

It is seldom that Bret Harte, in his correspondence, alludes to the personages of any of his works, and the mention of his latest book and the delicately humorous description of his favourite heroine 'Cressy' contribute to the interest of his amusing letter to Mrs. Boyd.

15, UPPER HAMILTON TERRACE, N.W.
November 29, 1889

MY DEAR MRS. BOYD,

Thanks for your charming letter of yesterday. You say many pretty things of 'Cressy' and 'The Carquinez Woods,' but I am afraid that your dear good Mamma is right in her criticism, when she alludes to the redundancy of 'passion,' and the tensity of 'satisfaction' she gets from my books! However, I am sending you to-day a copy of

'The Heritage of Dedlow Marsh,' my latest, which I think she may like. I think I may avow, with my hand on my heart, that I have at last written a volume which any young married woman can thoughtfully put into the hands of her innocent Mother! It is possible that it may be still unsatisfactory in conclusion, though greatly diminished in fervour. The fact is my characters *will not* do as they ought to do, at the end. I may give them the advantages of a perfect (my own) example; I may clearly point out to them what the virtuous reader expects! but they won't have it. Even Cressy, much as I loved her, turned her back upon me at the last moment, and skipped out of my pages with a man I had only just introduced to her!

Seriously, which means that the foregoing should be considered amusing, I took some pains with the scenery of Dedlow Marsh, and I wish an artist like your husband could have supplemented with his pencil what my pen failed to describe. I lived near it for three years, when I was much younger and more impressionable. The characters, as I used to *think*, were real. But I don't know that I would allow your husband to read 'Telegraph Hill.' There is a flippancy in the character of the heroine that it would be well for him to avoid.

I enclose for him a photograph, taken in the country last summer, as an exchange for the drawing he made of me. The lower limbs will awaken his Scotch sympathies; they have what may be called a 'Northern Exposure'! My face may not betray it, but my impression is that I was *cold!* Are you thinking of flying south again this winter? Your husband must let us know if he takes you through London.

With love to Aleck and the baby, always yours

BRET HARTE

For many years, and until his death, Bret Harte and his friend A. P. Watt used to exchange little gifts with the passing of each year, and the following little note accompanied those of Christmas, 1889.

LONDON, *December 24*, 1889.

MY DEAR MR. WATT,

Won't you kindly accept the accompanying trifle, if only as a token of my earnest wish to be associated in some way with your pleasant recollections of Christmas Day? In the hope that its feeble note may not be in discord with larger chimes, believe me, dear Mr. Watt, always yours

BRET HARTE

The first letters of 1890 are written from the seaside, where Bret Harte went to recuperate from another sickness, which handicapped him seriously in that work which, in spite of his need for rest, he was still obliged to keep at steadily, 'for eight hours a day, sick or not, in spirits or out of spirits,' as he says himself.

ROYAL HOTEL, VENTNOR, I. W.
February 4, 1890

DEAR NAN,

I was regularly laid up with the epidemic cold for three weeks — with an additional relapse — while I was waiting for my American remittances to make up your draft and letter. The remittances never came — for the syndicate is untrustworthy; and ill as I was, I was obliged to finish some work in any way to enable me to *telegraph* you the sum of the usual draft so that it would reach you in time. Of course, I had to forego my usual letter.

I am now here trying to get my strength again to work.

I think I am better — but the attack has left me very weak, and the doctor says I must be careful. I will write you again on the 15th. With love to the children, who must wait for a reply to their letters, always your affectionate

LIMICK

ROYAL HOTEL, VENTNOR, I. W.
February 19, 1890

MY DEAR ANNA,

I answered your telegram, and I presume you have got my letter before this. I am remaining here, though I am much better, because I can get through eight hours' work a day, which is absolutely necessary to finish the story I have in hand in time. Sick or not, in spirits or out of spirits, I must work, and I do not see any rest ahead. I will answer your letter and Frank's as soon as I have a moment's relief from this haste. I have to make up for those weeks when I was scarcely able to do anything, and there is a pile of proofs and business letters before me that are still untouched. There was a paragraph in the London newspapers about my being here, convalescent from the influenza, but I do not know whether it was copied in the American papers. It was by no means alarming, though, of course, it may have been garbled by copying of correspondents.

I forgot to say in my last letter that Jules Andrade came to the house while I was at Ripon and told Madame Van de Velde that he was in London to attend his mother's funeral. She died at a *maison de santé* in the suburbs. The husband died eight or nine years ago and I was with Jules at the funeral.

With love to the children and yourself, always

LIMICK

P.S. I have written so much lately that my hand is becoming more than ever illegible.

The three following letters are written to his friend Hatton, who collaborated with him in the dramatization of his story 'M'liss,' at which Bret Harte was busily occupied in the spare moments he was able to snatch from his other work. They give some interesting details on the costumes worn by the miners and children of the early Californian days, which show the extreme accuracy of detail to which he was always attentive.

ROYAL HOTEL, VENTNOR, I. W.
February 9, 1890

MY DEAR HATTON,

I am ashamed that I have let my work interfere with my acknowledgment of your charming letter. 'Praises from Sir Hubert . . .' but, no! I refrain from that hoary chestnut! What I was trying to say is that praise from a brother artist is not only recognition of merit, but of work. Thanks, old fellow, for saying such pleasant things very pleasantly and unaffectedly. No matter whether they are true or not.

The work that I am engaged on now is imperative in mood, and present in tense, or I should fly to 'M'liss' at once. But it is also the bread-and-butter that enables me to live in hopes of something better. It is the work first and 'play' afterwards of school ethics.

I don't think it will take long to lick that third Act into shape. I have the general idea in my mind, but my fingers are preoccupied with the story that must be finished before March 1st.

Yours always
BRET HARTE

P.S. The weather has been abominable! There is, in
this southern verge of this island, a diabolical east wind
blowing direct from the Channel. It has been blowing
four days with Arctic severity of temperature. It is so
d——d uncomfortable, I suppose it is doing me good!
B. H.

15, UPPER HAMILTON TERRACE, N.W.
Sunday

DEAR HATTON,

There is nothing particularly picturesque in the dances
of the school children, and Laura and Kerg might wear
French white-and-blue blouses, with patent-leather belts.
This was their gala dress. The smaller children usually
wore blue-and-white checkered pinafores ('aprons' we
call them in America), with sleeves — for work. But the
white blouses will keep up the summer heat of the play!
The only other 'picturesque dances' I can think of, for
women and children, are Spanish. One or two would do,
among the grouping: the usual *camisa*, chemise, and
saya, petticoat or (flounced) skirt, and *manta*, a black lace
shawl for the head and shoulders. Flowers — usually red
or yellow ones — for the hair. The American women
wore light print dresses, and the old-fashioned hand-
trimmed straw hats (flat) with ribbons — of forty years
ago.

California was a land of flowers and blossoms, and an
always pretty effect could be produced by them in every
scene. The children's dresses were usually smothered
with them inside and out.

Hope you enjoyed yourself at Brighton.
Yours always
B. H.

15, UPPER HAMILTON TERRACE, N.W.
Tuesday P.M. [*April* 8, 1890]

DEAR HATTON,

I'll try to draw some design of the schoolhouse, for your artist. I'm afraid, in the matter of *costumes*, my country-man on the 'Herald,' unless he has been in California, would make the usual mistake of all my illustrators, and most theatrical managers, by equipping the miners in *red* flannel shirts and old trousers thrust in their boots — like tramps.

Bonebreaker should have a Mexican *vaquero's* dress (*not a cowboy's*), with figured silk shirt, red sash, velvet jacket, and velvet trousers, open from the knee down, to show a white trouser underneath, and the edge trimmed with silver buttons and connected with a silver chain. He should wear huge silver spurs. The miners should wear white ducks (white jumpers and white trousers) and one or two with high rubber boots, like fishing boots. Re-member, please, that the thermometer on the river bars used to mark *100 in the shade;* and then think of the red flannel shirts and dark woolen trousers of the stage miner! The light-coloured bandanna handkerchief, thrown around their necks was helpful always to keep up the picturesque half-tropical appearance and kept them from looking *rowdy!*

Yours always

B. H.

P.S. The appointments and costumes should look wild and bizarre, but never look *coarse!* As a matter of fact, *they never did.* Their white ducks never got dirty, but got red from contact with the red soil. As many of them were refined and educated men, and scarcely any *labouring* men or *artisans* — they had, in spite of their long hair and mus-

tachios, refined and delicate hands, feet, and faces! But —
I have written all this before, until I am weary of it! And
yet they are always delivered over to me as common
workmen or field labourers.

B. H.

Bret Harte was considerably overworked, as his letters
home of this period plainly show, but he was always hopeful of a successful dramatization of one of his stories
which would procure for him the rest from the 'daily
grind of which he was so much in need. Unfortunately,
more than one disappointment awaited him in this direction, and 'M'liss' was not produced until much later.

15, UPPER HAMILTON TERRACE, N.W.
April 15, 1890

MY DEAR NAN,

I am enclosing the draft to-day, but I must again ask
you and the children to possess your souls in patience for
a little while longer before I attempt to answer all your
kind letters. I am just beginning to lift the burden of unfinished work from my shoulders — all that my illness
this spring left undone — and I hope by the first of May
to have an interval of rest. I have worked very hard since
the 1st of February, and even astonished my publishers
here! As soon as the weather changes, I shall leave London for some quiet place in the country till the most urgent work is off my hands. I hope by the 1st of May to
tell you something more of my play (which *ought to be* in
rehearsal by that time) — though its appearance may be
put off until later in the season.

I have a great deal to say to you about my prospects
for the summer and your own plans, but I must not enter
upon it now or I shall have no energy or heart for my

daily 'grind.' God bless you all! Tell the children to keep on writing to me; their letters are always welcome, and don't forget, yourself, to tell me everything — and *as often* as you can. *You* may be *preoccupied*, but you cannot possibly hate pen and ink as I do who live in it and by it perpetually! Always dear Nan, yours

FRANK

15, UPPER HAMILTON TERRACE, N.W.
May 16, 1890

MY DEAR NAN,

I have just returned from two weeks' absence in the country, where I went to work and recruit, for I am not yet quite strong. I do not think the change did me any good, and I fear I shall have to try some other locality in a few days. During the last week of my stay I was scarcely able to do my work, a serious thing to me with all my engagements.

I have just written to Frank and Mr. Boucicault in reference to a dramatization of 'The Luck of Roaring Camp,' which 'B' has suggested. I hope something may come of it. My own play of 'M'liss' I fear now will go over to the autumn before it sees the footlights for the first time. I am greatly disappointed, as I hoped to have it launched this spring. But the delay for a success is better than haste for a failure, and I, and my collaborateur, Mr. Hatton — whose daughter is to play in it — are, of course, anxious that *all* the chances shall be favourable.

I hope so. I am getting very weary of this monotonous work, though it is better paid here than in my own country, where I believe I should starve from all appearances if I depended solely upon my stories.

With love to the children, always, dear Nan, affectionately

LIMICK

15, Upper Hamilton Terrace, N.W.
May 16, 1890

My dear Frank,

I have asked Mr. Boucicault seventy-five dollars per week instead of sixty dollars — his offer for the use of the name, characters, and incidents of 'The Luck of Roaring Camp.' This is the *lowest* figure you suggest in your letter to me, and if the play is a *success* will be of little moment to him. However, if *you* think he *cannot* give any more, I will take his offer of sixty dollars, and I authorize you to tell him so if there should be any difficulty as to the terms.

More important to me is the consideration that he shall not use any of the characters or incidents in my story of 'M'liss,' nor of 'A Blue Grass Penelope,' nor of *any story* I have written within the last three years. This is only due to my collaboration with Mr. Joseph Hatton in my play of 'M'liss,' and Madame V. de V. in 'Penelope.' I cannot imagine, however, that Mr. Boucicault will require any of these as the characters he proposes to take from my 'other works.'

I am glad to find that you anticipate my judgment in your feelings in regard to any connection of yours with the play. As a mere matter of *business*, it is better that the *contract* should be made with *me*, and the *payments* likewise, even though I transfer the latter to your mother instead of my monthly drafts; and in regard to the new use of *your name* — if that is what Mr. Boucicault suggests — I cannot see what reputation that will give you except *he* takes *you* as collaborateur in dramatizing *my* story. I fear it would be more confusing than advantageous to the play.

If, of course, any of the material that Madame Van de Velde and myself imparted into the play is used by Mr. Boucicault, I shall pay Madame V. de V. for the use of her collaboration out of the royalty Boucicault pays me, and I therefore hope you will let me know if such is the case. She sends you kind messages and would have written, but says you owe her a letter. I have not been very well lately and have been obliged to go for two weeks to the country.

Your affectionate father
B. H.

A lady, Mrs. Colles, who had written Bret Harte enquiring into the origin of his story 'Thankful Blossom,' received the following interesting reply, in which he gives an account of the sources from which he drew the material of this charming story.

15, UPPER HAMILTON TERRACE
LONDON, N.W., May 31, 1890

DEAR MADAM,

In reply to your favour of the 14th inst., I fear I must begin by saying that the story of 'Thankful Blossom,' although inspired and suggested by my residence at Morristown at different periods, was not *written* at that place, but in another part of New Jersey. The 'Blossom Farm' was a study of two or three old farmhouses in the vicinity but was not an existing fact so far as I know. But the description of Washington's Headquarters was a study of the actual house, supplemented by such changes as were necessary for the epoch I described, and which I gathered from the State Records. The portraits of Washington and his military family at the Headquarters were drawn from Sparks's 'Life of Washington' and the best chronicles of the time. The episode of the Spanish Envoy is also historically substantiated, and the same may be said of the disaffection of the 'Connecticut contingent.'

Although the heroine, 'Thankful Blossom,' as a character is purely imaginary, the name is an actual one, and was borne by a (chronologically) remote maternal relation of mine, whose Bible with the written legend, 'Thankful Blossom — her book,' is still in possession of a member of the family.

The contour of scenery and characteristics of climate have, I believe, changed but little since I knew them between 1873 and 1876, and 'Thankful Blossom' gazed at them from Baskingridge Road in 1779.

I remain, dear Madam, yours very sincerely

BRET HARTE

Mrs. Henniker, the sister of the Marquess of Crewe, present Ambassador of Great Britain to France, was a great personal friend of Bret Harte. It is regrettable that at her death many letters which would have been of interest have been destroyed. The late Mrs. Henniker and Lord Crewe were children of the late Lord Houghton, whom Bret Harte had known when he was in America. The following letter is the only one that has been found in spite of the courteous efforts of her heirs in tracing others.

15, UPPER HAMILTON TERRACE
LONDON, N.W., *June* 17, 1890

MY DEAR MRS. HENNIKER,

I shall wait until you are quite settled at 'Culdicott' and your Ascot hurry is over, for a day's visit, but if I can run down for an hour or two at midday, some day before, I will let you know in time so as not to interfere with your day's plans. I should greatly like to meet your brother, if it can be arranged, and I suppose I can promise myself the pleasure of seeing your husband, who is on duty at Windsor, is he not? I met your aunt, Lady Galvy, at dinner the other night; we had met before, but I did not then know the relationship, and she talked of you very delightfully, and as appreciatively as she did of Venice, which is saying a good deal. It is something to be put on the same level with Saint Mark's! I am dining with her the first week in July. Won't you be running up to town about that time? I am afraid that as my neuralgia is chiefly in my head and face, 'massage' — at least anything short of a black eye — wouldn't be of much use. I fondly believed it was my teeth, and was joyfully rushing off to have them all extracted when the doctor stopped me.

Can you recommend anything amusing for me to read? It must be *amusing;* I am getting too old to find any pleasure in being made sad. Lately I have been trying to read serious and even scientific and philosophical books to 'improve my mind.' But I think I find gibbering and vacuously smiling ignorance preferable to responsible knowledge!

I am still at work on 'bespoken' tasks for publishers but I am going off at the end of the week for one or two days' 'country-house hunting' for my friends here.

Yours always
BRET HARTE

The two letters to Mr. Watt end Bret Harte's correspondence for 1890, which was a year of hard struggle and disappointment. There are in the following year only a few letters by which to follow him.

15, UPPER HAMILTON TERRACE, N.W.
Christmas, 1890

MY DEAR MR. WATT,

I am so sorry that the initials on the newspaper knife have been mistaken by the engraver, but after to-morrow this error can be remedied and the 'T' become a 'P.' It arose from my giving him the initials from *your signature* which certainly *did* resemble a 'T.' But you will accept it to-day with Christmas charity and good-will and the best intentions of even the engraver.

How can I sufficiently thank you, and express my admiration of the lovely vase you sent me! It is 'an urn,' a casket! and worthy to hold something more precious than Wine!

Believe me always, with best Christmas wishes, yours

BRET HARTE

15, UPPER HAMILTON TERRACE, N.W.
January 7, 1891

DEAR MR. WATT,

I am sending you herewith the paper-knife with the initial in the inscription properly corrected, and I think with no trace of this unhappy blunder. I had told the engraver, if necessary, to put on a new shield, but he declared that it was unnecessary, and the change could be made by a simple *additional* stroke of the 'graver.'

You were saying that you could *order* the Christmas number of the 'New York Dramatic News' for me. Will you kindly do so when it is convenient for you?

Yours always

BRET HARTE

The greater part of the summer was spent with the Van de Veldes in their country place, of which he speaks in the next letter to his wife, and where he was steadily working at his new stories.

CRANBOURNE COURT, WINDSOR FOREST
September 17, 1891

MY DEAR NAN,

I duly arrived here a few days ago — the Van de Veldes having taken this house for six weeks. They had it before — three years ago — and I dare say I have described it to you already. It is not far from London, in a part of Windsor Forest, and the town and castle of Windsor is only four miles away. The forest, with its old oaks and deer, is of course beautiful, but I would have preferred to have been farther from town and in some more bracing air! It's something, at least, to find a place where one's work is less difficult.

I am looking very anxiously for a letter from you. Since I wrote to the children, one is due, and I hoped it might come before I sent this draft. But I dare not wait longer. I must only hope that the Adirondacks have done you good, and that you are much better. I enclose a cheque for three hundred dollars — which includes the fifty dollars remaining of the extra one hundred dollars I promised you, and trust, dear Nan, that it has been as much satisfaction to you to receive it as it has been to me to be able to send it. God bless you all. With love to the children, always affectionately,

FRANK

Two short notes are all that can be traced until the end of the year. The first to Mr. Watt, the second to Jerome K. Jerome, the famous author, and editor of the 'Idler,' to which Bret Harte contributed.

15, UPPER HAMILTON TERRACE, N.W.
December 24, 1891

DEAR MR. WATT,

Many many thanks for your beautiful Christmas gift. The carving on the ring is, in itself, alone, a work of Art,

and even its delicacy does not interfere with its daily
utility for the 'needs' of

Yours gratefully   BRET HARTE

15, UPPER HAMILTON TERRACE
LONDON, N.W., December 26, 1891

DEAR MR. JEROME,

I am expecting to go out of town for a few days after
the holidays, or I should accept with great pleasure your
kind invitation to join the 'Idlers' at their first Club dinner. It is barely possible that I may be still here at the
date you fix, but I dare not *promise*.   Believe me

Yours most sincerely   BRET HARTE

In the early part of 1892, an epidemic of influenza swept
the entire continent, devastating families, and leaving
everywhere the mark of its terrible passage. While Bret
Harte escaped its more serious effects, his host and friend
was the unfortunate victim of an attack from which he
never recovered.

15, UPPER HAMILTON TERRACE, N.W.
January 23, 1892

MY DEAR ANNA,

I have been so poorly with a succession of colds that
my work is greatly in arrears and I have only just been
able to get the enclosed draft. I ought not complain, for I
have been in the midst of much more serious illness, re-
sulting from this dreadful influenza and the poison that
seems to be in the air everywhere.

Mr. Van de Velde, the head of this house, a middle-
aged man, whose strength and youthfulness I have always envied, has been lying critically ill, with nurses,
doctors, and consultations, and the whole household —
like many others — is ailing. I have given up for the
present my intention of going away, for I should not like

to fall seriously ill, as so many have, among entire strangers — with no relations here, and three thousand miles from my family. There is no place exempt from the scourge — although probably there may be spots where the weather is less depressing. Here it has been fittingly dark and gloomy; days when one exists only by artificial light and the streets at noon are like midnight.

London has well earned the title of the 'City of Dreadful Night!' The oldest Londoners remember nothing like it. Everywhere we hear of friends — whole households — stricken down.

My work is so far behind that I must keep all my strength for that. You must write to me more frequently; I was quite worried at receiving no Christmas letter till a few days ago; some of you certainly can find time to send me a few lines once a fortnight. I will write again soon.

I hope you and the children are keeping well. Eliza says she has had the *grippe* three times. It must be in some mild form. Always your affectionate

LIMICK

You do not say where Frank is. Is he still in Europe?

The portrait in question is the same that has been referred to previously in Bret Harte's letter to Mr. Watt.

15, UPPER HAMILTON TERRACE
LONDON, N.W., *January 26, 1892*

George B. Burgin, Esq.
Office of 'The Idler'
310 Strand, London

DEAR MR. BURGIN,

My hostess has a photogravure of John Pettie's (R.A.) oil picture of me, which was exhibited at the Royal Academy a few years ago, and at Berlin later.

The photogravure is signed by Mr. Pettie; and was given by him to Madame Van de Velde. She will lend it to you to be copied, although I cannot make out clearly from your note the form in which you wish to reproduce it, where and when!

The original hangs in the dining-room at No. 15, Upper Hamilton Terrace, where you may have seen it when you called: the photogravure is also on the wall in the drawing-room. If you wish to see it or send for it, let me know. Madame V. de V. will lend it to you, on your assurance that it will be carefully looked after. Believe me

Yours very sincerely

BRET HARTE

P.S. I am glad to hear of the great success of 'The Idler.'

B. H.

Two weeks after Bret Harte's last letter to his wife, Monsieur Van de Velde died, and the tragic circumstances that surrounded the misfortune of his friend's family are eloquently expressed in his next letter.

15, UPPER HAMILTON TERRACE, N.W.
February 20, 1892

MY DEAR NAN,

Since I last wrote to you of poor Van de Velde's illness, the end has come! He died on the 7th after six weeks' illness — yet unexpectedly as these things always are. It was a sad breaking-up of the household which his kindness and almost brotherly friendship did so much to make a possible home for me here so long among strangers. On the same day Madame's stepfather (Count de Launay) died at Berlin, and one of the saddest incidents of her double loss was when she was obliged to answer a telegram from her youngest daughter (who was nursing the Count) begging her to come to her help in the Count's extremity, by telling her — what she had been keeping from the poor child — that she could not leave the bedside of the dying father!

Madame has gone to Berlin with her eldest daughter to settle the Count's affairs and bring home her other daughter. I have been left in charge of the London house and my poor friend's children — rather, perhaps I should say they are looking after *me* as their poor parents did — until the others return. I do not know what will be the disposition of the family after that. Van de Velde's brother, from Brussels, was with him during his illness, and has just gone home, but it is probable that the family will still remain in England.

Throughout all this, with the shadow of disease and death everywhere one looked, this dreadful winter, I have, thank God! as yet, kept from any serious illness myself, and, beyond my usual neuralgia and dyspepsia, have suffered only from the depression of it. I am rejoiced to hear of your being so much better and stronger in health, and I thank you, dear Nan, for the pretty use you proposed to make of it! I might take a *little* part of it — if there was a surplus.

I send you the draft as usual enclosed. I am hoping for the children's letters. I will write again, should I be going away from London before I send the next draft. God bless and protect you all. Affectionately

LIMICK

In the following letter to Mr. Watt, referring to one he wrote in 1886, Bret Harte expresses again his appreciation of being relieved of the business part of his literary work through the valuable assistance of his literary agent.

15, UPPER HAMILTON TERRACE, N.W.
March 6, 1892

DEAR MR. WATT,

At your request I have looked over the letter I wrote to you six years ago, in grateful acknowledgement of your services to me as my literary agent. Very few of us, I believe, are able, even in that brief space of time, to look back with perfect equanimity on any previous epistolatory gush or effusiveness, and I am delighted to find nothing that I would alter of the full praise I gave you then, and nothing that our later continued relations have not fully endorsed and justified.

Believe me, dear Mr. Watt, yours most sincerely
BRET HARTE

The next two letters explain certain circumstances in the life of Bret Harte, and his plans for a united home.

15, UPPER HAMILTON TERRACE, N.W.
March 14, 1892

MY DEAR NAN,

I am still here, awaiting the return of Madame Van de Velde and the part of her family that were with her at Berlin. I am expecting them to-night, and, when I am relieved of my charge and the responsibility of looking after the orphans, I shall go to the seaside to recruit. I will then write to you more fully of myself and my plans. Meantime I enclose a note from Madame Van de Velde, which came yesterday. I suppose it is in acknowledgment of your sympathy which I had conveyed to her. She sent it to me to be addressed to you.

I have not heard from you since that letter, although I have received only a few days ago a nice long one from Jessamy — which I will answer as soon as I can get away from my work here. My health has been so poor that my writing is sadly in arrears, and I must try this year *some change* to prevent me becoming a confirmed invalid. My doctor wants me to go to Bath for my gouty tendency, and take the regular 'cure' of three weeks. But I am puzzled what to do, and shall, I think, consult others before entering upon an experiment of this kind. Everything is called 'gout' here, and the British doctor doesn't quite understand the American constitution, even when it has become partly acclimatized like mine. The 'cure' would have no reference to any other changes — as, for instance, my coming to America, or going on the Continent.

My love to the children; God bless and keep you all till our next meeting! Affectionately, dear Nan

LIMICK

P.S. I enclose the draft for two hundred and fifty dollars.

CAVENDISH HOTEL, EASTBOURNE
April 15, 1892

MY DEAR NAN,

Your kind, loving letter came a day after I last wrote you. First and foremost I want to say that I *never for an instant* even conceived of the girls coming here *without you*, and much as I want to see them, I would not have had them separated from you, even for the shortest visit. My idea has always been that we should be *all together* again, or if that were impossible that it was more important that *you and I* should meet, and that if there were any sacrifice, at first, it must be of the girls. That is why I have thought more of coming to America than I have of bringing you here; and the obstacles to the latter have only been the same *practical* ones that worry me now.

Cruel as it seems to weigh them against the love that prompted your letter and a love *I* feel, appreciate, and have always felt and appreciated, I am only kept from saying to you, 'Come at once, dear Nan!' by the thought that I could not, at this moment, see my way to make my invitation result in anything but a bitter disappointment. That I can *later* — perhaps in a month or two, or surely *this summer* — manage it, I am *quite confident and hopeful!* To come here to London to a hotel, or even to lodgings — living as you ought to live as my wife — even in the plainest way, would cost more than my income would permit, and much more than for me to come to New York — or rather to New Jersey or the country for an equal length of time. I have been able to live in London solely because I lived with the Van de Veldes, half as guest, under circumstances that enabled me to send you three thousand dollars a year. That three thousand dollars would not give you the same *comfort* here as in America. But it *may be possible* to find something, out of London, or in the vicinity where we could make at least a *temporary* home; for I should never consent to have my daughters educated or even reside permanently in England. Or, after a slight visit to London and the Van de Veldes, if they are in a new house in town or country, we could go to the Continent, where I would *first* find some place in Switzerland or Germany for a longer stay. Travel would be too expensive *at first*, until after we had tested what it cost us to remain comfortably in any one place.

This is what I am considering now and enquiring about, and of which I shall write you as soon as I return to London. I am a little better since my week's sojourn here, but I am yet far from strong. I go back next week. I still remain with the Van de Veldes until they move to a new house. With love to the children, always your affectionate

FRANK

I am hurrying this off to catch the post on Saturday, as there is a bank holiday and Good Friday hiatus at the Post Office.

Many references to the actor Dion Boucicault are found among the foregoing letters, in connection with his kindness to Bret Harte's second son. Together with Lawrence Barrett, he facilitated and encouraged him in the first steps of his theatrical career, and he also collaborated with Bret Harte in the dramatization of 'The Luck of Roaring Camp,' which he produced in New York, and in which he acted.

15, UPPER HAMILTON TERRACE, N.W.
Thursday A.M.

MY DEAR BOUCICAULT,

A sore throat kept me from calling upon you yesterday, as it will keep me, I fear, from going out to-night. If you still hold your generous intent of sending me a box, and will kindly retain it for a night or two later, till I am better, I shall be charmed — though I am sorry to miss the first night.

I will try to drop in to-morrow or Saturday, if I go out. Believe me, yours always

BRET HARTE

Mr. and Mrs. Boyd had now settled in London, where Bret Harte and they were to see a great deal of each other. This happily did not prevent them from exchanging frequent letters, of which the following is one written soon after their arrival.

15, UPPER HAMILTON TERRACE, N.W.
Friday

MY DEAR MRS. BOYD,

I take it that the Barrs are coming in any event, and that *I* may come in on Sunday to luncheon, if I don't go down to Wimbledon on Saturday for the week-end. This will suit me very well, is most thoughtful of you, and I dare say I will be able to come, as I am not very keen about suburban 'sleeping out' for two days, and believing it a change. Next week I hope we can arrange for the quiet little family dinner with yourself and husband, and perhaps theatre afterward.

Meantime I am sending you the 'Mystery of the Campagna.' I not only want 'to make your flesh creep,' as did the Fat Boy in 'Pickwick' (I hope soon to be able to sleep as he did also), but I want you to see how very powerfully written the story is, in the details of scenery, art, and local colour. 'The Shadow on the Wave' is far prettier, and as carefully done.

With kindest remembrances to your husband, whom I hope to see on Sunday, always yours

BRET HARTE

Although his children all seemed gifted in different ways, Bret Harte, while encouraging them whenever he saw fit, possessed a rare faculty of judgment, independently of his deep affection for them, which he uses in the following letters, the principal ones of this summer.

15, UPPER HAMILTON TERRACE, N.W.
July 18, 1892

MY DEAR NAN,

I have written to Jessamy by this post in reference to her article on the Adirondacks and her design for the

magazine, both of which I knew all about through the
papers (my usual source of information for family affairs!)
nearly a month before she wrote about it. Unfortunately,
through this kind of advertising the poor child does not
get a fair hearing and only the usual 'nothings' are said.

Personally *I* don't think the little article is anything to
be treated *seriously* or even as significant of *anything* —
except that it paid her twenty-five dollars — and, as I
wrote to her, I should be indeed glad if she were able to
get that amount for her pin-money frequently. The article itself is notable only for its freedom from the faults of
even better beginners — but it neither *promises* nor *denies*
anything. I should say (superficially) that she has many
friends who admire her — I do not mean to say undeserv-
edly — to whom she owes this kindness of a first presentation and *reception*. But it is rather early to run away
with an idea that she has any especial talent or even the
chance of a *vocation*. You have already been deceived
in that in regard to Frank. God knows I wish the dear
child success, and I have tried to write as much to her.

I am just waiting for the proofs of my long story, which,
after four months of dragging work, is at last off my hands.
As soon as that is read, I will write you again of the plans
for the summer and autumn.

With love to all, dear Nan, yours

                                          LIMICK

                              15, UPPER HAMILTON TERRACE, N.W.
                                        August 20, 1892

MY DEAR ANNA,

The accounts we received here of the terrible heat in
New York worried me greatly, and I am glad to find from
your letter that you were in the Alleghanies. I have been
away for a few days at Bushey Park, near Hampton

Court, and have come to town in the heat (which is excessive for London) just to arrange for the draft which I enclose. I have time to write but a few lines, and nothing yet to say of my plans except that their general outline *is unchanged*, and that I shall either arrange to come to New York or send for you and the girls this autumn. I am sorry that you have taken my remarks about Jessamy's article more seriously than I intended it: in fact, I did not consider *it seriously* at all. I am with you in believing that if she can do anything *at all* in the way of occupying herself and making a little money with her pen and pencil, it is not to be discouraged. It is very different from Frank's excursion into theatricals, which, as far as I can see, was worse than useless in its encouragement of everything from which he now suffers.

It is probable that my friends will not take a country house this summer, and, with my prospects for the autumn, I should probably not go with them. But I will write you again in a few days, when my present hurry over proofs, etc., has abated a little.

With love to all, and grateful thanks that you have all escaped illnesses from the terrible weather, always I am, Nan, your affectionate

LIMICK

P.S. I *did* receive Jessamy's photographs and thought that I had acknowledged them. They are very pretty, and I suppose *artistic* — though I do not care for æsthetic dressing. But it makes her look tall, and I suppose it is the fashion in America. I rather preferred, as far as my own taste was concerned, the little picture I have of her, standing in a garden.

PENMAENMAWR, *September* 17, 1892

MY DEAR NAN,

Your kind letter was forwarded to me from London to Wrexham in North Wales, where I have been staying with some friends for the last two weeks, only coming here to this little seaside watering-place for a change on my way to London. I had been so closely occupied during the spring and summer that I was very much rundown and, for the first few days in the bracing air of the Welsh hills, I was quite giddy and upset — scarcely enjoying either the scenery or the antiquities. I think I am a little better now — with the usual hope of feeling the beneficial effects of the change later on. My friend is a retired Liverpool merchant, and was a large mill-owner in Wales, but he has been with his wife many years in America; they have crossed the Atlantic thirty times! They know more of America, understand it and appreciate it, I am afraid, more than most Americans — at least of the slavish, flavourless, snobbish kinds I meet. They had a large house in London until the last year, and I frequently dined there; my present visit to them — which includes this little seaside trip — is the outcome of an old promise. The V. de V.'s, on account of their bereavement, and their purpose of leaving their London house, have not taken a summer house this season, but have visited relations and made separate excursions.

I was at first inclined to smile at your fears of the cholera and the dangers to Frank (who is or was in Paris) and myself, for there never was any epidemic here nor in Paris. But I am sincerely alarmed for you in New York, where I fear there has been less sanitary precaution than here. And the 'scare' has produced a rigid quarantine that has upset all commercial relations, to say nothing of the serious interruptions of passenger traffic. Had I been able to come to America this month, it would not have been very pleasant to have lain off Fire Island for two weeks. I will write again as soon as I return to London. My best love to them *all*, and tell the girls I will send them some Welsh views I have collected for them. God bless and preserve us all for a happy meeting, before long. Always affectionately

LIMICK

With the end of the year 1892, Bret Harte was the usual giver and receiver of Christmas gifts, which the next letters to Mr. Watt and Mrs. Boyd respectively accompany and acknowledge.

15, UPPER HAMILTON TERRACE, N.W.
December 24, 1892

DEAR MR. WATT,

I'm sending you a Doulton jug which I am told is intended for beer, or, possibly, that 'right gude willie waught,' of which your gifted countryman wrote. But just now it is filled to the brim with best wishes for a Merry Christmas and a Happy New Year, from yours always

BRET HARTE

15, UPPER HAMILTON TERRACE, N.W.
Christmas Day, 1892

DEAR MRS. BOYD,

The sketches are charming in their frames, and I am very grateful for mine, albeit I feel a little mean in taking it from you. But your gifted partner can make you another. The French album is just what I wanted, and is delightful.

I am glad that Stuart accepted his transfer from the

military to the naval forces with tranquillity and fervour. But I will confess to you (as a cautious Scotch mother, who will appreciate my discretion) that I was mainly influenced by the fact that the midshipman's cap could be utilized at the seaside, and other places, as an article of *regular wear*, while a guardsman's helmet might provoke criticism. Am I not thoughtful, and a treasure to any respectable and growing family?

I am glad that your husband 'tumbled' to the fly. Is it not a majestic insect? I knew he would appreciate its distinguished heavy respectability, and that pathetic suggestion, particularly in its frayed wing cases, of having seen better days!

With all the best wishes of the season, yours always

BRET HARTE

The first two months of 1893 have not brought us any letters of particular interest. Bret Harte had been very ill, with a series of attacks from his old complaint, which, combined with the strain of his increased work, had completely broken down his resistance. The following letters written from the home of his old friend James Anthony Froude show with what indefatigable energy he continued to work in spite of his condition.

CHERWELL EDGE, OXFORD
March 21, 1893

MY DEAR NAN,

I have been here only a few days and not long enough yet, I fear, to feel the benefit of a change, although my neuralgia is better, and I no longer have the night attacks that used to leave me sleepless. I am here with one of my oldest friends, dear Froude — who is, as you know, now the Professor of History in the University — and one of the biggest of the big 'Dons.' It was quite an honour to go to chapel with him yesterday, in his cap and gown.

I should perhaps enjoy it more if I were strong enough to accept the invitations and courtesies I receive, but I am still far from well, and can only sun myself in the park when the weather is fine, or creep about in the shelter of the cloisters. The place, I hardly need tell you, is venerable, poetical, and beautiful — but perhaps, in my sensitive condition, a trifle depressing!

I thought the picture cover by Jessamy very good indeed; the fact that it was thought good enough by artists and publishers to be used and *paid for* is sufficiently valuable criticism; but to my own taste it did not seem very *novel* in conception! I should so like to see some of her drawings from Nature. I think there can be no question about her talent for execution, or copying — and I am delighted and hopeful.

I do not know how long I shall remain here, but I will write you again before I leave. I am not even attempting to work, and am scarcely up to letter-writing.

With love to the dear children, always, Nan, your affectionate

LIMICK

15, UPPER HAMILTON TERRACE, N.W.
July 18, 1893

MY DEAR NAN,

After two or three months of great difficulty and slower progress, I seem to have recovered enough of my old vigour again to once more keep even with my work, and I have been writing hard and continuously ever since my last letter to you, hardly daring to stop, lest I should fall back into my former condition. I think I am much stronger — I know I am more hopeful — and it looks now as if I might be able to make some preparations toward our near meeting. My friends are not yet in their new house, and I am sending this still from the half-dismantled house in Upper Hamilton Terrace. I have only time to send the draft and close this, I hope, more cheerfully than I have my last letters.

With love to the girls, dear Nan, always your affectionate

LIMICK

At the end of 1893, Bret Harte's son Frank, who had been married a few years previously, came with his wife to settle in England, and Bret Harte was a frequent visitor to their home in Weybridge. The next few letters are addressed to him, and to Mrs. Boyd, and are amusing and happy reactions to the fatigue of his daily work.

109, LANCASTER GATE, W.
December 29, 1893

MY DEAR FRANK,

Very many thanks for that beautiful cigar-cutter which arrived here an hour or two after my return yesterday. It is quite too valuable and 'smart' a gift for an old fogey like me, but I reflect that it is 'portable property' and shall keep it! The monogram is at once obscure and beautiful!

Receive, my dear son, the distinguished consideration and profound esteem of your affectionate father

B. H.

109, LANCASTER GATE, W.
Thursday night, [*January 19, 1894*]

MY DEAR MRS. BOYD,

I am delighted to get a line from you *at last*, for I have been unable to come up to The Hut, since I parted from you and your husband a week ago. No, I haven't even had the change of going out of town, but have been very busy and preoccupied here. My son, who should have been settled in his new house by this time, has been disappointed by his house agent and has had to recommence his house-hunting. And I have had some old friends here on a visit. All of which has kept me active, but not lively.

I shall try to call to-morrow morning or afternoon, if only to satisfy myself that you and Aleck and the child can still talk, if you can't write letters.

Meanwhile, I am going to bother you and Aleck with the enclosed proofs, as far as they go, of the 'McHulishes' for the new volume. I have already corrected it (this is only a duplicate), but if there are any outrages in Scotch dialect or Scotch customs that, as an ignorant foreigner, I have passed over, please excise them mercilessly with your pencil. I have already ruthlessly torn away the *prayer*-book from the hands of the church-going Glaswegians and thrust a *hymn*-book there instead. But this was done a century ago.

Always yours
BRET HARTE

109, LANCASTER GATE, W.
Sunday night, [January 29, 1894]

MY DEAR MRS. BOYD,

I didn't go to Suffolk on Saturday, as I was very busy, and found that it was too far to go for the few days I could spare. I called on Friday with a little package of books for your journey, but, alas! the bird, or the Boyd, had flown! So I gave them to Aleck, who I grieve to say was wearing an air of indescribable bachelor jauntiness, and he promised to bring them to you. I hope he did so, and didn't reserve the best for himself. There was that in

his eye which revealed unsunned depths of hidden wickedness and made me suspicious.

I hope you are enjoying yourself in this lovely weather.
If I could only get away, I should run down to the Grand
or the Metropole, for a day and a night. I don't believe
the sea air would affect my temper badly for so short a
time.

Let me know when you and Aleck are returning.

Yours always

B. H.

109, Lancaster Gate, W.
March 15, 1894

My dear Son,

I did not send you the beautiful razors I got for your
birthday gift, as I remembered that your mother always
objected to my giving you knives and other edged tools,
and I was fearful that you might attempt to shave with
them. I believe there is also a superstition about the
giving of anything 'that cuts' unless one receives some
coin in exchange, and, as I should have expected a guinea
from you at least, and know I wouldn't get it, I abandoned
the razors as a gift offering.

I send you instead a beautiful pair of hard brushes for
your hair, with your initials in solid silver. I trust you
will accept them with my love — in a separate enclosure.

I was somewhat uncertain about your birthday being
on the 4th, so I selected them on the 5th, that they might
always remind you of the 6th in happy commemoration
of the 7th. I am sending them to you on the 15th so
that there shall be no mistake.

Believe me always affectionately, your credulous and
trusting father

B. H.

109, LANCASTER GATE, W.
March 27, 1894

MY DEAR MRS. BOYD,

I've just finished the book you asked me to read, and thank you for it.

I think you can praise it very fairly. It struck me as being realistic in the best sense, and a portrayal of character in a very wholesome, true, and at times *tender* fashion, and with a style utterly free from either the affectations of precision or brutality. If it was written by a woman, I should say it was very *gentlewomanly*, and if it was written by a *man*, I think I should still retain the epithet without disparagement! The only thing I do *not* like about it (and this is purely a personal taste) is the domination of sadness in the whole book, although it is not a *hopeless* nor a *cynical* sadness. It reminds me somewhat of Miss Wilkins in these recurring chords.

I thought it quite a stroke of genius to make the (so-called) ill-assorted marriage of the 'Hon. Stanbury' and the poor sick danseuse turn out happily for both, and to terminate only by her death. One is always looking for the woman to run away with some one else, or the man to grow neglectful or brutal (all in the interests of Mrs. Grundy!) that one feels that this ending may be true after all! 'Poor Miss Skeet' is still more delicately touched, and one feels that this poor woman's passion for passion and beauty might not be as ridiculous as the clergyman's wife thought, nor as dreadful as Mrs. Grundy would imply.

There, now I must go back to my own drivel, which I must finish by to-morrow. I will bring the book with me.

Yours always
B. H.

Bret Harte, like most other authors, was frequently receiving requests to allow certain of his poems to be set to music. The following is his charming reply to his friend Boyd, who had solicited this favour for an acquaintance. It precedes two other letters to Mrs. Boyd, that are delightful examples of his sense of humour, combined with clever though kindly criticism of contemporary books and their authors.

109, LANCASTER GATE, W.
Tuesday A.M. [*April* 3, 1894]

MY DEAR BOYD,

I once got sixty pounds from Chappell for some verses I wrote for Gounod, who set them to music, but this was a special thing. Most of the other composers who want to set my things to music are poor, or have *ten* children, or are *utterly* childless, or are old maids, or ladies who have had distinguished fathers leave them without a penny, or want to buy a piano, or to restore the east window in Poke-Stoges Church, and who simply feel that they *must interpret at any cost* (*mine* generally) the Christian soulfulness that my verses inspire in 'em. From them I sometimes get a five-pound note, or nothing. Generally nothing. And I am happy. What I am trying to say is that Mr. Partridge will probably have no difficulty in getting my permission for his friend when I know what the poem is.

I regret to say that I have found out that *you* are the one who is responsible for the late public statements that I am still good-looking. I have just received a letter from a very old friend in Rome, a spinster lady whom I knew ages ago in California. And she says — the italics are mine: 'I saw such a nice *idealized* picture of you *copied from the "Idler."* It was not only like a face in a dream, but a face to dream of! But I fear this will be too much for masculine vanity, and nothing but our long-enduring friendship makes me venture to say it.'

There! That lady saw me at Christmas, and didn't seem to find any dream faces lying around loose on me, but since she's seen your infernal drawing, this — this — is the result! Now I understand why your wife 'Injin-givered' me out of the original sketch.

You might say to your wife that she promised to let me know when she would go a-'Galleoying' with me, but she don't write. She said something vaguely about Wednes-day, but I have no longer any faith in her.

Don't let's play with her any more! I know a nicerer girl in the next street, round the corner, who don't go with her kind of boys, and I'll introduce you.

Yours always
B. H.

ROSENEATH, WREXHAM
Monday [April 16, 1894]

MY DEAR MRS. BOYD,

Aleck's letter must be answered first, as it came first, so tell him that I don't believe a word he says, and never did, that his undoubted talent for 'drawing' seems to include the long-bow, and that for a long time I refuse to 'pu' any gowans wi' him' and will not 'paidle i' the burn' with him on any account. Particularly as it has been raining here like 'anythink' and has been since I came!

As for yoursel', your story is more artistically con-cocted (like your sloe gin) — you had a longer time, you know, and you make poor Aleck fly his note first, like the raven that went out of the Ark and was drowned, before you ventured to send *your* dove with its olive branch.

But I forgive you — my nature is essentially humble

and forgiving—and will play with you when I come back. But let it be one of these games in which *I* am not always beaten.

The air here is very stimulating. I've got it on my nerves frightfully, and have lost appetite and sleep, but I am still hoping that after this 'upset' it will improve. If I can stand it, I shall stay a week or ten days in all. Thank you for the 'Nat. Observer'—I suppose you sent it. I can hardly believe I am at all like Sarah Grand. I'm afraid I'm more like Sarah Walker!

Yours always
BRET HARTE

109, LANCASTER GATE, W., Wednesday

MY DEAR MRS. BOYD,

I have only just got back from Weybridge. I have finished Howells's book. I think you may safely say it is a very pleasant social and political satire on American institutions and society, evolved from the *not very new* situation of a foreigner (the Altrurian) who comes from a country where the people have a gracious, ideal socialistic Republic of which the American one is proved to be only the insincere *beginning!* All this is told by *conversations* in which Mr. Howells—always Mr. Howells—is very imperfectly disguised as a banker, a manufacturer, a professor, a clergyman, a lady, and the foreigner himself. These people talk well, but seem to me rather colourless and even flavourless, and the scene takes place on the verandah of an American watering-place hotel, and in an American farmhouse, which you can't for the life of you see! The American woman, well drawn, but colourless too (you can't even see her *smart frock*, although you know she probably wore one), is Howellsian. There isn't a sensation of any kind in the book, nor an out-and-out laugh in its pages. You feel that it would be vulgar, and this is perhaps the crowning satire on American fashionable literature — because quite unconscious. And the most delicious touch, equally unconscious, is when Howells speaks of *himself*, 'the novelist,' as a writer of *romance!* Fully a third of the book is made up of a lecture delivered by the Altrurian, chiefly to the farmers and labourers. And in such excellent and even scientific English!

That's all! Please, Ma'am, may I go and play now? I am very busy to-day and am dining out, or I should try to tell you all this by word of mouth.

I hope you are 'keeping well' as we used to say in Scotland. Yours always

B. H.

The next two letters are written to Mr. Samuel S. McClure, editor of 'McClure's Magazine,' which had an article on Bret Harte by H. J. W. Dam.

109, LANCASTER GATE, W.
May 2, 1894

DEAR MR. McCLURE,

I have seen a paragraph going the round of the press, in reference to my future work, which I recognize as the concluding paragraph of Mr. Dam's interview with myself. It is word for word. Has his 'interview' been already published by you, and this merely a quoted fragment? Kindly let me know.

I have to thank you for the photographs of the illustrations of my works, and the interior of the Grafton Street room, but you will have to arrange with Mr. Dana in what manner they are to be distributed through his article. As far as I can remember, there was no allusion in his proof to the illustrations. *I* can add a line or two in reference to my illustrations and their work.

I have never received Mr. Goodman's sketch of me, and I don't quite understand what he eventually produced in place of the sketch in colour.

Yours very truly

BRET HARTE

P.S. Please address me care of my club, Royal Thames Yacht Club, 7 Albemarle Street W., for a day or two.

109, LANCASTER GATE, W.
May 4, 1894

DEAR MR. McCLURE,

I send, in a separate parcel, the photo of illustrations of my stories, etc., and have marked on the back of each the name of the story. But I do not find among them any copy of the most *original* and *valuable* pictures I sent; viz: Long's (R.A.) 'M'liss' and Pettie's Royal Academy picture of myself. It would be supremely ridiculous to leave out the only two really fine pictures of the collection, pictures which have never been copied before.

I have never seen Goodman's portrait of myself since he did it in colour. Have you not got a photo of it to send me? Please let me know.

I enclose herewith the photo of myself in a morning suit, which I had taken by Mr. Fall to supplement (if necessary) Mr. Goodman's portrait, in case it was not a satisfactory likeness.

Yours very truly

BRET HARTE

Bret Harte occasionally composed for his friends little sets of verses, and the amusing little poem written for Mrs. Boyd shows that he made good use of his stay at Glasgow and his knowledge of Scotch dialect. He also speaks, in the note that follows it, of his meeting with Lord Roberts, the famous English general, and Rudyard Kipling.

109, LANCASTER GATE, W.
Monday, 1894

MY DEAR BOYD,

I have just found the 'return' verses I wrote for you. I don't claim much for the *poetry* — it's the strict *accuracy* of Scotch epithet and description I was after. . . .

Yours always
B. H.

SCOTCH LINES TO A. S. B.
(From an unintelligent foreigner)

We twa ha'e heard the gowands sing,
  Sae soft and dour, sae fresh and gey;
And paidlet in the brae in Spring,
  To scent the new-mown 'Scots wha hae' (hay?)

But maist we loo'ed at e'en to chase
  The Pibroch through each wynd and close,
Or climb the burn to greet an' face
  The Steendhus gangin' wi' their jocs.

How aft we said 'Eh, Sirs!' and 'Mon!'
  Likewise 'Whateffer' — apropos
Of nothing — and pinned faith upon
  'Aiblins' — tho' why we didna' know.

We've heard nae mon say 'gowd' for 'gold,'
  And yet wi' all our tongues upcurled,
We — like the British drum-beat — rolled
  Our 'R's' round half the speaking worruld.

How like true Scots we didna' care
  A bawbee for the present tense,
And said 'we *will* be' when we 'were,'
  'Twas bonny, but it wasna' sense!

And yet 'ma frien'' and 'trusty frere,'
  We'll tak' a right gude 'Willie Waught'
(Tho' what *that* may be is not clear,
  Nor where it can be made or bought).

109, LANCASTER GATE, W.
Friday P.M. [*May* 4, 1894]

MY DEAR MRS. BOYD,

I am not certain yet if I shall go to Oxford to-morrow for over Sunday, but I will let you know if I do.

If not, I hope to tell you and Aleck all about the Astor 'Pall Mall' dinner last night, and of my meeting with some of my fellow craftsmen, especially Kipling.

I sat next to Roberts, not Arthur, but Lord 'Bobs,' a dear old chap. I am afraid he interested me more than our mighty intellect. For we are a conceited lot.

Yours always
B. H.

Some time previously Bret Harte had met the Earl of Compton, later Marquess of Northampton, of whom he subsequently became a close friend, and from the writing of the present letter up to the year of his death, he frequently visited him both at Compton Wynyates and at Castle Ashby. Bret Harte was always fascinated by the mediæval history of Europe, and the historic homes of England were always, on account of their past, a source of the greatest interest to him. More than any other, perhaps, this famous house, one of the oldest and most beautiful in England, was to leave the subtle imprint of its charm upon him. Reminiscences of these visits are found in 'The Desborough Connections' and 'The Ghosts of Stukeley Castle,' part of which were written there.

COMPTON WYNYATES

The historic estate of the Marquess of Northampton

COMPTON WYNYATES, KINETON
Saturday [July 2, 1894]

MY DEAR MRS. BOYD,

I was so sorry to leave London without seeing you on the day you were up for the first time. But my long put-off visit had to be made, and I am here at last until Monday night.

This is a most wonderful house, far beyond my conception of it. I cannot tell you of it now. Suffice it that I sleep in a bedroom *with two floors*, and a railing dividing them, with two steps leading up to the raised *dais*, like an actor. I have to come down these two steps to bed, and up two steps again to my dressing-table. The reason: I am just over the drawbridge, and the old portcullis is under my dressing-table. The house is a small edition of Hampton Court, only older and more picturesque.

I hope you are better and that you will keep well until my return. With love to Aleck, yours always

B. H.

The next letter to Mrs. Boyd, characteristic of Bret Harte's sense of fun, was written while staying with his son and daughter-in-law at Weybridge, during one of his short vacations from his work.

HURST GUITING, WEYBRIDGE, SURREY
Sunday [July 23, 1894]

MY DEAR BOYD,

Before writing a duty letter to your wife, I'm sending you a line privately, as I know the 'Missus' would lift your hair, old man! if she saw it. Well, it's just to say that things are 'booming' along just about the old gait since you left. The 'Fly-by-Nights' miss you, old Chappie! And as to the girls — my! Lotty B. and Katie S. want to know how the Scotch Laddie is gettin' on, and asked me if you remembered that supper at Romano's, and the dance afterwards — that night your wife thought you were at the Bible Society's dinner! — O you wicked!)

DEAR SISTER BOYD,

I am glad to hear that you like the new minister so well, and that his doctrine has none of the finalities and rank heresies of the modern school. It is so soul-satisfying that one's spiritual adviser is right both as to election and calling. I trust that my dear friend Aleck is more receptive of counsel in his peaceful Scotch home than I fear he was here.

I am sending him a copy of 'McClure's Magazine' (I am sorry to say that 'Baxter on the Free Kirk Council' has not yet arrived), with some painful illustrations of the 'Ingénue of the Sierras' which will probably gratify his worldly feelings of pride and revenge over my criticism of 'Johnniboy.' I would beg him also to observe the illustration at the beginning of the second instalment of 'Chu-Chu,' which is supposed to represent the pretty 'Consuelo,' in the 'Pall Mall Magazine.' He will be glad that Mr. Dove Keighly, the art editor, has not begged him to contribute.

I also send you a cutting which I will explain. It appears that my Carshalton friend was evidently deceived by the newspaper reports of my expected presence at the 'Keats' celebration, and sent a wreath for the bust, from 'Sappho of Green Springs.' This is the way the gallant reporter received it. Think of being called an *unromantic admirer* of B. H. — and the slur on her favourite heroine! I should have naturally taken no notice of it but *for that*. Being, I hope, 'a gent,' I could only sit down *after that* and write her a brief note *thanking* her. But it was a crushing paragraph.

I do not yet know what I am going to do during the next month. I have been staying here, over Sunday, with my son and his wife. The weather is most depressing, nothing but rain, and *no sun*, and the brief summer is slipping away. If you write to me, you had better address it to The Royal Thames Yacht Club, No. 7, Albemarle Street.

I will write again soon. Perhaps I may write to your husband.

Yours always
B. H.

Three more attractive letters to Mrs. Boyd, from London, Malvern, and his son's home, during a brief holiday which was mostly a convalescence, and during which he was, in spite of his broken health, working against time, are the only letters of interest during the summer of 1894.

109, LANCASTER GATE, W.
Saturday [August 18, 1894]

MY DEAR MRS. BOYD,

Although you and Aleck are a pair of gay but cautious Scotch deceivers, I am writing to admit that it was 'extraordinar' kind of you to take the trouble to write and wire me. But I had no hope, from the hour that I found you had arranged your outing entirely in reference to the 'dear child' — the central and omnipresent Stuart! — and were limited to places which you artfully knew wouldn't agree with *me!* So I gave up my fond dream of Savernake, or some pretty mountain village, where grown-up people could get some fresh air and quiet, and for which you remember I offered to get some sea-sand for the gentle Stuart to play with, and I was quite prepared for the telegram. But the wording of it (in my nervous condition) sounded awful! 'Sorry absolutely impossible for you,' was particularly depressing. The only 'cussing' I did was when I left your house and found I had been artfully deluded into the belief that you meant a *genuine* holiday. I grin with fiendish delight as I think it is probably raining now, and that Stuart can't go to the beach, and is probably crawling over you both in the back room over the butcher's shop, and eating unripe fruit on Aleck's drawings.

My son has taken a new house in Weybridge, and can't come with me on a trip as he promised. I have nothing before me but a week or so at Malvern, and after that I know not! I shall leave here on Monday. You can address me at the Club until I have a positive habitation. With love to Aleck, yours always

B. H.

IMPERIAL HOTEL, MALVERN
August 30, 1894

MY DEAR MRS. BOYD,

I have just found time to answer your charming but deceitful letter which was forwarded to me here from London, and I suppose this will find you back in St. John's Wood. *I have been very hard at work* ever since I have been here, and that is about all I can say, for I am afraid I am *not* getting much better or stronger for my sojourn here. It appears that the 'bracing' qualities of Malvern are only found by climbing (every day!) to the top of the highest hill, the Worcestershire Beacon, which would be equivalent to a drive to Hampstead from Lancaster Gate as far as time goes, and not so easy, while the hotel in which you live and breathe and eat and sleep stagnates itself on the hillside. But I have no time to look for any other places now, nor 'monkey' with excursions. All the excursions, by the way, are rather interesting, which after all is only saying that you have to get your pleasures elsewhere. The people in the hotel are mainly elderly invalids — so elderly and so invalidy that I, weak as I am! seem absolutely giddy and infantine beside them. They look upon me as a rather nice but dangerous boy. That is, the ones who don't know me. The others make a point of walking around with my books — from the circulating library — in their hands!

On my birthday — the 25th — I received a basket of hot-house fruit from the proprietor of the hotel, and sent to my sitting-room with his compliments. When I went down to dinner, I stopped to thank him, and asked him *how* he knew it was my birthday. He replied with some astonishment that he *did not know it!* — that it was a spontaneous gift, but instantly begged me to accept for my birthday a bottle of his best champagne with liqueurs and cigars to follow. It was awfully embarrassing, and I felt like a fraud, but I had to accept this *encore* present.

Don't expect me to feel the least sympathy or concern in your doings at the seaside! I have washed my hands of that ghastly fraud and deliberate deception. But I hope that Stuart paddles, and that the 'sly sea crabs' bite him; that he regularly overeats himself with unripe fruit; that you are thoroughly satisfied that artists are the best judges of places to go to, and that you and Aleck both managed to arrange for a little robbery (under insurance!) while you were away, and that you will both try to make me believe that you *went away* and *hurried back* entirely on *my* account.

I shall be here until Monday probably, and then — I don't know where I may go.

Yours always
B. H.

HARDUÉMONT, OATLANDS PARK
SURREY, *September* 19, 1894

MY DEAR MRS. BOYD,

I am sending you, in a separate parcel, the book and the newspaper clippings you so kindly lent me, and for which I have returned the ingratitude of keeping far beyond the decent limit. But my son got hold of 'The Red Robe' and I am only now able to wrest it from his eager hands. Besides, I hoped to be coming to London before this, and wanted to return it in person. But I have been keeping here at work; I was in London only on Saturday night late, and left before noon on Sunday, so that I had no time to avail myself of your hospitality.

I read your 'Burglary' and 'Hop-picking' articles *first*, and you know I mean no polite fiction when I say I thoroughly and actively enjoyed them. But as an old magazine and newspaper editor myself, I want to add that I think them the *very best* of their kind — and a kind that is rare in journalism — a combination of masculine brevity and concentration of subject with a feminine delicacy and poetry of observation.

The book is very good and took me quite out of myself, in that delightful land of romance where all unrealities are real, and we accept all history and all the past as pure fiction. I did not care for the conventional stage Richelieu, nor the conventional Don-Cæsar-de-Bazan-like hero (as I still love my Dumas and *his* inventions), but I thought his *conversation* very well managed and the book thoroughly spirited. It sent me to reading the 'Gentleman of France,' but I find the latter too like the other in idea and subject.

I hope to come up to London this week, but I will let you know. I have been a little better here, but, just as I am congratulating myself, I find myself doubled up with lumbago.

Now please don't tell me that you have been ill again, and are going away!

Always yours

B. H.

The remaining letters that can be traced to the end of the year are all addressed, with the exception of one to Mr. Watt, to his son Frank, and have a little of the same affectionate humour characteristic of those written years previously, when he was still a boy. Bret Harte and his son and daughter-in-law were devoted to each other, and he was always a regular and frequent visitor to their home.

109, LANCASTER GATE, W., *Saturday*

MY DEAR FRANK,

I rather expected that you would call here on Thursday, and therefore didn't write. I have such a loathing of this whole Boucicault business that I have waited until you and I could have an hour together and concoct a letter to your lawyer asking him to make a preliminary enquiry and *demand*. I would run down this afternoon to Weybridge (over Sunday), but I want to see John Hay, who is in London until to-morrow only, and I will make an appointment for some day and night early next week — if your wife is sure that she will not be inconvenienced.

I have been looking over my summer clothes, and find that I have not only reached the 'lean and slippered *pantaloon*' age, but that even my *coats* and *waistcoats* are *too large* for me. Now, my dear child, my usual method in such cases is to call in the aid of Messrs. Ikey Solomons & Co., whose magnificent advertisements in reference to 'gentlemen's cast-off clothing' you may have noticed in the daily papers, and who attend gentlemen 'at their own residences' with discretion and secrecy and the 'highest market prices.' I propose, therefore, my dear Sir, that *you* shall be my Ikey Solomons, and inspect, at your early convenience, and with your last quarter's allowance in your pocket, a few magnificent bargains. I can offer you Sir, the finest styles of tweeds, of good value and unimpeachable cut from the best West End tailors! I say nothing — perhaps it becomes me not to say it — in regard to the other advantages inseparably connected, interwoven and stitched, so to speak, in these garments. I could point out to you certain faultless tweeds in which you could travel from one end of England to the other without paying your bills — followed only by the admiring glances of the fair — which, as a younger and still unreflective man, might be of interest to you. I offer these — at low figures — five per cent off for cash. I need not say that the strictest secrecy will be observed.

With love to your wife and child and vicarious osculations. Attenuatedly, your ever affectionate father

B. H.

109, LANCASTER GATE, W.
Tuesday P.M.

MY DEAR FRANK,

My bag was really 'lifted' out of the brougham to-day while I was calling upon you. Lambert admits that he *might* have fallen asleep (I am sorry to say that is 'his custom of an afternoon') and undoubtedly some passing thief took that opportunity of 'boning' it from the seat beside the open window. I hoped that it might be only a slip of my memory, and that I had left it at Whiteley's or at home. But I quite remember now to have taken from

it the envelope of Boucicault papers as I got out of the
brougham.

Except for my silver flask, which was a present I have
kept for twelve years, there was little of value for the
appropriator. He can't poison himself with my homœopathic medicines. But I hate to have my belongings
pawed over by grimy fingers — and perhaps spread out
in an attic or a pawnshop!

I am telling you this only in case you should hear
anything of it in the neighbourhood. Your always affectionate papa

B. H.

109, LANCASTER GATE, W.
December 18, 1894

MY DEAR FRANK,

Just a line to say that Whiteley's cart will bring you
to-morrow a mechanical boat for Richard and a box of
tools for your youngest stepson. I shall send a book for
the eldest in a day or two. You will please keep them for
the boys until Christmas, and present them with my affectionate wishes. Everything is so hurried here toward
the holidays that one has to take the earliest opportunities.

I am afraid that for yourself and wife and house you
will have to accept that ten pounds as the free Christmas
gift of your affectionate father

B. H.

109, LANCASTER GATE, W.
December 23, 1894

MY DEAR MR. WATT,

I am sending you a whisky decanter (modern Venetian)
and a seal (a real Dutch antique), with a hearty wish for
your welfare and prosperity in the New Year, and the

kindest Christmas greetings (which are still older and more genuine!)

And I am thanking you in the same breath for your lovely Christmas gift of the silver cigar-case. It is very beautiful, and there is quite a fraternal embrace in its clinging curve to fit the body. It is a wonderful match to a flask I already have — and the two go quite around me! Thank you a thousand times.

Always yours

BRET HARTE

109, LANCASTER GATE, W.
December 26, 1894

MY DEAR FRANK,

Just a line to thank you so much for your very beautiful Christmas gift. All the same, you ought not to waste your substance in riotous living with marble paperweights for sumptuous offerings!

Your affectionate father

B. H.

The letters of the coming year are mostly to Mr. and Mrs. Pemberton and the Boyds, and contain many interesting details concerning Bret Harte's work as a playwright. In the following letter to Pemberton, he is not sanguine of the possibility of a good dramatization of 'The Judgment of Bolinas Plain,' which, however, in collaboration with his friend, matured into 'Sue,' by far the most successful of all of his dramatic efforts.

109, LANCASTER GATE, W.
January 15, 1895

MY DEAR PEMBERTON,

First: let me say that, during several visits lately to the vicinity of Birmingham, I have always been regretting that what I supposed was your *complete* removal to Broadway prevented me from renewing an old acquaintance. I am delighted *now* to find that you are dating your letter from the pleasant suburb where I once enjoyed your charming hospitality.

Now, as to the possible play that is in the little romance of 'Bolinas Plain': You know there is always the doubt if what is dramatic in ordinary *prose narrative* is equally dramatic in *theatrical representation*. The story is but a single *episode*, and I am afraid that much would have to be imported into it that might weaken its dramatic intensity.

But I am far from dissuading you to make the attempt, and perhaps we could *together* make something out of it, or I could at least make some suggestions regarding it. You might give me an idea of your conception. Perhaps we might talk it over. I think of coming up again to the vicinity of Birmingham, *next week*, and we might (if you are still there) meet at your home at Edgebarter.

With kind regards to your wife, yours always

BRET HARTE

Following upon the heels of the previous letter, we see that Bret Harte was now seriously engrossed in the idea of the new play, which up to the present was to be a great secret.

BIRMINGHAM, *January 26*, 1895

MY DEAR NAN,

I am afraid I am again remiss in writing, and even now I have had to have the draft, which I enclose, sent to me here at Birmingham where I have come on business. I have been busy ever since Christmas with a new story; it was a very tempting offer from a publisher, and I am even working at it now in my hotel while my other business is being despatched. *That* business is an offer from a well-known dramatist and manager who proposes to dramatize one of my short stories and *produce* it! It is one of my old illusions, as you know, but it has now been put in a more positive shape than any other offer I have had. However, I do not hope *much*, and shall not be disappointed.

I wanted to write before in regard to Jessamy's work, and Linley Sambourne of 'Punch' has promised to write me a letter in regard to her book of illustrations which might do her some good. I have had the opinion of many artists, and they all agree in praising her gracefulness and sense of prettiness in conception, but all think she has still much to learn about *drawing*. I like *all* her vignettes and bits of landscapes, and some of her figures are quite pretty in spite of their being 'out of drawing.' When I tell you that her work is much better than I *expected* — and her success in getting it placed with publishers still more than I conceived possible, from what I had seen of her other work — I have said all I can to *you*, but I shall say more to her when I write.

Thank you so much, dear Nan, for your pretty presents, which really arrived here *on Christmas day!* That book was simply marvellous and I have shown it everywhere. The velvet case was very beautiful. Tell Jessamy I think her photos very smart; they are much admired, but *I* prefer the one in the armchair. Where is the one of you? I sent you *my* decrepit, grey-haired, haggard portraits, that you may at least keep some idea of me — but you send me nothing! I hope when I write again I may send you further news of the play. I must close this now, as the post starts for Liverpool and America in half an hour. God bless you all, dear Nan, is the prayer and hope of your affectionate

LIMICK

The next two months were busily spent in frequent journeys between London and Birmingham — between the continuation of his regular work and the collaboration on the play.

109, LANCASTER GATE, W.
April 10, 1895

DEAR MRS. PEMBERTON,

After writing to you, I find, on enquiry at Paddington, that I could not arrive at *Broadway until Friday evening after dinner.* The regular trains on Good Friday are made to run with deliberate slowness and infrequency to atone for the wicked levity of excursion trains. It would be only a tantalization to come so far to have to return on Tuesday, and I was sorry that I had to wire you that I must postpone my visit until after Easter.

I have to finish some work before the three days' blight of the holidays descends upon London. Perhaps I was *too* sanguine and hopeful when I wrote you, for I *did* want to come. If you were only a little nearer, I should risk a Saturday to Monday visit. Let us hope that it is only a little deferred.

Yours always
B. H.

His next letter to a lady friend, Miss Chappell, written from the home of Lord Northampton, shows that he was all-absorbed in his rôle of dramatist, and speaks of his departure for Broadway, where Mr. and Mrs. Pemberton had moved from Birmingham. The little note that follows, to the same lady upon his return to London, is an example of the courteous and charming manner in which Bret Harte attended to the little social functions of his daily life.

COMPTON WYNYATES, KINETON
Tuesday

DEAR MISS CHAPPELL,

Just a line, to add to my previous letter, that I am leaving here, to-morrow, for Broadway, but I am not quite certain yet whether I shall also go to Birmingham, in which case I should not be able to come to you before *Tuesday* next. I will, however, wire to you from Broadway should I be able to come on Monday.

In great haste, yours very sincerely

BRET HARTE

109, LANCASTER GATE
May 6, 1895

DEAR MISS CHAPPELL,

I am so very sorry that I cannot avail myself of your generous offer, for I am engaged on Wednesday afternoon. And it seems so very ungracious to return the tickets, even at your own suggestion; but because I am myself unfortunate, I suppose I have no reason to prevent others from being made happy by your kindness.

Believe me, yours always

BRET HARTE

The heavy cold of which he speaks in the next two letters was to have much more serious effects than he realized. It was the beginning of the long illness which lasted, with brief abatements, for the remainder of his life, and which was the cause of his death, seven years later. The last letter to Mrs. Pemberton accompanied some presents for his friend's family, in souvenir of his stay at Broadway.

109, LANCASTER GATE, W.
June 19, 1895

MY DEAR PEMBERTON,

I stayed from Saturday to Monday at Cliveden, and, either from being walked off my legs through the woods on Sunday morning or blistered on a steam launch on the river in the afternoon, I somehow managed to develop as fine a cold as I could in *mid-winter!* I have been sniffling and coughing ever since, and my rheumatism is worse than ever. And this was the 'quiet Sunday' that Mr. Astor promised me!

I have not been able to work consequently since, with any comfort, but I hope to be well enough to start for Broadway on Saturday. Only please don't give me a 'quiet Sunday' nor expose me to the insincerities and inclemencies of an English summer, in the fond hope that it is doing me good! I will come to Honeybourne by the train you suggest, only I hope we haven't *far to ride*, as the jolting of a vehicle makes my neuralgia particularly lively and quite sets up my independent rheumatism. Pardon all these lamentable suggestions, my dear fellow, but I don't want to come to you an invalid. I sometimes think, in fact, that I ought not to inflict myself on anybody but a callous hotel-keeper, or a regular Gordon Hotel Company, Limited. I have an idea that Honeybourne is *farther* from Broadway than Evesham and a *longer drive*, and that you have dreadful ideas of showing me some *scenery!* Swear that you haven't.

Thank you so much for the clipping.

Yours always
B. H.

PYE CORNER, BROADWAY
WORCESTERSHIRE, *June 27,* 1895

MY DEAR ANNA,

I am sending you the draft to-day from this place where I am working on my 'play' with my collaborateur in his country house, and where I have come also in hopes of getting rid of a cold quite as severe as any I had last *winter!* I have no news from you; I have no news from Colonel Shepherd in regard to my lecturing tour in America. I shall wait until I hear something before writing again.

With love to the girls, always your affectionate

LIMICK

109, LANCASTER GATE, W.
July 3, 1895

MY DEAR MRS. PEMBERTON,

I am sending you a particularly hideous Japanese 'hat-rack' against that halcyon day when I might again 'hang up my hat' in your Worcesterian halls on some future visit. It is, however, a real novelty, though I don't know whether it isn't better fitted for the 'Museum' than the hall. But it can go in a 'dark corner' and frighten 'Phenyl' when naughty.

The other things are for the girls' 'Museum,' in which I took such a scientific interest. The skeleton is of 'George Washington when a child,' recovered at great expense from the ancestral vaults of the little church in Worcestershire, whose name I have forgotten, and you will kindly see that it is named as such. Attention may be called to the singular disproportion of the skull and the rest of the bony structure, showing the extraordinary cerebral development of the great American even at *that* early age. The skeleton was undoubtedly taken at the

great 'cherry-tree' epoch of his history, and a glance at
the frontal angles of the head will show the impossibility
of his 'telling a lie,' or indeed anything else at that time.
So the skeleton thus conveys that moral which should
underlie all scientific fact, and is especially suited for
'Museums' for the Young Person.

The entomological specimens consist of 'Spottybugi-
ana,' a singular Japanese variety, and the Skye Terrier
Spider, which is supposed to have been the one which
'frightened Miss Muffet away.' Examination of its
abdominal structure shows it to have lived exclusively
upon 'curds and whey' collected entirely from children.
These specimens are singularly rare, and unique, and are
presented with the writer's compliments to Madge.

I am trying to get you 'By Killarney's Rocks and Rills'
(or words to that effect) and will duly send it. I know
there was something else I promised and I am searching
the dim perilous depths of my memory for it. Perhaps
like Browning's Evelyn Hope, I shall 'wake and remember and understand,' sometime.

As Bret Harte admits, he had not been out of the British Isles for the past twelve years, and, as his health became worse, the doctors urged him to take a complete
rest somewhere on the Continent. He was at last contem-
plating a journey abroad, in company of a friend, Colonel
Collins. The benefit derived from a change of climate
would, however, be marred by the fact that, even for so
short a time, Bret Harte felt the impossibility of freeing
himself from his daily task. The real rest which he had
looked forward to for so long, he was never to know, for
the last years of his life were those in which he was forced
to work the hardest, wearied though he was by old age
and sickness.

My dear Mrs. Boyd,

You will smile at this familiar paper and wonder that in my wanderings I have got no farther from London than this. But I am here with my niece Miss Griswold and her friend and fellow traveller Miss Neale, and I have just despatched them to Warwick Castle to see the sights together, for I really cannot 'do' the old familiar 'shows' again! The house at Lancaster Gate is topsy-turvy, and the servants are going, and, like the dove that went out of the Ark, I find 'no rest for the sole of my foot,' and I am *en route* for *I don't know where yet.* I have many plans, but no preferences, nor any certainty of movement. Colonel Collins wants me to go to *Aix-la-Chapelle* with him, where he has to undergo the 'cure.' My niece wants me to go with her and her friend to Paris; perhaps I may combine both, and so — for a while — get out of this island; but all is yet unsettled. I shall, *I expect*, return to London day after to-morrow, then I may go to my friend Pemberton at Broadway for the week-end. I may go to Crewe, or I may go to Compton Wynyates — they are all 'on the cards.' But I do not see where I am to find the *rest* and *quiet* I am supposed to want. As my niece has her friend with her (who is an enthusiastic sight-seer and a worshipper of Gerty), they take the trouble of sight-seeing off my hands, and leave me to myself and that aforesaid 'rest.' They are both enthusiasts of a new kind of religious 'fad' which, they tell me, is sweeping America, called 'Christian Science.' They wonder I have never heard of it! Have you? They have books upon it, they expound it to *me*. Our conversation is not flippant nor wildly entertaining. My niece is serious, and her friend teaches *Latin* and cognate things in a seminary in Baltimore.

It was very nice of you to write to me, and overlook my long silence — which was only that I was greatly preoccupied with many things for the future which have to be settled *now*. And I never can write letters 'on the wing' — it always seems like having a protracted conversation on a street corner! I will write to you again as soon as I know anything definite of my movements. Do send me that book of Mallock's, if not too late. I should like to read it, though I may not agree with you about the hero. (I will afterwards send it to Mrs. Hindley and pay you the difference between the reduced market values! Eh, Sirs, but I am getting 'canny' in my old age.)

Give my love to your husband, and as much of it to Stuart as will do him good; — don't spoil him with sweets as is your fashion. Pity me in my roving loneliness.

Always yours

BRET HARTE

109, LANCASTER GATE, W.

August 2, 1895

MY DEAR MRS. BOYD,

I have been so busy with work, so bewildered by many plans, so erratic in my movements, that I have not had time to answer your kind and thoughtful letter, and even if I *had*, I could have given no satisfactory account of myself. If I was not pledged to Collins to come to Aix, I would seek out some quiet place in England where I could work. But the doctor says I *must not work* during my holidays; he says also that I must not linger at Aix longer than a week. My niece, who has been in Paris for a week, wants me to join her party (with a French nephew and *his* family) and come to Switzerland. My doctor also advises me, if I don't go to Switzerland eventually, I ought to go to Braemar in Scotland, and not work! — while Mr. Watt all the time is dangling before my eyes the engagements I must finish this year. It would not be strange if between these many stools I should come to ground somewhere in England after all. So you see I have not written about myself before, because I absolutely knew nothing about my own movements. . . .

I went to Broadway on business of the play, and to consult with my friend in regard to another suggested to me by a London manager and actor. I returned on Tuesday night only. It is very quiet and pleasant there, but my friends have a *small* house and a *largo* family.

I have not yet finished the 'Heart of Life,' for I thought the first volume very dragging and tiresome and I have only just survived that long-drawn funeral! Without entering upon any discussion with you as to the reality or even resemblance of the character of the hero to anybody, I think the great mistake of the author is in making him *serious* in regard to his weakness and even *sentimental* over it, and the still greater mistake of the *writer* taking it seriously. You may remember another character in which you saw *the same resemblance* in one of my stories, but I think *I* never treated him *seriously;* on the contrary, I make fun of him as he deserved. I think the story interminably long; I have only got as far as 'the introduction to Pansy,' who is the same woman as the one in 'The Human Document,' as inexplicable, and as unexplained.

I have been trying to find Aleck, but we have missed each other.

Always yours
BRET HARTE

LANGHAM HOTEL, PORTLAND PLACE
LONDON, W., *Thursday* P.M.

DEAR MR. WATT,

I enclose herewith the typewritten copy and manuscript of 'Bulger's Reputation.' Madame V. de V., who herself typewrote the first part of it, went to Switzerland before I completed it, and I am obliged to send you the simple manuscript of the end, which you will, however, see is also typewritten. It makes over four thousand words (I could not make it fit Mr. Roberts's order, but I think that both the 'Strand' and 'Idler' are willing to take something under their limit of six thousand words). Of course, as I cannot send the typewritten copy, I *must* see the printed proof before it appears anywhere. You will kindly make a note of it.

I have my foot in the stirrup and leave London, tomorrow, *en route* for Aix-la-Chapelle, though I may stop a day or two at Folkestone. You can acknowledge this by a line sent *to the house*, which will be forwarded when I have a foreign address.

In great haste, yours very truly

BRET HARTE

Bret Harte decided finally to go to Switzerland, which he had visited when Consul at Crefeld. Again, as then, his thoughts turned back to California, and his dearly beloved Sierras. 'I never knew before how I really loved them,' he writes, 'and how they have taken such a hold on my life.'

HOTEL BYRON
VILLENEUVE, SWITZERLAND
August 25, 1895

MY DEAR NAN,

At last, after being nearly twelve years in England without change of scene or climate, I have managed to get a

holiday for a few weeks in Switzerland. I wish it could be,
as the doctor orders, a complete *rest* and change, but, alas,
I must still work, only I hope to do so under better conditions, and perhaps freshened by the fine air of the lake —
although I am not 'up' in the bracing air of the high alti-
tudes. Some of my doctors think I am better out of an
exciting air and that I don't require much stimulation.
However, this is only an experiment, for, if I do not find
myself much better, I shall go somewhere higher up. This
whole country, you know, is simply given up to hotels and
pensions that invade the very crags of the mountains, and
give an artificial ballet-scena to everything. The dear old
Sierras, after all, are infinitely finer with their freshness,
their beauty, their absolute and wholesome rudeness and
sincerity, and I never knew before how I really loved them,
and how they have taken such a hold on my life; here
everything is grand and spectacular — but in the very
heart of the wilderness there is a suspicion of *drains* and
the smell of French cooking comes in at your window, with
the breath of the pines. I have never been to this more
popular and frequented part of Switzerland before. When
I was last on the Continent I went to Zurich and along
the Wallen See, which are not as tourist-haunted. I am
sending this to the London Bank with the request that
they will enclose a draft to you in another envelope beneath the one I shall address. You had better, however,
write to me to the care of 'The Royal Thames Yacht
Club, Albemarle Street, London,' and I can have the
letters forwarded to me to any change of address, as the
house at Lancaster Gate is closed while the family are
visiting their relations in Belgium and Berlin. I was a
few days in London and at Folkestone with Frank and his
wife before I left.

I wish, of course, I was with you in the Adirondacks

rather than here, but I have been very much alarmed at the effect of the recent hot weather — which has been phenomenal on the Continent and is certainly as extreme as anything I ever experienced at home. I will write you soon again; with love to the children, always your affectionate

LIMICK

Bret Harte was, during his so-called vacation, in almost daily correspondence with his literary agent, and was engaged on a new story, begun and completed during his stay in Switzerland. The following letter is addressed to Mr. A. S. Watt, who was associated with his father.

HOTEL BYRON
VILLENEUVE, *August 29*, 1895

DEAR MR. WATT,

I have to thank you for yours of 16th, 27th, and *26th* (the latter, as I only received it last night, may be misdated).

In reference to the German translation of 'Clarence,' I have not offered the rights to anybody and they are therefore *still for sale.* I think you ought to get twenty-five or thirty pounds for it, but the German publishers, specially when Jews, are very mean and not always *honourable!* They would think nothing of giving *your* price and then writing to me for a reduction, and delaying the whole thing until some time *after the book is published*; they having warned all the publishers off by saying they had a contract or were in treaty with you — and then, when there is *no competition*, offering you some niggard price. But perhaps you know their methods already. I should settle upon some good firm and give them no chance to delay about it.

I cannot remember what are the new volumes of Tauchnitz which are not accounted for in your father's recent advances to me (by pro. notes) on account. Perhaps you can let me know.

Yours very truly
BRET HARTE

P.S. I posted the corrected typewritten copy of 'Bulger's Reputation' to you yesterday. By the way, you did not tell me how many words it contained; did your typewriter count it?

B. H.

Although Bret Harte was sensitive to the grandeur of the Swiss Alps and the beauty of her lakes, yet, accustomed to the rugged magnificence of the West, so powerfully described in his works, he was shocked by the intensity of the tourist industry, and the impression of artificiality so cleverly depicted in the two delightful letters to Mrs. Boyd, written from Villeneuve and Geneva.

HOTEL BYRON, VILLENEUVE
LAC DE GENÈVE, September 5, 1895

MY DEAR MRS. BOYD,

I have been wandering ever since I left England on the 19th of August, and not only have I had no time to write to anybody, but have no address where I could receive letters, so that your pleasant birthday reminder reached me only a day or two ago. I came directly to Cologne without stopping at Aix, as I had intended, and met my friend there, with the son of one of his friends, and together we made some trips up and down the Rhine in the hottest weather I ever experienced in Europe, and the densest crowds I ever mingled with, out of an English bank holiday. Luckily they were *local* tourists, mostly German, and very good-natured, so for a few days we basked in the sun, and the *sauerkraut*, and the dear old smell of pipes and dregs of beer glasses, which reminded me of the old days. I found myself able to 'check off' the castles of the Rhine for my friends, and waved my handkerchief (to Collins's intense English disgust) to all the other boats that passed, just like old times. We parted at Bonn, he and his friend for England, and I the same night through Strasbourg into Switzerland, to Bâle and Lausanne, by Neuchâtel and on to Vevey, Montreux, Territet, Chillon, and Glion. I have been around the Lake (Leman), up the Territet-Glion railway (a kind of lift that gives you the sensation of being dragged upstairs by your coat-collar), and up to Rocher de Naye, about six thousand feet! All this I know gives you no idea of what I have seen, and what has particularly impressed me. This part of Switzerland is entirely new to me. I can only tell you that the photographs I send you are absolutely *true* in detail and effect, and that the character and even *defect* of the scenery here is that it looks as if it were artistically composed; all the drop-curtains, all the stage scenes, all the ballet backgrounds you have ever seen in the theatre exist here in *reality*. The painter has nothing to compose, the photographer still less; that *chalet*, that terrace, that snow-peak, is exactly *where it ought to be*. The view from the balcony at this moment is a picture hanging on my wall, not a view at all. You begin to have a horrible suspicion that Daudet's joke about all Switzerland being a 'gigantic hotel company' is true. You hesitate about sitting down on this stone terrace, lest it shouldn't be 'practicable'; you don't dare to knock at the door of this bright Venetian-awninged shop lest it should be only painted canvas. There is a *whole street* in

Montreux that I know I have seen a dozen times at the Grand Opera. The *people*, tourists of all nations, are the only thing *real*, and in the hotels, when they are in full dress at the balconies or salons, they look like — the *audience!*

Imagine all this in an atmosphere that is almost as unreal to a Briton or an American, an atmosphere perfect in lightness, in clearness, in absolute purity; two weeks of unclouded sunshine, unsurpassed sunsets, absolutely balmy nights, when you can sit out all night without a thought of imprudence — where going to bed seems the only thing stupid, and even improper! Since I left America I have never known what summer meant in all its fullness and graciousness. Of course, it isn't 'bracing,' no more than a *spectacle* would be, but I am afraid that it has forever spoiled me for the English climate! I dread going back. Imagine, I, who was quite content to hover over the English islands for twelve years, have suddenly developed a taste for wandering on the Continent!

And, strangest of all, I find my heart going back to the old Sierras whenever I get above three thousand feet of Swiss altitude, and — dare I whisper it — in spite of this pictorial composition, I wouldn't give a mile of the dear old Sierras, with their honesty, sincerity, and magnificent uncouthness, for a hundred thousand kilometres of this picturesque Vaud!

Of course, I don't know when I shall return. I am sending this to St. John's Wood, but if you answer it to this address within a week, I shall get your letter here.

With love to your husband, yours always

B. H.

GRAND HÔTEL DE LA PAIX
GENÈVE, *September 25, 1895*

My dear Mrs. Boyd,

It was very nice to think that my letter pleased you and that I *did* succeed in conveying to you — away off there in smoky London — the unalloyed and genuine delight that my surroundings of sunshine, scenery, and summer have given and are still giving me. For, although there is already autumn by the calendar, it is still ripe summer to the eye and all the senses; there is an absolute joy in mere existence; it is a comfort to get up in the morning with the air about the temperature of your own body; to have no concern as to what you shall wear to-day, except that it shall be the lightest. To grudge even the hours that you *must* sit down in a room to work (for one must work even under these conditions, and I have really written a great deal since I left England), and to enjoy your meals in the open air. This is quite enough to make my letters less grumblesome and more buoyant than usual, but when I read your letter the other morning, and grasped your suggestion of the *reason*, I almost laughed outright as I glanced around the table at the heterogeneous collection of uninteresting tourists.

Of course, I have met some pleasant people, and I have at least a chum, in a retired Indian Colonel, who has a civil post somewhere in India, but is here for his holidays. He is what you might imagine old Colonel Newcome would have been had he been *prosperous* and *happy* in his retirement. The dear old boy, for he is the real youthful one of our companionship, is going back to India to-morrow, and I am going with him as far as Lausanne, to see him *en route* for Brindisi. I shall miss him greatly. I met another charming old chap, of an old French type, in Baron de Blonay, a cousin of Madame Van de Velde's, who lives in the old Château de Blonay that was built in the tenth century, and who showed me the shields and arms of the old Crusaders around the walls of his dungeon-like hall. The old château is a smaller copy of Chillon, but much older. The old chap in his stately way, in spite of his white flannels, looks like an old Seneschal!

I thought I would *not* like Geneva, imagining it a kind of Continental Boston, and that the shadow of John Calvin and the old Reformers, or, still more, the sentimental idiocy of J. J. Rousseau and the de Staëls and Madame de Warens still lingered there. But I was agreeably disappointed in the place. It is gay, brilliant, and even as pictorial as the rest of the Lake Leman, and as I sit by my hotel window on the border of the lake, I can see Mont Blanc, thirty or forty miles away, framing itself in a perfect vignette! Of course, I know that the whole thing was arranged by the Grand Hotel Company that runs Switzerland. Last night, as I stood on my balcony looking at the great semi-circle of lights framing the quay and harbour of the town, a great fountain sent up a spray from the lake, three hundred feet high, illuminated by beautifully shaded *lime-lights*, exactly like a 'transformation scene.' Just then the new moon—a pale green sickle— swung itself over the Alps! But it was *absolutely too much*. One felt that the hotel company was overdoing it, and I wanted to order up the hotel proprietor and ask him to take it down. At least, I suggested it to the Colonel, and he thought it would do as well if we refused to pay for it in the bill.

But I am 'overdoing' the letter-writing, too. You do not tell me about yourself and Aleck, and what you are doing. Tell him I never regretted before that I was not a painter. Ask him if he ever saw an expanse of thirty miles of water exactly the colour of the inner shell of a mother-of-pearl oyster. *I* have!

Alas, I shall have to be returning soon to the dreadful months of the 'R's' and the oysters! Perhaps in ten days.

Always yours

B. H.

The last letter, written before his return to England, accompanied the manuscript of the story mentioned previously. His holiday had lasted a little over six weeks, and, in spite of the continual strain of work, he derived from the pure air and change of surroundings a temporary benefit.

HÔTEL BERNERHOF, BERNE
October 8, 1895

DEAR MR. WATT,

I enclose herewith the story for the 'Graphic,' entitled 'A Night on the Divide.' It runs a little over six thousand words. I have taken 'a bear incident' (although I have treated it *half humorously*), as the editor suggested. But it is the same grizzly bear that 'Miggles' made a pet of — and as such ought to find favour with the general reader. Kindly advise me of its receipt, but you had better address me at my club, 'The Royal Thames Yacht Club, No. 7, Albemarle Street,' in case I have left here.

Of course, I should like to see the proof of the story as soon as possible, even if it appears only a year hence.

Yours very truly

BRET HARTE

Bret Harte's new book 'Clarence' was completed shortly before his departure from England, and his comments on this work will no doubt be found interesting in view of the marks of appreciation with which its appearance was greeted in England.

109, LANCASTER GATE, W.
October 16, 1895

DEAR MR. WATT,

I am considerably mystified by the proofs you sent me of the 'Convert of the Mission,' and not a little indignant to find that the editor of the publication had treated my manuscript very much as Mr. John Camden Hilton treated his pirated edition of my works in England — i.e., *had broken up all my paragraphs into short French journalistic ones* — in order to gain length! I need not explain to *you*, who know something of composition, that this is as destructive of style as if he had substituted words of a greater length than the copy to *fill out a line!* It will amuse you also when you remember how these gentlemen resist paying for a few hundred words over the limit — even when the story requires it — on the ground that *length* is of no value to them!

But I have no desire to make your new clients any unnecessary trouble in 'measuring' and I shall alter the proofs to my original construction only when I think *their* style of paragraphing is a little *too obvious.*' I will reserve the others for the book reprint.

I am almost as surprised as I am gratified with the remarkable unanimity of praise in the reviews of 'Clarence.' Not that I didn't like my own work in it — but I did not believe the *story* would interest Englishmen. I wrote it as an *American* for *Americans*, to try and make them understand what was really fine and strong in their own history, instead of the usual pinchbeck imitations of English society novels — apart from any style of my own in rendering it, and I needn't tell you how honestly pleased I am — apart from being the author — to find that I was right. Perhaps you may remember my saying something to this effect to *you* when I conceived the story, which I may say to *you, now,* with equal confidence, as between ourselves, that *I don't think my own countrymen see it yet!* Funny! — isn't it?

One of the most remarkable things about these citizens is that while I, a Northern partisan in will and blood, have made a *partisan* story — the old *Tory*, *Southern sympathizing* journals have been loudest in their praises!

I only arrived here Monday night with, unfortunately, a bad cold, contracted *en route*. I may have to go North at the end of the week. But *I hope* you will find time to call here some morning.

In haste, yours very sincerely

BRET HARTE

P.S. I will make the corrections in the 'Convert of the Mission' at once, and send the proofs to you. I am glad that Mr. Joyce liked the 'Graphic' story — it was a happy thought — that 'Miggles bear'!

In the little note to Mrs. Boyd written from Castle Ashby, another property of the late Lord Northampton, Bret Harte admits that he has not been himself again since his return from abroad.

CASTLE ASHBY, NORTHAMPTON
Friday A.M. [*November 15, 1895*]

MY DEAR MRS. BOYD,

Only that I am returning this afternoon, and have another horrid cold, keep me from sending you an excruciatingly witty and delightfully sarcastic reply to your wicked insinuations. But one cannot be funny with a weeping eye, and nose — and, alas, I have never been light-hearted since Switzerland!

I may have to go away again for a day or two next week, but before that you will see me. Always yours

B. H.

At a moment when there was some tension between the two countries, Bret Harte had determined to return to America in the event of hostilities. The news was all the more perturbing to him for the reasons which Bret Harte explains, not without a deep regret, in the following letter to his wife. No one suffered more than he did from the lack of comprehension which he believed to exist toward him, on the part of his countrymen. The Earl and present Marquess of Crewe, the British Ambassador to France, and brother of the late Mrs. Henniker, was a great friend of Bret Harte, and it was from his home that the next few letters are written.

FRYSTON HALL
FERRYBRIDGE, YORKSHIRE
December 18, 1895

MY DEAR NAN,

I tried very hard to get the enclosed draft for three hundred dollars early, but it has only just followed me here, and I am posting it in great haste that it may reach you about Christmas time, so that you can use the extra fifty dollars for presents for yourself and the children.

I am here on a visit to the Earl of Crewe — the son of the late Lord Houghton, whom you remember breakfasted with us once at Eliza's in Fifth Avenue; and though I have often been invited before I have never yet succeeded in effecting my intention. Even now, I have only come on the promise of Lord Crewe that I should be allowed to work while here, and I have brought with me some unfinished manuscripts which I want to complete by Christmas, if I consent to stay during the holidays. Everybody here is very much excited over the President's Message, which they all believe means war between the two countries! Heaven forbid! — for all reasons — and not the least, the selfish one that it would be ruinous

Yours very truly

Northampton.

to my future, for I should, of course, no longer remain in England — the only place where I could earn my daily bread. For much as I love my own country — it does not love *me* sufficiently to enable me to support myself there by my pen!

God bless you and the children, Nan, with love and Christmas greetings from your ever affectionate

LIMICK

FRYSTON HALL
FERRYBRIDGE, YORKSHIRE, *Sunday*

MY DEAR FRANK,

I could not attend to my Christmasing before I left London, and, as I shall *not* be there on *Christmas* Day, I must trust to others to send the few little gifts I have selected for *you;* you know already what they are. I beg you will give the 'mechanical dredge' and the 'Great Wheel' to Richard with the Caldecott books, while the other books are for your stepsons, whose names I will write in them — the books! — some day when I am at your house. I have selected a Japanese work-basket table for your wife, which I trust will reach her safely and which she will accept with love and Christmas greetings from me.

Then, last of all, I enclose you a cheque! I am afraid you will not find it much — *I* didn't — but I have kept it all these weary months! — and it goes to you now with kindest Christmas wishes from your affectionate father

B. H.

FRYSTON HALL
FERRYBRIDGE, YORKSHIRE, *Sunday*

DEAR MR. WATT,

As I do not expect to be in London during the Christmas holidays, I fear I must slightly anticipate the occasion and, for once, trust to others to forward to you from me that usual little trifle which I hope is, however, a symbol of our larger friendship from year to year.

As a Scotchman, you will recognize my providence in sending you something 'for a rainy day'; as *my friend* you will accept it as a Christmas and seasonable offering from yours

BRET HARTE

The correspondence for the year ends with the next two letters, which find him back in London, settled this time in his own home, which remained his headquarters until his death.

74, LANCASTER GATE, W.
December 19, 1895

MY DEAR PEMBERTON,

I am sending you and your wife two Christmas gifts, which, however idiotic and useless they may be, you must accept in that real Christmas spirit which you, and such as you, have done so much to foster! The flower-vase stand your wife *must* find room for somewhere in the domain of Pye Corner; the revolving small book and newspaper stand *must* go into your study if *you* have to go out! Such are the sweet austerities of the season.

I always select something *Japanese* because I fondly believe you don't make 'em in Birmingham. But I am prepared to hear the reverse.

But they go to you with my heartfelt wishes for a happy Christmas for you and yours, and a hope that the New Year may bring you a fuller meed of happiness than the last.

Yours always
BRET HARTE

The play was now almost completed, and Bret Harte submitted it to his friend Sir Charles Wyndham, the famous English actor, whose advice he valued very highly. Bret Harte's ill-health was making his work daily more difficult, and yet he had never been so rushed in order to fulfil his engagements. The slow and careful manner in which he wrote, and the infinite pains devoted to the perfecting of every line that came from his pen, did not simplify his task. The next few letters are the only ones of interest that can be traced for the first half of 1896.

74, LANCASTER GATE, W.
December 30, 1895

DEAR MR. WATT,

I have just returned to London to find your very charming present, and the little note which adds lustre to it, until the tortoise-shell pink shines! Thank you most heartily.

Alas! I have not seen the sun since I left London two weeks ago — except in one or two English homes where I visited. On Christmas Day I looked out upon a Christmas-card landscape with *snow* — but the same grey sky over all!

Hoping to see you, with best New Year wishes to you and yours, always yours

BRET HARTE

Thursday night [January 10, 1896]

MY DEAR PEMBERTON,

A thousand and one thanks for that flashing paper-knife! It's a sword — a regular 'Excalibur' which I am afraid this puny arm is scarcely fit to wield! So its solid blade shall lie on my writing-table, and be as good as an extra candle against this awful London sky.

I met Wyndham last night at the theatre. He recognized me from the stage, as I was in a box with some friends, and sent for me to come to his dressing-room. I asked him about the *scenario*, and I find that he would like it to be very complete and full, so that he could grasp all the possibilities and see if there are *enough of them*.

Friday

I left this letter unfinished last night, as it was too late for the post, and I now have yours of the 9th. I shall do as you say, and send the manuscript to Wyndham *at once*, just as it is. At least we shall have his criticism. In haste, yours always

BRET HARTE

74, LANCASTER GATE, W.
March 31, 1896

MY DEAR NAN,

I have only just now been able to get you the draft, as I am working night and day to finish a long story which, when done, will, I hope, relieve me of the financial tightness I have been labouring under for half a year. If I had kept my health and strength, it would not have occurred, for, thank Heaven! I have always work enough ordered, but I have not been well since I left Switzerland, and it is not strange that a man nearing sixty should not be able always to do his *day's* work! I am afraid that I cannot get away for Easter either. In great haste, but with much love, always your

LIMICK

74, LANCASTER GATE, W.
May 26, 1896

MY DEAR NAN,

I have been through quite a siege of rheumatism, which is giving way now to one of my winter colds in the head and throat! For three or four weeks my right hand was so cramped and painful that I could hardly write, and the little finger is still so swollen at the second joint that it reminds me of my poor mother's hand in the later years of her life. The doctor says it is a kind of *gout* — and proposes that later I should go to some baths — here or on the Continent. It is too bad, as I have a big job of writing — a long novel on my hands — cramped as they are! I don't want to be a cripple quite yet, however, and I must try to get rid of my gout some way.

I suppose you know Frank is at Brighton — but if Madame V. de V. takes a country place (as she thinks of doing) she might let it to Frank and me, when she is in her town house, and doesn't require it. It would be a great change from London, which is always unsuitable to me in winter. I should have gone to Switzerland this last winter, but I dreaded being so far alone, and among strangers.

I am so sorry, Nan, to hear of your repeated illnesses. Surely what you call the 'grippe' must be very different from what we call the 'influenza' here — people don't have it *so many times!* They can't — it is too severe!

I enclose the draft which I had hoped to send you earlier in the month.

With love to all the children, always dear Nan, affectionately yours

LIMICK

74, LANCASTER GATE, W.
May 30, 1896

MY DEAR NAN,

I have had a very hard spell of work which I am just finishing, and I hope next month to send you the draft a little earlier. A good deal of this work has been done in the country, for I was really too exhausted to do it in town. Frank and his wife were with me, visiting Madame Van de Velde in her new country home — a little cottage in a very rural but very delightful part of Hampshire. I was consequently kept up by the pure air and healthful surroundings, and was enabled to do my work better. But holiday! — I have had none!

I and my collaborateur — a very pleasant literary man and dramatist of some ability — have completed a contract with an *American manager* for the production of a play we have written together. You may remember that I told you I was engaged upon it some time ago. We did not think to produce it first in America, but we thought it advisable not to lose the offer. I will write you the particulars later, but *please don't say anything about it yet.* I hope something may come of it to relieve me of this continuous strain. With love to the children, always, dear Nan, your

LIMICK

ARFORD HOUSE
HEADLEY, HANTS, *June 30*, 1896

MY DEAR NAN,

I am again late, but it could not be helped; I have not yet received the money for work done over two months ago — and yet my regular expenses go on. I am sorry, very sorry, that you should have been detained in Plainfield after the first of July, but it could not be helped. I have your letter of the 12th; if I do not regularly acknowledge their receipt, you know that I generally tell you if I *miss* one; though I am mortified to remember now that I never acknowledged the presents you sent me at Christmas, when I was delighted with them, and believed that I had told you so! I probably shall not hear from my play before October, but as soon as the manager writes me that it is ready for production I shall tell you, and if it is performed anywhere where you can see it I shall see that you have tickets.

I hope you will not think me rude to *your* friends if in enclosing these autographs I cannot help saying how utterly heartless, soulless, indelicate, insincere, and vulgar I hold the whole tribe of autograph-hunters, big and little, and how I loathe them! I could tell you so many stories of them — of their insolence and brutality, and their complete *want* of any sentiment of gratitude, respect, veneration, admiration, or even *knowledge* of the people from whom they expect these favours or of any feeling that could excuse their persistence — that you would not wonder at my extravagance. Some day I may tell these things publicly!

I am here at work, but the air is pure and the place rural and secluded, and I work better than in London. Sometime I may send you some photographs of it — taken by *myself* — when I am a little more proficient in the art. Alas! I have only a cheap instrument and am very bungling.

I do not know yet whether I shall go to Switzerland or not this autumn; it will depend much upon the amount of work I can get ready before.

I am sorry — yet I cannot help being amused with your accounts of the children's health. No wonder I cannot think of my daughters as grown-up young women — when they are continually being prostrated by infantile diseases! Thank Heaven! I have not yet been worried by Frank's 'teething.'

With great love to them, nevertheless, always your
                                                            LIMICK

Bret Harte always hoped to return to Switzerland, if only for a few weeks, but it was not possible for him to be so far from publishers, etc., so that his summer was spent in England, with brief visits to the country. The two letters to Mrs. Boyd are the only ones of this period.

74, LANCASTER GATE, W.
July 25, 1896

MY DEAR MRS. BOYD,

I have been very long in answering your pleasant letter, but I dare say you have forgotten it, while I have not — so I shall make no excuses! I came up to London from Hampshire about ten days ago, with a long list of engagements to wipe off in town, just as I had wiped off my drudge work in the country. I think I preferred the latter! For I find myself very quickly fagged out in town, and shall be glad to get away again.

Everything here looks prematurely worn out; this long drought has parched up the Park, where the leaves lie as thick as in October! The grass looks like the straw that is littered in the street before sick folk's houses — and it is only July! I know no one else writes this to you, for no one else seems to notice it as I do. They all rush around in that dreary race at the end of the season, and think of nothing else. But it is terrible to think of a bleak, leafless early autumn.

I have been, of course, to Broadway since I arrived and I shall go back to Hampshire for a while; then to Compton Wynyates if I don't go abroad — and then, but that's far enough to look ahead. As for you and Aleck, I don't suppose anything short of another robbery would bring you back to London, before you had 'served your time' in Scotland. I know you don't like it there; I never believed you did! But I am firmly convinced that you and

Aleck and all other self-righteous 'Scotch' people go up there every year as a kind of penance, to get absolution and 'indulgence' for your wicked gaiety in town! I never seem to really see you there enjoying yourselves — as you did at Winchelsea, for example!

I disbelieve in that strip of seashore where you picnic! I remember, with a shudder, some of the Scotch coast scenery — and your picnic must have much of the horror of a shipwreck! I can see you with a shawl on, cowering behind a rock, while Aleck with his only remaining match (the others have been blown out by the gale) tries to light a fire, and Stuart endeavours to wrest a floating Bath-bun from the yeasty waves.

After an hour of this 'privation and suffering,' you allow yourself to be rescued and creep home to a 'peat-fire,' with a cold in the head. Then you eventually return to London, and think St. John's Wood a Paradise!

I am only just now finishing Zola's 'Rome,' which you lent me. I read it at night when I go to bed, and regularly forget where I left off, and have to turn back the next night. At this rate, with careful obliviousness I may be able to make it last until I see you again. For all that, it's *very fine* — even if a little guide-bookish.

Let me know how long you can stand it in Scotland. With love to Aleck and Stuart, always yours

B. H.

74, Lancaster Gate, W.
August 31, 1896

My dear Mrs. Boyd,

I really believe that you intended your last letter to be a *birthday* letter to me, though you did not allude to it, and your date 'Sunday' was conveniently vague. Anyhow, it was pretty enough for a birthday present, and

much more original and interesting than most birthday
letters. I had my son and his wife with me in Hants, on
the 25th (you observe how artfully I supply *the date* that
you had forgotten), and I also received the usual congrat-
ulatory letters and telegrams.

This birthday party and some country teas have been
my only excitement. During the rest of the time I worked
and walked: it's a lovely locality for *both* occupations.
When I was tired of the monkish seclusion of my semi-
detached green-house study, I could lay aside my pen
and ramble through the loveliest and quietest lanes in all
England. Yes, even more quiet and remote than Winchelsea!

Of course this 'Sleepy Hollow' existence leaves me
little news to tell you, except that my play 'Sue' (the
collaboration with my Birmingham friend, Pemberton)
will come out in America on the 14th of September. A
noted American manager, Daniel Frohman (whom Aleck,
I dare say, knows), is to produce it in Philadelphia, and
his management, I am told, is a guerdon of its being well
acted and mounted. But after all that — who can tell?
I shall, however, be very content with a little money
from it.

I was up to town to-day on business, but I shall go back
to-morrow to 'Arford House, Headley, Hants,' to stay
until the 8th, and then I shall probably go to Compton-
Wynyates and Bushey Park for short visits. But I hope
to see you before then. And you must write to me as soon
as you arrive in London.

May I keep the 'Poker' book for a birthday present?
I haven't had a chance to read it yet.

Will it be wicked for me to say that, while you were
shivering at Kilconquhar, I have been basking in sunshine, and that even the showers of the past two weeks

are soft and balmy in Hampshire! That is my Parthian
arrow. Good-night.

I was sorry not to see Aleck, to whom I send love, but
it was his fault, not mine. Be sure to write. Yours always
                                                          B. H.

Miss Annie Russell contributed much to the success of
'Sue' by her graceful and clever interpretation of the part
of the heroine, which she again took when the play was
produced in London a year later. Both Bret Harte and
Pemberton had intended that it should be produced in
England first, and only later in the United States, but,
owing to the flattering offers made for its performance in
New York, this was reversed. Although a clever dramatization of 'Clarence' was also made, it was never produced. The next few letters are mostly connected with
the excitement of the play and with his observations concerning its success in America.

                                          ARFORD HOUSE
                              HEADLEY, HANTS, *October* 11, 1896
MY DEAR NAN,
    Your letter about 'Sue,' which I received two days ago,
was very appreciative and rather *charming*, although I am
still very uncertain about the actual *success* of the piece.
Of course, I have received the critical notices, some good,
some bad; and the letter from Mr. Frohman, announcing
the fact that *the actors* seemed to have made 'a hit' in the
leading rôles, but all is yet too vague for any reliance on
the future. You understand that I don't care for *criticism;*
that I am quite content if the papers abuse the play so
long as the audience like it, and the thing pays. For the
rest, I know it is a *wholesome* play, and my conscience is
clear. I am even quite willing that my *collaborateur*, Mr.

Pemberton, should receive *all* the praise for its success —
as he has worked very hard upon it, and it is *he* who succeeded in placing the play with Frohman, who, I dare
say, would not have looked at it in *my* hands — nor
would any other American manager have troubled himself about it. Mr. Frohman now writes to my *collaborateur* that it is 'booked for a tour,' and that is about all *I*
know of it. He communicates with Mr. Pemberton
directly, who in turn communicates with me. *I have not
sold my rights in it*, but expect to receive a share of its
profits as long as it keeps the stage. It is yet too soon to
even imagine what *that* will be, or if it will be anything.

I thought all your criticisms *very good* and just. I believe they (in New York) will try to work up a dénoue-
ment that shall be less hopeless and more satisfying to the
audience than it seems to be at present, and I believe that,
if either Pemberton or myself had seen the rehearsals, we
could have arranged it. You know we always expected to
produce it here first! If it is only a fair success in America,
we will still do it, if we can get as good an actress as Miss
Russell seems to be to take the part of 'Sue.' I should
have a better hearing here than in my own country. The
London audiences and critics are not afraid of being
thought *vulgar* if they like to hear of 'common' people or
American subjects. But that is all in the future. Meantime, I and Pemberton are hard at work on a dramatization of 'Clarence,' which we think will be much better
than 'Sue.'

I have barely time in my hurry to tell you how grieved
I am to hear of poor Dora's death — nor can I write to
poor Liza my sympathy at such a moment. But I will
later.

What terrible proportions that strange disease you call

the 'grippe' assumes in New York and particularly in our
family! I cannot comprehend it!

With love to the girls, always your

LIMICK

P.S. I am here for a week or two longer, but you can
still write to the Club, for I do not know how long I may
remain out of London.

ARFORD HOUSE
HEADLEY, HANTS, *October* 12, 1896

MY DEAR FRANK,

I have a lot of criticisms of 'Sue' — good, bad, and
indifferent — some of which I dare say you have seen in
the theatrical papers of New York. One and all agree that
Miss Annie Russell has made a 'hit' in the title rôle —
and I suppose Frohman, for that reason, writes to my
collaborator that he has booked 'Sue' *for the season's tour*.
You know better than I what that means; I suppose,
though, it ought to indicate that Frohman has some belief
in it.

The only *personal* knowledge I have of its quality and
reception is from a letter from my old naval friend Com-
mander Tobin, who went to see it, and said it was 'a
success,' that Annie Russell was 'lovely' in it (they all
agree on that), and that he had a talk and 'second drinks'
with the *stage manager!* who was 'wildly enthusiastic
about it.' The only other personal knowledge I have is
from your mother, who went to see it. Of course, she is
prejudiced! So she says it was 'lovely' — that 'every line
told with the audience,' and every bit of pathos '*had its
effect*'; that the trial scene and all the lynch law business
'went off splendidly!' Even if this was not merely her
loyal and kind prepossession for my work — and was

really the feeling of the audience — still, it does not make a play a success. I remember how I thought the audience was delighted with 'Sandy Bar,' and even at the Washington representation of 'Ah Sin,' I left the theatre thinking it a success!

Your mother's criticism of the demerits of the play in its rather hopeless ending (I am annoyed to find that the 'proper' New York audience don't like 'Sue' being reconciled to her husband), and her criticisms of the actors, I think, are very good. She says that Haworth doesn't understand 'Ira' and makes him utterly unsympathetic to the audience.

Let me hear from you! With love to your chocolate wife. In haste to catch the post, your affectionate papa

B. H.

74, LANCASTER GATE, W.
October 22, 1896

MY DEAR PEMBERTON,

The bowl has arrived and is beautiful! making even the dingy, foggy window of my room like a copper sunset! Thank you so much.

I am very sorry that you have been so unavoidably delayed with 'Clarence.' I am only afraid we may lose a chance to place it soon, or some one may try to anticipate it in America.

I have a letter from a lady in Georgia, U.S.A., asking if she may send me a dramatization of 'Thankful Blossom' — quite an old story — and writing to know if I would object to having it presented! Luckily, years ago, I dramatized that same story with Madame Van de Velde; and Irving and Bram Stoker saw it, but they both thought the subject of the American Revolution was not palatable to an English audience! In haste, yours always

B. H.

In spite of the apparent and real success with which 'Sue' met in America, it was not one financially in so far as Bret Harte and his friend were concerned, and Bret Harte, who had counted on being able to rest his pen for a while from the proceeds, was bitterly disappointed, as the following letters to his wife and son show.

74, LANCASTER GATE, W.
October 29,1896

MY DEAR ANNA,

I lost yesterday's (Wednesday's) post through not getting my draft from the bank before 6 P.M., and I fear this will not leave here until Saturday; I hope you received the previous draft by cable, without any trouble.

I have not very satisfactory news from my play; indeed, I dare say *you* hear more about it than I do. Mr. Frohman writes to my *collaborateur*, and has all his dealings with *him* directly. We have had accounts of the first four weeks' receipts and two *little cheques*, but no letter of advice or information since the one that told us that the play would be taken 'on tour.' I am afraid the election excitement will affect it very badly, but I still *hope*, Nan! It is something to have got the play *on* and fairly off before the public and I hope better luck for the next!

I am back again in London, in the fogs and smoke. I am afraid I cannot stand the whole winter here; year after year it seems the more terrible, and the days of semi-darkness harder to bear. Yet everything I get, in the way of criticism, advice, or comment, from America, tells me how utterly *alien* I and my writings have become in my own country — and how I must depend upon my appreciations and standing here. When Max Nordau, the celebrated German philosopher and novelist, lately wrote that I was the 'Columbus of American fiction' (whatever that may mean?), and that my own countrymen did not appreciate me sufficiently, I thought it might strike some echo in America — but, alas! I have not seen even an allusion to it in my American publishers' *advertisements!* — while here it was copied largely and discussed! I don't believe, Nan, that even *you* ever heard a word of it!

I have a sad, very sad, letter from poor Maggie, and a request for money. God knows I should be too happy to support her — but what can I do, beyond a few pounds a year!

Give my best love to the children, and let me soon hear from you. Always affectionately

LIMICK

74, LANCASTER GATE, W.
November 12, 1896

MY DEAR FRANK,

Certainly, you had better forward the manuscript to me *here*, and I will send it with a line to Pemberton. He is not very well and has been very much delayed in his work on 'Clarence,' but I dare say he can find time to give you an opinion.

If I were not thinking of going down to Arford House about the date you mention, I should certainly accept your hospitable offer, for I am far from well here. I suppose I got some kind of a chill, which has been an excuse for all the aggravated horrors of dyspepsia and nervous depression. I might be able to run down for a night — and should like to — before the 19th if you could put me up. Madame V. de V. has been very ill with a cold and confined to the house for some days, but she expects, as soon as she can get up, to go down to Arford to recruit.

I have very little from the play, an occasional cheque (also little) from my pal, which shows that 'Sue' is on 'tour.' I expect she is in Chicago now. Only one thing I know positively — that Miss Russell has made a hit as 'Sue.' There seems to be no difference of opinion on that point. But how far that will carry the play and how long it will keep up its vitality, perhaps you know better than I. And if the people will only go in sufficient crowds to the theatre to see *her*, I shall be satisfied.

You might drop me a line to say if it would be convenient for you to have me with you for a night, between this and the 16th. I am engaged on the 17th, Tuesday, and may go to Arford on the 19th.

With love to your wife and a box of chocolates from Whiteley's, your always affectionate father

B. H.

74, LANCASTER GATE, W.
December 17, 1896

MY DEAR FRANK,

Madame V. de V. tells me that you have the manuscript of 'A Blue Grass Penelope,' which she lent you to read some time ago. Will you please send it to me, if possible by *return post*, as, if I go to Broadway on Saturday, I should like to take it with me. She also wants the manuscript of her dramatization of Edward Hunt's novel (she gave me the name, but it has slipped my memory at the moment, although I have read it long ago) — but this you can send later.

I have had to buy a new *fur coat* — so I am not so keen (as the weather is) about getting a covert coat, at least for the present. But I will go and see your friend later. You say you are pleased with yours — that it is a good coat 'for the country to walk in'! I would prefer to have one that I could *walk in, myself*, as I fear that the one that would suit 'the country to walk in' would be *too large* for me. But enough of this frivolity; I have been Christmas shopping all day and am dazed and tired. By the way, if any little parcels for your children find their way, punctually, to Caversham, keep them until you get a letter from me later, explaining who they are for. I have addressed everything to your wife. In great haste, your affectionate 'poppa'

B. H.

Bret Harte's favourite hobby was amateur photography, and in this he had the collaboration of Miss May Pemberton, the daughter of his friends, with the results described in the delightful letters which ensued. Miss Pemberton was also of valuable assistance in typing the much rewritten manuscripts of her father and Bret Harte in their dramatic work.

Arford House
Headley, Hants, Sunday

My dear Miss May,

I am quite envious of your photographic success. The little Kodak picture of your sister is wonderfully good, and shames my feeble efforts in the garden at Broadway, except the ones where I 'snap-shotted' the 'snap-shooter' herself, and brought down you and the dog with one barrel! Alas, the Mary Anderson de Navarro group turned out a failure, and the sublime patience your father and mother are showing in the most atrocious photographic situations brings tears to my eyes. Your mother, however, has a certain reserved melodramatic look in her eyes, as if she were 'biding her time.' I shall dread coming again to Broadway! Thanks for the prompt expedition of the third act. You must be 'steeped' in drama by this time.

With love to all at Pye Corner, yours always sincerely

Bret Harte

ARFORD HOUSE
HEADLEY, HANTS, *November 23, 1896*

DEAR MISS MAY,

Thank you so much for the small, indefinite pictures of me and the huge, distinctive one of your father's foot! It may be a foolish, human weakness, but I *should* have liked (as the plates are small) to have had *one* plate *all to myself*. But I am thankful all the same.

Do you keep a set of small plates with his foot in the corner — a sort of perpetual reminder — a kind of *ex pede Herculem?* You know *I* don't mind, but it must be disconcerting and *ominous* to the average *young* man whom you take!

Give my love to your father and mother, and believe me, yours always

BRET HARTE

74, LANCASTER GATE
LONDON, W., *Thursday*

DEAR MISS MAY,

I send you the photographs I spoke of, and, in a separate parcel, a magnesium light for photographing at night or on a dark day. You must hold the magnesium light, with its reflector, in your hand so as to throw the light on any object (including your father's foot, of course) or any part of the room you wish to show. You light the end of the little magnesium ribbon that projects from the holder, and 'pay it out' by the crank.

I am told that some people light *the whole of the ribbon at once*, to get a stronger and more protracted light. But as this is always accompanied by the sudden disappearance of the house and the spectators and the operator, and the calling out of the village fire-engine, perhaps you had better not try it. Your parents might object. And for a young lady, it might seem somewhat *ostentatious*.

Best otherwise, and Boyd assures me it is perfectly safe.
Yours always

BRET HARTE

It was sometimes a hard struggle to make ends meet,
when, in addition to the support of his wife and family, he
had perpetual demands from relatives, to which his kind-
hearted nature never failed to respond. Now that he was
an invalid, and in his old age, when his daily life and that
of his family depended upon his power to continue working, it is not surprising that, in spite of his indomitable
courage, he was at times very much discouraged. It had
been his greatest hope that a financially successful play
would enable him to look ahead with more equanimity,
and in this he was only to be bitterly disappointed.

74, LANCASTER GATE, W.
December 18, 1896

MY DEAR NAN,

I hoped to be able to send your draft so that it might
reach you *before* Christmas, but I have been disappointed.
Yet I trust you will get it during the holidays, and that
you will get some present for yourself and the girls with
the extra fifty dollars. I wish it were more, but I am trying to send poor Maggie something, and, if I can, something for Eliza too. I get occasional cheques for my share
in the play of 'Sue' — but it is not much, though I am
very grateful for it — even *that little!* Perhaps my next
play may be a greater success!

May you and the girls have a very Merry Christmas is
the loving wish, dear Nan, of your affectionate

LIMICK

P.S. The draft only came an hour ago, and I am hurrying to catch this Saturday's post, which will account for
my haste.

To the outer world Bret Harte showed only a bright and humorous side, and the next two letters to Mr. Watt and Mrs. Pemberton show his thoughtful memory of them in his little presents for Christmas and the New Year.

74, LANCASTER GATE, W.
December 29, 1896

DEAR MR. WATT,

I was delighted with the sleeve links; they could have gained nothing by a monogram!

I am glad you like the aneroid barometer; I thought that and the thermometer only in natural succession to the umbrella I gave you last year! So, whatever weather the New Year bring you, you are equipped for both, just as I know you are equal to whatever fortune it may dispense. But that it may be the *best*, is surely the wish of

Yours always

BRET HARTE

74, LANCASTER GATE, W.
January 20, 1897

DEAR MRS. PEMBERTON,

I find I haven't a copy of 'The Mission Bells of Monterey' with me here, but I will get one from Chappell and Company, and send it to you. Meanwhile, I am sending 'What the Chimney Sang' and the 'Cantala.'

I have also ventured to pick out for you a *little lantern* for the 'dark corner' behind the stairs, where the hats and coats are so effectually hidden. It is very artistic, in the sense that it doesn't give much light and is of very little use, but I believe that the *colouring* is all right and *in harmony*, and it will effectually delude your visitors into the belief that they are getting *their own* coats and hats, until they have got them on and are gone away. But, as you said of the stove that was 'so warm in colouring' (but didn't give out any heat) — it really looks as if *it gave light!* It has a kerosene lamp; I know that to be perfectly artistic it ought to have only a candle and a gutter! But you can remedy that. I would suggest a limp wax Christmas candle, afflicted with the 'rinal spinal curvature.'

Alas! I arrived here to find the lovely frost all gone, and only the regular deadly chill of the damp English weather. But I am glad, for your sake, that the frost has gone! When I think of that bitter night when you proudly showed me the monumental chill of your conjugal bedroom — as chastely impressive as a family vault — shivers still go down my back! All that night I lay awake and thought of you and your husband lying there rigidly, like the effigies of a stone crusader and his wife in some country church — at your feet that perfectly hopeless and ineffective hot-water bottle!

The lantern goes to you via Evesham by rail to-day; judging from the post, it ought to reach you certainly before the close of the century.

Yours always sincerely
BRET HARTE

The first six months of the new year are again represented only by the two following letters to Mr. and Mrs. Boyd, written at long intervals, but both from the country. Bret Harte was always happy when he could get away from the crowded city into the country, and he gives in these letters charming descriptions of the coming spring and the pleasure he derived from the beauty of his surroundings. The clever and amusing caricature of Bret Harte as a bishop reproduced here was made by his friend Boyd, in reference to the 'Clothing Club meeting' and village entertainment at which Bret Harte was asked to preside and to which he humorously alludes in his next letter.

too sudden
or severe in
its results
One ought
not to
relinquish
all at once
the calm delights
of the bowie-knife
and gaming-table
for the fevered
excitement of
a clothing
Club!
I have put
my fears in a
pictorial form
and I trust it
may act as
a warning.
I have been
troubled with
bad dreams
during my

illness and this
is probably one
of them.
With this I
send you a
Ludgate which
has an article
on Emval the
picturesque
and forsaken
mansion you
spoke of.
Is it not?
I hope we
shall be able
to see you
soon.
Any afternoon
you can look
in, do
Yours most faithfully

BRET HARTE AS A BISHOP
Caricature by A. S. Boyd

ARFORD HOUSE
HEADLEY, HANTS, *February 28*, 1897

MY DEAR BOYD,

You might have been certain that had I been in town I should have called long before this, with or without the faithful Lambert. But I have been *here* for two weeks — getting the London fog from my eyes and throat, and avoiding 74, Lancaster Gate, while some changes are being made in my chimney. It's a little early to be here, and I am a little rheumatic, but I have had the rare pleasure of seeing the spring *begin* under the impulse of two or three days of June-like sunshine. It sent the bees into the crocus chalices ('to improve each shining hour'), and some butterflies sauntered down the garden walks without their overcoats. It was very pleasant to go out each day with the confidence that something pretty would 'turn up' in hedge-rows. Of course, socially, it was *deadly dull*, although I had some of my friends with me, but with 'teas' with neighbours we managed to get on, and I consented to take the chair at a village entertainment! I always had an idea that a chairman on these occasions was somebody who said, ''Armony, gents! 'armony,' and that 'Mr. So-and-So would now oblige'! But we were very decorous and genteel. On my way to the entertainment I thought of telling the audience that I didn't know what the 'Clothing Club' was, but I was assured, by the presence of the Rector, that there was nothing in the *performance* that would suggest the *necessity of one!* The dear man nearly fainted from shock, so I sat up in the chair and was good — though I know he was in mortal terror of what I might say during the evening.

I am sorry to hear of your wife's trials through Stuart's illness, and her own slow recovery. Tell her I often thought how she would enjoy the 'coming in of spring' in a place like this. It is so really and truly rural here, and the air is a blending of the hilltops and the sea — only twenty miles away! No wonder that, despite my 'rheumatics,' I prolong my stay until next Saturday.

Yours always
BRET HARTE

ARFORD HOUSE
HEADLEY, HANTS, June 15, 1897

MY DEAR MRS. BOYD,

I was delighted to see your handwriting again, though I fear it is all I shall see of you until *after* this wild, bewildering Jubilee, which I am trying to evade, is over.

Then I shall return to London, and — then, of course, you will be going away!

I have been here with my son and his wife, and during the past week with my Birmingham collaborator in playwriting, Mr. Pemberton, and *his* wife. There are no 'Duchesses' here — nothing above a baronet; but there are woods, real pine woods — and glorious sunshine and real summer!

I drove yesterday through a forest of oaks — every step of which recalled the 'Arden' of Shakespeare and one expects Rosalind or Jaques to slip out from some mossy trunk. It is called of men 'Alice Holt,' and belongs to the Crown, and is really a wild and trackless, almost virgin forest.

What are processions — and crowded London — and 'sassiety' to this!

Yours always
B. H.

How faithful Bret Harte was to the traditions of his country is seen from his interesting allusion to the 'Sons of the Revolution,' and to his pride in being the descendant of a Revolutionary soldier.

ARFORD HOUSE
HEADLEY, HANTS, *June* 19, 1897

MY DEAR NAN,

I have succeeded in getting the draft earlier this month, and I hope you will receive it by the 1st July as I am hurrying this off to catch the post to-morrow. Frank and his wife have been visiting here with me and lately I have had my dramatic collaborateur, Mr. Pemberton, and his wife here also through Madame V. de V.'s kindness — as I had some work to do with Pemberton. I am afraid 'Clarence' has been anticipated here by Gillette's 'Secret Service,' or at least put off, as *two* American plays on nearly the same lines wouldn't succeed. I think I told you that Frohman wouldn't take 'Clarence' for America — because he said the war plays are overdone. P. and I have some hope of bringing out 'Sue' *here*, but it is only a hope — and we have no Annie Russell to ensure its success. We are also at work on another play — a dramatization of my 'Mæcenas of the Pacific Slope,' which will be offered to Frohman.

I am keeping out of London and the confusion and snobbery of the Jubilee. I am sorry to say that my countrymen — the Americans in London — are among the most vulgar and ostentatious in their display. I shall not go up for the Jubilee. I detest crowds, and a London crowd has not even the humour of an American crowd to make it bearable. As for seeing the Royalties together — the few I *have* seen are not striking enough to make a spectacle, and I am afraid I have no other feeling about them.

I am sorry that my being away from London has prevented my seeing Maggie's married daughter 'Maud Wyman Eburts,' who is in England and who has written to me. But I may see her later — after the sawdust and orange peel of the big Jubilee show is swept out of London and people have recovered their senses.

I have been very *proud* and pleased by a letter I have received from a Mr. Thomas, of Council Bluffs, who writes to me that in making researches for the 'Sons of the Revolution' he has discovered that his *great*-grandfather was my *great-great*-grandfather (on my mother's side) — a Revolutionary soldier — whose daughter also married a Captain Truesdale, a Revolutionary officer — so that I am a 'Son of the Revolution.' I remember my mother had often talked of her Revolutionary ancestors, but it was odd to receive this confirmation from a stranger. I don't know what the 'Sons of the Revolution' are as *a society*, but I am much more pleased, I am afraid, than if I had been told that I had a peer among my ancestors — or had come into a little property through a distant millionaire.

I hope you will enjoy your outing at Norfolk, and, though you may not believe it, I wish I could be there this summer! We had a few days of quite hot weather like an American summer — and then a drop of twenty degrees *in one night* into the usual chilly, damp English summer. Yet we believe that it is only in America that we have these sudden changes. With best love to the girls, your affectionate

LIMICK

The principal reason of the interest of Bret Harte's letters in general is explained in the following one to Mrs. Boyd, in which he confesses to that same creed which governs all his literary work; care and absolute sincerity, which prevented him from ever writing what he did not esteem to be the genuine expression of his thoughts. No letters of his are lacking, therefore, in that something which make them all worth while, both in depth of pathetic feeling as well as in humorous kindliness.

ARFORD HOUSE
HEADLEY, HANTS, August 15, 1897

MY DEAR MRS. BOYD,

I don't know how to apologize to you for leaving your kind letter from Dorset so long unanswered. I may as well be frank (no perfectly fresh and novel excuse offering itself) and say that I *did* have time to write before, only that I was finishing a little story in which I was much interested and preoccupied, and, that instead of writing to you in the intervals, I wrote to unimportant people — business folks and otherwise — *business* letters, the flattest social letters, answers to invitations, and even one or two duty letters. My vague reason for this was that I did not, and *do* not feel like writing to you unless I am perfectly free and untrammelled — and wholly like myself — as I fancy you would certainly detect my 'attitude' in my letters, and I know *I* would myself, and loathe myself for it. I have an idea that all this sounds utterly feeble and the weakest of evasions — but there is a heap of truth in it for all that! Did *you* never have anything that you ought to do, that you *wanted* to do, that you expected to do, that was all right to do — and yet, for some unexplained reason, you preferred to do something else that was *pour passer le temps*, or perfunctory?

And here's half my letter gone in the apology I didn't intend to give! I have just finished, as I said before, a little story for the 'Graphic,' and I'm going up to London on the 17th. Besides writing, I have been teaching myself to 'develop' my own photographic plates, and I haven't a stick of clothing or an exposed finger that isn't stained. I sit for hours in a dark-room feeling as if I was a very elderly Faust at some dreadful incantation, and come out of it, blinking at the light, like a Bastille prisoner. And yet I am not successful! I have plates that are wonderful in image and polychromatic in tint, but all 'over' or 'under' developed. I print well enough, but in 'toning,' my prints have a dreadful way of vanishing completely (as perhaps some other things that I have printed will do!) and I am left with a faded scrap of paper. You may not lend a sympathetic ear to this, but I know Aleck will!

I have finished and thoroughly enjoyed Miss Kingsley's book. What a wonderful and inexhaustible sense of humour she has! Did I tell you (no, of course, I haven't seen you since) that at Compton Wynyates I met a Mrs. Green (widow of the historian Green — see 'A Short History of the English People') who was the bosom friend of Miss Kingsley, and they were thinking of taking a little house *together* in the country. She, Mrs. Green, acted as amanuensis to her dying husband when he was winding up his life and his book at the same time, and she developed some disease of the hand, like 'writer's cramp,' and cannot use a pen since.

This is a long but worthless letter. But I'll tell you more when I see you. ('I could be twice as stupid to please your worship!') Drop me a line when you get this, to 74, Lancaster Gate, where I expect to be on Tuesday.

Yours always

B. H.

Bret Harte's rare moments of leisure were at this time entirely devoted to the photographic hobby, and the three letters to his son are mostly connected with the difficulties encountered in that domain, together with a few references to his play.

ARFORD HOUSE
HEADLEY, HANTS, *March* 31, 1897

MY DEAR FRANK,

I am sorry that I shall miss the chance of seeing you in town, for I will probably remain here a week longer and I shall then go to Pemberton's at Broadway to stay over Easter. My neuralgia was very bad when I came here, but I think it has yielded much in the pure air and sunshine.

I have no news, not even of 'Sue.' Frohman hasn't written to Pemberton for three weeks and we do not know whether 'Sue' survives or not. Have you seen anything in the New York dramatic papers about her? Frohman has 'Clarence,' but has not written regarding it.

I think something of trying to do the 'developing' of such photographs as I may take here. Mr. Beck has furnished me with a portentous list of the things I need; I have been downstairs to see the 'dark-room' — and the construction doesn't look pleasant! You might draft me some 'Hints to a Young Developer.'

The Hastings, mother and daughter, are here — but are not very cheerful. Madame V. de V. says she hopes you will come, with your wife, some time later — in summer. I am going to town for a day or two before I go to Broadway to spend Easter with Pemberton.

With best love to your wife and babies, your affectionate papa

B. H.

ARFORD HOUSE
HEADLEY, HANTS, *August 25*, 1897

MY DEAR FRANK,

Very many, many thanks for the handsome birthday present I got from you and your wife 'jointly.' The handkerchiefs *are* large — but then, as the Scotchman said of his friend: 'I hae gran' accommodation!' Tell your wife I appreciate the 'marked' initials, fully.

I am here, and will stay here a couple of weeks longer, when I expect to make a little visit to the Froudes, who live near you, somewhere, in the vicinity of Reading. I am writing, as usual, and my only *recreation* is photography — my only *trouble* 'developing.' I have been singularly unfortunate, but have at last traced my trouble (by test) to a diabolical 'ruby lamp' which 'fogs' all my plates in 'developing,' as well as in putting them in the camera. And my toning was something weird — I used to get every colour of the rainbow on my prints, and then the whole thing would vanish like a bursting bubble.

I hope to see you soon, even if I do not come for another 'happy day' on the river. I think my neuralgia is better — but I am not sure of risking it and your patience again.

With love to your wife and babies, always your affectionate papa

B. H.

ARFORD HOUSE
HEADLEY, HANTS, *September 23*, 1897

MY DEAR FRANK,

If you can find the negative of the enclosed, will you print me two or three copies, or, if you haven't time, send the plates to me, and I will do the printing and return the plate if you want it? The 'toning' I will also do, though it is usually something wonderful to contemplate.

I also send you a little photo, posed, photographed, developed, printed, and *toned* by me! It is 'Tommy' and a child of the neighbourhood (lest you should *not* distinguish them in their high artistic combination!). The *vignette* effect is produced by a bit of cardboard in printing. The 'tone' is all my own — wrong possibly, but beautiful to me!

I have no news. I am working here now after visiting two or three friends — one (the Froudes) near Reading, but not near enough for me to have dropped in upon you. Annie Hughes wants to play 'Sue,' but can't get a theatre. All the other plays are as yet uncertain.

With love to your wife, your affectionate papa

B. H.

In the death of James Anthony Froude in 1894, Bret Harte had lost one of his most intimate friends, for whose intellect and culture he had the greatest admiration. His History of England, as well as his other works, had made his name famous in America, where Bret Harte knew him before coming to Europe.

ARFORD HOUSE, *September 23, 1897*

MY DEAR NAN,

I hope I am sending this draft in good season. I am still in the country as I fancy I work better there, and as I grow older I find myself not *so well* in London. I spent a few days near Reading, with one of Froude's daughters, but the household has never seemed the same to me since my dear friend's death. Froude and Lord Houghton were the *two Englishmen* that were equally a part of my American life, and now Froude is dead, and the late Lord Houghton's son is the Earl of Crewe — and even the name is forgotten.

I wish I were able to buy you that house at Norfolk! Of all the places that you have told me of I seem to fancy this most, and understand it. What do you think it could be bought for? If my ship of plays ever comes home, I might do it! But everything here is only *promised*. An actress here will take 'Sue' and play it in London *if* she can get a theatre. Frohman *promised* to do his best to dispose of 'Clarence' and 'Rushbrook'!

I am having my first autumn cold, for the weather has suddenly relapsed into the usual English dampness, and I am sneezing and shivering as if it were really winter. With love to the children, always your

LIMICK

Christmas and the birthdays of his wife and children never went by without the offering of little gifts, accompanied by some kindly little note such as the one below. In the letters that follow it, he speaks of the rehearsals of 'Sue,' which had just been brought over from America, and in which Miss Annie Russell was again to take the leading rôle. The play ran up to the end of July, over six months, and was again a great success with the public, but not financially to the extent that Bret Harte had hoped.

74, LANCASTER GATE, W.
December 14, 1897

MY DEAR FRANK,

You will, of course, be perfectly surprised to hear that I have got — as a Christmas present for yourself and wife — a pair of Indian 'Ji Jam' curtains (the plural is 'Jim Jams') of the beautifullest old gold and navy blue imaginable. I don't know *how* I came to think about getting them! — but I did! Although you have never heard of them, or I dare say never seen 'em, perhaps you can make use of them for your drawing-room! It's quite a novel idea.

Yes, I hope to come to you on Christmas, unless I have a 'command' to Osborne or Sandringham — where, of course, you know private feelings must give way! Perhaps, if I am able to come, we might go to the theatre, as before, and I should bring my own 'fizz.' In great haste, your affectionate papa

B. H.

74, LANCASTER GATE, W.
January 2, 1898

MY DEAR FRANK,

When I go anywhere to stay overnight, I usually leave behind me so many articles of value that I make it a point to *try to take* some trifles from my host (like that copy of the magazine you prematurely discussed) to ensure the prompt return of my own articles! It seems to be quite successful, so I shall look forward to your bringing me my articles when you come to Arford House. I am impelled also to enclose to you this fragment of rare old lace which I found in my handkerchief case, but which I think belongs to the dressing-table in the bedroom I occupied. I also lost heavily at 'Nap' in your house — but I do not expect *that* returned to me. I am very noble about these things!

I don't intend to send that gong until after your return. I might keep the neighbourhood awake!

With love to your wife and family, always affectionately your papa

B. H.

74, LANCASTER GATE, W.
January 30, 1898

MY DEAR FRANK,

Certainly, I will ask Frohman for stalls for you and your wife next Friday. He has asked me for a list of those of my friends whom I would like to have.

I have seen Miss Russell and have attended *one* rehearsal of the play. She is very charming; I can quite understand her popularity in America, and certainly there is no *ingénue* on the *English* stage comparable to her. But at the rehearsals I was pleased to see that other American actors were equally good in their rôles, and while the play has certain inherent defects it is by no means as bad as the American critics make it. The lynch trial was wonderfully good — and unless I am mistaken in what I know of English audiences, it will 'go' with them.

I ought to be at Miss Froude's at Padworth Croft to-day, but I have been rewriting one of the scenes this morning and have to go to a rehearsal to-morrow, so my visit to Aldermaster may go by the board. In haste, with love to your wife, your tired 'popper'

B. H.

Bret Harte frequently encountered difficulties, such as those he refers to in the following letter, in addition to the many other causes of vexation from pirated editions of his works, and desecration of his stories, as in the case of 'M'liss.' Yet nothing could be kinder than his warning by which he finds means to convey a message of sympathy to an unknown person.

74, LANCASTER GATE, W.
June 13, 1898

DEAR MADAM,

The enclosed letter, although addressed to *my name*, at the Garrick Theatre, is evidently not intended for *me*, but for some person, who, I am sorry to have to inform you, is using a name to which he has no right. Some years ago the late Mr. Pigott, Licensee of Plays, informed me that the manager of a theatre near Manchester was using my name. As I am the only Bret Harte in existence, I wrote to this manager and he admitted that he had *adopted* the name for business purposes, but assured me that he would not use it again. As you seem to know him, and have business relations with him and his partner, it would be well for you to make known to him the contents of this letter, and inform him that if he continues to use my name he may encounter more serious legal difficulties than the present misapprehension.

Believe that I am very sorry for your own difficulties, which I have been accidentally made cognisant of through the mistaken address, and that I trust you will see your way out of them.

Yours very sincerely
BRET HARTE

Bret Harte's son had suggested that a slight alteration in the structural composition of the play would render 'Sue' more effective for stage production. It was not, however, his own opinion or that of Frohman, the producer. Some changes were, however, made, in collaboration with Mr. Pemberton, before the play was produced in England.

AVERLEY TOWER
FARNHAM, SURREY, *July* 24, 1898

MY DEAR FRANK,

As you said you wanted tickets for Saturday night *only if it* were the last night of 'Sue,' and, as I saw by the bills that it would be played until Tuesday next, I didn't think it necessary to send for them. The entire company leave for America on the 27th (the next day), so 'Sue' will have played up to their last night in England. You ask me about the success of the play. The *financial* returns have been very disappointing to Pemberton and myself — particularly as we always *heard* that the house was *full*. I suppose it must have been paper.

As Bucknall proposes to take 'Sue' *on tour* through the provinces — *without Miss Russell and the American company* — I suppose he must think there is something in the *play itself* with all its 'structural defects.' These I modified as well as I could before the play went into the evening bills, but the actors didn't think it necessary — you know they are apt to be poor critics of anything but their *own* parts — and as the audience seemed to enjoy the play equally with or without these changes, I hardly think the financial returns were affected by *them*. They say it was the *lateness of the season*. Your affectionate papa

B. H.

AVERLEY TOWER
FARNHAM, SURREY, August 4, 1898

MY DEAR FRANK,

I have been trying to finish some work before going to Compton Wynyates to-morrow, where I shall spend a few days, or I should have answered you before.

Regarding 'Sue,' Frohman is as astounded as I am, but is much more cheerful over it, and says if the company could have remained he would have kept playing it 'right on.' I don't agree with you that any *structural* defect covered the bad houses. If it had, the play would still have drawn *a few good houses at* FIRST, on account of the praise and advertising it received, and the effect would have been shown in the *falling-off* of receipts. People *could not* judge of a play — whether they were disappointed or not — without going to see it *first* — and they simply didn't go! The few adverse criticisms of its quality *as a play* do not affect the average theatre-goer as a rule — if there are other things talked about. My only conjecture as to the cause is that the average theatre-goer did not care to see *that kind of a play;* i.e., the plot as told in all the newspapers!

As to the *structural* defects of the play — and what they were — is a distinct question. The third Act, altered as you suggest, would certainly have made *another* play of it, but I am not prepared to say that it would have been as original a one — nor, as you infer, that it would have been a better-paying play. I made a great many alterations in the second and third Acts — though the actors didn't want *anything changed!*

However, Pemberton writes me that Frohman has already had offers from *Australia* and *South Africa* for it, and *Germany!!* It is to go on a tour in September, I believe. Before then, perhaps, *if they will let me,* I will make some other changes.

Remember me to your boys in holidays and with love to your wife, always your affectionate papa

B. H.

In the peace and quiet of Compton Wynyates, he opens his heart in the touching letter to his wife in which he admits for the first time the great disappointment 'Sue' has been to him and his profound discouragement.

COMPTON WYNYATES, KINETON
August 8, 1898

MY DEAR NAN,

It was very foolish and inconsiderate in me not to write to you for so long a time, but ever since I heard of the possibility of my play of 'Sue' being brought out in London — ever since I saw it in rehearsal — ever since it made an *artistic* success here — and during its run for a month at one of the West End theatres, I have been *waiting* and *hoping* to be able to tell you that it was also a *financial success for me! Alas!* I have been once more cruelly disappointed; in spite of the praises of press and audiences; in spite of the attractions of a perfect actress, like Annie Russell, and a splendid company — in spite of everything that goes to make the success of a play — *it never paid!* I cannot understand it — my collaborateur cannot understand it — the manager, Mr. Frohman, is equally bewildered and confounded, although he is much more *satisfied* with the money he has undoubtedly *lost,* and the artistic success the play has gained, than we are. I need not tell you how *for six weeks* I had hoped to delight and astonish you with news of a good fortune that would spare me all the trials and troubles I have had lately over my literary work — and how deeply disappointed I have been! I have had no heart to write to you, or to Jessamy regarding her affairs, and even now I can only congratulate her upon finding a husband who can take the place of her father and his precarious fortunes. It is hard to face this fact, which for the last six months I have been trying to avoid.

I will try to send your next draft by the middle of this month. I am visiting one of my old English friends here, but I shall return to London next week. Write to me soon, no matter how remiss *I* am, or how hopelessly I write. I am always, dear Nan, your affectionate

LIMICK

The last two letters of the year are to his son, with presents for all of his numerous household, and to Mr.

Watt with the annual exchange of gifts which was kept up until Bret Harte's death.

74, LANCASTER GATE, W., *Wednesday*

MY DEAR FRANK,

I am sending to you to-day a parcel of books for the children, which you will apportion according to their tastes: the picture books for the little ones and the 'Boys' Annual' for the two big ones — to be given to them, like Cap'n Cuttle's watch, 'jointly.' In one of the parcels you will find a cigar-cutter (a perfectly useless trifle from Thornhill's) — for yourself.

In separate packages from Whiteley's are a china service for your wife, and a box of cigars for yourself, a mechanical cat for the baby, and a theatre for Richard. Perhaps I may have a chance to add a box of chocolates for the 'chocolate girl.' I am also returning the large shears you loaned me at Arford — with some gloves and some particularly offensive neckties for the big boys. The packages are large and imposing to the eye; they are not much, but they go with a great deal of love to you and yours and the best of Christmas greetings from your affectionate 'popper'

B. H.

P.S. If I don't go out of town for the week-end, I *might* come down at Christmas 'to dine and sleep,' as they say at Windsor. Yours

B. H.

74, LANCASTER GATE, W.
December 23, 1898

DEAR MR. WATT,

It is not altogether sheer vacuity of invention that makes me send you *another* umbrella for our fond and foolish interchange of Christmas gifts; I know you must have worn out or lost the one I gave you long ago — perhaps even forgotten I ever gave you one — and it will be of some real use to you! I wish I could say as much for the two other trifles that go with it, but you surely can make room for *another* calendar for 1899 — somewhere among the many you will have, and you *can* chain up the little gun-metal and turquoise pencil I send you, and make it handy. I know this because *I*, who have *six* pencils (one of which was one of your earliest Christmas presents), never have one in my pocket, because I don't take this precaution! and honest enough!

But in any event, they enable us both — at this season — to look back at the years we have been friends! With all seasonable wishes for you and yours, always sincerely yours

BRET HARTE

The first interesting letter of 1899 is written in March to his friend Pemberton, and shows that, in spite of all the misfortune they had met with in the theatrical world, Bret Harte was still determined to achieve his desire to write a good play. 'M'liss,' however, was according to his opinion not so adaptable as other of his stories, nor so well suited to the part of the actress who was to play the part of the heroine of that beautiful story.

THE RED HOUSE
CAMBERLEY, SURREY, *March* 9, 1899

MY DEAR PEMBERTON,

I had hardly time to acknowledge your last letter, as I had posted down here to Madame V. de V.'s new country home to finish some work in a great hurry.

I had no idea that 'Sue' would be produced again in

America, and I wanted to alter that last Act before it was played again. This I must and *shall* do if there is any hope of its being brought over here once more.

Who played 'Sue?' What kind of a company was it? But I dare say you know no more about it yet, unless you have access to the American dramatic papers.

As I told you, the Mauriers came to see me. They wanted me to do 'M'liss' for them, and Mrs. Maurier was to send me *her* idea of what she wanted done. But it may be very difficult for me to construct something without running over the lines on which Hatton and I worked, and I have not seen him yet. I tried to make her understand that the episodes of the *story* would not make episodes of a *play* — as, for instance, M'liss's declaration of heterodoxy at the end of a chapter! Besides, the charm of M'liss is that she is a mere *child*, and it is very difficult for a grown actress to represent such a character — in love!

I hope to be able to come to Pye Corner at Easter. The weather will not prevent me, for I know that the country at Easter is wilfulness and caprice itself. But I will let you know in due season. With love to you all, yours always

B. H.

74, LANCASTER GATE, W.
March 30, 1899

MY DEAR PEMBERTON,

I was very sorry that I had to wire to your wife this morning that I had to forego the pleasure of coming to Pye Corner this Easter. I am very, very busy with work that must be finished just after the 5th, and, as I should really lose a day in coming and another in going, I should have but two days with you, even if I dragged my work with me, which I don't want to do! So I am afraid, my dear friend, that I must wait a later opportunity when you and I are less hurried. I might be able to come to you on the 14th, when I shall have my work finished and would have more time to spend on travelling. I want to see you very much to talk over our hapless plays!

Miss Anne Sturghes sent me a sketchy *scenario* of 'M'liss,' from her point of view. It had some good things in it, but I wrote her that I much doubted the success of 'M'liss' as a play, and advised her to read 'Cressy,' where the heroine was much more effective and in better dramatic surroundings — and a little *older!* I have my doubts of a heroine who in one act is a girl at school, and charming through her ingenuousness, and in the next a loving woman.

With best love to all at Pye Corner, and wishing you a happy Easter from my drudging desk at 74, always yours

B. H.

In January, 1898, Mrs. Bret Harte came to England and made her home with her son and daughter-in-law. Although they did not live together, Bret Harte frequently went to see her and stayed at their son's house. There is a certain lassitude in the following letter to her, in which one sees the tremendous strain of his work, which made it impossible for him to be absent from it a single day.

74, LANCASTER GATE, W.
March 30, 1899

MY DEAR ANNA,

I'm sending you a cheque for thirty pounds for this month's remittance. I have dated it *to-morrow* to give the bank time to receive a draft from me, which I only got this morning, and unfortunately I have had no balance for some days to my credit.

And now, I am dreadfully sorry to say that I cannot come to Caversham to-morrow, but that I must stay *here* and work, morning and night, to finish a story for which I have got a partial advance. I have had to wire to Pemberton at Broadway, where I expected to spend my Easter holiday, for I *cannot really spare the time to go and come* — which would mean nearly *two days* out of that brief vacation of four. I cannot even spend *the day* at Caversham, but must plod at my work here until it is finished. But I expect to be free by the 15th April, and then I will come. I am sorry to disappoint you again — but it is really harder upon me than you.

In great haste, with love to Ethel and Frank, to whom I am writing, your affectionate

LIMICK

74, LANCASTER GATE, W.
April 25, 1899

MY DEAR FRANK,

I don't know what you will think of me — perhaps everything but the truth — that I have been working here night and day since I last wrote you, and that really I could not spare myself a single day's leisure. As I cannot afford to take my own time in writing as I did formerly, I must work hard and continuously to meet my expenses week by week! Still, I do hope with some certainty to get a day off at the end of this week or the first of next. I will always write or wire to you in good season.

I had not forgotten that gong which I promised your wife for the new house, but I could not find a suitable *hanging* one. When I did — I sent it. I was really too busy to write to your wife about it.

I suppose all this is difficult to comprehend. But, alas! I no longer work with the readiness of youth — nor, I fear, even of middle age. If I turn aside from my work for a single day, it is with the greatest difficulty that I can take up the thread again. So my only resource is to *keep* at it until it is finished.

Tell your mother why I didn't write, and with love to all, your affectionate papa

B. H.

74, LANCASTER GATE, W.
June 1, 1899

MY DEAR ANNA,

I enclose a cheque for thirty pounds for May. If this weather will keep as pleasant for a few days longer, until I shall not be quite so hard pressed for time, I will run up for a day. Tell Frank I have just seen Frohman to-day, and have given him 'M'liss' to read. He also is delighted with my suggestions about changing the last Act of 'Sue.' From what I can gather, they are very nervous about trying Miss Russell in anything new after her success in 'Sue,' but the poor little lady is quite ill — and the 'Bugle Mystery' in which she now appears is a farcical thing, after the failure of 'John Ingerfield.'

Tell his wife I am so sorry to hear of her household afflictions, and I hope the cook is better. Thank her for her letter to me. Tell Ethel that after Frank has taught her to bicycle, she can teach me. With love to all, your affectionate

LIMICK

It was a busy summer spent mostly in London, with short visits to the country when ill-health made it impossible for him to continue his work in town. The next few letters to his wife and son reveal the difficulty which sickness was creating in his former capacity for work, and the feeling of the decline in his indomitable spirit slowly coming upon him.

74, LANCASTER GATE, W.
June 8, 1899

MY DEAR FRANK,

Thank you and your wife ever so much for your thoughtful offering of the 'first roses' of Warren Heights. They were compressed so tightly in their narrow box that I had to draw them out with a corkscrew! But that, I suppose, is a particularity of 'first roses' — being shy and reluctant! After I got them fairly together again, with the aid of a spoon and my hat-brush, I put them in a bowl, where they looked very pretty — exactly like a mint julep! But I knew they were roses, for all that. Tell your wife how I thank her for remembering me, and that I am quite lost in admiration of your skill in packing them. Nobody would ever have supposed that little narrow 'Sozodont' box *contained roses*, no, not even after they were taken out! That was the distinct charm of their packing.

I suppose you have read what the papers said of 'The Cowboy and the Lady.' It seems to have been a very clumsy imitation of my work, and distinctly an outcome of 'Sue,' although Frohman, only a day or two before, unmistakably told me it was nothing of the kind!

The whole thing is incomprehensible to me — and even to Miss Annie Russell, whom I saw to-day. She is returning to America without playing anything! although she was brought over by Frohman to do 'The Mysterious Mr. Bugle' or 'Catherine.' She cannot understand it at all — and her own treatment by F. is equally purposeless and mysterious. Truly the ways of the managers are past all finding out . . . !

I have yet another spell of work to do, but it will not take very long, and then I hope to come down and see you. In haste, with love to all, your affectionate papa

B. H.

CAMBERLEY, *August 26,* 1899

MY DEAR ANNA,

Just a line to thank you and Ethel for the very handsome (far *too* handsome!) book you sent me for my birthday. I am glad it was something *cheerful* as well as handsome, for these birthdays, as the years go on, are no laughing matter. I never was so impressed with the lapse of years as when you forwarded to me Z's *Son's* letter, asking my intervention for *that* Son's grown-up Son!!

I hope you will enjoy yourself at Eastbourne; I, alas! never liked it and never could enjoy myself there. Like Brighton, Bournemouth, Hastings, etc., etc., it is London again, with London people and London's ways, by the sea! But that is also the Thames difficulty!

I found London so hot I could not stand it more than half a day. With love to all, yours affectionately

LIMICK

CAMBERLEY, *September 30,* 1899

MY DEAR ANNA,

I am enclosing the cheque for thirty pounds for next month. I expected to be in London this week, but I am staying here to finish some work. It should have been done before this, but during the bad weather I was fit for very little, and now, at the end of my vacation, I find myself obliged to do double time to make up arrears of work. Everything lags with old age!

I am glad to hear through Frank that you enjoyed your stay in Eastbourne. I have made only one visit since I came here. I expect to go to Broadway soon, but I shall come to London first — and I hope to Reading also — before that. Thank Frank for his letter to me and say I will answer it soon. With love to Ethel and Frank and his wife, always your affectionate

LIMICK

74, LANCASTER GATE, W., Sunday

MY DEAR FRANK,

I returned to London only a few days ago — having been quite laid by the heels with an attack of lumbago for nearly a month! I suppose you know nothing about it — or you would have sympathized with me, and I hesitate to tell you, even now, lest you should burst into retroactive tears!

Do you come to London once a week as formerly? Could you and your wife come in to tea some day? Let me have a line.

I am still very rheumatic, but for a while I was really quite crippled — and went around like the doddering old man on the stage who revisits the home of his boyhood with a stick. With love to Aline, your senile parent

B. H.

Only in rarer letters to old friends does he regain a little of his old self in the expression of that strong sense of humour which was the undercurrent so closely interwoven with the pathos of his life, and of which his letters to Mrs. Boyd are such delightful examples.

CHERWELL EDGE, OXFORD
Sunday evening [October 23, 1899]

MY DEAR MRS. BOYD,

You will not be surprised to know that, after all, I didn't leave London until Saturday! I had another day of work.

But I found Oxford still here, and actually saw the very hotel where we all lunched and the shop where your husband and I bought the weather glass, and even one or two of the Colleges that remained, although *we* went back to Leamington!

But, alas! it is 'term time' now, and on Saturday the streets were full of boating flannels and knickerbockers. Some day I must try to see the undergraduate *at work*. I never see him except coming from or going to football, lawn tennis, cricket, or the boats, or sitting in his window.

But to-day it rains, and is Sunday, and that unhallowed combination is too much for him!

I have come to the conclusion that as an ornament a cap-and-gown is not a success. The wearer generally goes off so dreadfully at the *feet!* Like that dancing gentleman of Dickens, whose enjoyment never seemed to get above his waist, the ecclesiastic illusion of this young gentleman never seems to get below his *knees*. His prosaic sturdy British ankles in flapping trousers are indecently exposed. There is a strong suggestion of his highly respectable British mamma in a moment of indecorous haste that is blood-curdling.

I found my host and hostess very much upset by my non-arrival in time for two dinner-parties, so I find I *may* have to stay a day or two longer than I intended. I never can make things arrive like other people.

I hope Mr. Boyd got the 'Hacienda' drawings to his own satisfaction — they were certainly to *mine!* In haste, yours always

BRET HARTE

The next few letters close his correspondence for the year.

74, Lancaster Gate, W.
November 2, 1899

My dear Anna,

My book is only just published, or I should have sent it before.

I am going this afternoon to Castle Ashby to stay with Lord Northampton for a few days before he goes away to Egypt. As soon as I return, I will make my promised visit to Warren Heights. As I told Frank I should have gone there after returning from Camberley, but I waited to have my visit when you were all together. In haste, but with love to all, yours affectionately

Limick

74, Lancaster Gate, W
December 2, 1899

My dear Anna,

I enclose the cheque for thirty pounds for December. I will try to send you a *little* more a few days before Christmas — for Christmas expenses — but I fear it will not be much, as I have not been doing much work lately, owing to illness. And now I am in the middle of my first cold this season and am 'stuffy' and 'coughy' — and aching with neuralgia in the head. The weather has turned frosty with a black, poisonous, smoky fog that makes any inhalation a smart. I am glad you are out of it at Brighton!

Tell Frank — I would write to him, but I am pressed for time — that I have been greatly interested in his account of his house at Brighton, and hope to see it soon.

With love to all, and looking forward to seeing you before the time for Christmas greetings has come, always your affectionate

Limick

74, Lancaster Gate, W., *Friday P.M.*

Dear Mr. Watt,

The only drawback to your pleasant note was the suggestion that you didn't smoke — and, alas! the little Christmas gift I had selected for you was a musical travelling cigarette van, for going round the table after dinner! Still I know you *have* smokers at your hospitable board *sometimes* — and I still venture to send the little toy. It *may* be filled with sweets!

At all events, I have freighted it, already, with my best wishes for you and yours at Christmas, New Year, and all times!

Yours always sincerely
Bret Harte

74, Lancaster Gate, W.
December 27, 1899

Dear Mr. Watt,

I was out of town on Christmas Day and had no chance before to tell you how delighted I was with your happily conceived Christmas gift. I smoke so much that I can only use *very mild* cigars — which are difficult to get of any quality — and I congratulate your son on his judgment in procuring for me the minimum of strength with the maximum of excellence! May you both receive as much pleasure in the coming year as you are giving me.

I am glad to hear that the cyclist with his little smoker's van did not impede the festal traffic of your dinner table. Wishing you again the Happiest of New Years, yours always sincerely

Bret Harte

The first two years of the new century were to be the last of Bret Harte's life. His illness was cancer of the throat, although he did not know it, nor did any of the physicians who attended him, until it was too late. The following letters are to his wife and son, and are concerned mostly with details of his daily life.

CAMBERLEY, *March* 1, 1900

MY DEAR ANNA,

I expected to be in London before the 1st, but I have been detained here quite crippled by neuralgia and rheumatism for the last two weeks. I think I caught a cold at Pemberton's at Broadway on my last visit, and the weather and, I suppose, *old age* make me particularly sensitive! From what I hear, you have not had particularly bright weather at Brighton either!

I enclose the cheque for thirty pounds for March. I hope to come to see you at Brighton soon after my return, if the weather is at all propitious.

I have, thank Heaven! not yet been kept from work — the neuralgia only affecting my lower limbs (like sciatica), and I have been writing ever since I left London. It's almost *all* I can do! ... With love to all and *hope* to see you soon, yours affectionately

LIMICK

P.S. I expect to leave for London in a day or two.

CAMBERLEY, *May* 2, 1900

MY DEAR FRANK,

I have been waiting to send the cheque for May, before answering your note with press cutting (which by the way I had already seen). Thank you all the same for sending it! Romeike is not always certain. I also hoped to make an appointment to come to Brighton *this week*, but I had promised Miss Froude, who has just returned from America, to come to her place beyond Reading from Friday next to Monday. If, however, you are not leaving Brighton until the 31st inst., I think I can manage to come about the 15th or thereabouts for a day or two. I believe the sea-air may pick me up, at least, if I do not stay long enough to 'stir up my liver,' and I have been quite crippled again with neuralgia or rheumatism — whatever it may be, for the doctor isn't quite certain — and have been scarcely able to work. Altogether it has been a trying spring to me.

I am very sorry to hear of your mother's illness, though I hope that pleuro-pneumonia, which is a dreadful thing, was a big name for it, but I am glad she is better, if only from a heavy cold. It must have been trying to your wife and Ethel at Easter time, but I hope you are all — invalid and nurses — better now.

I may have to see Frohman next week, as I have been writing a new first scene to Act 3 of 'Sue.' Perhaps you may remember that I told you I was going to change it, so as to show Sue and Wyand escaping after the murder and the discovery by Sue of Wyand's selfishness and perfidy, and then separation!

I have written to Frohman about it, and he was pleased, and has said that he would, in future, have it played with that change.

If you write, *after Thursday*, you can send 'Care of Miss Froude, Padworth Croft, Reading'; but *after Monday* send to 74, Lancaster Gate.

Your affectionate papa
B. H.

PYE CORNER, BROADWAY
WORCESTERSHIRE, July 1, 1900

MY DEAR FRANK,

I am enclosing the cheque for July, which you will please give to your mother, to whom I will write later. I am leaving here on Wednesday, but I shall probably go directly to London now, and I fear that I cannot come this week to Caversham. I know you will *all* be on the river during the 'Henley Week,' and I should rather come to you when that dreadful cockney festival is over. It *used* to be a nice idea — that excursion to Oxford — and I should like it, but that also would be pleasanter later. And let us hope we should have some better weather. Here it is quite chilly — and looks like late spring — and feels like late October.

With love to all, and in haste to catch the Sunday afternoon post, your affectionate father

B. H.

74, LANCASTER GATE, W.
July 27, 1900

MY DEAR FRANK,

After having been half-baked at Camberley, I came here to be stewed, but the thunderstorm this afternoon has cleared and cooled the air a little. I was glad to get your letter, and shall be glad to come to Warren Heights too. I couldn't come after being at Broadway, for I had to go back to work — and I supposed, too, that you had visitors for that dreadful Henley period. Indeed, I am wondering now, as the holidays are coming (if not already here) where you can put me — with a house full of your boys from school! However, if you will let me telegraph you on the day I can come, I will try it, very soon. Possibly I may get a chance to-morrow —over Sunday; if so, you will get a wire from me, following your receipt of this. If that *won't do*, don't hesitate to wire me at once.

With love to all, your affectionate papa

B. H.

P.S. At Whiteley's to-day I despatched some chocolates to your wife. They're for *her* only, so don't *you* try
to 'swipe' any!

It was always a great pleasure to Bret Harte when some
reunion brought him in contact with the old friends of his
American life. In the following letter to his son, he whim-
sically looks back upon the days of his meeting with
Howells, who, it will be remembered, received Bret Harte
in Boston upon his arrival from California, and with
Osgood's partner, John Spencer Clark, whom he meets
again after thirty years.

74, LANCASTER GATE, W., *July 29*, 1900

MY DEAR FRANK,

I suppose you did not *expect greatly* a telegram from me
yesterday, but until now *I* fully expected to send one!
But at twelve o'clock I got one from Mr. Clark, of Boston,
who is over here, and has been trying for the past two
weeks to see me. So I threw Caversham over for the
Langham, and a ten o'clock breakfast this morning, to
meet this old countryman of mine whom I have not seen
for *thirty years!*

I don't think you remember him, but your mother will.
He was Osgood's old partner in the old Osgood-Boston-
Howells-Cambridge days. You surely remember Cambridge — and our staying with the Howells! Osgood and
I used to treat him as an 'old fogey' — far too old-fashioned and stiff for us — and, lo and behold! here he was at
breakfast — looking unchanged — with scarcely a grey
hair in his head — not a day older in appearance, and
poor Osgood dead these five years, and *I* a doddering old
Grandfather Whitehead!

But what I am writing to say is that I will try to come

up *early this week* for a day or two, and will wire you before. In great haste, your always affectionate papa
B. H.

Bret Harte had a great admiration for the talent of his friend Boyd, and always thought that his knowledge and comprehension of his literary work would enable him to illustrate better than any one else his stories.

74, LANCASTER GATE, W.
July 31, 1900

MY DEAR BOYD,

You must have thought me dreadfully 'empressé' with my urgent notes and telegrams, but I sent the latter after I arrived in town, as the business on which I came was important, and I had no time for what I found was a fruitless journey to the Wood of St. John. I merely wanted you to make under my eye, and 'voice,' a little sketch to be shown to a regular scene-painter for a scene in a play of mine to be produced a little later, and the manager was in a hurry to get everything ready in advance. It was quite impossible for me to *write* a description of what I wanted, and already my collaborator had employed an artist at Broadway to make a sketch which I did not think at all comprehensive or true to my conception. It was only a woodland scene — but a *California woodland,* with trees like columns, five feet in diameter (*stage* feet — really twenty-five or thirty actual size!), and glimpses of the sunlit cañon beyond, and afar the Sierras snow-line. That is what *I* wanted. The artist pictured a pretty little plantation of firs, such as one sees at *Weybridge!* It was charming in colour and arrangement, but it wasn't what I wanted. I told them all to leave it to me, and rushed off to London to find you flown! My manager is extravagant and is determined to have (painted by the best scene-painter) a perfectly Californian woodland landscape, no matter what it costs, and does not want a brother manager to put his finger on a detail that is not correct.

I thought that, if you and I sat down together, you with your colour box and pencils, and I with a large and knotty club (to be wielded if occasion required), we *might* make a sketch to give the scene-painter an idea — unless one of us fell. So perhaps it's just as well we didn't meet!

I'm *really* sorry, as I think you know my ideas, and I know you can do my 'people.' I suppose now I shall have to see the scene-painter myself, and make suggestions to him directly. I am glad, however, that you and your wife are out of this awful, dusty, sticky, stifling, and perspiring London — even if you are in *dour* Scotland.

Tell your wife I never received any letter from her after I saw you all last. Mrs. Cosgrave (my landlady) wrote to me some time ago that she had mislaid a letter for me, but thought that, from the similarity of handwriting *to my own*, it was from my son! It might have been from your wife; — *she* writes a small hand with that uncertainty of outline which (I am told) indicates high genius and imaginative power! Anyhow, *I* didn't get her letter.

With best love to her and condolences for your recent loss, yours always

B. H.

P.S. I need not tell you that the play is at present a secret. That was one reason why I wanted to get you to participate confidentially in the work.

How intensely appreciative Bret Harte was always of any remembrance of him is seen from the charming letter written to his son and daughter-in-law, to thank them for little birthday presents which they had sent him.

AVERLEY TOWER
FARNHAM, SURREY, *Saturday* P.M.

MY DEAR FRANK,

Thank you so very, very much for remembering my birthday with that box of incomparable cigars! Knowing how expensive they are, I limit myself to one cigar a day. This should make the box last nearly a month. Call it a month, and you will readily see that, if you send me a box a month, twelve will last me till my next birthday! This should be an inducement to you.

Say to your wife that I hardly know how to thank *her* for that beautiful nightgown-case, shirt-case, dining-table cover, slipper-case, fancy waistcoat, and pillowslip combined which she sent to me. It is awfully pretty. And how perfectly scented it was! 'All the perfumes of Araby'! I found the servants outside the door of my room smelling it through the keyhole; it disseminated a languishing odour through the open window to the third and fourth storeys. When I take it in the train with me — in my dressing-bag — haggard City men lean their heads out of the window and say to each other, 'How beautifully the country smells.' When I opened the package here, the roses on the balcony turned pale with envy and withered on their stalks, the jasmine on the porch shut up, and the honey-suckles stopped 'suckling'! Where did she find that perfume! Tell her that it is so sweet that it attracts wasps and bees and I have to 'fly-paper' my chest of drawers.

But seriously — it is not only a thoughtful, lovely present for my birthday, but it and the cigars make me feel reconciled to growing old and gradually becoming your doddering, wheezing, rheumatic old papa

B. H.

Although much had already been written concerning Bret Harte and his work, his friend and dramatic collaborator, T. Edgar Pemberton, decided to write a biography of him. Bret Harte finally consented, although he had a strong dislike for any form of publicity, even as flattering a one as this. He was, however, very sensitive to the clever and delicate fashion in which Pemberton undertook the work, and agreed to write, in accordance with his friend's request, a letter as preface. This letter has been included with the two that follow in connection with this work.

THE RED HOUSE
CAMBERLEY, SURREY, *August 23, 1900*

MY DEAR PEMBERTON,

I should have to refer Mr. Scott to Mr. Watt, who knows how far my engagements would permit my writing for him, the terms, etc. I am working very hard now (and even in the country here, on holiday), enough to keep my nose to the grindstone for a month or two!

I am glad and cheered to see your welcome hand again, even with its unbroken record of family affliction! You could give points to Job, for *he* was troubled with no executor's work of his deceased kindred. No! I did not laugh, even at the cab. But I fancy you feel like the Western man who, returning home after an unsuccessful pursuit of Indians who had stampeded his cattle and burnt his barn, found that a cyclone had removed his home and scattered his family indifferently into far distant counties. Only a babe, his latest born, smiled at him from the forks of the sole remaining tree in the district. Then the Western man laid down his gun, and, looking at the babe, said, 'Yes! *I agree with you*, this *is* perfectly ridiculous!'

Yours always

B. H.

THE RED HOUSE
CAMBERLEY, SURREY, *August 27*, 1900

MY DEAR PEMBERTON,

You have done your self-imposed, self-denying task *wonderfully, generously, delicately well!* This is all I have time to say now, after a hurried rush through it, for I am nearly distracted with work — but I shall read it again to-night. I have taken but one other into our confidence — Madame V. de V.; she has read it, and is delighted with its kindness, tact, and skill, and bids me tell you so! I do not think it requires any prelude, but you shall have 'that letter' for all that.

But let me *implore* you to beg your printer to *display his title-page* in some other way than in that monumental, half-ecclesiastical, wholly *funereal* fashion! He seems to have taken the idea from some flat tombstone — and not an *old* one at that, but some frightfully new one with white marble black-edged vault, commemorating 'the rich man' in the new cemetery. Don't give the critics a chance of saying that we are both *buried* in that book — as its title-page would imply! Even taking a less *funereal* view of it, it looks like the cross on the cover of an osten-tatious book of 'Common Prayer,' carried (with a tall hat) to church on Sundays.

Thanks also for your letter and the screen, which has not arrived here yet, but I suppose was sent to Lancaster Gate. I will write you again in a day or two. I am just sending off some copy to Mr. Watt, and must repeat my thanks hastily, but heartily, for all your kindness.

Yours always

B. H.

P.S. I like the *black lettering* of the title-page, for all that.

74, Lancaster Gate, W.
August 31, 1900

My dear Pemberton,

History affords many noble examples of sacrifice upon the altar of Friendship, but none, I believe, comparable to your own. When it was discovered that a biography of me was to be published without my consent, and that I had no legal power to prevent it, you offered to preclude the process by taking upon yourself the task of writing it, and by accepting a responsibility which might include the sneers of my enemies, the pity of my friends, and even the criticism of myself. I had been left the alternative of taking my own life in an autobiography, had you not, Sir, in a moment of Roman exaltation, proffered the point of your own honourable sword, which had never been drawn in ignoble action, for me to run upon.

What I am trying to say is that I honestly thank you, even if, in looking over your pages, I shall be conscious, upon an equally classical authority, that I ought to be already dead to have so much good said of me, for there is still the chance of my trying to live up to your charming ideal of your friend

Bret Harte

This amusing, interesting, and clever letter to Mrs. Loyd, written from the country, gives a good example of his 'fun,' together with his sound, sensible criticism of a certain form of literature.

The Red House
Camberley, Surrey, *August 29, 1900*

My dear Mrs. Boyd,

Many thanks for your birthday letter, and all its kind and liberal wishes. Yet, like you, I have a sneaking regret for that *lost* letter — probably because it is *lost* (such is human nature), but I think a good deal because a letter is never a *real* letter until it has been received and read; it's an unexpressed thought to all intents — a silenced voice. I always pity the 'dead letters' that are returned to one through the post-office — they are *really* ghosts of letters only, that are sent to haunt you — their purpose has never been fulfilled. For all this touching sentiment I am afraid that your letter went down some drain in the Bayswater Road; my landlady confessed that she was hurrying to shelter in a pelting shower and had the letters in her hand. So we can imagine that unfortunate missive emerging from the sewers and the Thames mud, into the Channel, thence to the Ocean, and thrown to gladden the heart of some shipwrecked sailor on his desert island!

Thank you for the book also; I have not read it yet, but have seen it reviewed. I agree with you — 'that way madness lies.' Oddly enough, I wanted to make a 'Condensed Novel' of Marie Corelli, and was recommended to read 'Ziska'! I did so. It evidently is akin to 'The Gateless Barrier,' in its wild extravagance, its imagination that is utterly lost to any sense of the ludicrous. 'Ziska' is really a parody itself — and in the same excruciatingly ludicrous lines as 'The G. B.' must be. And these ladies all seem to forget, as well as their critics, that that sort of thing has been done before — much better — by better hands. It's not even novel. If you have never read 'Ziska,' I will send it to you.

I've been told by an admirer of 'The G. B.' that the heroine ghost is *materialized by degrees* — I suppose a leg one day, and an arm another; but I don't know if the features come as consecutively or not. And they say that she refused to *eat*. She should have been consistently offered *spirits*. But I am dying to read it.

Yes, I have been very busy with my legitimate work — and have had to drop my 'play-ing.' I am doing some more 'Condensed Novels' for an American magazine, and I have two stories promised of which I have not written a line — nor yet selected a subject; and they are writing to me now for a 'title' for one of them. So I know you will forgive me for this hurried scrawl; the thousand things I have forgotten to say, my sympathy with you in your mother's illness, and my hopes that you will come back soon, recruited and happy.

I am going to Reading this afternoon to my son's — but you had better write, if you answer this, to 74, Lancaster Gate, whence, if I should not yet have arrived from Reading, it will be forwarded to me.

With love to Aleck, yours always

B. H.

Bret Harte's health was becoming weaker, and he complains of suffering greatly at the hands of the dentist, who, with the doctors looking after him, had no knowledge of the seriousness of his illness and was treating him in a perfectly useless manner. The following letters, mostly to his son, in which one sees the loving care with which he chose the little Christmas offerings for each member of his numerous family, especially his grandchildren, close the letters for the year. Bret Harte's wife and daughter were in Paris, where the latter was studying singing.

74, LANCASTER GATE, W.
November 14, 1900

MY DEAR MRS. BOYD,

I have only just returned from the country, where I have been developing a full-blown cold, the seeds of which I managed to pick up the last day or two that I was in

London! If that, and the dentist, to whose tender solici-
tude I have also returned, will leave me sufficiently sane
and capable, I will take pleasure in coming to your charming gathering on Sunday afternoon. I owe a debt of gratitude to your friends, as you know, the latest being Mr.
Jacobs, whose 'Many Cargoes' I read a few weeks ago
with a pleasure quite new.

Like the wife of that delicious parish constable in
'Dandy Dick,' you're picking up 'a nice lot o' friends' for
Aleck!

Hoping that this mixed weather has not prevented
you from 'keeping well,' as we used to say in Glasgow,
always your

B. H.

74, LANCASTER GATE, W.
December 11, 1900

MY DEAR FRANK,

I am still bothering with the dentist, or I should have
answered your kind invitation for Christmas before. I
think I shall be able to come — I know I should be glad
to!

Meantime, I wish you would give me a hint or two —
as we are sensible practical human beings — as to what
little things the boys might want for Christmas. Books,
ties, gloves (even razors!) come in handy for the elders,
but Richard and Geoffrey trouble me. One doesn't like
to duplicate *toys* (in Geoffrey's case), and I am afraid
Richard is getting beyond them.

Could you make any suggestion for your wife — beyond
chocolates!

I am hard at work when I am not at the dentist's —
and generally I am too tired to go out at night — so it is
rather dull here. In haste, but with much love to all, your
affectionate papa

B. H.

74, LANCASTER GATE, W.
December 18, 1900

MY DEAR FRANK,

I am sending off to-day the tool box for Richard (and it *ought* to be useful for *yourself*, as the tools are Sheffield make, and not cheap!) — and also a separate fruit set (china again!) for your wife, which should have been packed with the other china.

I hope it will come safely. I have an umbrella for you (which is being engraved) — so — for Heaven's sake! — don't tell me you've just got one or you *never* use one! It has a hook handle, which is very serviceable to hook on your arm (à ia Colonel Starbottle) when you want to use *both hands*. I am picking up some little things for the bigger boys! In haste, your affectionate papa

B. H.

74, LANCASTER GATE, W., *Wednesday*

DEAR FRANK,

I made a row at Whiteley's this afternoon about that bicycle toy, but it ended only in my getting another toy, of a less active kind (which goes by hand), for Geoffrey. Please give it to him for me — whenever it comes — which ought to be soon.

I got to London only twenty minutes late, but saw nothing more of the theatrical contingent I travelled with. However, I was in time for my dinner, and no worse for my journey. To-day it is *freezing hard!*

Give my love to all. Tell your wife I forgot to take my Christmas card and she must send it to me. In haste, your affectionate papa

B. H.

74, LANCASTER GATE, W.
December 22, 1900

MY DEAR ANNA,

I am enclosing a post-office money order for five pounds for Christmas presents for yourself and Ethel. I wish I could send more, but we are so perilously near the *first of January* that I dare not run the risk of making that payment and the music teacher's bill late, and I should like you to be able to pay *promptly*.

I am glad to hear from your letter that you were getting on so well, and I expect that when I see you you will have quite forgotten to speak English. The Christmas visit to Paris for me, alas! is quite out of my power — as a matter of expense — and time. And I am still under the dentist's hands. The plates are very difficult to fit — and are an enormous worry to me; *more* than the teeth filing and 'pulling.' (I did *not* take gas, by the way; I prefer the pain to that dreadful stuff!)

I will write you again, about the 1st. I hope and pray you and Ethel may have a very happy Christmas, and a hopeful outlook for the New Year. With love and sympathy and all good wishes to you both, affectionately

LIMICK

P.S. I had not time to get a draft from the bank, and had to get a post-office order. You will have to sign your name *Anna Harte*, in full, for they demand the *first* name by some absurd rule, even for married women.

74, LANCASTER GATE, W.
December 22, 1900

MY DEAR MR. WATT,

I was quite touched the other day to see that you were still faithful to the umbrella I gave you — I *know not* how many Christmases ago! It seems to have lasted you through the stress of many years, and I thought I would send you something this time for the smiling days to come. Won't you, therefore, make me happy by accepting the gold-headed *pencil* stick I am sending you. It is rather a 'smart' and *youthful* affair (but I do not see why you and I should not be able to carry these things off quite as well as the youngsters!), and the pencil in the handle is supposed to give it a practical utility above mere 'smartness.' At all events, it goes with all the friendly greetings and sympathies we have exchanged these many years, and my hearty wishes for a Happy Christmas and New Year to you now.

Yours always

BRET HARTE

P.S. I thought *I* was a little early, but I have *already* to thank you for your very thoughtful and charming gift which came last night; you could not have hit my taste more acceptably.

B. H.

Although courageously fighting his own terrible sickness, he is full of sympathy for his friends, whose son had been dangerously ill with scarlet fever in Paris.

74, LANCASTER GATE, W.
January 6, 1901

MY DEAR MRS. BOYD,

I am very much ashamed not to have answered your husband's letter before, but I was very hard at work on some writing that the dreadful holidays had arrested, besides being half sick from my visits to the dentist's — whose work, alas! is not yet finished. All this is very selfish, I know, and ought not to have prevented me sending you a line of sympathy, but I thought you had met your misfortune very promptly and masterfully — and all the circumstances were providentially good. I knew there was no danger to your boy, with both his parents with him, and the isolation and fresh air of Versailles would do him good. Then it was wonderful that you were enabled — *both of you* — to carry your work with you there, and make it (if it is not too much to say) *almost* a *holiday* change from beastly London! I have in my mind a case (in my own knowledge) of a mother who was telegraphed to that her son was lying *very ill* at a Parisian hotel — and the disease was declared scarlet fever. She took the night boat, alone, arrived to find a furious landlord and an officious commissary of police, and a demand that the child should be taken away *at once* (which would have been fatal!). She barricaded herself in the room with the child, and finally was allowed to isolate herself and *the rest of the rooms on that passage* (at a tremendous price), and there she fought the illness with no other help than her doctor. When the child had recovered sufficiently to be moved, she was presented with a bill for *fumigating the entire wing of the hotel*, and for *new furniture* for the two bedrooms she had occupied. I believe *you* would have done all this for your boy's sake, but isn't it lucky you did not have to?

I do not know much of Paris, and what I do know of it I don't particularly like! I am very unlike most of my countrymen in that respect. I have been to Versailles and Fontainebleau with friends on excursions, painting tours, etc., etc. But you will tell me all about it when you return.

I must stop this scrawl before it becomes entirely illegible. I am writing in frost and fog, and on a London Sabbath day!! Think of it, you two — in sunshine and life — in Paris! With love to Aleck, yours always

B. H.

His rapidly failing health and physical weakness was making the amount of work unceasingly to be accomplished a very hard struggle. Yet it was absolutely necessary for the maintenance of his family that he should work along with indomitable courage and energy, never daring to stop for fear he should not be able to continue.

CAMBERLEY, SURREY
February 1, 1901

MY DEAR ANNA,

I enclose a draft for thirty-seven pounds for this month's remittance. I would have written to you before, but I was hard at work in London until a few days ago — when I was glad to be able to escape it for a little while. I have still trouble with my teeth, but a still greater trouble with my dentist's bill — which he rendered the other day for *forty-two pounds!!* Think of it! over *two hundred dollars* for two or three months' suffering, and two plates which I still can hardly use! It seems to me most *exorbitant* — but he is a *countryman,* and tells me that the English dentists of the same class charge sixty pounds for the same work. I would have infinitely preferred to have had nothing done — and have lived on slops, soups, and jellies! My wretched body is scarcely worth the sum I am spending on it.

Your presents came at last, and I told Frank to explain to you how the delay seemed to have occurred. You could have sent them by *parcels post* as cheaply and more securely. But they were very pretty, and I thank you and Ethel heartily for them. I promised Ethel I would answer her letter, but I was too worried and low-spirited to write. I shall go up to London again after the hysterical sight-seeing of the Queen's funeral is over — for I shall have to see the dentist once more. You can write to me to Lancaster Gate, to let me know that you have received the draft safely. I have heard from Frank since his arrival at Paris, and I suppose you are all enjoying yourselves together. In haste, yours affectionately

LIMICK

74, LANCASTER GATE, W.
March 5, 1901

MY DEAR ANNA,

I received money for this draft on Saturday only, and on account of the intervening Sunday I could not get the draft before, but I hope it has given you no inconvenience. I will try to send the next remittance through some other Paris banker, as you wish, but I had no chance this time.

I have been suffering from my teeth greatly, although since my dentist sent me that inordinate bill I have avoided such *expensive* relief. I wish I had never been tempted to go to my *dentist* at all. I could not have been more uncomfortable than I am — and at least I would not have had to pay for it. I hope you are all much better than when you wrote last; I have, thank Heaven! been so far free from colds this season; my teeth probably left no room for other disturbances.

I am hurrying this off in hope that it may catch the first Paris post. With love to all, your affectionate

LIMICK

CAMBERLEY, *April 2,* 1901

MY DEAR ANNA,

I am very sorry to hear how badly you have all suffered from this terrible spring weather — and particularly of

Ethel's trouble with her throat. But *that* she seemed to be subject to all winters in America, as I remember from the tenor of your letters; and it appears to me a very serious thing both for her vocal studies now, as well as for her profession of singing — if she is ever able to pursue it. As for the other colds (with more or less indications of influenza), everybody here has had them, and among my London friends I cannot count any who have not been laid up, sometimes seriously. I, too, caught a severe cold about a month ago — which attacked *my* weakest part, my jaws, teeth, and digestion; and for weeks I have not been able to eat anything but slops and 'spoon victuals' that required very little mastication. I kept on going to the dentist until I had to see the doctor, who told me it was partly from a chill and derangement of the whole mucous membrane. I came here yesterday on my way to Broadway to spend Easter with Mr. Pemberton, but, if the weather — which has been mending — should prove worse again, I should not dare to go farther North. Pemberton's house is very draughty, and the position exposed, and I am — from insufficient diet — rather weak yet.

I have not heard from Frank, so I do not know if he has yet returned to Caversham — or I might have stopped there on my way to Evesham, via Reading.

Everything in the country is over a month behind the regular season and the wind is bitter — and incessant. I hope you managed to keep warm in Paris. *I* never could in winter — and I was there in one of the severest — when the snow seemed to shrink Paris to half her size; the widest streets had only a single track in the centre — and fires were built on the street corners!

Let me know when you receive this, if only a line to acknowledge the draft I enclose, and send it to 74, Lan-

caster Gate, where it will be forwarded to me wherever I
am. Always affectionately your

LIMICK

74, LANCASTER GATE, W.
April 22 (but it might be July), 1901

MY DEAR FRANK,

I caught a bad cold — my first real sniffling, feverish
cold of the year — during that treacherous Easter week
of hail and high wind and rain at Broadway — and was
miserable afterwards, besides being very anxious about
my poor friend, who was very ill indeed. Altogether it
was a most dismal Easter, and I haven't got over it yet.
This sudden tropic weather (it was seventy degrees in my
bedroom last night) has made me very limp and seedy,
and I am going to Camberley to-morrow to pick up, although Madame V. de V., who is there, tells me it is quite
hot there too. I hope to run over to see you at Caversham,
before I return — perhaps on my way down to London
again. With love to your wife (you can tell her I attrib-
ute my last cold to the want of that Christmas muffler)
and believe me your affectionate papa

B. H.

P.S. Excuse the above blot from a pen.

The letters are no longer as enthusiastic as formerly.
One feels the fatigue of his illness and relentless work upon
a constitution that had never been strong, and upon a
will power which was courageously fighting against them.
Yet he always finds a kind and humorous word to bring
to others the cheer of which he was the most in need.

74, LANCASTER GATE, W.
Wednesday P.M.

MY DEAR FRANK,

Whiteley has sent the hammer and mallet (I hope they *were* the tools that are missing! I'm rather dubious about it), and I have added something for the boys — a new 'biograph' and lantern, which they say is very good. (I wish I had seen it *before* Christmas, but I could not resist buying it *now*.) It is exactly on the principle of the big biograph. If it works all right, I shall have to come up for a day and night to see it! It may be more interesting than the pantomime was!

Your mother answered my letter, giving me full description of the two little Parisian gifts she sent me, and according to her statement everything was perfectly packed, *sent*, and *registered*, and they have promised at the French post-office to refund her the full value of the articles if they are not delivered in *eight days* hence! So we must wait. No one knows whether the trouble was in the French or English post.

Bougry has given them a receipt for his first payment, which they sent me. It is written *in pencil on his visiting card*. He says he never 'makes out bills.' I point out to him that it is hardly a valid receipt — in pencil. B. seems a bit of a *poseur!*

With love to your wife and children, your always affectionate papa

B. H.

74, LANCASTER GATE, W., *Wednesday*

MY DEAR FRANK,

I did not answer your last, as I thought I should see you on your way through London. I wish I could come to you to-night, but I knew you and your wife must be in the throes of packing for Paris.

The soap came all right, for which many thanks; the *Paris Quinze package* arrived the next day — *just three weeks on the journey* by 'Grand Vitesse' and 'Carter Paterson & Co.' for which I paid extra 1/6. I enclose you the outer wrapper to put amongst your things to give to your mother, in case she wants to make a scene with the express company. And to think all this while I was making a row at the *post-office* here!

I shall remember all your suggestions when I see B——, whom I expect to meet in a day or two. But you know, better than I, what reliance can be placed upon actors or stage managers, and that a combination of the two — as with B—— makes an unknown quantity that you cannot predict anything from. Fancy his reviving 'Peril' too!

I shall write to Ethel to-day or to-morrow in answer to her last letter. Give my love to your wife and tell her I was sorry not to see her before she left; you can tell her that amusing story about the delay of the Christmas presents from Paris and sarcastically allude to a certain muffler which is still on its way from Caversham *via Southampton, San Francisco,* and *Hong Kong,* care Carter Paterson & Co. and Pickford Van to your old papa

B. H.

74, Lancaster Gate, W.
Saturday P.M. [1901]

My dear Frank,

Thank you for your prompt note and the full particulars of 'Pangbourne.' I am afraid I should not hesitate a moment at any expense that could procure me a day and night free from pain and discomfort, but, alas, the doctor will not let me go away *until my throat is better.* You speak of my 'face' troubles (neuralgia and teeth), but you

forget that I have an *ulcerated sore throat* with swollen
tonsil, and this, I suppose, is the matter of supreme consideration with him. It was better yesterday, but to-day
it is paining me again, and I shall have to see him to-
morrow or Monday. In haste with love to all, your affectionate and long suffering papa

B. H.

CAMBERLEY, May 2, 1901

MY DEAR ANNA,

I am very sorry to hear from Frank of your illness, and
I hope that whether you really had *pleuro-pneumonia* or
only a lung cold, *with pleuritic pains,* you are quite safely
over it. Only you should be very careful in this excessively
trying weather — for I suppose it is the same at Brighton
as here — with the sun and shade sometimes showing a
difference of ten to twenty degrees! It was sixty-five degrees here one afternoon, and there was a heavy frost at
night. As for me, I am alternately crippled with neuralgia and heavy with dyspepsia as the weather changes.
I have been scarcely able to *work* when I was not able to
walk. I suppose it is partly gout, though the doctor
doesn't seem to know.

I have written Frank that I shall try, and really *hope to
accomplish,* a little visit to Brighton about the 15th, now
that I know you will be there until the 31st May. I would
have come this week (if it were convenient to Frank and
his wife), but I did not feel like travelling that far, and
had promised Miss Froude to come to her place just beyond Reading. With love to Ethel, who I hope has kept
well, and all the family, your affectionate

LIMICK

Mr. Pemberton, who for long had been an invalid, was
taken very seriously ill, and it was a cause of great anxiety

to Bret Harte, who was greatly attached to him and valued very highly his friendship. Bret Harte, although he did not know it, was the more dangerously ill of the two, and his friend survived him many years.

CAMBERLEY, *May 5*, 1901

MY DEAR ANNA,

The draft which I enclose is a little late again, as, however prompt *I* may be, I find I cannot always get *business* people to be as prompt. But I hope a few days makes no difference with you.

I thank you for your last two letters, and I am glad the *family health* is better, although Ethel's throat trouble is unfortunate, to say the least, for her studies. But she ought to get enough practical knowledge of M. Bougry's methods and technique to be of avail to her in *teaching*, which is the most I dare hope for. I am not surprised that you do not like Paris: I never thought you would — but it was your desire to go there on account of Ethel's studies.

I spent a very miserable Easter with my friend Pemberton, who became dangerously ill while he was taking his holiday at his house at Broadway. He is a man who has been all his life fighting an incurable disease (Bright's disease) and who has been a marvel to the doctors, who tell him he should have been dead fifteen years ago! In spite of this he has lived on — an *indomitable worker*, a perfectly cheerful, generous, noble spirit — the prop and mainstay of a large family — a character almost incredible out of fiction — as all his friends agree. It was horrible and pathetic to see him, at last, perfectly helpless and crushed under an attack of bronchitis, which, in his condition, might at any minute prove fatal through complications. I stayed until he was a little better — but his wife writes to me that he is frightfully weak, and the doctors are very anxious. During my stay there the weather was frightfully changeable, and I suppose I was imprudent, but I got a severe chill, and the day I left I was so feverish and prostrated that, if Frank had been at Reading, I think I should have broken my journey to London and stopped a day or two with him. But I managed to get through, and after a week in which I could not work, I came out here. I have been to London once on business — but I have not seen Frank since his return. My teeth still trouble me, and I have lost my appetite and loathe all food. This naturally does not give me much strength or inclination for *work*. I am afraid I cannot put it down to dyspepsia any more — nor dodge the fact that it is age!

But this is quite enough about myself. I hope to see Frank in a few days and hear something more of you, but let me have a few lines when you get this to say how you are; I hope a great deal better. Always your affectionate

LIMICK

It was not an optimistic outlook that dictated the following letter to his wife, in which he again urges, as at frequent intervals throughout his life, a certain carefulness which seemed to be lacking, as though he began to realize that the time might not be remote when he would no longer be there to take care of them.

CAMBERLEY, *May 29*, 1901

MY DEAR ANNA,

I am sending you the draft for thirty-seven pounds today, which ought to reach you by the 1st June, as you requested. It was rather difficult for me to get it even then, and you must not mind my telling you that it has been *extremely hard* for me to make the payment of seven pounds extra, any month, for the music lessons from the

French teacher. I hope and trust it has been of some practical utility, for I really could not have kept it up any longer! My income, far from increasing, is continually becoming more and more uncertain, and if any of those illusions, such as are likely to befall Ethel in the prosecution of *her* profession of singing (such as used to befall *you* when you were engaged in the choir, in our younger days) should *befall me* — in *my* profession, Heaven knows! where we should be landed!

I could not get a *substitute* to *write* for me. With the ailments I have, I am writing much more slowly each year — and I have *no income* but from my pen. You must forgive my repeating this, but I do not think either you or Ethel or Frank realize it in your plans, or consider how precarious is the living I am making.

I had a bad cold, but I spent Whitsuntide with Miss Froude in the country and I think it benefited me. I had a Saturday to Monday visit, the week before, to Mr. Astor at his beautiful place 'Cliveden.' I came from Miss Froude's *here*, on my way to London, though, if the weather keeps warm, I may return again. I have not been to Caversham yet, but I shall keep that until you return.

Let me know when you return, and when you get this. Write to 74, Lancaster Gate, where I shall probably be when this reaches you. In haste, with love to Ethel, your affectionate

LIMICK

Their visit to Paris ended, Mrs. Bret Harte and her daughter returned to England to stay with her son, to whom the following letter is addressed.

THE RED HOUSE
CAMBERLEY, SURREY, *June 25, 1901*

MY DEAR FRANK,

This is the only chance I have had to say *when* I would be able to come to Caversham. It will be on my way to Compton Wynyates, where I am going for a few days on Thursday, 27th. I quite broke down in my work in London, and had to come here to finish it, and have been writing hard ever since. I shall be at Caversham in the morning and catch the train to Banbury at about four o'clock P.M. If you will *not* be there, send me a wire on receipt of this; otherwise, shall come Thursday. If I don't come to C. I shall probably go to London on Wednesday P.M. and then to Banbury the next day, if I can find time.

I have a great deal to do, and very little time to do it in. I hope your mother is better and that you are all quite well and more settled. With love to all, your affectionate papa

B. H.

The letters to his son and his wife written during and upon his return from Compton Wynyates, where he had been staying with his old friend, are acknowledgments of kind presents which he had received for his birthday, which was the last of his life.

COMPTON WYNYATES, KINETON
August 28, 1901

MY DEAR FRANK,

I started for my long-delayed visit here so soon after my birthday that I had not time to write and thank you and Aline for your charming presents. I was delighted with the cigars, which are much milder than any I can procure, and, I fear, more *expensive* than I can afford. But they are, nevertheless, acceptable. Tell your wife I thought the long-looked-for muffler atoned for its delay with its elegance; it is a beautiful piece of silk, and quite worthy of the handsome monogram she worked for it.

Tell her that, before the cold weather sets in, I shall be tempted to use it as a decorative table-cover — on rare occasions when I have company! It's too beautiful to keep entirely to myself. The little match-box from Paris was very unique; so, alas! must be the matches that go in it, for it will not harbour a 'gross English' wax match. But it's a pretty table ornament for all that.

I'm surprised that you think of leaving Eastbourne on the 17th. Why? But I hope to see you before that time. I might get in a Saturday to Monday visit, but I should hate Eastbourne for a longer time. With love to your wife, your affectionate papa

B. H.

CAMBERLEY [*September 3, 1901*]

MY DEAR FRANK,

If you can get me another box of cigars like in colour and mildness the one you sent me for a birthday gift, please do so, and I will send you the money. Lest you have forgotten the *brand*, I give it to you for your guidance: 'Punch' from Valle & Co., Havana.

I have only returned from Compton Wynyates, whence I wrote you, the other day; but you may send the cigars to Lancaster Gate, as I expect to come in to see the dentist if he makes an appointment for me this week.

Please give the enclosed to your mother, and with love to Aline, your affectionate papa

B. H.

CANTERBURY, *September 3,* 1901

MY DEAR ANNA,

I am sorry the enclosed cheque is a day or two late, but I wrote to Frank that I could not send it until I returned from Compton Wynyates, where I was having my brief holiday. I intended to go directly thence to the dentist's for another three or four days of discomfort! but he could not make an appointment then — and I have the dismal prospect still before me.

I think the change did me good, although my poor host's wife is evidently in the last stage of her mysterious paralysis — which has lasted so long. It was consequently very depressing to me, although the cheerfulness and courage of both wife and husband are unabated. It is an awful irony of fate that surrounds them in their beautiful home, where they have everything they wish for — but the one essential thing!

As soon as I have the dentist and a little unfinished work off my hands, I will run down to Eastbourne. With love to Ethel, your affectionate

FRANK

Bret Harte was becoming steadily worse, and almost incapable of the work at which he so courageously kept. Yet, as he himself admits, he dared not lay it aside, fearing no longer to have the strength to take it up again.

CAMBERLEY, *November 1,* 1901

MY DEAR FRANK,

Tell your mother I would write her a line with the enclosed, but I am desperately finishing some work which should have been completed *yesterday* but for sore throat and weakness. I suppose I ought really to be abed instead of working, but I must keep at it while I can. I will write again, and if I am well enough will be in town early next week. With love to all, your affectionate papa

B. H.

THE RED HOUSE
CAMBERLEY, SURREY, *November* 3, 1901

MY DEAR MRS. BOYD,

Ever since I received your little note of the 19th September, I have been so hard at work that I am obliged to put aside everything but the most urgent *business* letters. The work was greatly delayed, too, by illness, and yet I was unable to come to London to see the doctor and dentist until it was finished. I fully expected to be in London, certainly, on the 1st November.

All this must extenuate my silence so movingly depicted by your husband in his sketch of 'the Bretar Baby' and 'Brer Rab-boyd,' just to hand. Only I fear the 'Bretar Baby' is not as patient as he was in the fable.

What shall I say about the very beautiful Versailles Christmas book, that you and Aleck have, like Cap'n Cuttle, made over to me 'jintly'? I can't say I have read it yet, for I am buried up to the eyes in proof and copy, but I have glanced over the illustrations and find all the old charm.

How 'blessed among women' are you, to be able to turn your domestic tribulations to such delightful account! I wish I could make something as charming out of 'Nine Months with a Dentist,' or, 'In Surrey with a Sore Throat and an Unfinished Manuscript.' I expect to be in London next week, and hope to see you. With love to the Hut Dwellers, yours always

BRET HARTE

The struggles and bitter disappointments, so valiantly supported throughout his terrible illness, were to culminate in a still greater blow through the sudden death of his eldest son Wode, a few weeks previous to the following letter. It was, indeed, a tragic closing to the last year of his life, and the pathetic little note written from his sick bed, yet ever so kind and thoughtful, shows how deeply he was crushed.

74, LANCASTER GATE, W.
December 22, 1901

MY DEAR ANNA,

I am sending you the draft for January a little earlier, as the holidays intervene. I also add *five pounds* to it, which I beg you expend in such presents for yourself and Ethel as may be suitable. God knows it is a sorrowful Christmas — for you — for both of us. Happy only to the *one who has gone* — but I hope you will not forget the living, for all that. I am too ill to make any shopping, and I shall send something to Frank to purchase some presents for his family.

With love, hope, and heartiest wishes for the season, to you and Ethel, always your affectionate

LIMICK

74, LANCASTER GATE, W.
December 25, 1901

MY DEAR ANNA,

I was greatly touched with yours and Ethel's pretty Christmas present, and yet a little worried that you should have taken all that trouble for *me* when you have had so much else to think of. *I* was unable to select anything for *anybody*, as I have been so distracted with pain and sleeplessness for the last three weeks that I have been confined to the house — and quite helpless for any exertions. A persistent sore throat (relaxed) has been added to my troubles — and is supposed, with the neuralgia, to be caused by my teeth. But I don't think the doctor nor the dentist really know. As soon as I am able I will come to Battersea, and as soon as the dentist will let me I will try to get out of London.

With love to all, and again thanking you for your thoughtful gift, yours

LIMICK

Yet he does not forget the little gifts that it has been his custom all these years to exchange with Mr. Watt, and there is a ring of truth in the last paragraph of the letter which accompanies them. He has, however, been remembered by all those who knew him, and whose affections he seems, indeed, always to have kept.

74, LANCASTER GATE, W.
December 24, 1901

DEAR MR. WATT,

It becomes more difficult each year to make a selection of some little offering for you — and this year my neuralgia has restricted my shopping — but I hope there is still room on your desk for a *stamp-box* and an envelope-opener — or at least for the Christmas greetings and friendly affection that go with them. The style of envelope-opener is new, and original, and quite strong enough to open a sardine box, or some of the cloth-backed envelopes that are now made. I hope you won't mind the sentimentalism of the legend! I think our chance for being remembered in the future is the luck we have had in keeping the affections of our friends.

With best wishes for a Merry Christmas and a Happy New Year, yours always

BRET HARTE

With the new year, Bret Harte's illness became so serious and so painful that, in spite of his extraordinary energy, he was obliged to forgo all work. This is the last letter to his son that can be traced, asking him and his wife to come to see him.

74, LANCASTER GATE, W.
January 6, 1902

MY DEAR FRANK,

You must forgive me for not acknowledging and thanking you before for the delightful 'Dramatic Sequels.' But I have been so miserably ill, with an ulcerated throat added to my neuralgia (all supposed to be a part of my dental troubles), that I have not known what to say to your enquiries. I intended to go to the seaside, but the doctor will not let me go away until my throat is better. And the throat is *sluggish* in healing.

Perhaps the best and kindest thing for you to do would be to come here — you and Aline, as you suggested — to tea to-morrow afternoon. You could see and talk with me — as far as my *defective* plate *and* sore throat would permit the latter. Let me have a line in reply.

Your affectionate papa
B. H.

With the following letter to his wife ends the long correspondence exchanged between them, which forms the vital part of this intensely human and pathetic life-story.

74, LANCASTER GATE, W.
January 17, 1902

MY DEAR ANNA,

Your little note was very kind and sympathetic, and I know you would do all you could for me in my illness if you had the opportunity. I thought you might have had that — if I had come to 'Pangbourne,' as it at one time seemed probable, but the doctor thinks I had better go to

BRET HARTE'S LAST PHOTOGRAPH
Taken in 1902, a few months before his death

the *seaside* for a more *decided* change, and I am going to Southsea to-morrow for a few days. Had you been in the country this winter with Frank, I should have probably been with you, and you would have had an invalid on your hands! My principal trouble now is a very sluggish *sore throat* (ulcerated) which puzzles the doctor with its slowness of improvement, although he says now it is mending.

If the air of Southsea does *not* improve me — or even if it *does* — I still hope to come down to Tunbridge Wells while you are there. With love to all, your affectionate

LIMICK

One other letter still has been traced. It is a short note to Mrs. Boyd written the day of his departure for the seaside, where he yet hoped to recuperate some of his lost strength. His 'foot was in the stirrup,' as he perhaps not unconsciously wrote, for his health was fast failing, and, a little over three months later, he at last found the peace and rest which he had so ardently and intensely longed for.

74, LANCASTER GATE, W.
Saturday A.M. [*January* 18, 1902]

MY DEAR MRS. BOYD,

Your pleasant note and invitation, alas! comes to me the day I am leaving for Southsea; the doctor having thought my throat sufficiently improved to enable me to take this little change of air. I have been very poorly, or I should have looked in at The Hut, but I will do so on my return in a few days. Pardon this brief line, as my 'foot is in the stirrup.'

Yours always

BRET HARTE

THE END

the seaside for a more decided change, and I am going to Southsea to-morrow for a few days. Had you been in the country this winter with friends, I should have probably been with you, and you would have had an invalid on your hands. My principal trouble now is a very sluggish sore throat (ulcerated) which puzzle the doctor with its slowness of improvement, although he says now it is mending.

If the air of Southsea does not improve me — or even if it does — I still hope to come down to Tunbridge Wells while you are there. With love to all, your affectionate

VANCK

One other letter still has been traced. It is a short note to Mrs. Boyd, written the day of his departure for the sea-side, where he yet hoped to recuperate some of his lost strength. His foot was in the stirrup, as he perhaps not unconsciously wrote, for his health was fast failing, and a little over three months later, he at last found the peace and rest which he had so ardently and intensely longed for.

74, Lansdowne Cres. W.
Sunday aft. [January 14, 1861]

My dear Mrs. Boyd,

Your pleasant note and invitation, alas! comes to me the day I am leaving for Southsea; the doctor having thought my throat sufficiently improved to enable me to take this little change of air. I have been very poorly, or I should have looked in at The Hut, but I will do so on my return in a few days. Pardon this brief line, as my 'foot is in the stirrup.'

Yours always

DION HAYNE

THE END

INDEX